Polish National Cinema

Polish National Cinema

Marek Haltof

Berghahn Books
NEW YORK • OXFORD

Published in 2002 by

Berghahn Books

www.berghahnbooks.com

Library of Congress Cataloging-in-Publication Data
Haltof, Marek.
  Polish national cinema / Marek Haltof.
    p. cm.
  Includes bibliographical references and index.
    ISBN 1-57181-275-X (cl. : alk. paper)—ISBN 1-57181-276-8 (pb. : alk. paper)
    1. Motion pictures–Poland–History I. Title.

PN1993.5.P55 H35 2002
791.43'09438–dc21   2001043587

British Library Cataloguing in Publication Data

A catalogue record for this book is available from
the British Library.

Printed in the United States on acid-free paper

Contents

Illustrations

Figures

Acknowledgments

I would like to thank the Polish Scientific Research Committee (Komitet Badań Naukowych) for supporting this work with a generous grant.

In the course of writing this book, I received help from a number of friends. I wish to thank Jane McCullough, Joanna Topor, and the anonymous reader at Berghahn Books for their comments, and Simon Rokiski, Dr. Peter Kanelos, and Dr. Wacław Osadnik in assisting this book in various ways. Special thanks go to Dr. Bohdan Nebesio and Dr. Allan Boss for their meticulous reading of the text and editorial comments. I am particularly thankful to Shawn Kendrick, an editor for Berghahn Books, who made numerous insightful suggestions.

My thanks also go to Professor Alicja Helman (Jagiellonian University in Cracow), Professor Ewelina Nurczyńska-Fidelska (University of Lódź), Professor Edward Możejko (University of Alberta), Dr. Mirosław Przylipiak (University of Gdańsk), the Polish film critic Jan F. Lewandowski, and friends at the Jagiellonian University in Cracow. I would like to thank my wife Margaret Haltof for her unfailing support and valuable comments on the manuscript.

I am grateful to the staff of the National Film Archives in Warsaw, Grzegorz Balski and Robert Mazurkiewicz in particular, for their generous assistance, as well as for providing the majority of the illustrations reproduced in this book. Other still photographs come from Jan F. Lewandowski's collection and my own collection.

I have presented shorter versions of a few chapters of this volume at film and Slavic conferences in Canada and the United States. Different versions of some chapters have been published previously. The chapters "National Memory, the Holocaust, and Images of the Jew in Postwar Polish Film" and "Polish Films with an American Accent" appeared in *The New Polish Cinema*, edited by Janina Falkowska and Marek Haltof (London: Flicks Books, 2002). The chapter "The Representation of Stalinism in Polish Cinema" appeared in *Canadian Slavonic Papers* 42, nos. 1–2 (2000): 47-61. The chapter "Polish Cinema before the Introduction of Sound" employs a segment on early Polish film theory taken from my "Film Theory in Poland Before World War II" published in *Canadian Slavonic Papers* 40, nos. 1–2 (1998): 67–78. Reprinted with permission.

Introduction

Over the last several years, I have developed an academic interest in Polish film and media. Being a native of Poland (now living in the United States), this was a natural evolution: Polish cinema is a part of my cultural background and university education. Despite the importance of Polish cinema, there are only two books in English dealing with its history: Bolesław Michałek and Frank Turaj's *The Modern Cinema of Poland*,[1] and Frank Bren's *World Cinema 1: Poland*.[2] There are also books focusing on narrower topics, for example, on celebrated filmmakers from Poland, such as Andrzej Wajda[3] and Krzysztof Kieślowski,[4] and on the most recent (post-1989) trends in the Polish "cinema in transition."[5]

This volume provides the first comprehensive study of the Polish national cinema from its beginnings to the year 2000. It reexamines, from a contemporary perspective, vital issues in the history of Polish cinema such as the Polish School phenomenon. The book discusses neglected problems, including screen representation of the Stalinist years, and incorporates a discussion on cinema industry practices in Poland. Although it employs a chronological framework in the first eight chapters, this book does not purport to be a typical historical study of the development of Polish film. Instead, it deals with characteristic features and elements, recognized locally and internationally as distinctively Polish—what one might call a recognizable "national accent." The focus is on full-length narrative films, although the book occasionally comments on Polish television films, documentaries, and animated films.

To write on Polish cinema is not an easy task. One has to take into account the specificity of Poland's history; the different stages of development of Polish cinema are usually related to changing political situations in Poland. From this perspective, it is feasible to distinguish films made in the Polish territories during the absence of the Polish state (before 1918), the cinema of interwar Poland (1918–1939), the cinema of communist Poland (1945–1989), and films made after the return of democracy in 1989. It is also necessary to take into account Poland's borders, which have changed throughout history. After the three partitions (in 1772, 1793, and 1795), Poland was wiped off the map in 1795 and divided among its three powerful neighbors, Russia, Austria, and Prussia, until the end of World War I. Polish films thus reflect the history of a land in which national insurrections resulted in military defeat, the presence of occupying forces, and the suppression of Polish culture. The partitions of Poland, including the fourth one in 1939 between Soviet Russia and Nazi Germany, defined the character of Polish nationalism—its pro-Catholic stance and antiauthoritarianism, and its romantic vision of history.

As a result of this political situation, cinema and other arts had to perform specific political, cultural, and social duties. Without a state, without an official language, Polish territories were unified by the Roman Catholic religion, a common heritage and culture, and a spoken language. Before 1918, Polish territories were on the peripheries of the three European superpowers. Their economy remained poor and underdeveloped, with a high illiteracy rate, especially in the Russian-controlled sector.[6] Consequently, it was not the press but the cinema that performed an educational role for a number of people, the literate as well as the illiterate.

To write about Polish cinema before 1939, in particular, is a difficult task. Little is known about films produced at the beginning of the twentieth century. The majority of early Polish films have been lost. A number of films and documents related to film production before World War II in Poland were destroyed during the war, especially during the Warsaw Uprising of 1944. Due to the absence of several primary sources (films), a researcher has to reconstruct the picture of Polish cinema before 1939 through miraculously preserved artifacts—pieces of films, articles, reviews, still photographs, film posters—most of which are held today at the Polish Filmoteka Narodowa (National Film Archives) in Warsaw. An expert on early Polish cinema, Małgorzata Hendrykowska, stresses this arduous investigative task by titling her book on the origins of cinema in Poland *Śladami tamtych cieni* (*Following Those Shadows*).[7]

Before the fall of communism in 1989, little had been written about early Polish cinema. The communist authorities preferred to promote the picture of prewar "bourgeois Poland" as a land of commercial cinema and disrespect for art films. They also did not want to mention several prewar films that were anti-Russian and anti-Soviet; these films were neither released nor discussed in the People's Republic of Poland. One faces similar difficulties when dealing with the communist period. Polish sources published before 1989 often suffer from restrictions that had been imposed by the oppressive communist ideology. Frequently, they testify more about the nature of "cultural politics" in Poland than about the aesthetic or political impact of these films or their true popularity.

The necessity to reevaluate the postwar period in Polish cinema also applies to Western scholarship, which, in several cases, was at the time interested only in describing and understanding the political "other." Polish cinema has familiarized audiences with its political context. This context and the relationship between film and politics in Poland have been so self-evident for many film critics that they frequently serve as a preconceived methodological approach. In film criticism, Polish film exists mostly as an expression of Polish history and of political and social tensions, and rarely as a discipline in its own right. The distinguished

Polish filmmaker Kazimierz Kutz writes bitterly: "Polish cinema in years past, propelled by anticommunism of the West, benefited from the permanent discrediting, because the theme had been always more important than the style. It never had to compete intellectually; we were allowed to enter salons in dirty boots to describe communism, which the public wished a quick death."[8]

For Western viewers, Polish film frequently serves as an introduction to communist politics, to the nature of the totalitarian state, to censorship and its repercussions—the Aesopian reading. It is, however, important to see films as films, not political statements playing some role in the demolition of the communist system. By perceiving them merely as political tools, willingly or not, we situate them among other remnants of the past. Milan Kundera's comment is appropriate in this respect: "If you cannot view the art that comes to you from Prague, Budapest, or Warsaw in any other way than by means of this wretched political code, you murder it, no less brutally than the worst of the Stalinist dogmatists. And you are quite unable to hear its true voice."[9]

* * * *

Since the mid-1980s, the concept of national cinema has been much debated in film and cultural studies. Many writers have theorized the idea of a nation, nationalism, and national identity, most often returning to the much-quoted book by Benedict Anderson, *Imagined Communities*.[10] National cinema as a multidimensional theoretical construct appears in Thomas Elsaesser's book on German, Susan Hayward's on French, Andrew Higson's on English, and Tom O'Regan's on Australian national cinemas, to name just a few examples.[11]

While I am cognizant of the theoretical complexities of the issues involving national cinemas, for the purpose of this volume I have adopted a simple and functional definition of Polish national cinema. In the book I examine films that fulfill at least two of the following criteria: works made in Poland (or on the Polish territories before 1918), in the Polish language, and by Polish filmmakers (filmmakers living in Poland, regardless of their nationality). Also, I examine international coproductions with significant Polish contribution (director and part of the crew), as was the case of Kieślowski's Polish-French films. For this very reason, *Polish National Cinema* does not include a discussion on Polish diasporic filmmakers, that is, directors, cinematographers, and actors working outside of Poland. Their films made in Poland are discussed in the book, whereas their international careers are only briefly covered in notes.

Outside of Poland, only a comparatively small canon of Polish films is known. Some names, films, and canonical movements, such as the Polish School and Cinema of Moral Concern, are privileged and stand for the Polish cinema as a whole. Rather than provide close textual analysis of films that have already been seen outside of Poland at international film festivals and discussed by scholars, I prefer to present an extensive factual survey of Polish film in general. Less familiar films and names are included to show the richness of Polish cinema and to build a more complete, balanced picture. It is my hope that more detailed and theoretically minded studies in English will soon follow.

The book is divided into eleven chapters. The first eight chapters cover the development of Polish cinema in chronological order—the periodization chiefly reflects the political changes occurring in Poland. The opening two chapters discuss Polish cinema from its origins to the outbreak of World War II. The first, dealing with silent cinema, stresses that cinema in Poland has a history essentially as long as that of other countries, and that the restoration of the Polish state in 1918 created conditions for the development of national art. The chapter discusses major silent films, the Polish version of the Hollywood star system (Pola Negri and Jadwiga Smosarska), and local film criticism and theory, which attained a comparatively high standard and an original profile. The second chapter focuses on commercial sound films (adaptations of the national literary canon, commercially oriented melodramas, and comedies), as well as on "artistic cinema" propagated by the START society. Attention is also given to cinema in Yiddish—films made in Poland but fashioned primarily for the American market.

Chapters 3 and 4 examine aspects of the period immediately after World War II (Poland had no feature film production during the war): the political construction of Polish national identity, the beginnings of the nationalized cinema between 1945 and 1948, and the poetics of Polish socialist realist films made during the Stalinist period (1949–1956). The focus is on the close connection between film and politics: film's cultural and political significance, political indoctrination, and the pressures within a nationalized film industry.

The Polish School phenomenon (1956–1964), which emerged on the wave of the post-Stalinist thaw, is addressed in chapter 5. This section of the book discusses a new generation of filmmakers who shared similar postwar experiences and contested the socialist realist dogma. This chapter is intended as a polemic to the existing mode of interpreting the Polish School phenomenon as a reflection of the politics and historical complexities of the region. I argue that given the diversity of films constituting this movement, it is necessary to approach that period differently and analyze artistic and nonartistic determinants, unique (tinted by politics) reception of films in Poland, and foreign filmic influences. I consider often neglected works, such as films about everyday problems, with their stylistic references to American *film noir* and Italian neorealism. Attention is also given to individual films that, due to their uncompromising style, usually exist somewhere on the margins of the movement.

Chapter 6, which deals with the period after the Polish School (1965–1975), analyzes films by established authors (Kazimierz Kutz, Jerzy Kawalerowicz, Wojciech Has, and Andrzej Wajda), as well as by the newly emerging "personal directors," such as Jerzy Skolimowski and Krzysztof Zanussi. This period is characterized by stricter censorship, the popularity of adaptations of the Polish literary canon, and the growing acceptance of Polish "popular cinema." Chapter 7 moves the discussion to the late 1970s, the Solidarity period (1980–1981), and the years after the implementation of martial law in December 1981. The last chronological chapter, "Landscape after Battle," discusses the political changes after the year 1989, which marked the end of the era of a fully subsidized and centralized Polish film industry.

Polish National Cinema ends with three topical chapters covering the representation of the Stalinist years, the representation of Jews and the Holocaust, and the new action cinema. These chapters focus primarily on films made after 1989 and serve to broaden the last chronological segment.

Notes

1. Bolesław Michałek and Frank Turaj, *The Modern Cinema of Poland* (Bloomington: Indiana University Press, 1988).
2. Frank Bren's *World Cinema 1: Poland* (London: Flicks Books, 1986).
3. For example, Bolesław Michałek, *The Cinema of Andrzej Wajda* (London: Tantivy Press, 1973), and Janina Falkowska, *The Political Films of Andrzej Wajda: Dialogism in* Man of Marble, Man of Iron *and* Danton (Providence and Oxford: Berghahn Books, 1996).
4. For example, Geoff Andrew, *The "Three Colours" Trilogy* (London: BFI Modern Classics, 1998); Paul Coates, ed., *Lucid Dreams: The Films of Krzysztof Kieślowski* (London: Flicks Books, 1999); Christopher Garbowski, *Krzysztof Kieślowski's Decalogue Series: The Problem of the Protagonists and Their Self-Transcendance* [sic] (Boulder: East European Monographs, 1996; distributed by Columbia University Press in New York); Annette Insdorf, *Double Lives, Second Chances: The Cinema of Krzysztof Kieślowski* (New York: Hyperion, 1999).
5. Janina Falkowska and Marek Haltof, eds., *The New Polish Cinema: Industry, Genres, Auteurs* (London: Flicks Books, 2002).
6. In 1897, 69.9 percent of the population were illiterate. Małgorzata Hendrykowska, "Was the Cinema Fairground Entertainment? The Birth and Role of Popular Cinema in the Polish Territories up to 1908," in *Popular European Cinema*, ed. Richard Dyer and Ginette Vincendeau (London, New York: Routledge, 1992), 118.
7. Małgorzata Hendrykowska, *Śladami tamtych cieni: Film w kulturze polskiej przełomu stuleci 1895–1914* (Poznań: Oficyna Wydawnicza Book Service, 1993).
8. Kazimierz Kutz, "Swojski pejzaż," *Kino* 9 (1996): 54.
9. Peter Hames, *The Czechoslovak New Wave* (Berkeley: University of California Press, 1985), 142.
10. Benedict Anderson, *Imagined Communities: Reflections on the Origin and Spread of Nationalism* (London: Verso, 1983).
11. Thomas Elsaesser, *New German Cinema: A History* (London: British Film Institute, 1989); Susan Hayward, *French National Cinema* (London: Routledge, 1993); Andrew Higson, *Waving the Flag: Constructing a National Cinema in Britain* (Oxford: Oxford University Press, 1995); and Tom O'Regan, *Australian National Cinema* (London: Routledge, 1996).

Polish Cinema before the Introduction of Sound

Watching films made then, one may think that authentic life withered in front of the gates of film production companies. As a consequence, cinema became the only-of-its-kind reserve of local stereotypes, obsessions and phantasms.

Alina Madej[1]

Polish cinema has a history essentially as long as cinemas elsewhere. The first screening in the Polish territories with the Lumière brothers' Ciné-matographe took place on 14 November 1896 in Cracow's municipal theater; the program consisted of some of the films from the first Lumière screening in Paris.[2] But the public was already familiar with moving images before this screening organized by the Lumières' representative. As early as mid-1895, Thomas Alva Edison's Kinetoscopes had been introduced in several major Polish cities, and therefore Poles credited cinema's discovery to Edison.[3]

At the beginning of the century in Poland, as elsewhere, films were shown during public fairs among other wonders of nature. A typical program consisted of documentaries, news, and historical reenactments.[4] Films performed important educational and nation-building functions for Polish audiences. In the absence of the Polish state, these films portrayed images of other Polish cities (now part of different countries), and covered important national events such as mass gatherings at funerals of great Polish artists (for example, the memorial services of writers Stanisław Wyspiański in 1907, Eliza Orzeszkowa in 1908, and Bolesław Prus in 1912). Films also recorded the celebrations of important national moments in history, such as the 1910 Cracow commemorations of the 1410 Grunwald battle against the Teutonic Knights, won by the combined Polish and Lithuanian forces.

Like other countries, Poland had its own cinematic inventors such as Jan Szczepanik and Bolesław Matuszewski. Piotr Lebiedziński and the Popławski brothers (Jan and Józef) collaborated on the construction of an apparatus that recorded and projected pictures, which they called "Zooskop Uniwersalny." With the help of "Zooskop," they recorded a number of short scenes on glass plates in the early 1890s. In 1896 another Polish scientist and inventor, Kazimierz Prószyński (1875–1945), created his own camera, the Pleograph.[5] In 1902, the perfected Pleograph was employed by Prószyński to produce the first Polish narrative film, a simple, single-shot feature, *Powrót birbanta* (*The Return of a Merry Fellow*), which introduced one of the most important prewar actors, Kazimierz Junosza-Stępowski (1882–1943). Regular film production in Poland started, however, some years later with adaptations of the national literary canon, commercially oriented melodramas, and comedies.

In 1908 a short comedy, *Antoś pierwszy raz w Warszawie* (*Antoś for the First Time in Warsaw*, Joseph Meyer), produced by the owner of a Warsaw cinema theater *Oaza*, introduced another actor, Antoni Fertner (1874–1959). On the screen he created a fun-loving chubby character from the provinces, Antoś, an extension of his own popular theatrical and cabaret performances in Warsaw. After being seen in a number of comedies as Antoś, Fertner became the first recognizable "star" of Polish cinema. During the war between 1915 and 1918, he continued his career in Russia working for, among others, Alexander Khanzhonkov's studio.[6] Fertner's favorite brand of comedy was farce. Slapstick comedy was never popular in Poland. Farce, coupled with musical comedy, flourished in the 1930s, again with Fertner, though now in strong supporting roles.

A different genre of film was introduced in 1908 with a film called *Pruska kultura* (*Prussian Culture*, makers unknown), which introduced a vital area of Polish prewar cinema: "patriotic pictures." The term applies to films set predominantly in recent history that show struggles against Poland's mighty neighbors and efforts to preserve Polish culture and language in the absence of the Polish state. The prototypical "patriotic picture," *Prussian Culture* shows the Prussian Poles suffering under the process of Germanization at the turn of the century, and portrays their struggles to preserve their national heritage and to stop German colonization.

A great number of films produced before World War I were directed against the most oppressive of the occupiers—the Russian tsarist regime. According to Tadeusz Lubelski, these melodramatic versions of "patriotic kitsch," such as *Ochrana warszawska i jej tajemnice* (*The Secrets of the Warsaw Police*, 1916, Wiktor Biegański) or *Carat i jego sługi* (*The Tsarist Regime and Its Servants*, 1917, Tadeusz Sobocki and Józef Galewski), laid the foundations for future national art and became an important part of Polish culture.[7] One of the main accusations that had been raised against early Polish film producers was the lack (or decline) of patriotic themes in locally made films. Other allegations dealt with the decline of public morality and the endangered physical health of the youth.

Following the tradition of the French *film d'art*, theatrical actors began to appear in Polish films to give the new medium a much desired aura of artistic status. In Polish territories, however, theater was not only the domain of high art, but also the respected guardian of national values. Artists were called on to play the roles of educators of the masses and defenders and propagators of national culture. Such a task had been extremely difficult to combine with the requirements of popular culture. In spite of that, a surprisingly large number of well-known Polish writers had been either writing specifically for cinema (e.g., Gabriela Zapolska) or allowing their works to be adapted for the screen (e.g., Henryk Sienkiewicz, Eliza Orzeszkowa, and Stefan Żeromski).

Adaptations of works published at the beginning of the century created another important trend in Polish cinema. The year 1911 marks the production of several films based on recently published, much discussed works by Polish authors: *Dzieje grzechu* (*The Story of Sin*, Antoni Bednarczyk), based on Stefan Żeromski's novel; *Meir Ezofowicz* (Józef Ostoja-Sulnicki), based on Eliza Orzeszkowa's work; and *Sąd Boży* (*God's Trial*, Stanisław Knake-Zawadzki), based on Stanisław Wyspiański's drama *Sędziowie* (*Judges*). Since only fragments of *Meir Ezofowicz* are preserved today at the National Film Archives in Warsaw, and the only source of knowledge about these adaptations remains a number of press reports and reviews, it is difficult to discuss their merit as films. We know that they were box-office successes, effectively competing with imported films. Although they touched on such problems as the assimilation of Jews (*Meir Ezofowicz*), they attracted viewers primarily with their sensational, "forbidden" topics (*The Story of Sin*) and the exoticism of the portrayed community (*God's Trial*).[8]

Filmmakers in Poland were eager to popularize the national literary canon, and looked for stage-tested scripts that, apart from signs of high art, contained melodramatic and sensational plots. Their choices had been dictated by the preferences of the Polish viewers. With the exception of the 1912 adaptation of Sienkiewicz's *Szkice węglem* (*Charcoal Sketches*), produced as *Krwawa dola* (*Bloody Fate*, Władysław Paliński), other films were adapted from previously popular stage plays or operas. All of them were closely linked with the Polish historical and cultural contexts. Unlike *film d'art* in France, in Polish productions "costume was not an indication of theater, a peculiar reference to 'genuine art,' but the sign of the presence of Polish culture."[9] This may explain the popularity of the faithful adaptation of *Halka* (1913, Karol Wojciechowski), from the Polish national opera by Stanisław Moniuszko. Another popular film, adapted from a celebrated play by Władysław Ludwik Anczyc, *Kościuszko pod Racławicami* (*Kościuszko at Racławice*, 1913, Orland), was an epic production with thousands of extras that portrayed the defeat of the Tadeusz Kościuszko Insurrection of 1794 by a combined Russian and Prussian army. This film had also been screened outside of Poland, for Polish emigrants in the United States and Canada.[10]

Both locally produced films and foreign films that had Polish themes, or were based on Polish literary classic works, proved to be box-office successes in the Polish territories. One of them was a lavish Italian spectacular *Quo Vadis?* (1913) by Enrico Guazzoni, based on Henryk Sienkiewicz's 1905 Nobel Prize winning Polish novel. The preference of Polish audiences for films narrating their history or referring to Polish culture had been often exploited by film distributors, who did not hesitate to alter titles or subtitles to find an audience.[11]

The most significant single influence on early Polish films was exercised by Danish melodramas, which were widely distributed in Poland, especially contemporary "decadent" melodramas starring Asta Nielsen and directed by Urban Gad. Polish filmmakers imitated their sensational and tragic stories. They also attempted to portray formerly forbidden topics: sexuality, prostitution, and the world of crime. For example, in *Wykolejeni* (aka *Aszantka, Human Wrecks/The Led Astray*, 1913, Kazimierz Kamiński and Aleksander Hertz), one finds the familiar story, also exploited in later Polish films, of a young girl from the province who comes to a big city and is corrupted by its decadence and lack of moral principles. The influence of Danish films began to wane during World War I; gradually, German films, including expressionist films, started to dominate the Polish market.

A significant number of early films made in the Polish territories were productions in Yiddish, the language of over ten million Jews living in Eastern Europe and in Jewish diasporas in the United States.[12] Interwar Poland was a multinational state, with national minorities (Jewish, Ukrainian, Belarusian, German, etc.) comprising more than 30 percent of the total population. The census based on language, conducted in 1931, shows that Poles accounted for less than 70 percent of the population. The Jewish minority (speaking Yiddish as the first language) comprised 8.7 percent, and was behind the Ukrainian-speaking minority of 14 percent.[13] In the capital city of Warsaw (the center of Polish film production), Jews accounted for about 38 percent of the population in 1914, as much as 50 percent in 1917, 26.9 percent in 1921, and 28.4 percent in 1931.[14]

In 1913, out of sixteen films, six were productions in Yiddish based mostly on popular plays by Jacob Gordin, such as *Der Unbekannter* (*Stranger*) and *Gots Sztrof* (*God's Punishment*), both probably directed by H. Fiszer.[15] Warsaw became the center of Yiddish cinema during World War I with such production companies as Siła (Power) founded by Mordkhe Towbin, and Kosmofilm, headed by Shmuel Ginzberg and Henryk Finkelstein. Films in Yiddish had been popular in the 1920s, especially works produced by Leo Forbert's studio, Leo-Film, and photographed by Forbert's cousin, Seweryn Steinwurzel. Steinwurzel quickly gained the reputation as arguably the best prewar cinematographer working on both Yiddish and Polish films. Forbert's production *Tkies Kaf* (*The Vow*, 1924), directed by Zygmunt Turkow, with the famous Esther Rokhl Kamińska ("the Jewish Eleonora Duse") and her daughter Ida Kamińska (Turkow's wife), was hailed by, among others, a Polish critic, Andrzej Włast, who praised its on-location scenes, commenting that they were done "with a great feeling of photogeneity."[16]

Jewish films and themes were appreciated by Poles and other nationalities living in prewar Poland, who enjoyed their exoticism, reliance on metaphysics, and social themes, such as the Jewish participation in Polish history and the problem of assimilation. Among these films is Jonas Turkow's *In Poylishe Velder* (*In Polish Woods*, 1929), which employs well-known Jewish and Polish actors to tell a story about Polish-Jewish unity during the January Uprising of 1863 against tsarist Russia.

Studio Sfinks (Sphinx)

Film production in the Polish territories before World War I remained the domain of economically feeble, ephemeral studios. This situation continued even after the war. For example, 321 feature films produced in interwar Poland (between 1919 and 1939) were made by as many as 146 film production companies. Ninety of them ended their existence after making their first picture, and only twenty-five were able to make more than three films.[17]

The studio Sfinks, established in 1909 and headed by Aleksander Hertz (1879–1928), dominated the film landscape in prewar Poland.[18] In 1914, Hertz merged with another studio, Kosmofilm, the most important studio between 1912 and 1914.[19] With the outbreak of World War I, when other film studios went bankrupt, Hertz established international contacts with Russian and German companies. These connections helped him to survive on the market and to broaden his sphere of influence. The number of films made in the Polish territories increased during the war. The new Sfinks production and distribution company, headed by Hertz and Finkelstein, established a virtual monopoly. Sfinks produced, among others, several "patriotic anti-Russian pictures" that reflected the spirit of the times, such as the aforementioned *The Secrets of the Warsaw Police*.

Before the end of the war, the studio, which relied heavily on its own version of the star system, was immersed in a crisis. It had lost its two biggest stars, Pola Negri (Apolonia Chałupiec) and Mia Mara (later known as Lya Mara; actual name Aleksandra Gudowiczówna), who moved to Germany in 1917. Due to the lack of Polish statehood and a solid film industry, it was common for Polish artists to be active outside of the Polish territories, especially in Berlin, Moscow, and, to a lesser degree, Vienna. Moscow attracted a number of Polish actors and filmmakers, including world-famous puppet animator Władysław Starewicz and such directors as Ryszard Bolesławski and Edward Puchalski. Opportunities for Polish artists were not confined to the neighboring capitals; for example, actresses Helena Makowska and Soava Gallone (Stanisława Winawerówna) had successful careers in Italy.

In spite of the growing competition on the Polish market, the early 1920s belonged to Hertz's Sfinks and its continuing strategy, which recognized the commercial appeal of stars. Hertz was also responsible for launching the career of his new star, Jadwiga Smosarska. At the beginning of the 1920s, he produced a series of melodramas, known as the "Sfinks golden series," with Smosarska as the lead. These were films like *Tajemnica przystanku tramwajowego* (*The Tram Stop Mystery*, 1922) or *Niewolnica miłości* (*The Slave of Love*, 1923), both directed by Jan Kucharski. Portraying the dangers facing young women, these moralizing films exploited sensational themes under the umbrella of "educational films."

Sfinks dominated the mainstream Polish cinema with its combination of patriotic and melodramatic features: the utilization of national themes and mythologies, the exploitative treatment of "educational" topics, and borrowings from Hollywood (sensationalism, dynamic action, stars). One of Hertz's films produced in 1926, *O czym się nie myśli* (*The Unthinkable*, Edward Puchalski), contains almost all of the aforementioned features: the sensational title, love that goes beyond class borders (a successful musician from a wealthy family gets involved with a worker's daughter), and "the girl with the past," who (to make it worse) is suffering from a venereal disease (the film was intended to campaign against sexually transmitted diseases). And finally, it has love and betrayal mixed with the necessary patriotic theme (the protagonist takes part in the Polish-Soviet war of 1919–1920).[20] Although the studio lasted until 1936, Hertz's premature death in 1928, at the age of forty-nine, marks the end of the first period of Polish cinema.

Polish Stars: Pola Negri and Jadwiga Smosarska

Hertz's biggest discovery was certainly Pola Negri (1897–1987), a "Polish Asta Nielsen"—a young, photogenic, and energetic star with a modest background in dancing and theater. In a series of unsophisticated but popular melodramas, starting with her debut, *Niewolnica zmysłów* (*The Slave of Sin*, aka *Love and Passion*, 1914, Jan Pawłowski),[21] she created a Polish femme fatale who attracts and then destroys her lovers. The eight melodramas that Negri made for Sfinks are frequently set in the exotic Warsaw underworld, and peopled with streetwise characters and outlaws—those driven by passionate love and suffering from its destructive power. In the only surviving film, *Bestia* (aka *Kochanka Apasza*; *Beast*, 1917, Tadeusz Sobocki and Józef Galewski), as well as in *The Slave of Sin*, the female character played by Negri is killed by her jealous former lover. Another film, *Żona* (*Wife*, 1915, Jan Pawłowski), is described by a reviewer in 1915 as "the tragedy of a wife who loves her husband but, after a long internal struggle, has to accept a disgraceful proposition from her husband's supervisor because she is afraid that he may lose his job. She confesses her mistake to her husband, and then takes her life."[22] Negri sealed her popularity with a series of films made by Sfinks in 1917, known as *The Mysteries of Warsaw*, which referred to real-life Warsaw criminal activity and erotic affairs.[23]

The Sfinks origins of Negri's stardom, as well as the beginnings of her career in Germany, are less well-known than her career in the United States. Thanks to her role in the pantomime *Sumurun*, produced in 1913 by Ryszard Ordyński for a Warsaw theater, Negri moved in 1917 to Berlin to play the same character in Max Reinhardt's stage production.[24] Between 1917 and 1922, she starred in approximately twenty German films. Her career, however, accelerated after she met Ernst Lubitsch, who directed her in two internationally famous films, *Madame Dubarry* (*Passion*, 1919) and *Sumurun* (1920), which enabled her to move with him to Hollywood.

After Pola Negri's departure for Germany, Jadwiga Smosarska (1898–1971) became Sfinks's leading star in the 1920s, and she remained one of the major stars into the 1930s. Unlike Negri's aggressive, caricatured women, Smosarska specialized in characters who embodied a number of clichéd Polish female virtues. Her protagonists were patriotically minded, romantic, well-bred, and beautiful, yet suffering the pangs of unhappy, often tragic, love. She started her career by playing supporting roles in propagandist "patriotic pictures" dealing with the Polish-Soviet war, such as *Cud nad Wisłą* (*Miracle on the Vistula*, 1921), directed by Ryszard Bolesławski.[25]

Characters played by Smosarska in "patriotic pictures" are in line with the Polish romantic female stereotype, which was, and still is, present in a number of Polish films. In Polish iconography, originated during the period of Poland's partition (1795–1918), a female character stands for suffering, pain, and subordination—the symbol of the suffering country.[26] This iconography also stresses that women are responsible for preserving the national heritage, since the public sphere, usually the domain of men, is taken by the occupiers. The symbolic Polish woman represents a peculiar form of Polish patriotism, which is a combination of the martyrological—she sacrifices her own welfare for the country (images of numerous mothers sending their sons to meet their death and glory in a series of national uprisings)—and the religious—she is reminiscent of Mary suffering after Christ's crucifixion. The mythologization of a female character in Polish culture, the stress on her dignity, often leads to her monumentalization and one-dimensional representation, since "while making choices, she always takes into account the interest of the country, and even the simplest household duty gains exceptional importance as being part of a sacred service for the enslaved country."[27]

Jadwiga Smosarska achieved fame later when she appeared in a number of melodramas produced by Sfinks, such as *The Tram Stop Mystery* and *The Slave of Love*. Polish critics no longer compared her with Asta Nielsen (which, at that time, was the highest compliment a Polish actress could get),[28] but rather with less theatrical and more and more popular American actresses, chiefly Lillian Gish. For instance, in *Iwonka: tajemnica starego rodu* (*Iwonka: The Mystery of an Old Lineage*, 1925, Emil Chaberski),

Figure 1.1 Pola Negri. Publicity still

she plays an innocent Gish-like character in love with a handsome ulan lieutenant (mounted cavalry officer), her savior. In this and other works, the studio Sfinks succeeded in creating a mélange of patriotic and melo-dramatic films that reinforced clichés dealing with Polishness. The setting of the action of *Iwonka* in so-called Kresy (Borderlands, Polish Eastern Provinces), and images of noble young girls from country manors who parade with their handsome ulans, are present in a number of subsequent films.

The peak of Smosarska's career is certainly the box-office hit of the 1920s: *Trędowata* (*The Leper*, 1926), directed by Edward Puchalski and Józef Węgrzyn, and adapted from the best-selling novel by Helena Mniszkówna. (Mniszkówna's popular romance had almost no competition in Polish literature, which was then highly didactic and obsessed with history.) The film offers an unsophisticated love story that goes beyond class borders and is free from the political and social responsibilities that restrained "serious" Polish literature. The title of the film refers to the female protagonist, Stefcia Rudecka (Smosarska), a young teacher in mutual love with the nobleman Waldemar Michorowski (played by Bolesław Mierzejewski). Under Stefcia's civilizing influence, Waldemar leaves his life of revelry and becomes a responsible man. She is, however, rejected by his family and his class, and treated like a leper. Due to the intrigues instigated by Waldemar's circle, Stefcia becomes ill and dies before their scheduled wedding. As one of the Polish critics noted about this narrative: "[Mniszkówna] employed the pattern so simplified and categories so general that apparent banality had been changed into mythology."[29] The apparent lack of originality and the fact that the action takes place among the Polish rich and famous made the film attractive to "ordinary" viewers. This may explain a number of subsequent imitations of Mniszkówna's writing, as well as many adaptations for the screen of her other works.[30]

Figure 1.2 Jadwiga Smosarska and Bolesław Mierzejewski in *The Leper* (1926), directed by Edward Puchalski and Józef Węgrzyn

Film Industry after 1918

The restoration of the Polish state in 1918 created conditions for the development of national art. After the war, however, there was practically no film industry in Poland. The postwar period was affected by the presence of economically feeble Warsaw-based studios, a few outdated films, high tariffs and taxes, and ineffectual distributors based in former partition territories. In 1921 twenty-seven million inhabitants lived in Poland, including 69.2 percent Poles. The number of cinema theaters was around four hundred.[31] During the interwar period, the number of cinemas per number of inhabitants situated Poland at the very low end of the scale in Europe, above only Albania and Yugoslavia. In Poland, there was one cinema for every 46.4 thousand inhabitants, compared with 12 thousand inhabitants in Germany, and 9.5 in Czechoslovakia.[32] The situation had moderately improved toward the end of the 1920s with 727 cinemas in operation.[33] Undoubtedly, the economic backwardness, as a result of the period of partition, and the unstable postwar political and economic reality that Poland experienced after 123 years of nonexistence contributed greatly to this situation.[34]

The poor Polish economy, inflation, and huge differences in the economic development of various parts of the country contributed to the imposition of heavy taxes on the owners of cinema theaters. The municipal tax on movie passes was at 50 percent in Warsaw in 1919, and as much as 100 percent in 1920. Such measures led to the decline of attendance, to the sporadic closing of cinemas, and, finally, to an unusual protest strike by cinema theater owners in 1923. Taxes were lowered to 75 percent in 1926, and were lowered again in 1931 (when they oscillated between 10 and 60 percent, depending on the film).[35] Taxes had been reduced on Polish "patriotic pictures," which may partly explain the popularity and rate of recurrence of such pictures in prewar Poland.

American films, including films by D. W. Griffith, entered the Polish market after the war and became hugely popular. According to Kristin Thompson, American films dominated the Polish market and contributed 39.4 percent of all screened films in 1924, 52.9 percent in 1925, and as much as 70.6 percent in 1926.[36] Flooded by American films, Polish authorities tried to impose a ten-to-one contingent plan (ten imported films for one Polish production), which did not materialize due to the pressure from Hollywood on the Polish minister of foreign affairs and the minister of the interior.[37]

Although Polish screens in the mid-1920s featured American films, immediately after World War I, critics and viewers in Poland preferred European films over American products. Occasionally, American films (including films by D. W. Griffith) had been promoted as German films or compared to German films to find viewers in Poland. Later, films by Griffith and Chaplin and some American genre films (thrillers and William S. Hart's Westerns) took the Polish screens by storm. In 1925 some American studios, including Fox and Universal, established their distribution offices in Poland.[38]

The mid-1920s also marked the return of French films, including critically acclaimed impressionist films. In 1925 French films held 20 percent of the Polish market, and German films, 15 percent.[39] In spite of the geographical closeness, the number of Soviet films on the Polish market was extremely small due to political censorship in Poland. Postwar Poland was a country traditionally suspicious of ideas coming from its communist neighbor, so it is not surprising to note that in 1925 Soviet films had only 0.4 percent of the Polish market; Sergei Eisenstein's *Battleship Potemkin* and Vsevolod Pudovkin's *Mother* had not been released on Polish screens.[40]

Genre: Patriotic Films

Immediately after World War I, "patriotic films" became a staple of Polish cinema. Heavily promoted by the new Polish state, these films referred to recent wartime experiences and emphasized the role of the Polish Legions and their commandant, Marshal Józef Piłsudski, in regaining independence.[41] The historic fear of Russia was expressed in a number of films dealing with the Polish-Soviet war, such as *Miracle on the Vistula, Bohaterstwo polskiego skauta* (*Heroism of a Polish Boy Scout*, 1920, Ryszard Bolesławski), and *Dla Ciebie, Polsko* (*For You, Poland*, 1920, Antoni Bednarczyk). Films confronting the recent Polish-German history were scarce, but did exist. For example, the turbulent modern history of industrial Upper Silesia, with its series of risings against German rule, was the topic of the propagandist *Nie damy ziemi skąd nasz ród* (*We Will Not Give Up Our Land*, 1920, Władysław Lenczewski). Another film, the well-received *Bartek zwycięzca* (*Bartek the Victor*, 1923, Edward Puchalski), was the adaptation of Sienkiewicz's novella about the struggles to preserve Polishness under the German rule, and starred the famous Polish wrestler Władysław Pytlasiński.

In the mid-1920s, Polish "patriotic films" had been evolving in two directions: political melodrama and historical reconstruction. The first group, films such as *Miłość przez ogień i krew* (*Love through Fire and Blood*, 1924, Jan Kucharski), has been aptly summarized by the authors of the first volume of the *History of Polish Cinema*, who describe it as follows: "In search of an attractive script the producers were ready to reach for whatever themes, ideas, programs, atmosphere, political news; they treated them in the manner of cheap pulp fiction."[42]

Historical reconstructions include films made chiefly after Marshal Piłsudski's coup d'état in May 1926, during the so-called period of *Sanacja* (literally, period of moral purification). These films mythologized Piłsudski, his Legions, and the patriotic tradition they represented. Frequently, they dealt with the January Uprising of 1863 against tsarist Russia, or with the 1905 revolution in the Russian-controlled part of Poland. The ideology of the 1863 and the 1905 heroic struggles served the newly emerging mythology of Marshal Piłsudski's Legions well. The regaining of independence in 1918 was portrayed in Polish historiography as a result of the earlier efforts by the young and desperate patriots.[43]

The former assistant of Robert Wiene, Józef Lejtes (1901–1983), directed one of the best examples of "patriotic films," *Huragan* (*Hurricane*, 1928, Polish-Austrian production). Its story of suffering and intrepid struggle is told through tableaux-like compositions, modeled on Artur Grottger's series of sketches titled *Polonia* (1863) and *Lithuania* (1864–1866). Grottger's powerful visions of the uprising—stressing its heroic and tragic dimension and patriotic fervor, and the pain of the defeat—virtually replaced the factual knowledge about the 1863 insurrection. Grottger and painter Jan Matejko are often credited as being responsible for influencing the Polish national imagery. Grottger's works frequently overshadowed later literary attempts to retell the events of the year 1863. In the interwar period, Polish films followed Grottger's version of the events and his manner of portraying patriotism and pathos, as well as religious and patriotic symbols. As Alina Madej rightly points out, Grottger's imagery, as seen in its theatricalization of mise en scène, actors' poses, and lighting, had overtaken the film. In so doing, the director Lejtes follows the long Polish tradition of staging "live paintings," usually allegories of abstract concepts (such as "Poland," "freedom"), or the "apotheosis" of important historical figures.[44]

References to Polish painting tradition aside, the martyrological national drama by Lejtes also contains elements of dynamic Griffithian editing and melodrama. The love story between a young insurgent, Tadeusz Orda (Zbigniew Sawan), and a proud noblewoman, Helena Zawiszanka (Renata Renée), is set against the backdrop of the January Uprising. Rather than following the unwritten rules of melodrama, *Hurricane* ends tragically, as do many Polish historical dramas: after learning about his lover's death at the hands of the Russians, the insurgent dies a heroic death, attacking the enemy with a group of his compatriots. The final call to arms and the suicidal charge, however, bring some hope. They symbolically link the events of 1863 with the year 1918, creating a connection with another group of insurgents: the victorious Piłsudski's Legionnaires.

A combination of the patriotic and the melodramatic is also present in a number of other films that tell the story of the January Uprising. Some of them are literary adaptations, for example, *Rok 1863* (*Year 1863*, 1922, Edward Puchalski), based on Stefan Żeromski's novel *Wierna rzeka* (*Faithful River*).[45] The same approach, with the addition of the assimilationist discourse, is also discernible in a group of Yiddish films, addressed primarily to Jewish audiences: *In Polish Woods* and Henryk Szaro's debut in Yiddish, *Lamed wow* (*One of 36*, 1925). Furthermore, the return of recent history is also seen in a small group of films about "Piłsudski's road to Poland," such as *Mogiła nieznanego żołnierza* (*The Grave of an Unknown Soldier*, 1927) by Ryszard Ordyński (1878–1953), and *Szaleńcy* (*Daredevils*, 1928, rereleased in 1934 in the sound version) by Leonard Buczkowski

(1900–1967), a film which was awarded the Grand Prix and Gold Medal at the World Exhibition in Paris in 1929.

The *Grave of an Unknown Soldier* contains many elements of another group of Polish films: dramas inspired by metempirical phenomena, such as metempsychosis and telepathy, and peopled by demonic characters (and also by mediums and ghosts). German influences, sometimes described in Poland pejoratively as mabuzeria[46] (inferior imitations of Fritz Lang and early Paul Wegener dramas), are apparent in several films: *Blanc et noir* (1919, Eugeniusz Modzelewski, scripted by Dimitri Buchowetzki and with him in the leading role), *Syn szatana* (*Satan's Son*, 1923, Bruno Bredschneider), *Orlę* (*Young Eagle*, 1927, Wiktor Biegański), and *Mocny człowiek* (*Strong Man*, 1929, Henryk Szaro).

German *Kammerspielfilm* influences are noticeable in Juliusz Gardan's *Kropka nad i* (*The Final Touch*, 1928) and *Policmajster Tagiejew* (*The Police Chief Tagiejew*, 1929). The latter was based on Gabriela Zapolska's novel and produced by Leo-Film, which emerged as the strongest film studio after Sfinks. Toward the end of the 1920s, however, Polish films were not being compared to German cinema; now the comparison was to American film. For instance, Henryk Szaro's *Czerwony błazen* (*Red Jester*, 1926) was praised by critic Leon Bruno, who noted that this fine film bears "the signs of the good American school, assimilated by the clever and talented disciple."[47] The much praised beginning of another film, Leonard Buczkowski's debut *Daredevils*, was "indeed American" for one of the reviewers.[48]

Adaptations and Personal Style

Polish cinema has been known for its close bonds with national literature. At the beginning of the century, literature provided an abundance of patriotic and social themes not only for the stateless nation, but also for the emerging national cinema. It also gave Polish cinema some respectability among audiences and helped to grant cinema the stature of art. Adaptations of the national canon remained very popular in the second part of the 1920s. Literary works by, among others, Stefan Żeromski, Józef Ignacy Kraszewski, Adam Mickiewicz, and the Nobel laureates Władysław Reymont and Henryk Sienkiewicz had been scripted by notable contemporary writers and adapted for the screen.

The most prestigious productions include *Ziemia Obiecana* (*The Land of Promise*, 1927) codirected by Aleksander Hertz and Zbigniew Gniazdowski, and *Pan Tadeusz* (1928) by Ryszard Ordyński. The former, adapted from Reymont's novel, commemorated the twentieth anniversary of Hertz's work as a film producer. The latter, *Pan Tadeusz*, adapted from Mickiewicz's national book-length poem, became the focal point of the celebrations of the tenth anniversary of Polish independence. Although very popular among the audiences for their faithfulness to the esteemed literary sources, these films had rarely been praised by contemporary critics, who frequently faulted the trivialization of the original, the literariness of the film, the lack of originality, and, usually, the lack of professionalism.

The 1920s also marked the appearance of the first directors with recognizable personal style. Probably the most interesting of them was the actor-writer-director-producer Wiktor Biegański (1892–1974), who started his career in 1913 with *Dramat Wieży Mariackiej* (*The Drama of the St. Mary's Church Tower*, unreleased). In 1921 he coestablished a film cooperative, Kinostudio. He became the founder of the Warsaw Film Institute in 1924, which produced a number of prominent Polish prewar stars such as Nora Ney, Adam Brodzisz, and Maria Bogda. Biegański was also responsible for launching the career of his assistants, future leading Polish directors, including Michał Waszyński (1904–1965) and Leonard Buczkowski.

Biegański is primarily known for a series of melodramas that usually deal with the themes of betrayed love, rape, and, eventually, the revenge of the deceived.[49] He is also known for the innovative use of locations that perform an important dramatic role in some of his films, for example, in his works set in the Tatra Mountains, such as *Otchłań pokuty* (*The Abyss of Repentance*, 1922) and *Bożyszcze* (*The Idol*, 1923). Unlike other producers, Biegański tried to pursue personal, independent projects and paid a heavy price for it. Situated on the periphery of the mainstream cinema, his films were well received by the critics but ignored by audiences and attacked by the government for their lack of "patriotic" and nationalistic themes. The critics praised his works for their dynamic montage, painterly mise en scène, and ability to tell a story visually. They also commented that Biegański had been influenced by the German expressionist and the French impressionist cinema.[50]

Another important influence discernible in Biegański's works comes from prerevolutionary Russian cinema, chiefly films produced by Alexander Khanzhonkov's company. This influence, present in particular in Biegański's most popular film, *Wampiry Warszawy* (*The Vampires of Warsaw*, 1925), is apparent in his films' rich mise en scène, slow pace, tragic denouements, and stress on psychologization—all of these traits are characteristic of films made by Yevgeny Bauer for Khanzhonkov. Biegański's later films, made before the advent of sound, for instance, *Kobieta, która grzechu pragnie* (*The Woman Who Desires Sin*, aka *When a Wife Cuckolds Her Husband*, 1929), had been less popular with the critics.

Toward the end of the 1920s, a new group of directors emerged, including Józef Lejtes, Leonard Buczkowski, Henryk Szaro, Michał Waszyński, and Juliusz Gardan. They dominated Polish filmmaking in the 1930s by producing some of the best examples of Polish prewar cinema. For example, the prolific Waszyński, who made as many as thirty-nine films from his 1929 debut, *Pod banderą miłości* (*Under the Banner of Love*), to the 1939 *Włóczęgi* (*The Tramps*), is responsible for films that are considered the most representative of Polish films of the 1930s. The change of guard also indicates the origins of a new sensibility and a novel, more professional, approach to cinema.

Early Polish Film Theory and Criticism

In interwar Poland, film theory and criticism formed an original and interesting domain of thought, not limited to incorporating ideas from abroad, but proposing its own concepts. In contrast to the first Western European theorists, who tried to define the specificity of cinema, Polish authors were more interested in film's place in society and its cultural role.

Although the film industry was economically weak, film theory and criticism flourished during the first years of independence. According to Marcin Giżycki, the mediocrity of film production in prewar Poland provided the impetus to campaign for artistic cinema.[51] Between the two world wars, Polish intellectuals and artists went through a peculiar "film fever,"[52] as Giżycki calls it, which was quite incompatible with the current stage of development of local cinema. The result of this "creative fever" deserves more careful analysis.

The first texts written by a Pole on cinema appeared as early as 1898; they were Bolesław Matuszewski's two studies, "Une nouvelle source de l'Histoire" (A New Source of History) and "La Photographie animée" (Animated Photography), published in French, in Paris.[53] These were pioneer texts, arguably on a world scale, which aimed at presenting the practical possibilities of film to the world of science and government institutions. Though now almost forgotten, these works were well received and debated in many French journals.[54]

Matuszewski (1856–1943?), a well-known Warsaw photographer and cameraman, probably worked for the Lumière brothers in Poland, France, and Russia, where, in 1897, the tsar awarded him the title of court cinematographer. As a cameraman traveling across Europe, Matuszewski was interested primarily in the recording function of film as an eyewitness to history. Film, according to Matuszewski, provides new research methods for the science of history by supplying it with "direct vision." In his studies, he considers "living photographs" capable of truthful documentation of reality. Unlike traditional photography, which is capable of distortions and falsifications, "living photographs" can present only "absolute truth."[55] This opinion, interestingly, Matuszewski grounds on the technical impossibility of altering thousands of pictures (frames).

Matuszewski, regarded in Poland as the pioneer of scientific cinema, stresses cinema's educational and cultural role in bringing nations together. He postulates the creation of film archives, a "storehouse of historical cinematography," functioning as a "new source of history." He also calls for the publication of a professional film journal devoted to technical and cultural aspects of cinema. Given his practical and theoretical interest in documenting rather than reproducing reality, Matuszewski marginalizes, as might be expected, the narrative opportunities of cinema. He follows the Lumières' line of the development of cinema, namely, of those who "believe in reality."

After Polish independence was regained, the social and cultural implications of cinema became of prime importance. The lack of a strong film industry probably explains the interest in cultural rather than purely cinematic issues. The majority of writers on cinema, while agreeing on the medium's entertainment role, stressed the complexity of the filmic phenomenon and noted its documentary, cultural, and educational functions. Like other "silent theorists," Polish writers compared cinema with other arts in order to elevate cinema to the status of art. They also stressed those properties of cinema that were unique to the new medium.

Unlike in France and the Soviet Union, where cinema was mostly discussed by practitioners associated with the film industry (in other words, by people interested in aesthetic issues), in Poland film attracted primarily the interest of critics who were not professionally involved in film production and evaluation. These were mainly writers, literary and art critics, art historians, and educators. The majority of critics were not academic teachers or scholars per se, as was the case with many German film theorists. We may partly attribute the lack of serious discussions of the formal aspects of cinema to the critics' social and educational interests and their ignorance of cinema's aesthetic problems.

An important influence and a continuous point of reference for early Polish film writers was provided by the German theoretical legacy. Not only did the German language occupy the position of a principal language of Central Europe, but also Germany, "the land of theory," as Walter Bloem writes (without exaggeration),[56] provided stimuli for theoretical debates and engaged Polish critics and writers with its polemics. In the 1920s, Polish writers and literary critics started to be more interested in cinema's aesthetic issues, and French influences became more discernible, especially the impact of avant-garde concepts. The assimilation of ideas from the French filmic impressionist movement of the 1920s enabled an actor turned critic and then filmmaker, Leon Trystan (1899–1941), to develop his own concept, which focuses on the specificity of film. Although Trystan did not produce a theoretical book on cinema, he attempted to develop a coherent film theory in his articles.

Trystan popularized the French impressionist avant-garde theory of Louis Delluc and Jean Epstein.[57] In his works published between 1922 and 1924, Trystan propagates poetic cinema: cinema that is avant-garde, "photogenic," influenced by the concept of "film as music."[58] The concept of *photogénie (filmowość)*, part and parcel of "pure cinema" consisting of movement alone, occupies a central position in Trystan's writings. He pronounces that "a theorist dealing with film aesthetics should consider a movement itself, a movement as a movement, with the exception of 'content' ..., he should deal only with formal values of cinema."[59] When compared with other Polish theorists of that time, Trystan is more preoccupied with aesthetic issues; this is the reason why he was attacked by other, more culturally inclined critics, including Karol Irzykowski. As a filmmaker, Trystan made seven feature films between 1926 and 1938. In the first two, made in 1927, *Kochanka Szamoty* (*Szamota's Lover*) and *Bunt krwi i żelaza* (*The Mutiny of Blood and Iron*), he tried to follow his theoretical premises; he combined melodrama with "photogenic" scenes that enhanced the atmosphere and created suspense. The later films were commercial undertakings. His last film was made in Yiddish and codirected with Joseph Green—*A Brivele der Mamen* (*A Little Letter to Mother*, 1938) had its premiere in the United States after the war.

There is no doubt that the first original work and the crowning accomplishment of prewar Polish film theory was Karol Irzykowski's *X Muza. Zagadnienia estetyczne kina* (The Tenth Muse: Aesthetic Problems of Cinema), published first in 1924.[60] Well known in Poland, but still limited only to readers of Polish, this book could have played an important role in the development of classical film theory if it had been translated.

Karol Irzykowski (1873–1944), a literary critic and writer and one of the most important figures on the Polish literary scene, followed other early film theorists and tried to overcome some prejudices against cinema. As early as 1913, Irzykowski was already writing, in a manner reminiscent of Emilie Altenloh, the German author of the first serious sociological study on cinema,[61] that "a contemporary European goes to the cinema but is ashamed of it."[62] Even though Irzykowski proudly states that he does not quote others because cinema is still "the field untouched by thinkers" and, therefore, he is "the source,"[63] his theoretical study is partly influenced by the German theoretical tradition. He refers primarily to works by Konrad Lange, Hermann Häfker (the author of probably the first monograph on film aesthetics),[64] and Rudolf Holzapfel. Irzykowski also debates the concept of *photogénie* expressed by Epstein and Delluc and propagated in Poland beginning in 1922 by Trystan. Last, but not least, Irzykowski's book contains numerous references to prominent Polish critics and theorists such as Leon Belmont, Stanisław Brzozowski, and Tadeusz Peiper.

According to a number of film scholars, Irzykowski's study belongs to the most important works of film theory produced in the 1920s.[65] *The Tenth Muse*'s obscure status outside Poland is interpreted by Paul Coates as being the consequence of its "accidental" formulation in Polish, which resulted in "its exclusion from the ranks of the world's imperially-disseminated languages" due to "the fierce jealousy with which Poles hug their national culture to themselves."[66] Yet this cannot be the sole reason. The aphoristic writing of Irzykowski, so different from the academic works of German theorists, contributed to the lack of popularity of his work. Coates aptly compares Irzykowski's style to that of Jean-Luc Godard. Furthermore, Coates implies that there is, in fact, "no 'Irzykowski line' on cinema: simply a labyrinth of interlocking lines the reader is invited to extend beyond the confines of the book."[67]

The fact that *The Tenth Muse* was written concurrently with the development of cinema (the volume's first chapter was finished in 1913) gives it a personal flavor; the book resembles an intellectual diary. Irzykowski is aware of all of the problems an innovative theory has to face. In the introduction he writes that he has purposely left many questions unanswered and is not afraid of contradictions because his intention is not to "transform theory into a system."[68] The personal character of *The Tenth Muse* is probably one of the main reasons why Irzykowski's work never received the wide acclaim and readership as did, for instance, the systematic study by Béla Balázs,[69] published in the same year.

Unlike many of his contemporaries, Irzykowski focuses on the artistic possibilities of film rather than on its present, imperfect stage of development. When compared with the other arts, states Irzykowski, cinema's unique feature is the visibility of movement of material forms, illustrating man's struggle with matter. In the very first paragraph of the introduction, he defines film as "the visible association of man with matter."[70] This laconic and complex pronouncement, the nucleus of his theory, already appears in 1913. Developing the man-matter dichotomy he writes: "The 'man and matter' formula, in any case, simply corresponds to the optical relations between things in a film: in a film, matter is generally an immobile part, an inert background, whilst it is man who triggers movement, change and unrest."[71]

Irzykowski believes that by capturing reality that has not been processed artistically ("naked nature, not covered by a network of human concepts"),[72] film allows the viewer to uncover the world free from misrepresentation of concepts and words. In line with the German theorists influenced by Gestalt psychology (e.g., Hugo Münsterberg), Irzykowski stresses the roles of memory, conscience, and imagination, which enable cinema to penetrate our inner world. As Jadwiga Bocheńska appropriately points out, as early as 1903, Irzykowski was already paying a great deal of attention to the mystifying role played by both conscious and subconscious processes in his experimental antinovel *Pałuba*. Echoing Bergson, Irzykowski claims that cinema imitates the mechanism of human perception and, furthermore, simulates human memory, imagination, and conscience. In this context, film is viewed as being capable of reproducing with equal adequacy external reality and internal processes, even without the direct participation of an artist.[73]

Taking into account Irzykowski's emphasis on the uniqueness of the cinematic medium, it comes somewhat as a surprise to find that he places it outside contemporary aesthetics. In spite of his sympathy for cinema, and the lack of any intellectual prejudice against cinema, the reason for situating cinema outside of the domain of aesthetics is quite pragmatic: by employing concepts of traditional aesthetics, chiefly works by Rudolf Holzapfel, Irzykowski cannot prove that film is truly an art form. Instead, he claims that, from the point of view of contemporary aesthetics, film belongs to "inauthentic" arts, which work with the given materials of nature, such as gardening, the art of the actor, or pedagogy. The decisive factor, however, that contributed to Irzykowski's stand was most likely the influence of Konrad Lange, a German authority who refused film the status of art. Lange asserted that the moving picture is only a mechanical reproduction of reality, a nonartistic illusion.[74] Irzykowski claims, however, that film does not necessarily have to be considered art to perform its function as "a filter of reality." Its main task is to register the world around us. The only instance, Irzykowski believes, in which film may be considered an art form, in line with contemporary aesthetics, is the case of cartoons, which belong to both the realms of painting and film. In a cartoon, a metaphor of reality, an artist has full control over the entire creative process.[75] Yet the author of *The Tenth Muse* discusses mainstream narrative films, not cartoons.

Irzykowski's study, like many other once innovative, now historically important works, still remains unknown to the English reader already familiar with great systematizers like Balázs or Arnheim and famous filmmakers and theoreticians such as Eisenstein or Pudovkin. Irzykowski's motivation in producing his theoretical study was to influence the course of Polish cinema. Yet, in spite of his importance and broad readership in Poland (there were numerous reprints after the war, in 1957, 1960, 1977, and 1982), Irzykowski's ideas had only limited influence on cinematic practice and on the dominant mode of theorizing and film criticism.[76]

Notes

1. Alina Madej, *Mitologie i konwencje. O polskim kinie fabularnym dwudziestolecia między-wojennego* (Cracow: Universitas, 1994), 9.
2. Małgorzata Hendrykowska, *Śladami tamtych cieni. Film w kulturze polskiej przełomu stuleci 1895–1914* (Poznań: Oficyna Wydawnicza Book Service, 1993), 115. Władysław Banaszkiewicz and Witold Witczak, *Historia filmu polskiego 1895–1929*, vol. 1 (Warsaw: Wydawnictwa Artystyczne i Filmowe, 1989), 34.
3. Małgorzata Hendrykowska, "100 lat kina w Polsce: 1896–1918," *Kino* 12 (1997): 45.
4. Discussed extensively in Małgorzata Hendrykowska's "Was the Cinema Fairground Entertainment? The Birth and Role of Popular Cinema in the Polish Territories up to 1908," in *Popular European Cinema*, ed. Richard Dyer and Ginette Vincendeau (London: Routledge, 1992), 112–126.
5. For information in English on Kazimierz Prószyński, see Marek Hendrykowski's text, "Kazimierz Prószyński and the origins of Polish cinematography," in *Celebrating 1895: The Centenary of Cinema*, ed. John Fullerton (London: John Libbey, 1998), 13–18. Details concerning technical aspects of pleograph can be found in Banaszkiewicz and Witczak, *Historia filmu polskiego*, 48–50.
6. Jerzy Maśnicki and Kamil Stepan, *Pleograf. Słownik biograficzny filmu polskiego 1896–1939* (Cracow: Staromiejska Oficyna Wydawnicza, 1996), entry "Fertner" [no page numbers]. Antoni Fertner appeared in more than thirty Russian films, earning the nickname "the Russian Max Linder."
7. Tadeusz Lubelski, "Film fabularny," in *Encyklopedia kultury polskiej XX wieku: Film i kinematografia*, ed. Edward Zajiček (Warsaw: Instytut Kultury and Komitet Kinematografii, 1994), 119.
8. Hendrykowska, *Śladami tamtych cieni*, 183–200.
9. Ibid., 206.

10. Ibid., 205; Banaszkiewicz and Witczak, *Historia filmu polskiego*, 72.
11. Hendrykowska, *Śladami tamtych cieni*, 137 and 164–166; Banaszkiewicz and Witczak, *Historia filmu polskiego*, 91–92.
12. Marek and Małgorzata Hendrykowski, "Yiddish Cinema in Europe," in *The Oxford History of World Cinema*, ed. Geoffrey Nowell-Smith (Oxford: Oxford University Press, 1996), 174–175.
13. Neal Ascherson, *The Struggles for Poland* (London: Michael Joseph, 1987), 59.
14. Edward D. Wynot, Jr., *Warsaw Between the World Wars: Profile of the Capital City in a Developing Land, 1918–1939* (New York: Columbia University Press, 1983), 106 and 108.
15. Stanisław Janicki, *Polskie filmy fabularne 1902–1988* (Warsaw: Wydawnictwa Artystyczne i Filmowe, 1990), 14–18. Małgorzata Hendrykowska provides different numbers: nineteen films, including eight in Yiddish. Hendrykowska, *Śladami tamtych cieni*, 206.
16. Eric A. Goldman, *Visions, Images, and Dreams: Yiddish Film Past and Present* (Ann Arbor: UMI Research Press, 1983), 20. The 1924 version of *The Vow* is lost. The Polish National Film Archives in Warsaw has the sound version of *The Vow* released in 1937, directed by Henryk Szaro, and with Zygmunt Turkow in the leading role. This version was released in the United States as *A Vilna Legend*. Ida Kamińska is known to the Western viewer for her role in the Oscar-winning Czechoslovak film, *The Shop on Main Street* (1965) directed by Ján Kadár and Elmar Klos.
17. Edward Zajiček, *Poza ekranem. Kinematografia polska 1918–1991* (Warsaw: Filmoteka Narodowa and Wydawnictwa Artystyczne i Filmowe, 1992), 10.
18. In her memoirs, Pola Negri writes that "Of the several small companies in Warsaw, Sphinx was the only one approximating any artistic standards." Pola Negri, *Memoirs of a Star* (New York: Doubleday, 1970), 113.
19. Banaszkiewicz and Witczak, *Historia filmu polskiego*, 88.
20. Since this film is lost like many others, I owe its plot summary to Banaszkiewicz and Witczak, *Historia filmu polskiego*, 190–191.
21. Some Polish sources list Pola Negri's Polish films as directed by the leading Sfinks director, Jan Pawłowski. Other sources indicate the producer, Aleksander Hertz, as responsible for all of the films. Władysław Banaszkiewicz, "Pola Negri. Początki kariery i legendy," *Kwartalnik Filmowy* 1 (1960): 37–80.
22. Originally published in *Nowa Gazeta* 450 (1915): 3. Quoted from Banaszkiewicz and Witczak, *Historia filmu polskiego*, 121.
23. *Tajemnica Alei Ujazdowskich* (*The Mystery of Ujazdowskie Avenue*), *Arabella*, and *Pokój nr 13* (*Room No. 13*), all directed by Tadeusz Sobocki and Józef Galewski.
24. Jan F. Lewandowski, "Zagadkowa Pola Negri," *Kino* 7–8 (1997): 24. Lewandowski notes that Negri's role in Ordyński's *Sumurun* was a turning point that helped to establish her career in Berlin; it proved to be more important than her films. Pola Negri also stresses the importance of Ordyński's pantomime in her autobiography. Pola Negri, *Memoirs of a Star*, 119–129. It has to be noted, however, that Sfinks' films featuring Negri were distributed in Germany.
25. Ryszard Bolesławski [true last name: Srzednicki; in the U.S. known as Richard Boleslawski, 1889–1937] later became a successful Hollywood director with such films as *Rasputin and the Empress* (1933), *The Painted Veil* (1934), and *The Garden of Allah* (1936).
26. Discussed extensively in Elżbieta Ostrowska, "Obraz Matki Polki w kinie polskim: mit czy stereotyp? *Kwartalnik Filmowy* 17 (1997): 131–140. Also in Ostrowska's "Filmic Representations of the 'Polish Mother' in Post–Second World War Polish Cinema," *European Journal of Women Studies* 5 (1998): 419–435.
27. Ostrowska, "Obraz Matki Polki," 133.
28. Halina Bruczówna, one of the leading stars of Sfinks, recalls that most actresses considered "the most perfect model to be Asta Nielsen." Banaszkiewicz and Witczak, *Historia filmu polskiego*, 122.
29. Tadeusz Walas quoted from Alina Madej, *Mitologie i konwencje*, 38.
30. Helena Mniszkówna's novels have been adapted by Juliusz Gardan in 1936 (*The Leper*), by Henryk Szaro in 1937 (*Ordynat Michorowski*), by Michał Waszyński in 1938

(*Gehenna*), and later, after the war, by Jerzy Hoffman in 1976 (*The Leper*). The 1927 version with Smosarska is lost.

31. Banaszkiewicz and Witczak, *Historia filmu polskiego*, 136 and 140.
32. Ewa Gębicka, "Sieć i rozpowszechnianie filmów," in Zajiček, ed., *Encyklopedia kultury polskiej XX wieku*, 420.
33. Banaszkiewicz and Witczak, *Historia filmu polskiego*, 216.
34. The violently disputed borders with Polish neighbors were finally settled at the Riga Treaty, signed in March 1921, which ended the war between Soviet Russia and Poland (1919–1921). The defeat of the Soviet army, led by General Tukhachevsky, at Warsaw, known as the *Cud nad Wisłą* (Miracle on the Vistula), occupies a place of prominence in Polish mythology and, consequently, in Polish film.
35. Wynot, *Warsaw Between the World Wars*, 282.
36. Kristin Thompson, *Exporting Entertainment: America and the World Film Market, 1907–1934* (London: British Film Institute, 1985), 136.
37. Kerry Segrave, *American Films Abroad: Hollywood's Domination of the World's Movie Screens from the 1890s to the Present* (Jefferson and London: McFarland, 1997), 46–47.
38. Banaszkiewicz and Witczak, *Historia filmu polskiego*, 141 and 177.
39. Jerzy Płażewski, "Film zagraniczny w Polsce," in Zajiček, *Encyklopedia kultury polskiej XX wieku*, 328.
40. Ibid. Contrary to popular opinion, Soviet cinema had some admirers in Poland. One of the leading Polish prewar critics, Stefania Zahorska, was known as a promoter of films in which imaginative form matches "humanistic content," the ideal of which she found in the montage cinema of the Soviets, especially that of Eisenstein. Her stand was far from common, given the situation in Poland after the Polish-Soviet war.
41. When Polish independence was proclaimed on 11 November 1918, Józef Piłsudski became the commander in chief of the Polish armed forces and the provisional head of state.
42. Banaszkiewicz and Witczak, *Historia filmu polskiego*, 185.
43. Madej, *Mitologie i konwencje*, 148–149.
44. Ibid., 140–141.
45. *Year 1863* was remade in 1936 as *Wierna rzeka* (*Faithful River*, 1936) by Leonard Buczkowski. The third version was produced by Tadeusz Chmielewski in 1983, but due to political restrictions (the unfavorable portrayal of Polish-Russian history), it was not released until 1987.
46. Lubelski in Zajiček, *Encyklopedia kultury polskiej*, 120. The term *mabuzeria* refers to Fritz Lang's *Dr Mabuse, Der Spieler* (1922).
47. Quoted from Jerzy Maśnicki and Kamil Stepan, "100 lat kina w Polsce: 1921–1928," *Kino* 1 (1998): 53
48. Ibid.
49. Since all films by Biegański are lost, the only source of information remains the reception of his works by critics. See Maśnicki and Stepan, *Pleograf*, entry "Biegański" [no page numbers]. Also Maśnicki and Stepan, "100 lat kina w Polsce," 51.
50. Maśnicki and Stepan, "100 lat kina w Polsce," 51.
51. Marcin Giżycki, *Walka o film artystyczny w międzywojennej Polsce* (Warsaw: Państwowe Wydawnictwo Naukowe, 1989), 15.
52. Ibid., 15.
53. Bolesław Matuszewski, "Une nouvelle source de l'Histoire (Création d'un dépôt de Cinématographie historique) (12 pages) and "La Photographie animée, ce qu'elle est, ce qu'elle doit être" (88 pages), both published by Matuszewski in Paris in 1898. They were first published in book form in 1995 by the National Film Archives in Warsaw: Bolesław Matuszewski, *Nowe źródło historii. Ożywiona fotografia, czym jest, czym być powinna* (Warsaw: Filmoteka Narodowa, 1995). This edition of Matuszewski (in Polish and in French) has the following on its cover: "Pierwsze w świecie traktaty o filmie" [First in the world treatises on film].
54. Reviews are included in the 1995 Polish edition of Matuszewski's works (1995), appendix 3.

55. Matuszewski, *Nowe źródło historii*, 57.
56. Walter Bloem, *Seele des Lichtspiels. Ein Bekenntnis zum Film* (Leipzig-Zurich, 1922); translated into English by Allen W. Porterfield as *The Soul of the Moving Picture* (New York: E. P. Dutton and Company, 1924), xiii.
57. Louis Delluc, *Photogénie* (Paris: Éditions de Brunoff, 1920); Jean Epstein, *Bonjour cinéma* (Paris: Éditions de la Sirène, 1921).
58. For example, Leon Trystan, "Fotogeniczność," *Ekran i Scena* 10–11 (1923); "Kino jako muzyka wzrokowa," *Film Polski* 2–3 (1923).
59. Leon Trystan, "Rytmizacja ruchu w kinie," *Almanach Nowej Sztuki* 2 (1924): 57. Quoted in Banaszkiewicz and Witczak, *Historia filmu polskiego*, 253.
60. Karol Irzykowski, *X Muza. Zagadnienia estetyczne kina* (Cracow: Krakowska Spółka Wydawnicza, 1924). Quotes from the fourth edition prepared by Jadwiga Bocheńska (Warsaw: Wydawnictwa Artystyczne i Filmowe, 1977). Fragment in English translation by Paul Coates, "The Tenth Muse (Excerpts)," *New German Critique* 42 (1987), 116–127. The phrase "the tenth muse," propagated by Karol Irzykowski, was, and still is, broadly employed in Poland to address cinema.
61. Emilie Altenloh, *Zur Soziologie des Kinos. Die Kino-Unternehmung und die sozialen Schichten ihrer Besucher* (Jena 1913), 96. Reference made by Andrzej Gwóźdź in his *Niemiecka myśl filmowa* (Kielce: Szumacher, 1992), 30.
62. Karol Irzykowski, "Śmierć kinematografu," *Świat* 21 (1913). Later included as the opening chapter in his *The Tenth Muse* (1977), 35.
63. Irzykowski, *X Muza*, 26 and 28.
64. Hermann Häfker, *Kino und Kunst* (Munich, 1913).
65. For instance, Paul Coates, "Karol Irzykowski: Apologist of the Inauthentic Art," *New German Critique* 42 (1987): 114; Alicja Helman, "Polish Film Theory," in *The Jagiellonian University Film Studies*, ed. Wiesław Godzic (Cracow: Universitas, 1996), 11; Zbigniew Czeczot-Gawrak, *Zarys dziejów teorii filmu pierwszego pięćdziesięciolecia 1895–1945* (Wrocław: Ossolineum, 1977), 150.
66. Coates, "Karol Irzykowski," 114.
67. Ibid.
68. Irzykowski, *X Muza*, 27.
69. Béla Balázs, *Der sichtbare Mensch, oder Die Kultur des Films* (Vienna, 1924).
70. Irzykowski, *X Muza*, 26.
71. Ibid., quoted from Paul Coates's translation, "Karol Irzykowski," 118.
72. Irzykowski, *X Muza*, 40.
73. Jadwiga Bocheńska, *Polska myśl filmowa do roku 1939* (Wrocław: Ossolineum, 1974), 105–107.
74. Konrad Lange, *Das Wesen der Kunst. Grundzüge einer realistischen Kunstlehre* (Berlin, 1901). The same comments about film being a nonartistic illusion were repeated in Lange's studies published several years later.
75. Irzykowski, *X Muza*, 248–254.
76. Irzykowski's importance and relevance to contemporary Polish film practice can be seen in the 1981 creation of the new experimental production collective, the Karol Irzykowski Film Studio in Łódź.

2

The Sound Period of the 1930s

The introduction of sound and the disintegration of the existing international film market were perceived by many European nations as an opportunity to break the hegemony of Hollywood. The demand for pictures in national languages was enormous, and some Central European countries—Czechoslovakia, for example—quickly took advantage of it. There was, however, no immediate national film production renaissance in Poland; the sluggish economy, worsened by the global economic depression, proved to be an obstacle. Although the first sound film was screened in Poland in 1929 (*The Singing Fool* with Al Jolson), the period of transition was slow and difficult. Since Poland did not introduce any protectionist measures, as did neighboring Czechoslovakia, Germany, and Hungary, the majority of pictures released in Poland were in foreign languages, predominantly English. This gradually alienated the Polish viewer, and, as a consequence, cinema attendance dropped drastically in the early 1930s; by 1932 it had decreased 30 percent when compared to 1929 and 1930.[1]

The advent of sound had been treated with suspicion in Poland, as well as in other parts of the world. At the beginning of the 1930s, the majority of Polish cinema theaters were not adapted to screening sound films. Excessive taxes did not encourage theater owners to invest in converting their theaters to play sound. Local films were thus produced in both silent and sound versions. The government later tried to intervene, issuing a regulation in 1936 that established lower taxes and preferential treatment for locally produced films.[2] Nevertheless, as late as 1938, eighteen silent cinema theaters still remained in operation. For the approximately thirty-five million inhabitants of Poland, the total number of cinema theaters was low at 807.[3]

Polish audiences favored Polish films, so at the beginning of the 1930s there were attempts to disguise Hollywood films as national products. Paramount's studio in Joinville near Paris began to produce multilingual films, including films in Polish, in 1930–1931. The leading Polish theatrical and film director, Ryszard Ordyński, and a group of distinguished Polish actors, such as Kazimierz Junosza-Stępowski, Bogusław Samborski and Aleksander Żabczyński, became involved in the production of several films that later had little resonance in Poland. The mechanical method of producing multilingual films and the lack of the Polish context, landscape, and theme contributed to the box office failure of and modest critical response to these films. The problem was not solved by the introduction of the dubbing technique. Hollywood films dubbed in Polish and produced by, among others, the newly established dubbing center in Joinville encountered mixed response in Poland. Given the heritage of the partition period—the high illiteracy rate—dubbing could have become a solution. On the other hand, the high costs of dubbing and nationalist concerns, expressed by a number of Polish intellectuals, made subtitling more popular. After the initial period, characterized by the predominance of dubbed films, Polish viewers came to favor subtitled foreign-language films, and this viewing preference remains unchanged today.[4]

The problems with imported films created a niche for the national cinema—films set in the Polish landscape, focusing on Polish history and mythology, and spoken in the national idiom. In the latter half of the 1930s, Polish films thus generated four times more viewers than foreign films.[5] The first Polish sound picture was, however, truly an international endeavor. *Moralność pani Dulskiej* (*The Morality of Mrs. Dulska*), which premiered on 29 March 1930, was based on a Polish drama by Gabriela Zapolska; was directed by a Russian director working in Vienna, Bolesław Newolin; was produced by Austrian and Polish Jews (Bolesław Land and Maurycy Herszfinkel); and starred Marta Flanz (Land's wife) and Dela Lipińska (Newolin's wife). Both actresses, who did not speak Polish, were dubbed. To make the picture complete, the cinematography had been done by the Italian Giovanni Vitriotti and the set design by the Czech Emil Štepánek. The quality of the sound-on-disc, recorded at Syrena Record in Warsaw, and its imperfect synchronization were harshly criticized by the Polish press.[6]

The first 100 percent Polish talking picture (with sound also recorded on disc) premiered in October 1930. Michał Waszyński's *Niebezpieczny romans* (*Dangerous Love Affair*) had been produced in four languages—French, English, German, and Polish—and starred one of the most popular prewar actors, Bogusław Samborski, known as "the Emil Jannings of Polish film."[7] Another film, *Każdemu wolno kochać* (*Anybody Can Love*), a musical comedy released in February 1933 and directed by Mieczysław Krawicz and Janusz Warnecki, is generally regarded as the first Polish film with sound-on-film (optical soundtrack).

Before World War II, the Polish film industry centered in Warsaw. As many as sixty-three out of the sixty-seven films made before 1918 and 258 of the 267 full-length films completed during the whole interwar period were made in the Polish capital.[8] Warsaw possessed not only a vibrant artistic community but also a group of entrepreneurs, mostly of Jewish origin, who were willing to risk their money and invest in the erratic film business. In the 1930s, the most important (though still small by Western standards) film companies were mostly in Jewish hands: Sfinks, Leo-Film (owned by Maria Hirszbein and Leo Landau), Blok-Muza-Film (Henryk Gleisner, Leopold Gleisner, and Emil Kac), Rex-Film (Józef Rosen), Feniks (Felicja and Leon Fenigstein), Libkow-Film (Marek Libkow). The only significant Polish-owned company remained Urania-Film, which was controlled by one of the best-known prewar Polish actors, Eugeniusz Bodo (1899–1943).[9]

The economically weak studios tried to promote their own stars, yet, as a rule, they relied on the established theatrical actors. Since the industry was based in Warsaw, a city with an abundance of theaters and cabarets, trained actors were readily at hand. The theatrical actors brought to the screen personae that they had already formed on stage; they rarely ventured beyond their established image. The producers routinely cast a small group of Warsaw artists in a clichéd manner; furthermore, they expected them to flesh out the narrative with their theatrical/cabaret signatures—songs, dances, and comic dialogues. As a result, a number of Polish actors reappear in several films, delivering predictable lines that verge on self-parody. For instance, the comic actor Stanisław Sielański appears in strong supporting roles as a sly dog, a servant, and a provincial hillbilly; one of the busiest prewar actresses, Mieczysława Ćwiklińska, specializes in upper-class matrons and mothers; and Antoni Fertner plays good-natured, well-to-do fathers. The popular melodrama *O czym się nie mówi* (*Something You Do Not Talk About*, 1939, Mieczysław Krawicz), based on a 1909 novel by Gabriela Zapolska about prostitution, serves as a good example of typecasting. In this film, several actors bring previous theatrical and filmic roles to the screen: the Polish femme fatale Ina Benita stars as a prostitute; cabaret actor Ludwik Sempoliński appears as a fun-loving person; one of the best prewar dramatic actresses, Stanisława Wysocka, plays a poor yet decent widow; Stanisław Sielański repeats his stunt as a provincial bumpkin in Warsaw; Mieczysław Cybulski and Stanisława Angel-Engelówna once again appear as leading characters—honest, yet tested by tragic circumstances.

Unquestionably, the Polish version of the star system reflected the state of the Polish film industry. Although the Warsaw stars became the center of attention for audiences and numerous film magazines, stardom as a film institution never fully developed in Poland due to the instability of the local film industry and the necessity to rely on theatrical actors. The reliance on stage actors subjected Polish prewar cinema to excessive theatricalization that was evident not only in the performances, but also in the prevalence of the verbal over the visual, and the predominance of long and medium shots that were often executed with an immobile camera.[10]

Warsaw was crucial for Polish cinema for another reason: even though it had only 10 percent of all movie theaters in Poland, the city generated as much as 33 percent of the total box office.[11] This figure is reflected in the choice of filmic themes related to Warsaw, in the settings, and in the type of humor popular in Warsaw cabarets and revue theaters. It is fair to say that Polish interwar filmmaking clearly became a Warsaw societal affair.

It was uncommon for films to be produced outside of Warsaw, but the results were often promising. One example is *Biały ślad* (*White Trail*, 1932), a silent film set in the Polish Tatra Mountains that was directed and filmed by Adam Krzeptowski (1898–1961). With its romantic plot played out against the backdrop of beautiful yet dangerous mountains, *White Trail* clearly resembles the *Bergfilme* (mountain films) of Arnold Fanck. The movie narrates an uncomplicated story about unrequited love, relying entirely on quasi-documentary footage of the mountains. The protagonist of *White Trail*, a young mountaineer, falls in love with a girl who has just returned from her schooling in the city. She, however, loves another man, a handsome mountain climber. The film's climax occurs when tragedy strikes: an avalanche nearly kills two of the principals. More important than the frail story, however, are the film's dynamic images of skiing competitions, the constant use of moving (skiing) camera, and the narrative relevance of the panoramic mountain scenes. The story is told visually—a rarity in old Polish cinema.

Krzeptowski's film was very well received at the first Venice Film Festival in 1932, and was generally praised by the Polish critics, though also considered amateurish (this was the feature debut of Krzeptowski with a cast of nonprofessional actors). From today's perspective, however, this amateurish quality makes *White Trail* a unique Polish production. Its cinematography and visual style in general make it very different from the photographed stage plays that predominated at the time. Krzeptowski's next (and last) film set in the Tatra Mountains, *Zamarłe echo* (*Dead Echo*, 1934), disappointed the critics: though they praised the visual aspects of the film, they harshly criticized its melodramatic story.[12]

Another film set outside of Warsaw offers an almost ethnographic experience. Set in the southeastern part of prewar Poland, in the Hutsul region, *Przybłęda* (*The Vagabond*, 1933, Jan Nowina-Przybylski) provides a glimpse of exotic local culture. The story tells of an attractive outsider, Maryjka (Ina Benita), who is chased by the local men and almost lynched by the villagers for hiding a man, another outsider. Although *The Vagabond* undeniably delivers an outside view of the culture, with its stylization and superficial folklore (villagers are portrayed parading in their Sunday-best clothes), it nevertheless offers a refreshing experience in the context of prewar Polish cinema. It leaves behind the pretentious salons of Warsaw and the cabaret milieu of many Polish films to search for new photogenic settings rarely seen before on the screen. The best parts of *The Vagabond* consist of documentary-like scenes, the work of one of the most talented prewar Polish cinematographers, Albert Wywerka. This film also elevated to stardom one of the most interesting actresses of prewar Polish cinema, the blond femme fatale Ina Benita (1912–1943). The character she played in her next film, *Hanka* (aka *Oczy czarne; Dark Eyes*, 1934, Jerzy Dal), was nearly the same as the one she played in *The Vagabond*. Benita is, however, better known for her films made in the late 1930s: *Gehenna, Serce matki* (*Mother's Heart*, 1938), and *Something You Do Not Talk About*. Arguably, her best screen performance is the role of a river barge captain's daughter in *Ludzie Wisły* (*The People of the Vistula*, 1938), which will be discussed later in this chapter.

Patriotic Films

In the 1930s, patriotic films still featured significantly in the Polish repertoire. The events of 1905, the January Uprising of 1863, and the formation of the Polish Legions remained popular themes on Polish screens. As in the 1920s, a typical patriotic picture referred to the atrocities committed by the Russians before and during World War I. Its melodramatic plot, usually revolving around the theme of love suffering due to the intrusion of politics, was commonly coupled with an unsophisticated picture of history. The purpose of "them" (Russian bureaucrats, officers, and the like) was to offer a stereotyped and evil background against which the impossible love played out. In films such as *The Police Chief Tagiejew* and *Serce na ulicy* (*Heart on the Street*, 1931), both directed by Juliusz Gardan, the "them" intervened like the elements in disaster films. In spite of forced happy endings (a requisite of the melodramatic formula), patriotic films taught that personal life and love had to be sacrificed "at the nation's altar"; individual yearnings had to be silenced for the common good. The stories told in "patriotic pictures" are an idealized take on Polish patriotism.

One of the early Polish attempts to produce talking pictures, *Na Sybir* (*To Siberia*, 1930), directed by Henryk Szaro, is a typical example of the "patriotic genre." Partly a sound film (with sound sequences recorded in Berlin), it offers a "patriotic love story" set during the turbulent period of 1905 and afterwards. *To Siberia* tells the story of a young student turned freedom fighter, Ryszard Prawdzic, alias Sęp (Adam Brodzisz), who hides outside of Warsaw after a successful attempt on the Russian governor-general's life. While working as a private teacher in a country manor, he meets an equally patriotically minded woman, Rena Czarska (Jadwiga Smosarska).[13] When Prawdzic unexpectedly returns to Warsaw, Czarska follows him, and they meet by chance at the moment of his arrest. She then follows him to Siberia and organizes his successful escape.

To Siberia closely emulates silent filmic examples of patriotic (anti-Russian) works. This is evident in the portrayal of the principal antagonist, Colonel Sierov, played by Bogusław Samborski (who specialized in such roles), and in the film's didactic overtones. This is also apparent in the film's episodic structure, being an illustration of patriotic tales combined with images of the peaceful Polish countryside. Jadwiga Smosarska plays a stereotypical Polish noblewoman whose actions are motivated equally by patriotic feelings and by her love for Prawdzic. The framing scenes heighten *To Siberia's* edifying premise. The film opens with a brief introductory lecture that stresses the importance of the 1905 revolutionary events in Polish history, and ends with Prawdzic's father-in-law (Mieczysław Frenkiel) reminding two grandchildren that they can live in a free Poland thanks to the bravery of their father.

Due to its popularity among audiences, *To Siberia* was imitated by a number of later films, whose reliance on clichéd images and situations sometimes borders on the comedic. The star of *To Siberia*, Adam Brodzisz, often appeared in other patriotic films at the beginning of the 1930s. Since his debut in Józef Lejtes's *Z dnia na dzień* (*From Day to Day*, 1929), this popular and photogenic actor[14] starred in, among others, *Uroda życia* (*The Beauty of Life*, 1930, Juliusz Gardan), *Dziesięciu z Pawiaka* (*The Ten from the Pawiak Prison*, 1931, Ryszard Ordyński), and *Młody las* (*Young Forest*, 1934, Józef Lejtes).

The majority of "patriotic pictures" are trapped by their own conventions and clichés. For instance, Ordyński's *The Ten from the Pawiak Prison* refers to actual events that took place in 1906, but alters them to fulfill the demands of patriotic melodrama. The film tells the story of the attempts of the PPS (Polish Socialist Party) to free its ten members who were arrested and kept in the infamous Pawiak prison. This film propagates the official version of patriotism, popular among audiences and the ruling elite, and changes the historical facts to make the film more appealing to the public, as well as to please Marshal Piłsudski and his government.[15]

In a number of other films, the historical events are modified as well, not only to accommodate the melodramatic love story, but also to suit the current political situation. For instance, Michał Waszyński's *Bohaterowie Sybiru* (*The Heroes of Siberia*, 1936) narrates the story of Polish POWs and exiles in Siberia in 1918. On hearing about the formation of Polish military forces, they travel through war-torn Russia. One of the Polish officers makes a comment that could be stolen from Marshal Piłsudski's political speech: "A strong army is the decisive factor securing the welfare of a citizen, the development of education and arts. Herein lies the sense of the state." Such observations, using history to comment on the current state of affairs, are frequent in Polish cinema and are not limited to the "patriotic genre." The national pride that developed from the newly regained freedom and from the interwar economic development is featured in a number of Polish films. In Leonard Buczkowski's *Rapsodia Bałtyku* (*The Baltic Rhapsody*, 1935), two young navy officers on a warship (played by Adam Brodzisz and Mieczysław Cybulski) look with pride at the newly built Baltic port in Gdynia near Gdańsk (Danzig). While the camera cuts between the medium shot of the two officers and long shots of distant Gdynia, the following conversation takes place:

– "Our shore! Look! What power comes from this Gdynia.
– "And do you remember what it looked like fifteen years ago!?"

– "And now ..."

– "The profound effort of our nation made this miracle. You know ... I feel somehow strangely moved when I look at this, our only gateway to the world. And I think that the same happens in the heart of every Pole."[16]

Polish prewar films are not afraid of using pathos to express the martyrological events from the past, or to present the current achievements; they also portray the euphoria resulting from reclaimed freedom. Nevertheless, the events of 1905, the battlefields of World War I, and the Polish-Soviet war often serve merely as exotic backdrops for action films or melodramas. This is the case, for instance, with *Krwawy Wschód* (*Bloody East*, 1931) by Jan Nowina-Przybylski, which was advertised as the first epic war film with sound. In this film, the Polish-Soviet war serves as a background for a familiar love triangle: in the trenches, an officer confesses to his friend that, while recuperating in a hospital, he fell in mutual love with a nurse. He shows her picture to his friend, who recognizes the nurse as his own wife. The husband volunteers for a difficult mission and dies securing the happiness of his friend.

Another brand of "patriotic pictures" features films, set in distant times, that promote popular and nationalistic versions of Poland's history. Frequently, these films refer to popular paintings or sketches and mythologized stories. In the Polish context, these were safe choices. Polish audiences had (and still have) a predilection for stylized, safe history, as if it were an illustration of common historical knowledge. This version of history, which reinforced rather than questioned national myths, was well received by audiences but, as a rule, attacked by critics for these very reasons. Polish history, mythology, and the landscape seemed to be enough to attract Polish viewers regularly exposed to Western (mostly Hollywood) films. Edward Puchalski's *Przeor Kordecki: obrońca Częstochowy* (*Abbot Kordecki: The Defender of Częstochowa*, 1934) may serve as a good example. This film refers to the Polish-Swedish war (known as the "Swedish Deluge") that took place between 1655 and 1660, and was mythologized in popular historical accounts, first of all, by Henryk Sienkiewicz in his epic novel *The Deluge*.[17] During the "Swedish Deluge," the monastery at Częstochowa, led by the Abbot Kordecki, successfully defended itself against the Swedish troops. Alina Madej writes that the film had been constructed so that "its every element refers to the commonly known national *universum*. The defence of the monastery at Jasna Góra supports the myth that the country has the highest, sacred value. This myth is expressed by ostentatious religious-patriotic imagery, and the love story motif developed in a mawkish-lyrical tone."[18]

At the beginning of the 1930s, Józef Lejtes, arguably the best Polish director of the interwar era, quickly gained a reputation for his cinematic treatment of recent Polish history. In *Dzikie pola* (*Wild Fields*, 1932), he deals with the fate of Polish soldiers trying to return to their country from Russia after the end of World War I. Another critically acclaimed film,

Córka generała Pankratowa (*General Pankratov's Daughter*, 1934), officially directed by Mieczysław Znamierowski, but in actual practice by Lejtes,[19] refers to the political unrest in 1905. With its superb cast (Nora Ney, Franciszek Brodniewicz, and Kazimierz Junosza-Stępowski), Seweryn Steinwurzel's camera, Henryk Wars's musical score, and Lejtes's adroit use of the conventions of melodrama applied to the events of 1905, it became one of the best-known examples of mid-1930s Polish cinema.

The events of 1905 are also the setting of two other well-received films by Lejtes: *Young Forest* and *Róża* (*Rose*, 1936). The former, the best film of 1934, according to the readers of the weekly magazine *Kino*,[20] deals with the conflict between Polish students and their Russian teachers. The latter, an adaptation of Stefan Żeromski's novel, focuses on the story of the Polish Socialist Party members and their fight against the tsarist regime. Unlike other directors of "patriotic pictures," Lejtes does not let the films' romantic subplot overtake the story. He avoids national stereotyping, provides a more complex characterization of the Russians, and in *Young Forest* illustrates the Polish-Russian solidarity against the tsarist regime.

Lejtes was not interested solely in recent Polish history; some of his other films refer to more distant mythologized events in Polish history. His *Barbara Radziwiłłówna* (1936), with Jadwiga Smosarska in the leading role, portrays the love story between the king of Poland, Zygmunt August, and Barbara from the noble family of Radziwiłł. Another historical epic, *Kościuszko pod Racławicami* (*Kościuszko at Racławice*, 1938), deals with an event that has a permanent place in Polish mythology: the 1794 national insurrection led by Tadeusz Kościuszko.

Comedy

Very few of the 117 feature films produced in Poland in the 1920s can be classified as comedies.[21] Patriotically oriented melodramas dominated in the 1920s, but the mid-1930s belonged to comedy. Polish popular cinema began to be controlled by people associated with Warsaw musical theaters and cabarets. From that milieu came popular actors, such as Adolf Dymsza and Eugeniusz Bodo; composers, including Henryk Wars; and directors, for example, Konrad Tom, who was also an actor. The use of the same group of actors, mostly coming from the popular Warsaw cabarets Qui pro Quo and Banda (The Band), and of similar themes sometimes gives the audience a sense of déja vu. Actors such as Kazimierz Krukowski, Tola Mankiewiczówna, Zula Pogorzelska, and Aleksander Żabczyński are put in clichéd situations taken from musical theater and frequently perform their well-known cabaret numbers on screen. The targets of Polish comedies remain "the terrible middle class" and the provincial hillbillies. The comedies frequently verge on caricature in their use of grotesque characters and names. The theatrical roots of many films resulted in an emphasis on dialogue and music at the expense of composition of frame and editing, for these were mostly musical comedies consisting of hit songs composed by the popular Henryk Wars.[22]

By and large, Polish comedies employed the structure of musical theater, farce, and Viennese operetta, or they imitated German comedies. A typical, unsophisticated narrative centers on two attractive lovers who, with the help of secondary characters (mostly played by comic actors), overcome difficulties and are united in the finale. Other types of narratives utilize the Cinderella story and the theme of mistaken identity. The poor are disguised as the rich in *Jego ekscelencja subiekt* (*His Excellency, the Salesclerk*, 1933), and the rich are veiled as the poor in *Jaśnie pan szofer* (*His Excellency, the Chauffeur*, 1935), both directed by Michał Waszyński, and both starring Ina Benita and Eugeniusz Bodo. The theme of mistaken identity is also prominent in comedies about women masquerading as men, for example, *Czy Lucyna to dziewczyna* (*Is Lucyna a Girl?* 1934), directed by Juliusz Gardan, with Jadwiga Smosarska and Eugeniusz Bodo in the leading roles.

Adolf Dymsza (Adolf Bagiński, 1900–1975) is certainly the symbol of Polish prewar comedy. At the beginning of his career, Dymsza appeared in a number of supporting roles that were well received by both the public and the critics. He was usually cast as a working-class or streetwise character who could outwit anybody. This character, a Warsaw sly dog named Dodek, was the continuation of a characterization featured in Dymsza's earlier cabaret performances.

After a series of memorable supporting roles, for example, in one of the biggest successes of 1933, *Anybody Can Love*, Dymsza's later films were typical star vehicles, written specifically for him and accommodating his type of humor and screen persona. Sometimes he was paired with other well-known comic actors, for example, with the "Czech Groucho Marx,"[23] Vlasta Burian, in a Polish-Czech coproduction, *Dwanaście krzeseł* (*Twelve Chairs*, 1933), directed by Michał Waszyński and Martin Frič. The protagonists of this film are in search of twelve used chairs because $100,000 is hidden in one of them. The differences in comic styles and the situational and verbal humor caused by the language barrier are the prime sources of humor in this film.

The stock situations and characters from Polish "patriotic pictures" returned in the mid-1930s, though this time as parodies, in two comedies starring Dymsza: *Antek Policmajster* (*Antek, the Police Chief*, 1935), and *Dodek na froncie* (*Dodek at the Front*, 1936), both directed by Michał Waszyński. Frequently voted the best Polish prewar comedy, *Antek, the Police Chief* is set around the year 1905 and deals with a Warsaw sly dog, Antek Król (Dymsza), who is chased by the Russian tsarist police for a trivial crime. Escaping by train, he finds himself in the compartment of a drunken and sleeping Russian police chief, who is traveling to his new post in one of the provincial towns. Antek steals the police chief's uniform, takes on his identity, and performs his role in the tradition of Nikolai Gogol's best short stories. Even when Antek's true identity is revealed, he is let free by the governor (Antoni Fertner), who is afraid of disgracing himself. The situational humor, the mockery of the martyrological dimensions of earlier "patriotic pictures," and the presence of known actors in supporting roles (Maria Bogda, Mieczysława Ćwiklińska, and Konrad Tom) made the film a success with audiences. Other films featuring Dymsza, such as *ABC miłości* (*ABC of Love* (1935), *Wacuś* (1935), and *Bolek i Lolek* (*Bolek and Lolek*, 1936), all directed by Michał Waszyński, although box-office successes, were never as popular as *Antek, the Police Chief*. The weak scripts of these films, built around unsophisticated cabaret numbers, did not enable Dymsza to develop his screen personality.

The crowning achievement of prewar Polish musical comedy remains *Zapomniana melodia* (*Forgotten Melody*, 1938), directed by Konrad Tom and Jan Fethke. This comedy of errors offers a fresh and unpretentious filmic experience. The well-executed script by Fethke, Ludwik Starski, and Napoleon Sądek introduces a lively and logically developed plot. Stefan (Aleksander Żabczyński), who is in love with Helenka (Helena Grossówna), is mistaken for the son of a cosmetic firm owner who competes with the company owned by Helenka's father (Antoni Fertner). Helenka's father, afraid of the competition, destroys the recipe for his new product, but first memorizes it with the help of a melody that he later forgets. In the film's climax, he recalls the "forgotten melody" while listening to Stefan's song to his beloved Helenka.

Forgotten Melody was cast with an ensemble of popular actors, including Grossówna, Żabczyński, Fertner, Jadwiga Andrzejewska, Michał Znicz, and Stanisław Sielański. It neither relies on a star performance, nor resembles popular cabaret sketches—the Achilles' heel of a number of prewar Polish comedies. The Polish prewar reviewers aptly noted a similarity to American musicals, mainly to the well-received films featuring Universal Studio's star, Deanna Durbin.[24] Today, this film is chiefly remembered in Poland for its musical pieces composed by Henryk Wars to the lyrics of Ludwik Starski.

Melodrama

In Poland, as well as in other countries, melodramas continued to be popular due to their sensationalism and story lines that dealt with "forbidden" aspects of life. The theme of prostitution and "white slavery" appears in *Uwiedziona* (*The Seduced*, 1931, Michał Waszyński); drug addiction in *Biała trucizna* (*White Poison*, 1932, Alfred Niemirski); alcoholism in *Dusze w niewoli* (*Imprisoned Souls*, 1930, Leon Trystan, with the legend of Polish theater Ludwik Solski); and sexuality in *Dzieje grzechu* (*The Story of Sin*, 1933, Henryk Szaro). As a rule, these films recycle the cautionary story about the dangers young women face when they try to follow their dreams to earn money and have a career overseas. A separate group of now forgotten films consists of works labeled by Małgorzata Hendrykowska as "exotic

Figure 2.1 Adolf Dymsza and Maria Bogda in Michał Waszyński's comedy *Antek, the Police Chief* (1935)

kitsch."[25] *Głos pustyni* (*The Sound of the Desert*, 1932) and *Czarna perła* (*Black Pearl*, 1934), both directed by Michał Waszyński, are set in exotic places (North Africa and Hawaii, respectively), and are abundant with clichéd narratives concerning brave and intelligent Poles and backward locals.

The treatment of women in Polish melodramas oscillates between presenting them as femme fatales in the tradition of Pola Negri's silent features made for the Sfinks company, and as vulnerable figures at the mercy of the environment. The former representation, which is not very popular in Polish cinema, can be seen in *Zabawka* (*The Toy*, 1933), directed by Michał Waszyński. The title refers to the female protagonist Lulu (Alma Kar), a Warsaw cabaret star, who is invited to a country manor by a wealthy landowner. The landowner's son and a local Don Juan both fall in love with Lulu and pay for it. The name of the protagonist and the theme of the film suggest G. W. Pabst's influence (Louise Brooks as Lulu in *Pandora's Box*, 1929), and this inspiration had been emphasized by one of the scriptwriters of the film.[26]

The destructive role of the city woman is a common filmic theme that is present in one of the most successful early sound films, *Cham* (*The Boor*, 1931), directed by Jan Nowina-Przybylski and based on Eliza Orzeszkowa's novel. This melodrama, set in rural Poland, draws on the familiar clash between the corrupt city and the pastoral country. As in *Sunrise* (1927), the classic by F. W. Murnau, the woman from the city seduces a village man (this time a single man). *The Boor* narrates a love story between a former prostitute, Franka (Krystyna Ankwicz), and a good-natured fisherman, Paweł (Mieczysław Cybulski). Paweł forgives Franka not only for her past, but also for her marital affairs and her attempt to poison him. He also defends her against the angry villagers. Franka despises him as *cham* (the boor), cannot stand his good-hearted nature, and drowns herself, leaving him alone with her daughter.

Much praised by Polish critics, *Wyrok życia* (*Life Sentence*, 1933), directed by Juliusz Gardan,[27] portrays its female protagonist, Hanna (Jadwiga Andrzejewska), as a victim of hostile circumstances. While in prison, after being convicted of killing her child and sentenced to death, she relates episodes from her life to her female defense lawyer, Krystyna (Irena Eichlerówna). From Hanna's stories we learn of her lonely childhood, brief unhappy love, and hard material conditions. Poverty forces her to abandon her child (who drowns), in the hope that it will be found and taken care of by somebody else. When Hanna's lawyer manages to get her out of prison and invites her home, it appears that Krystyna's husband is the father of Hanna's child. When Hanna learns that he really loves Krystyna, she leaves their house.

Stylistically, *Life Sentence* uses many elements of expressionist cinema and the poetics of silent cinema, which, for more ambitious Polish filmmakers at that time, was "a kind of defence against the abuse of words in standard talkies."[28] The opening sequence, for example, juxtaposes the prosecutor's uplifting words about children with images of a father punishing his child. What follows are the scenes of the jurors returning to their daily business, the neon lights announcing "the evening of laughter," and the paper with the news about the trial disappearing into a gutter. In spite of this opening sequence, with the film moving toward social drama, the melodramatic conventions quickly overtake the story. In *Life Sentence* social and economic conditions are not to blame for Hanna's misfortune, but rather her lack of social skills and her own immaturity.

One of the biggest box-office hits of the decade became *Pod Twoją obronę* (*Under Your Protection*, 1933), scripted and directed by the experienced Edward Puchalski.[29] It narrates a story about a Polish pilot, Jan Polaski (Adam Brodzisz), who is working on an invention that has caught the interest of foreign spies. In mysterious circumstances, his plane crashes the day before his wedding to Maryla (Maria Bogda).[30] Paralyzed but cared for by his faithful fiancée, he travels to the holy picture of the Black Madonna in Częstochowa, where he is miraculously cured. The combination of a simple melodramatic plot and a strong religious content (the choice of Częstochowa) proved to be an enormous success with audiences.

A number of popular films in the 1930s were adaptations of well-known literary works—classics of literature and pulp fiction alike. An early sound film by Ryszard Ordyński was loosely adapted from Henryk Sienkiewicz's novella *Janko Muzykant* (*Johnny the Musician*, 1930). Sidestepping Sienkiewicz's stress on social injustice, Ordyński produced a formulaic film about a career against all odds. A young shepherd boy, Johnny, himself a talented musician, steals a fiddle from a country manor, is caught, and is sent to a juvenile detention center. Later, with the help of his inmates, who support his talent, he breaks out, and in Warsaw finds success as a musician.

Józef Lejtes is known for his skillful adaptations of celebrated contemporary novels: *Dziewczęta z Nowolipek* (*The Girls from Nowolipki*, 1937) and *Granica* (*Line*, 1938), based on the novels by Pola Gojawiczyńska and Zofia Nałkowska, respectively. *The Girls from Nowolipki* portrays the dramatic stories of four young women: Bronka (Elżbieta Barszczewska), Franka (Jadwiga Andrzejewska), Amelka (Tamara Wiszniewska), and Kwiryna (Hanna Jaraczówna), who live in the same working-class Warsaw building. The multiplicity of realistic details, the complex psychological pictures of four women, and the portrayal of their aspirations, which are verified by the prose of life, made this film not only a box-office success, but also a cultural event.[31]

Line offers a fatalistic story of a man, Zenon Ziembiewicz (Jerzy Pichelski), torn between two women: his lover Justyna (Lena Żelichowska) and his wife Elżbieta (Elżbieta Barszczewska). Lejtes is more interested in the tragic dimensions of the triangle than in the social issues permeating Nałkowska's novel (Justyna is a simple woman from the village, Elżbieta a sophisticated one from the big city). Żelichowska's performance as Justyna stresses the tragic aspect of her character and makes her an intricate persona, vulgar and tender at the same time, suffering from the extremes of love and hate for the man with whom she has had an ongoing affair.

Figure 2.2 Stanisława Wysocka (right) and Lena Żelichowska in Józef Lejtes's *Line* (1938)

The melodramatic conventions and sentimental narrative are also present in adaptations of pulp fiction, box-office successes based on the novels of Helena Mniszkówna, Tadeusz Dołęga-Mostowicz, and Maria Rodziewiczówna. Dołęga-Mostowicz's books, in particular, became extremely popular in the late 1930s. One of his adaptations, *Znachor* (*Quack*, 1937), directed by Michał Waszyński, remains for many the symbol of Polish popular cinema in the 1930s. The story concerns a well-known surgeon, Rafał Wilczur (Kazimierz Junosza-Stępowski), who loses his memory and lives as a tramp for many years. He eventually settles in a village and helps the locals as a quack. Later, due to some happy coincidences, he regains his memory, as well as his previous social standing and material status.

The popularity of this film helped to produce the sequels, *Profesor Wilczur* (*Professor Wilczur*, 1938), again directed by Waszyński, and *Testament Profesora Wilczura* (*Professor Wilczur's Last Will*, Leonard Buczkowski), which was made before the war but not released by the Germans until 1942. Equally popular were melodramas based on Mniszkówna's writings—the new version of *Trędowata* (*The Leper*, 1936) and an adaptation of Rodziewiczówna's novel, *Wrzos* (*Heather*, 1938), both films directed by Juliusz Gardan. *The Leper* introduced a new pair of popular screen lovers, Elżbieta Barszczewska and Franciszek Brodniewicz, while *Heather* introduced Stanisława Angel-Engelówna.

A New Sensibility: The START Group

An important part of the Polish critical, and later filmmaking, scene, the Society for the Promotion of Film Art (START)[32] was established in Warsaw in 1930 by, among others, Jerzy Toeplitz, who became a famous film historian, and the notable Polish filmmakers Wanda Jakubowska, Eugeniusz Cękalski, Jerzy Zarzycki, Aleksander Ford, Jerzy Bossak, and Stanisław Wohl. This was a dynamic cine-club that promoted ambitious, "artistic" cinema through screenings, lectures, and seminars, as well as articles published in almost all of the major Polish journals. The young members of START were primarily cultural educators who were interested in changing the landscape of film production in Poland. In an article published in Warsaw in 1932, the board of the Society explicitly pointed out that the main task of the group was to "popularize and propagate a few valuable films, to discredit and boycott worthless cultural productions, and to awaken interest in film as a first-class educational component."[33]

The START members began their careers by attacking commercial Polish productions while promoting art cinema. Regarding cinema—and for that matter, all arts—as more than just entertainment, they were united by "the struggle for films for the public good," which was the START slogan from 1932. Under the influence of Soviet filmmakers, the START activists considered film to be a socially useful art. In an extensive press campaign, the START members raised fundamental problems concerning Polish cinema and provided some solutions for improving the situation. They believed that the only chance to have an artistic cinema was to have an enlightened audience. By educating the public, they hoped to limit the production of mediocre films and to create audiences ready to accept truly creative, even experimental, cinematic works.

The only member of START with some film experience was Aleksander Ford (1908–1980). His much praised debut, *Legion ulicy* (*Legion of the Street*, 1932), was one of the first films showing a realistic picture of everyday life coupled with elements of social commentary. Ford's film, which focused on Warsaw street boys who sell newspapers, was well narrated, devoid of the stereotypical sentimental features that permeated Polish narratives, and realistic to the point of "foretelling neorealism."[34] An attempt to reflect the atmosphere of the street was more important for Ford than the story itself. The realistic aspect of *Legion of the Street*, enhanced by the casting of young nonprofessional actors, certainly presages Ford's documentary beginnings. The young director, then only twenty-four, was hailed, by the leftist press in particular (he was a known communist), as the most promising Polish director.

Ford's film, like many others, is now lost. Stills, publicity materials, reviews, and articles held by the Polish National Film Archives prove that this film was well received by the majority of reviewers. It was voted the best film of the year by the weekly *Kino* readers. One critic commented: "Among domestic productions, this film is a kind of curiosity. It is neither an illustration of a novel nor photographed theater, but a genuine film, born out of cinematographic elements such as movement, visual approach to phenomena, riveting photography, editing, etc."[35] Other ventures by Ford into mainstream cinema were less successful. The authors of the second volume of *The History of Polish Cinema* note that the combination of the conventions of traditional cinema and communist messages produced a "pretentious style" that was "anachronistic in its modernist avant-gardism."[36]

After the disintegration of the START group in 1935, its former members attempted to make films that reflected their interest in socially committed cinema. In 1937, some of the START members, including Ford, Cękalski, and Wohl, established Spółdzielnia Autorów Filmowych (the Cooperative of Film Authors). Their two productions, *Strachy* (*The Ghosts*, 1938), directed by Eugeniusz Cękalski and Karol Szołowski, and *The People of the Vistula*, directed by Aleksander Ford and Jerzy Zarzycki, are among the finest achievements in Polish prewar cinema.

The Ghosts, set in the Warsaw world of cabarets and musical theaters, is an adaptation of Maria Ukniewska's semiautobiographical novel. The film's dialogue was cowritten by well-known Polish poets Konstanty Ildefons Gałczyński and Władysław Broniewski, and the cast included, with the exception of the newcomer-dancer Hanka Karwowska, some of the finest prewar actors: Eugeniusz Bodo, Józef Węgrzyn, Jacek Woszczerowicz, and the hardest-working star of the Polish prewar cinema, Mieczysława Ćwiklińska. The safe choice of two legends of Polish theater, Węgrzyn and Woszczerowicz, to play supporting roles proved to be a success. The old bombastic and alcoholic Russian dancer Dubenko (Węgrzyn), who dies during the film, and the mysterious illusionist Srobosz (Woszczerowicz) remain the strongest characters in the film.

The story of *The Ghosts* deals with two young female friends who work in a chorus line for a second-rate revue theater. The more pragmatic Teresa (Hanka Karwowska) has an up-and-down affair with the star of the show, Zygmunt Modecki (Eugeniusz Bodo). The sentimental and vulnerable Lilka (Jadwiga Andrzejewska) cannot bear the pressures and intrigues surrounding her and, in an act of desperation, commits suicide. The specific nature of the portrayed world and the aura of scandal that accompanied the publication of Ukniewska's novel undeniably attracted Cękalski and Szołowski. Despite their avant-garde backgrounds and leftist convictions, their approach to cinema can be best described as mainstream with a tendency to experiment.

The theme of *The Ghosts* has little to do with the lofty ideals of the START group, yet the film's visualization contains traces of the group's search for the new language of film. With its tendency toward symbolism and melancholy, and a dark visual style (due to night-time settings), Stanisław Wohl and Adolf Forbert's cinematography reflects the strong influences of French poetic realism. *The Ghosts* also exhibits a number of slightly old-fashioned avant-garde devices: rapid, sometimes rough montage;

Figure 2.3 *The Ghosts* (1938), directed by Eugeniusz Cękalski and Karol Szołowski. From the left: Hanka Karwowska, Jan Kreczmar, and Eugeniusz Bodo

superimposed images to portray dream sequences; and voice-over narration to comment on the state of the protagonist's mind. The film is distinguished by its feeling of authenticity, and by very well-choreographed and executed dance numbers, a rarity in Polish cinema.[37]

The second production of the Cooperative of Film Authors, *The People of the Vistula*, based on Helena Boguszewska and Jerzy Kornacki's realistic novel *Wisła* (*Vistula*), is known for its realistic portrayal of the marginalized groups of society. The melodramatic aspect of this film focuses on Anna (Ina Benita), the daughter of the barge owner on the Vistula River, who is in love with a handsome petty thief from the shore, Aleksy (Jerzy Pichelski). The true heroine of the film, however, is Matyjaska, the tragic, struggling owner of another barge, who is played by one of the leading prewar theatrical actresses, Stanisława Wysocka.

This film is set in the milieu of Jean Vigo's *L'Atalante* (1934) and also bears some features of Vigo's masterpiece: glimpses of social conditions, a love story on a river barge, the life on the shore contrasted with that on the barge. Like Vigo, the makers of *The People of the Vistula* employ a number of traveling shots, evoke the beauty of life on the river, and show sympathy for the portrayed community. Stanisław Lipiński's cinematography commands attention from this film's dynamic opening sequence: the low-angle shots against the sky, the moving camera, and the portrayal of river life in the manner of a folk ballad. The realistic depiction is somewhat compromised by the intrusion of the staged "bar scenes," which were forced on Ford and Zarzycki by the film producers.[38]

Films in Yiddish

The richness and uniqueness of prewar Jewish culture in Poland is reflected in the thriving Yiddish cinema of the 1930s. Films in Yiddish were made in Poland but were primarily fashioned for the American market. The first Yiddish films known to have been produced in Poland, such as *Der vilder Foter* (*The Cruel Father*, Andrzej Marek), appeared in 1911.[39] In the 1930s they became an important part of the Polish film scene. The first sound film in Yiddish, *At Chejt* (*For Sins*), directed by Aleksander Marten, the former student of Max Reinhardt,[40] however, was made as late as 1936.

A Polish-born American, Joseph Green (Józef Grinberg), is known for a number of films produced in Poland that depict Jewish life in Eastern Europe. Green's works include his well-received musical comedy *Yidl mitn Fidl* (*Yiddle with His Fiddle*, 1936), with the American-Jewish actress Molly Picon, based on Konrad Tom's script and codirected by Green and a Polish director, Jan Nowina-Przybylski. Shot mostly on location in Kazimierz Dolny, a historic town with well-preserved architecture, this film is today chiefly remembered for its music, written by the American Abraham Ellstein. It tells the story of a girl (played by Molly Picon), dressed as a boy fiddler, and three other *klezmorim* (musicians) touring the Jewish quarters of small Polish towns. When the girl falls in love with one of the musicians, she has to reveal her true identity.

One of the best-known examples of the flourishing Yiddish cinema in Poland is the Yiddish classic *Der Dibuk* (*The Dybbuk*, 1937), directed by Michał Waszyński, a film adapted from a popular play by S. An-sky (Shloyme Zanvil Rappoport). Deeply rooted in Jewish folklore and mysticism, and heavily influenced by German expressionist theater, this film about unfulfilled love is frequently listed as one of the masterpieces of prewar European cinema.[41] *The Dybbuk* portrays the world of nineteenth-century Eastern European Hasidim—the world of traditional superstitions—and couples it with a melodramatic aspect. It offers a metaphysical tragedy in the spirit of *Romeo and Juliet*.

The list of Joseph Green's successful productions also includes his *Der Purimshpiler* (*The Purim Player*, 1937), codirected with Jan Nowina-Przybylski, and, in 1938, *A Little Letter to Mother*, codirected with Leon

Trystan (Chaim Lejb Wagman). Ten films in Yiddish were made in Poland between 1936 and 1939. Although they frequently employed the familiar features of musical comedy and melodrama, their strength lies in their reliance on Jewish folklore and metaphysics, and the flair of authenticity in their portrayal of the Jewish *shtetl* life in Poland. As Eric A. Goldman writes, these films "left us a legacy for centuries to come and a record of a life that would be no more."[42]

Notes

1. Barbara Armatys, Leszek Armatys, and Wiesław Stradomski, *Historia filmu polskiego 1930–1939*, vol. 2 (Warsaw: Wydawnictwa Artystyczne i Filmowe, 1988), 15.
2. Taxes for Polish films were as low as 5 percent in Warsaw and 3 percent outside of the capital, compared with 60 and 35 percent respectively for foreign films. Furthermore, cinema owners had a chance to benefit from an additional 25 percent reduction of taxes on foreign films if their screening time of Polish feature films was not less than 10 percent. Ibid., 16 and 42.
3. Ibid., 14 and 17.
4. Subtitling is a common practice in modern Poland, both in cinema theaters and on television. On television, however, subtitles are often replaced by the voice of a reader over the original dialogues, so that the viewer can also hear the original language version.
5. Edward Zajiček, *Poza ekranem. Kinematografia polska 1918–1991* (Warsaw: Filmoteka Narodowa and Wydawnictwa Artystyczne i Filmowe, 1992), 17. In the 1930s, however, Hollywood clearly dominated the Polish market, comprising 77 percent of all foreign films in 1934 and 61 percent in 1938. The remaining films mostly came from Germany, France, and Austria (Viennese comedies). See also Jerzy Płażewski, "Film zagraniczny w Polsce," in *Encyklopedia kultury polskiej XX wieku: Film i kinematografia*, ed. Edward Zajiček (Warsaw: Instytut Kultury and Komitet Kinematografii, 1994), 329.
6. Discussed by Jerzy Maśnicki and Kamil Stepan, "100 lat kina w Polsce: 1930–1933," *Kino* 2 (1998): 47–48.
7. Armatys, Armatys, and Stradomski, *Historia filmu polskiego*, 239.
8. Figures from Edward D. Wynot, Jr., *Warsaw Between the World Wars: Profile of the Capital City in a Developing Land, 1918–1939* (New York: Columbia University Press, 1983), 280–281.
9. Edward Zajiček, "Kinematografia," in idem, ed., *Encyklopedia kultury polskiej XX wieku*, 53.
10. Alina Madej, *Mitologie i konwencje. O polskim kinie fabularnym dwudziestolecia międzywojennego* (Cracow: Universitas, 1994), 60.
11. Wynot, *Warsaw Between the World Wars*, 281.
12. Jerzy Maśnicki and Kamil Stepan, *Pleograf. Słownik biograficzny filmu polskiego 1896–1939* (Cracow: Staromiejska Oficyna Wydawnicza, 1996), entry "Krzeptowski" [no page numbers].
13. The symbolic meaning of several Polish screen names may escape the attention of a non-Polish-speaking viewer. They not only display the nationality or class background of a protagonist, but frequently signal the features of his or her personality. For example, the name "Prawdzic" designates somebody who believes in truth, someone who can be trusted (*prawda*=truth). The name "Czarska" is close to "charm" (*czar* in Polish).
14. Adam Brodzisz (1906–1986) graduated from Wiktor Biegański's Warsaw Film Institute in 1927, and received his first acting opportunity in 1929, after winning "the contest of the photogenic" organized by the *Warsaw Evening* newspaper. Maśnicki and Stepan, *Pleograf*, entry "Brodzisz" [no page numbers].

15. *The Ten from the Pawiak Prison* was based on the account of Colonel Jan Jur-Gorze-chowski, the chief organizer of the 1906 action. Ferdynand Goetel's script, however, focuses on the melodramatic story of a young freedom fighter (played by Adam Brodzisz), and changes historical events. For example, to make their deed more heroic, the ten patriots in this film are arrested for the terrorist act against the military police general, and not for participating in anti-Russian demonstrations. The premiere of Ordyński's film was attended by the Polish officials, including Marshal Piłsudski.

16. *The Baltic Rhapsody* belongs to a popular group of so-called "sea movies" (*filmy morskie*) such as *Under the Banner of Love*, directed by Michał Waszyński, and *Wiatr of morza* (*The Wind from the Sea*, 1930), directed by Kazimierz Czyński. The newly gained access to the Baltic Sea after World War I gave rise to this group of films.

17. Henryk Sienkiewicz's *Potop* (*The Deluge*) forms his well-known historical trilogy with *Pan Wołodyjowski* (*Pan Michael*, aka *Colonel Wołodyjowski*) and *Ogniem i mieczem* (*With Fire and Sword*). Jerzy Hoffman adapted this trilogy for the screen in 1969 (*Pan Michael*), 1974 (*The Deluge*), and 1999 (*With Fire and Sword*). These works will be discussed later in the book.

18. Madej, *Mitologie i konwencje*, 118. The monastery at Częstochowa, the Polish holy sanctuary, houses the icon of the Black Madonna (the Virgin Mary). The term *Jasna Góra* (literally, Bright Mountain) refers to the monastery.

19. Józef Lejtes was hired to direct *General Pankratov's Daughter*. Mieczysław Znamierowski acted as an assistant director and as a producer. To be credited as a director, he gave up his salary. Jerzy Maśnicki and Kamil Stepan, "100 lat kina w Polsce: 1934–1937," *Kino* 3 (1998); 47.

20. Armatys, Armatys, and Stradomski, *Historia filmu polskiego*, 257.

21. Stanisław Janicki, *Polskie filmy fabularne 1902–1988* (Warsaw: Wydawnictwa Artystyczne i Filmowe, 1990), 28–67.

22. Henryk Wars (1902–1977) provided musical scores for as many as forty-three films between 1932 and 1939. Ibid., 78–131. His numerous prewar hits include one of the best-loved songs, "Miłość ci wszystko wybaczy" (Love Will Forgive You Everything), performed in a 1933 film, *Szpieg w masce* (*The Masked Spy*, Mieczysław Krawicz), by Hanka Ordonówna. Prewar film music was also produced by such popular composers as Jerzy Petersburski, Władysław Daniłowski (Dan), Władysław Szpilman, Roman Palester, and Jan Maklakiewicz.

23. Josef Škvorecký, *All the Bright Young Men and Women: A Personal History of the Czech Cinema*, trans. Michael Schonberg (Toronto: Take One Film Book, 1971), 22.

24. Armatys, Armatys, and Stradomski, *Historia filmu polskiego*, 304.

25. Małgorzata Hendrykowska, "Polak walczy z dzikusami. Kicz egzotyczny w polskim kinie międzywojennym," *Kino* 9 (1996): 22–23 and 31.

26. Coscriptwriter Andrzej Łomakowski, quoted in Armatys, Armatys, and Stradomski, *Historia filmu polskiego*, 234–235.

27. *Life Sentence* was voted the best film of the 1933–1934 season. Ibid., 226.

28. Ibid., 28.

29. *Under Your Protection* was in fact directed by Józef Lejtes, but because of his Jewish origins, his name had to be removed from the credits in order to please the Catholic Church, the patron of this "Christian film." It played for twenty-one continuous weeks in one of the biggest Warsaw cinemas, the Apollo. This was an unprecedented story. At the climax of the film, the miracle at Częstochowa, a number of viewers knelt and said prayers. Ibid., 244–245.

30. Maria Bogda and Adam Brodzisz, popular prewar actors, were an actual off-screen couple (married in 1930).

31. The reviewers praised the composition of the film and the harmony of the narration, and stressed that in Polish cinema *The Girls from Nowolipki* became the first "stylistic directorial success." Zbigniew Pitera, "Twórcy sztuki filmowej," *Srebrny Ekran* 12 (1937). Quoted from Armatys, Armatys, and Stradomski, *Historia filmu polskiego*, 286.

32. Stowarzyszenie Propagandy Filmu Artystycznego Start. From 1931, officially known as Stowarzyszenie Miłośników Filmu Artystycznego START.

33. "Film polski na bezdrożach," *Głos Stolicy* 87 (1932): 5. Quoted from Jadwiga Bocheńska, *Polska myśl filmowa do roku 1939* (Wrocław: Ossolineum, 1974), 174.
34. Tadeusz Lubelski, "Film fabularny," in Zajiček, ed., *Encyklopedia kultury polskiej XX wieku*, 127.
35. Stefania Heymanowa, quoted from Maśnicki and Stepan, "100 lat kina w Polsce: 1934–1937," 50.
36. Armatys, Armatys, and Stradomski, *Historia filmu polskiego*, 226.
37. In 1979 Stanisław Lenartowicz made *Strachy* (*The Ghosts*), a television series of four episodes also based on Maria Ukniewska's novel.
38. The producers were afraid that Ford and Zarzycki intended to make an uneventful, realistic film about the life of "simple people." Boycotted by the owners of cinema theaters, who despised Ford and his political convictions, the producers decided to shorten the documentary-like scenes, which created the ballad-like atmosphere of this film at the expense of staged "bar scenes." Ibid., 270.
39. Janicki, *Polskie filmy fabularne*, 11.
40. Maśnicki and Stepan, "100 lat kina w Polsce: 1934–1937," 49.
41. For example, by Parker Tyler in his *Classics of the Foreign Film: A Pictorial Treasury* (Secaucus, N.J.: Citadel Press, 1962). For some insightful comments, see Ira Konigsberg, "The Only 'I' in the World: Religion, Psychoanalysis and the Dybbuk," *Cinema Journal* 35, no. 4 (1997): 22–42. According to Konigsberg, the restored version of *The Dybbuk* premiered in New York in September 1989. "The dead were returned to life, and a culture long vanished, wiped out by the Holocaust, was resurrected on the screen" (page 23).
42. Eric A. Goldman, *Visions, Images, and Dreams: Yiddish Films Past and Present* (Ann Arbor: UMI Research Press, 1983), 109.

3

Polish Films—Whose Dreams?

Cinema and the Political Construction of
Polish National Identity after World War II

◞

The development of Polish cinema was brutally halted in 1939 when the Polish state ceased to exist. Nazi Germany attacked on 1 September, then Soviet armies invaded from the east on 17 September, thus completing the fourth partition of Poland. Unlike a number of other countries, whose film production was maintained at the prewar level, or even increased at the beginning of the 1940s, Poland had no feature film production during the war.

The Germans maintained the cinema theaters in Poland after September 1939 for profit, as well as for propagandist reasons. The repertoire consisted of prewar Polish comedies, some features that were made before the war but were not distributed, and a handful of films finished after the outbreak of war. German films and a small number of Spanish and Italian films dominated the market. Propagandist films such as the infamous *Menschenleben in Gefahr* (known in Polish as *Żydzi, wszy, tyfus [Jews, Lice, Typhoid Fever,* 1942]),[1] anonymously produced in the General Gouvernement (the Polish Protectorate), did not constitute the majority of screened films, yet their presence prompted the Polish underground to try to implement a boycott of movie theaters. The slogan "*tylko świnie siedzą w kinie*" (only pigs go to the cinema) had been followed by actions, such as the use of stink bombs, to discourage Poles from going to movies. In spite of that, the call to boycott cinemas was unsuccessful. In 1941, films screened in the Polish Protectorate had a total of twenty million viewers (including fourteen million Polish viewers) and were shown in 124 cinemas: eighteen for Germans only, sixty-two with separate screenings for Poles and Germans, and forty-four for Poles only.[2]

The Polish underground not only tried to discourage people from visiting movie theaters, but also punished filmmakers and actors who collaborated with the Germans during the war.[3] For instance, Igo Sym, a popular prewar actor, was executed for spying, for acting in Gustav Ucicky's anti-Polish *Heimkehr* (*Return Home*, 1941), and for recruiting other Polish actors to appear in this film. In retaliation, the Germans sent a group of distinguished Polish actors, including Leon Schiller and Stefan Jaracz, to Auschwitz. Another tragic story involves arguably the best Polish prewar actor, Kazimierz Junosza-Stępowski, who was killed in 1943 by the members of the Polish Home Army (Armia Krajowa, AK), while trying to protect his wife, a Gestapo informer.[4]

* * * *

During the war, a number of established Polish filmmakers lost their lives. Henryk Szaro, the leading prewar director of Jewish origins, was killed by the Gestapo in 1942; the actor Eugeniusz Bodo, for some the symbol of commercial Polish cinema in the 1930s, was killed by the Soviets in a concentration camp in 1943.[5] The losses were enormous, including directors such as Leon Trystan and Juliusz Gardan, and actors such as Stefan Jaracz, Ina Benita, Tadeusz Frenkiel, Michał Znicz, and Franciszek Brodniewicz.

Although some filmmakers survived the occupation in Poland, including scriptwriter Ludwik Starski, director Leonard Buczkowski, and actor Adolf Dymsza, the majority left after September 1939. Michał Waszyński, Seweryn Steinwurzel, Ryszard Ordyński, Józef Lejtes, and Jadwiga Smosarska, among others, found themselves in the West and never returned to Poland.[6] Others, mostly filmmakers associated with prewar leftist groups, survived the war in the Soviet Union and created a film unit Czołówka (Vanguard) within the Polish Tadeusz Kościuszko First Division, which fought alongside the Red Army. Aleksander Ford, Jerzy Bossak, Stanisław Wohl, and Ludwik Perski, all prewar START members or followers, returned with the Red Army as officers in the Kościuszko Division.

Polish filmmakers abroad documented the struggles for Poland and also created anti-Nazi propagandist works. For instance, Eugeniusz Cękalski made compilation propagandist films in England, some of them narrated by known British actors such as Leslie Howard (*The White Eagle*, aka *A Nation in Exile*, 1941) and Sir John Gielgud (*Unfinished Journey*, 1943).[7] An experimental propaganda work by Franciszka and Stefan Themerson, *Calling Mr. Smith* (1943), also received some attention. A small group of filmmakers was active in well-organized film units that had been created by the Polish army in the West. Some of the best prewar Polish filmmakers—directors Michał Waszyński, Konrad Tom, and Józef Lejtes; leading cinematographer Seweryn Steinwurzel; and prewar hit-maker and composer Henryk Wars—documented the route of the Polish divisions and their battles against the German troops. The only Polish feature film produced during the war, *Wielka droga* (*La granda strada* [*The Big Road*, 1945–1946], with a premiere in Rome in 1946), had been made in Italy by Waszyński (director), Tom (script), and Wars (music).[8] Using documentary footage from the battle of Monte Cassino, the film narrates the melodramatic story of two lovers separated by war.

Geopolitics

The new political system that was forcefully imposed after 1945 onto the Polish organism replaced one dreaded system with another. Traditionally disliked and feared, Poland's eastern neighbor, with its communist ideology, started to leave its mark on Polish life. This led to the gradual Sovietization of Polish life, to Poles being subjected to the rules of the communist minority operating under the umbrella of the Soviet Union, and to the rejection of any links with the prewar, "bourgeois Poland."

In addition, the Polish borders changed dramatically. Poland moved to the west, at least geographically. It lost its eastern territories, Kresy, places immortalized in patriotic tales by, among others, Henryk Sienkiewicz in his epic historical novels. As compensation, Poland gained new territories in the west and the north, with new borders set on the Odra (Oder) and Nysa Łużycka (Neisse) Rivers, the so-called *Ziemie Odzyskane* (the "Regained Lands"). Due to the migration from the east to the west, from villages to cities, Polish people needed to be incredibly mobile. The migration, the changed borders, and the losses caused by the war visibly altered the Polish landscape. After the war, Poland became an almost ethnically homogeneous society: the majority of Polish Jews were killed; Germans were forced to resettle behind the Odra River border; and Ukrainians and other nationals who populated the eastern provinces were now part of the Soviet Union. Poland started to become an ethnic and a religious monolith, with the majority of the population being Roman Catholic (Poland had been a multinational society, with Poles comprising 68.9 percent of the total population in 1931).[9]

Before the war, and throughout history in general, the Polish identity had been created by interactions with Poland's powerful neighbors and with many national minorities living within Poland. The important aspect of national self-definition had been lost. Instead, Poles were deprived of contacts with other nationalities due to political isolation, poverty, communist propaganda, and travel restrictions.[10] Furthermore, they were also isolated within the Soviet bloc, similar to a group of other Central European nations.

Attempts to create a new national identity began with the rewriting of Polish history from the communist (Marxist-Leninist) perspective. This became a history that stressed the "progressive" tendencies in the Polish past and presented the new, politically correct version of troubled Polish-Russian relations. In spite of attempts to erase traces of traditional Polish identity and to reinterpret Polish history, certain aspects, important for the national identity, still remained. Arguably, the most important aspect continued to be the role of the Roman Catholic Church in preserving Polishness, especially during the period of Poland's partition (1795–1918). The Catholic religion played a significant role in defining and strengthening the Polish character. Throughout the ages, Poles fought with a number of enemies representing different religions, from Islamic Turks to Orthodox Russians. Polish nationalism, identified with the Roman Catholic Church, always focused on national freedom being paramount, to be defended at all costs; it demanded personal sacrifice for national causes. In trying to change the nature of Polish nationalism, communist authorities fought a losing battle. They failed to replace nationalism with internationalism, religion with ideology, and Polish romanticism with revolutionary spirit.

Loss of Continuity: Film Industry

In the new geopolitical situation after the war, numerous filmmakers chose permanent emigration rather than return to a Soviet-dominated Poland. Some of the established prewar figures continued their careers in the West, such as composers Bronisław Kaper and Henryk Wars; directors Michał Waszyński and Józef Lejtes; and the experimental filmmakers, the Themersons.[11] As a consequence of their decision to remain abroad, their postwar careers were rarely mentioned in Poland.

Postwar Poland, renamed the Polish People's Republic (PRL), started its existence by gradually erasing links with prewar Poland.[12] Reliable information about the prewar period had virtually disappeared from school curricula and was replaced by accounts of the class struggle and the larger-than-life communist movement. The silence over certain nationally sensitive and important issues and the harsh criticism of others created a conviction that everything was to begin anew in a social and cultural void.

The same applied to cinema. Although the leading postwar film figures started their careers before the war, they attacked the prewar film industry and the dominant film culture of that period. Jerzy Bossak, the editor of the newly established magazine *Film*, stated in 1946: "In prewar Poland there were no good films, not just because there was no difference between the maker of films and the maker of artificial jewelry, but also because we did not know how to make films and look at them.... Today we have to create conditions in which Polish film can flourish."[13] Leonard Buczkowski became the only established prewar film director to be able to make films in communist Poland. Interestingly, some of the first and most popular postwar films were made by the prewar professionals who had associated with the *filmowa branża* (film trade), much criticized by START members.

The negation of prewar achievements paralleled the mythologization of certain marginal, yet politically more appropriate, trends, in particular the role of the START group. Some START members, headed by Aleksander

Ford, entered Poland with the Polish army from the Soviet Union and immediately seized power. Ford and his START colleagues controlled the nationalized post-1945 Polish film industry, both as decision makers and filmmakers.

There was only one Polish film organization in existence immediately after the war, Wytwórnia Filmowa Wojska Polskiego (The Polish Army Film Unit), and it was attached to the political department of the army. Its task had been not only to provide documentation of war activities (frequently biased and unreliable), but also to capture film equipment and film stock left by the Germans, and to take care of the surviving movie theaters.[14] Polish filmmakers who affiliated themselves with the Polish army coming from the east were able to take some advantage of UFA's technical supplies, in both Berlin and the Lower Silesia, where the Germans had stored their film equipment. The equipment and confiscated films enabled the establishment of a film studio in Łódź (the only Polish city with an infrastructure intact).[15] Before the end of 1945, the studio in Łódź was ready to produce films.

The film industry was nationalized on 13 November 1945. Film Polski (Polish Film, the national board of Polish film) was established as the sole body producing, distributing, and exhibiting films in Poland. From 1945 to 1947, Aleksander Ford was the head of the organization. He accumulated power and ran the board in an almost dictatorial manner.

Film Polski controlled the production and distribution of films, yet during the first years after the war, there was some room for other film organizations. For instance, in 1947 the cooperative Kinor had been established by some of the surviving members of the Jewish filmmaking community, who started to make films in Yiddish with the help of facilities provided by Film Polski.[16] The task of Shaul Goskind, Natan Gross, Adolf Forbert, and two comic actors, Israel Schumacher and Shimon Dzigan, who returned to Poland in 1948, was to document Jewish life in Poland. In 1947 Goskind produced a documentary, *Mir Lebn Geblibene* (*We Are Still Alive*), and in 1948 the first postwar narrative film in Yiddish (and the last Yiddish film made in Poland), *Unzere Kinder* (*Our Children*). Both films were not approved for screening by the Polish authorities.[17] After the creation of the state of Israel in 1948 and the implementation of Stalinist rules to cinema in 1949, there was no place for American-funded Kinor in Poland; the majority of its members emigrated to Israel.

The damaged and outdated infrastructure remained the biggest problem for the nationalized film industry. In 1945 only approximately 230 cinema theaters were functional, and by 1947 that number had risen to 599. The first three years after the war were considerably liberal as far as the repertoire of Polish cinema theaters is concerned, in spite of the domination of Soviet war films such as *Raduga* (*Rainbow*, 1944) by Mark Donskoi; the musical comedy *Volga-Volga* (1937) by Grigori Alexandrov was genuinely popular in Poland. In 1946, 158 films remained in distribution, including 53 prewar Polish, 84 Soviet, 16 English, and 5 French films.[18] In

1948, there were 99 films on Polish screens: 33 American, 23 Soviet, 18 French, 16 English, 7 Czechoslovak, and 2 Italian films.[19] Some of the best films of the decade were screened in Poland, including *Citizen Kane* (1941), *Alexander Nevsky* (1938), and *Rome, Open City* (1945).

Following the Soviet example, the Polish communist government paid particular attention to the "cinefication" (*kinofikacja*) of rural areas by building new cinema theaters and by creating mobile cinemas (*kina objazdowe*). The number of permanent cinema theaters climbed rapidly from 762 in 1949 to 2,033 in 1952, but, interestingly, the number of viewers remained virtually the same.[20]

Apart from the infrastructure, the biggest problem facing the Polish film industry was the shortage of filmmakers and the lack of skilled professionals due to war losses and emigration. To change that, the Young Filmmakers Workshop was founded in Cracow, a city virtually untouched by the war. Its first graduates included future prominent filmmakers Jerzy Kawalerowicz (b. 1922) and Wojciech J. Has (1924–2000). The crucial step, however, was the establishment in 1948 of the later famous Film School in Łódź, which began to dominate the Polish film industry in the mid-1950s with such talented graduates as Andrzej Wajda (b. 1926), Andrzej Munk (1921–1961), Kazimierz Kutz (b. 1929), and Janusz Morgenstern (b. 1922). In 1955, as many as 158 graduates of the Film School worked in the national film industry, with the total number of active film professionals being 228.[21]

The ambitions of the communist government and Film Polski were very high, yet very few feature films were made within the first ten years after the war: two in 1947, two in 1948, three in 1949, four in 1950, two in 1951, four in 1952, three in 1953, ten in 1954, and eight in 1955.[22] No feature film was released in 1945–1946, largely due to censorship and the impossibility of dealing with certain sensitive issues, such as the theme of the 1944 Warsaw Uprising and the role of the underground Home Army. Many scripts were subjected to severe criticism and endless rewrites. Others were produced and immediately shelved—for example, *Dwie godziny* (*Two Hours*), by Stanisław Wohl and Józef Wyszomirski, was made in 1946 but not premiered until 1957—or released in mutilated versions, as happened to Jerzy Zarzycki's *Miasto nieujarzmione* (*Unvanquished City*, 1950).

First Films

Given the complexities of the Polish past, it comes as no surprise that history, recent history in particular, is the traditional topic of Polish postwar films. Memories of World War II haunt Polish cinema and, like many traumatic experiences, return powerfully on the screen. As early as 1947, Leonard Buczkowski's *Zakazane piosenki* (*Forbidden Songs*), generally regarded as the first postwar Polish film, highlights this obsession.

Forbidden Songs was made by a group of leading prewar filmmakers. The film was directed by Buczkowski, who made nine feature films before the war; scripted by Ludwik Starski, whose name had been associated with the best-known prewar comedies; and photographed by the experienced Adolf Forbert. This film fulfilled the expectations of many Polish audiences and had 10.8 million viewers within the first three years of its release (average attendance was then high at five million viewers per film).[23] Even today, *Forbidden Songs* remains one of the most popular Polish films ever, with fifteen million viewers.[24]

This episodic film narrates an anthology of songs popular in Warsaw during the occupation. Although well liked by the audience, *Forbidden Songs* was reproached by communist authorities and film critics for its lack of political involvement, its stereotyping, and the false picture it projected of the occupation. As a result, it was taken off the screens, remade, and then rereleased in 1948. The new version embraced stronger political accents and portrayed a darker picture of the occupation (with an emphasis on German brutality), stressed the role of the Red Army in the "liberation" of Warsaw, and provided better developed psychological motivation for the characters' actions. From today's perspective, however, this film is historically important as the first postwar Polish film.

Other early narrative films also pay tribute to the victims of the war. In her landmark film *Ostatni etap* (*The Last Stage*, aka *The Last Stop*, 1948),[25] Wanda Jakubowska (1907–1988) shows the monstrosity of Auschwitz-Birkenau and draws on her firsthand experiences while portraying the "factory of death" (she was interned in Auschwitz and Ravensbrück). With its dramatization of the camp experience, *The Last Stage* establishes several images easily discernible in subsequent Holocaust narratives: the dark, "realistic" images of the camp (the film was shot in Auschwitz); the passionate moralistic appeal; and the clear divisions between victims and victimizers.

The Last Stage suffers, however, from several weaknesses inherent in many later projects that aimed at the impossible task of re-creating the horror of the Holocaust, including the melodramatization of situations and characters due to a dependence on mainstream narrative patterns, and the use of inspiring endings. For instance, *The Last Stage* presents an ideologically correct version of the times by introducing the dignified figures of a brave female Russian doctor and female Russian officers, by emphasizing the role of the Russian army in the liberation of the camp, and by stressing the role of the communist resistance in Auschwitz. Marta Weiss (Barbara Drapińska), a Jewish interpreter in the camp, dies a martyr's death while uttering: "You must not let Auschwitz be repeated." Her dying words are juxtaposed with the image of (presumably Soviet) planes over Auschwitz. Undoubtedly, *The Last Stage* reflects more the postwar political atmosphere, and less the reality of the camp.

This internationally acclaimed film, which marks the birth of the Polish postwar film, encountered problems while being made. According to

Figure 3.1 A scene from Wanda Jakubowska's *The Last Stage* (1948)

Jakubowska, only Stalin's personal approval enabled her to pursue this project. Authorities in Poland were supposedly afraid of similarities between the Soviet and German concentration camps, and preferred not to touch the sensitive topic.[26] Jakubowska also faced aesthetic problems while making this first major film about the horror of the camps. For example, she tried to reach large audiences at the expense of naturalistic scenes. She comments that "the camp reality was human skeletons, piles of dead bodies, lice, rats, and various disgusting diseases. On the screen this reality would certainly cause dread and repulsion. It was necessary to eliminate those elements which, although authentic and typical, were unbearable for the postwar viewer."[27]

Today, in spite of its powerful imagery, *The Last Stage* may seem archaic and artificial, in line with the official cultural policy and the dominant aesthetic modes of the late 1940s. Tadeusz Lubelski attributes the "overaesthetization" of several camp images to a Russian cinematographer, Boris Monastyrski, who had filmed equally "unreal" images of war in Donskoi's *Rainbow*.[28] Yet these images of camp life (e.g., morning and evening roll calls on the *Appellplatz*) reinforced the depiction of Nazi concentration camps and are present in a number of subsequent American films, including *Sophie's Choice* (1982, Alan Pakula) and *Schindler's List* (1993, Steven Spielberg). Certainly, to this day *The Last Stage* remains a seminal film about the Holocaust, a prototype for future Holocaust cinematic narratives.[29]

Like *Forbidden Songs*, *Ulica graniczna* (*Border Street*, 1949) was made by prewar professionals (scriptwriters Ludwik Starski and Jan Fethke), headed by the former avant-garde director Aleksander Ford (who had criticized the professionals before the war). The film was produced mostly at the well-equipped Czech Barrandov studio and with a Czech contingent that included cinematographer Jaroslav Tuzar and art director Stefan Kopecky. The straightforward, well-made, and realistic (although studio-made) *Border Street* deals with the wartime predicament of Polish Jews and shows the partitioning of Warsaw by the Germans into Jewish and Aryan quarters. The film gives a vast panorama of Jewish and Polish characters living in a building on the street that becomes the border of the ghetto.

The original screenplay by Ford stressed the hostile attitude of Poles toward Jews.[30] The final screen version, modified by Ford after severe criticism of his project, presents not so much the divisions but the solidarity between Jews and Poles across the wall (real and symbolic) dividing the city. The anti-Semitic sentiments of many Poles, however, are not suppressed in the film. In addition to images of Poles risking their lives to help the ghetto dwellers and to support the 1943 Warsaw Ghetto Uprising, *Border Street* also shows Poles denouncing Jews to the Germans out of malice or in the hope of getting their vacated apartments. Ford succeeds when portraying the annihilation of his own people. Like Jakubowska, he soothes the pessimistic tone of the film with an edifying final voice-over urging the solidarity of all people as the means of destroying man-made barriers.

Figure 3.2 Tadeusz Fijewski (in the middle) in Aleksander Ford's *Border Street* (1949)

* * * *

In terms of box office, the period immediately after the war certainly belonged to Leonard Buczkowski. In his next postwar film, an unpretentious comedy, *Skarb* (*Treasure*, 1949), he employed the prewar star Adolf Dymsza and two young leading actors who started their careers in *Forbidden Songs* (Danuta Szaflarska and Jerzy Duszyński). The film features topical Warsaw humor and the poetics of prewar comedies, coupled with postwar problems (e.g., the lack of housing).[31] Tadeusz Lubelski points out that "among all the films made after the war in Poland, *Treasure* had the most communicative features, typical of classical Hollywood cinema. The film was an example of an impersonal product, made by the crew of professionals identified with a certain style (prewar film trade), with decisions made to target the expected needs of audiences. And the public appreciated it."[32]

The audiences appreciated the lack of open didactics and the presence of actors who repeated their prewar typecasting (Adolf Dymsza and Ludwik Sempoliński). *Treasure*'s intentional artificiality, however, was considered by a number of critics as anachronistic in an age of neorealism and *film noir*. Yet the film's artificiality, coupled with the fact that *Treasure* was devoid of explicit political references and portrayed conventional characters in stock situations, contributed to its popular appeal in the highly politicized climate of postwar Poland.

As if in a fantasy world, the representatives of different classes and generations do not clash in Buczkowski's film, but coexist in their futile search for a treasure hidden in their building. Instead of a treasure, the protagonists find an unexploded bomb, but they are saved by the poster-like workers. This ending of *Treasure*, as noted by Lubelski, shows the forces of "the new world order"—communism.[33] Films made in the next several years belong to these billboard characters.

Notes

1. Under the pretext of being an "educational film" (typhoid fever prevention), *Menschenleben in Gefahr* propagated racist, anti-Semitic views.
2. Compared with fifty-seven million Polish viewers in 807 cinema theaters before the war. Edward Zajiček, *Poza ekranem: Kinematografia polska 1918–1991* (Warsaw: Filmoteka Narodowa and Wydawnictwa Artystyczne i Filmowe, 1992), 36. Jerzy Płażewski, "Film zagraniczny w Polsce," in *Encyklopedia kultury polskiej XX wieku: Film i kinematografia*, ed. Edward Zajiček (Warsaw: Instytut Kultury and Komitet Kinematografii, 1994), 332.
3. In the postwar period, a small group of Polish filmmakers and actors, for example, Bogusław Samborski, who appeared in *Heimkehr* (he left Poland after the war), were on trial for collaborating with the Germans. Others, for example, Adolf Dymsza, who performed in Warsaw's theaters during the war, underwent verifications and sometimes symbolic punishment.

4. The name of Kazimierz Junosza-Stępowski is inseparably linked with the prewar Polish cinema. He started his career in 1902, acting in the first Polish films produced by Kazimierz Prószyński, and continued until the war, making several films per year (as many as ten in 1938), including some of the best-known prewar Polish works. His wife, who survived the assassination attempt, was killed nine months later. Jerzy Maśnicki and Kamil Stepan, entry "Kazimierz Junosza-Stępowski," *Pleograf. Słownik biograficzny filmu polskiego 1896–1939* (Cracow: Staromiejska Oficyna Wydawnicza, 1996), entry "Stępowski" [no page numbers]. In 1989 Jerzy Sztwiernia made *Oszołomienie* (*Daze*), a feature film inspired by Junosza-Stępowski's life and the circumstances of his death.

5. The tragic circumstances surrounding the death of Eugeniusz Bodo are the subject of Stanisław Janicki's documentary film, *Eugeniusz Bodo: Za winy nie popełnione* (*Eugeniusz Bodo: For Crimes Not Committed*), made in 1997 for the Polish State Television. The title of this film refers to Eugeniusz Bodo's film made in 1938, *For Crimes Not Committed*.

6. Ryszard Ordyński worked with Lubitsch on his *To Be or Not to Be* (1942). After the war, Michał Waszyński directed two feature films in Italy; acted as an assistant director on Orson Welles's *Othello* (1952); worked as an art director on, among others, *Roman Holiday* (1953, William Wyler) and *The Barefoot Contessa* (1954, Joseph L. Mankiewicz); and acted as the executive producer of *El Cid* (1962, Anthony Mann). Maśnicki and Stepan, *Pleograf*, entry "Waszyński" [no page numbers].

7. Jolanta Lemann, *Eugeniusz Cękalski* (Łódź: Muzeum Kinematografii, 1996), 104.

8. Teresa Rutkowska, "Film polski na świecie," in Zajiček, *Encyklopedia kultury polskiej XX wieku*, 309.

9. Norman Davies, *Heart of Europe: A Short History of Poland* (New York: Oxford University Press, 1984), 104.

10. The figures are apparent. In 1952 barely two thousand Polish citizens traveled to the West. Among them, only fifty-one were private citizens allowed to visit their families abroad. Quoted from Tomasz Goban-Klas, *The Orchestration of the Media: The Politics of Mass Communications in Communist Poland and the Aftermath* (Boulder: Westview Press, 1994), 84

11. The most successful had been Bronisław Kaper, who in 1930 moved to Germany and then to the United States. He composed music for numerous films, including works by such known directors as John Huston, King Vidor, George Cukor, and Arthur Hiller. Kaper was awarded an Academy Award in 1953.

12. This breaking of continuity is not a unique Polish experience. The most discussed examples include post–World War II Germany and Russia after the October Revolution.

13. Quoted from Tadeusz Lubelski, *Strategie autorskie w polskim filmie fabularnym lat 1945–1961* (Cracow: Wydawnictwo Uniwersytetu Jagiellońskiego, 1992), 39.

14. Alina Madej, "100 lat kina w Polsce: 1938–1945," *Kino* 4 (1998): 50.

15. As Alina Madej writes, the main UFA studio was captured by the Soviets. The Polish emissaries seized film materials from small private companies. Ibid., 50.

16. Eric A. Goldman, *Visions, Images, and Dreams: Yiddish Film Past and Present* (Ann Arbor: UMI Research Press, 1983), 147–151.

17. For an illuminating account in English, see Ira Konigsberg, "*Our Children* and the Limits of Cinema: Early Jewish Responses to the Holocaust," *Film Quarterly* 52, no. 1 (1998): 7–19. According to Konigsberg, *Our Children* premiered in Tel Aviv in 1951. This was the "first film to confront the issue of whether the Holocaust is a suitable subject for art" (13).

18. Bolesław Michałek and Frank Turaj, *The Modern Cinema of Poland* (Bloomington: Indiana University Press, 1988), 3.

19. Płażewski in Zajiček, *Encyklopedia kultury polskiej XX wieku*, 333.

20. Ibid., 336.

21. Michałek and Turaj, *The Modern Cinema of Poland*, 18.

22. Figures are from Stanisław Janicki, *Polskie filmy fabularne 1902–1988* (Warsaw: Wydawnictwa Artystyczne i Filmowe, 1990), 139–152.

23. Ewa Gębicka, "Sieć kin i rozpowszechnianie filmów," in Zajiček, *Encyklopedia kultury polskiej XX wieku*, 433.

24. In a recent poll conducted by a newspaper, *Gazeta Wyborcza*, and a weekly, *Antena*, *Forbidden Songs* ranks after Andrzej Wajda's *The Land of Promise* and Jerzy Hoffman's *The Deluge* in the drama category. *Gazeta Wyborcza* (24–26 December 1999), 42.

25. *The Last Stage* was Jakubowska's second film. Her first work, *Nad Niemnem* (*On the Niemen River*, codirected with Karol Szołowski), was finished shortly before the war, but never had its premiere, which had been scheduled for 5 September 1939. All of the film's prints were destroyed during the war.

26. Tadeusz Lubelski, "Generalissumus płakał" [interview with Wanda Jakubowska], *Film* 18–19 (1990): 53. In a different interview, Jakubowska stresses that the head of *Film Polski*, Aleksander Ford, proved to be another obstacle for her project. Alina Madej, "Jak powstawał *Ostatni etap*" [interview with Jakubowska], *Kino* 5 (1998): 13–17.

27. Wanda Jakubowska, "Kilka wspomnień o powstaniu scenariusza (na marginesie filmu *Ostatni etap*)," *Kwartalnik Filmowy* 1 (1951): 43.

28. Lubelski, *Strategie autorskie*, 81.

29. See a discussion in Stuart Liebman and Leonard Quart, "Lost and Found: Wanda Jakubowska's *The Last Stop*," *Cineaste* 22, no. 4 (1997): 43–45.

30. Alina Madej, "100 lat kina w Polsce: 1945–1948," *Kino* 5 (1998): 49–50.

31. Leonard Buczkowski is credited in the film as "Marian Leonard," the punishment for making a number of short films for German companies during the war. The penalty was in effect after *Forbidden Songs* and lasted three years. Jerzy Pelz, "Zaczęło się w cukierni ojca ...," *Kino* 7 (1984): 14–20.

32. Lubelski, *Strategie autorskie*, 60.

33. Ibid., 65.

4

The Poetics of Screen Stalinism
Socialist Realist Films

> Both fascist and communist totalitarianisms are, in a sense, a parodic imitation of religion.... The totalitarian system fights religion to replace it, and to become a "religion"; therefore, it proposes its own version of revelation, its own vision of salvation, and its own type of ties between people that resemble the mythical bond in religion.
>
> *Rev. Józef Tischner*[1]

In Polish history, Stalinism is a term that refers to the postwar period beginning in 1949 and ending in October 1956. During that time, the one-party rule and the strict Soviet control of all aspects of Polish life[2] created a small totalitarian replica of the Soviet state. The Polish communist leader, Bolesław Bierut, was a faithful follower of Stalin—more accurately, his obedient political puppet.

The Soviet model imprinted its mark on the arts. The postwar period in Polish arts was dominated by the socialist realist doctrine, detailed in the Soviet Union by Andrei Zhdanov at the First All-Union Writers' Congress in 1934. The doctrine of socialist realism demanded the adherence to the Communist Party line, the necessary portrayal of the class struggle (the struggle between old and new), the emphasis on class-based images, the rewriting of history from the Marxist perspective, and the elimination of "reactionary bourgeois" ideology.

The Polish version of socialist realism was outlined in a speech delivered in December 1947 by Bolesław Bierut. It was officially approved in December 1948 at the "unification congress" of the Polish Workers Party (PPR) and the Polish Socialist Party (PPS), which saw the formation of the Polish United Workers Party (PZPR).[3] In November 1949, the so-called congress of filmmakers met at Wisła, a small resort in the Beskidy Mountains, to enforce the doctrine of socialist realism (this was preceded by similar gatherings, with similar results, of other arts organizations). The Wisła Congress condemned cosmopolitan and bourgeois tendencies supposedly present in Polish cinema, such as disregard for class struggle, nationalism, and revisionism. The speakers at the congress, including party apparatchiks, critics, writers, and filmmakers, criticized previously made films such as *Forbidden Songs, Treasure, Border Street,* and *The Last Stage* for their lack of "revolutionary spirit." Some of the two hundred participants in the congress later stressed that they had to compromise under political pressures, and blamed the atmosphere of the Stalinist period or their blindness. But research shows that in many cases the initiative belonged to filmmakers who willingly went down the socialist realist path.[4] For the START members, for instance, this path was the continuation of their prewar political beliefs and the struggle for socially and politically committed cinema.

The political climate of the 1949 Wisła Congress certainly demonstrated that Stalinism was flourishing. For instance, the first Polish exhibition of portraits of work leaders took place in August; socialist realist plays dominated Polish theaters; and the new Polish literary genre, "novels about production" (*powieść produkcyjna*), came into prominence. The explicit titles of the novels tell their whole stories: *Traktory zdobędą wiosnę* (*Tractors Will Conquer the Spring*) by Witold Zalewski, or *Przy budowie* (*At the Construction Site*) by Tadeusz Konwicki.

As in the Soviet model, the reality in Polish arts was portrayed "as it should be," with clear divisions between the forces of progress, personified by a positive hero, a model to be emulated, and the dark forces of the past, embodied by a cunning opponent of the new, a model to be wary of. One of the leading political figures of the time, the feared minister of public security, Jakub Berman, expressed the political goal facing Polish artists: to use arts as a political weapon. In his 1951 speech he advocated taking "aim at kulak and speculant, spy and saboteur, American warmonger and neo-Nazi."[5]

Cinema, like other arts, was treated as an instrument in the political struggle. Soviet films, rarely shown in Poland before the war for political reasons, started to dominate Polish screens after 1949. Polish cinema theaters were divided at that time into two categories: the "festival theaters," which showed Soviet films almost exclusively, and the second category, theaters that screened films mostly from other socialist countries.[6] It was difficult, however, to fill Polish screens with contemporary Soviet films alone; during the last years of Stalin's life, only a few films had been made, and these were mostly epic propagandist works. With the help of classic Soviet works, such as *Battleship Potemkin,* and films from the communist bloc countries, the "progressive films" constituted 78 percent of the Polish repertoire. That repertoire, however, was not numerous: between 1951 and 1953 only between sixty-four and sixty-six new titles were shown yearly in Polish movie theaters.[7]

Polish films did not contribute a significant percentage. Only thirty-four feature films were made in Poland between 1949 and 1955, among them thirty-one that followed the socialist realist formula. They all shared thematic and stylistic affinities, provided the same didactic messages, and created similar protagonists. The exceptions, according to the Polish scholar Grażyna Stachówna, were as follows: Andrzej Wajda's *Pokolenie* (*A Generation*), Jan Rybkowski's *Godziny nadziei* (*The Hours of Hope*), and Andrzej Munk's *Błękitny krzyż* (*Blue Cross*). These three films were all made in 1955, and were forerunners of the Polish School.[8]

With the invasion of Soviet films came the gradual elimination of Western films on Polish screens. The restrictive policy also included Italian neorealist films. Particular attention was paid to the latter by Włodzimierz Sokorski, the Polish minister of culture at that time, who attacked Italian neorealism as a "primitive exhibitionism of humankind's lowest instincts, the most hideous forms of cruelty, sadism, and superstition," which "has nothing whatsoever to do with a scientific analysis of life; it has to do with employing (what we have observed in fascist art) a naturalistic method to promote false, insolent arguments."[9] As a result of the rejection of Western films, there was not a single American film shown in Polish movie theaters for more than seven years. For instance, in 1951 there were only six Western films in distribution in Poland (two French, and one Dutch, Finnish, Italian, and English), and only eight in 1952 and 1953.[10]

Socialist Realist Films

The dominant theme of socialist realist films—that of the class struggle—is developed, for instance, in the classic *Dwie Brygady* (*Two Brigades*, 1950), made by the students of the Łódź Film School and supervised by Eugeniusz Cękalski. *Two Brigades* was adapted from *Grinder Karhan's Crew* (*Parta brusiče Karhana*), a play that Mira Liehm and Antonin J. Liehm have called "one of the most primitive Czech plays of the time."[11] The film tells a story about two brigades and two forms of Stakhanovite[12] competition: workers in a factory try to increase production, and actors in a theater attempt to adapt the workers' effort for the stage. The message provided by the film is quite straightforward: art is an imitation of life, but life as it should be, not life as it is. In the process of learning about the "true workers and the true factory life," the young actors (the old ones oppose them) gain new consciousness and, as a consequence, their "new style of acting" slowly emerges. Authenticity in *Two Brigades* means realistic detailed set design and crude stereotyping. Oddly enough, this film won the Karlove Vary Film Festival as the best experimental film. The trite presentation of the struggle between the old and the new in two disparate fields (factory and theater) apparently was the reason for this award.

Eugeniusz Cękalski, one of the leaders of the START group, who spent the wartime period working on documentary films dealing with the Polish cause in France, England, and the United States, is also responsible for another classic socialist realist work, *Jasne Łany* (*Bright Fields*, 1947).

This film, which heralded the socialist realist poetics in Polish cinema, is set in a village symbolically called Dark Fields. Its story line and its schematic propagandist content are formulated by the film's positive hero, a village teacher, whose message is that "Dark Fields must change to Bright Fields."

Bright Fields is abundant with socialist realist clichés and stereotypes, and contains explicit propagandist messages. In the artificial and chaste love story, the young and progressive protagonist, teacher Stępkowicz (Kazimierz Dejmek), marries a local girl. She functions as a reward for his support of the communist ideology, which brings the lovers together. The film also portrays a treacherous attempt on the teacher's life, organized by a group of black marketeers, and shows a cluster of negative characters populating the screen, such as the rich miller and the reactionary former teacher Leśniewski (Andrzej Łapicki), who is associated with the Polish government-in-exile in London. In the film, a politically disoriented, yet talented, young boy represents the generation that has a chance to thrive in the new political reality.

As Tadeusz Lubelski writes, the film was rejected by the audience and by the authorities as antipropaganda, and became "the inglorious legend of Polish cinema."[13] A number of other films were badly received by both the public and the critics. For example, *Gromada* (*The Village Mill*, 1952), directed by Jerzy Kawalerowicz and Kazimierz Sumerski, lasted only a couple of weeks on Polish screens. Another film, *Niedaleko Warszawy* (*Not Far from Warsaw*, 1954), by Maria Kaniewska, which "perfectly reconstructed on the screen the socialist realist formula," was in 1954 voted by some critics the worst Polish film ever made.[14] The poor box office of these films proved that in an environment tightly controlled by the guardians of the official ideology, it was almost an impossible task to produce a film that people would want to see yet that at the same time would advocate "the need to struggle for peace, to enhance productivity at work, to hate imperialism, and to love the communist leaders."[15]

One of the attempts to produce a politically correct, yet popular, film was Leonard Buczkowski's *Przygoda na Mariensztacie* (*An Adventure at Marienstadt*, 1954), the first Polish film in color. This film also revolves around the work competition but combines it with gender politics. Its narrative structure has all the components of a typical, socialist realist drama: work competition portrayed with a melodramatic aspect, the postwar reconstruction of Warsaw, the social advancement of the working class (the realization of a slogan "the masses will enter the city"), and new women who are not afraid of leaving their traditional roles to compete with men.

The film opens with a symbolic image of a small stone being crushed by a bulldozer. The camera then pulls back to show a bulldozer leveling the ruins of Warsaw. With uplifting music, the scene cuts to the image of Warsaw's new construction site, Marienstadt. A montage sequence shows the bricklayers working there; with the help of low-angle shots, they are presented as heroic figures silhouetted against the blue sky. Almost every frame in that sequence closely resembles Polish socialist realist paintings. Another dynamic montage sequence shows young people going to Warsaw. They carry red banners and slogans, and sing "To idzie młodość" (Here Comes Youth), the emblematic song of the 1950s. These first images of the film establish the relationship between youth and Warsaw, between energy and the new ideology.

The film's female protagonist, Hanka Ruczajówna (Lidia Korsakówna), moves to Warsaw from a small village and becomes a bricklayer in a females-only brigade. Although the main theme in the film is work competition, the reasons that Ruczajówna moves to Warsaw are primarily romantic/personal. During her first brief visit to Warsaw, as a member of a folk ensemble, she had befriended one of the handsome socialist leaders of the work at the Marienstadt, Jan Szarliński (Tadeusz Szmidt). She does not remember his name, and knows only that he produces more than 300 percent of the norm. She soon finds him after seeing his huge portrait exhibited on the wall. As if to present the bricklaying job in an attractive light, the film offers yet another explanation for Hanka's move to the city. A brief glimpse of her backward village, which is shown in the manner of nineteenth-century realist paintings, completely justifies her decision.

Figure 4.1 A scene from a socialist realist comedy, *An Adventure at Marienstadt* (1954, Leonard Buczkowski). Lidia Korsakówna as Hanka Ruczajówna in the middle

An Adventure at Marienstadt is set in postwar Warsaw. Instead of a realistic portrayal of the city being rebuilt from ashes, it depicts "the official optimism" of the party authorities. This is the world in which work is life. "New women" from villages take "men's jobs" and seem to like them. The world presented on the screen resembles a hastily colored postcard, an image further enhanced by the presence of the Polish folk ensemble Mazowsze.

Buczkowski's film was an effort to produce a socialist realist comedy —a difficult, if not impossible, task in a time of gray seriousness and mandatory optimism. In the Stalinist period there was no room for satire or for laughter at issues commonly reserved for serious treatment (the only exception was the so-called "constructive laughter"). In spite of that, *An Adventure at Marienstadt* has proved to be one of the most popular films screened in postwar Poland, having had more viewers than, for example, *Popiół i diament* (*Ashes and Diamonds*, 1958, Andrzej Wajda) and *Star Wars* (1977, George Lucas).[16] *An Adventure at Marienstadt* features witty dialogue (script by Ludwik Starski) and popular songs (by the founder of Mazowsze, Tadeusz Sygietyński), which certainly have helped the film's popularity.

Polish films made during the Stalinist period also include biographical features, both good and bad. For instance, *Żołnierz zwycięstwa* (*Soldier of Victory*, 1953), a film by Wanda Jakubowska, delivers a propagandist biography of General Karol Świerczewski.[17] The film covers forty years of Świerczewski's life (beginning with the revolution of 1905), and introduces a number of other historical figures, including Lenin, Stalin, and the Cheka (Soviet secret police) founder Dzerzhinsky, while portraying a multitude of then current political topics, such as spying, fascism and imperialism, and other elements of Polish internal politics. Even the presence of some of the most prominent Polish actors, including prewar stars such as Jacek Woszczerowicz and Jan Kurnakowicz, and of new, emerging talents, such as Gustaw Holoubek, Tadeusz Janczar, and Władysław Hańcza, cannot save the film. It has to be noted again that Polish filmmakers examined certain themes to please the authorities. In many cases, these themes illustrate the filmmakers' political convictions (e.g., in Jakubowska's case), political opportunism, and naiveté.[18]

Some directors, however, were able to produce biographical films of certain merit that were devoid of overtly propagandist elements. Critically acclaimed in Poland and abroad in the 1950s, *Młodość Chopina* (*The Youth of Chopin*, 1952), by Aleksander Ford, traces five years of the composer's life. This epic production differs from Hollywood biographical films that usually tell stories of struggling and misunderstood geniuses; it also varies distinctly from Soviet epics, with their stress on ideological/class sources of artists' inspirations. The episodic *The Youth of Chopin* portrays Chopin (Czesław Wołłejko) as a young artist inspired by Polish history and culture—the sources of his music.[19]

Socialist Realist Characters

The representative Polish films of the Stalinist period are similar to classic Soviet examples,[20] but tone down the extreme didacticism of the latter. They also deal with the process of gaining political consciousness. In such films, a (usually young) protagonist acquires political knowledge thanks to the guidance of the party authorities. That knowledge enables him or her to understand the complexities of the class struggle, to embrace the new ideology (always presented as a "natural" stage of historical development), and to improve his or her vigilance toward external and internal political opponents.

The "positive heroes" are usually mature party workers, security force officers, workers, or ideologically correct teachers of proper (peasant or working-class) origins. Their class background is often stressed by employing last names that indicate their peasant/working-class origins. Apart from the proper background and working-class mannerisms of speech and behavior, the schematic hero has to be straightforward, open, smiling, and wise, though not necessarily well educated (the higher the level of education, the more one has doubts, and a communist hero should have none). Another feature characterizing the hero is his asexuality; he is interested only in chaste relationships that are governed by politics rather than sensual love. The protagonist has no private life and no desire to have one. Rarely shown alone, he is usually seen at work or at political gatherings.

The mature, positive protagonist commonly guides the younger one, who is typically good-natured yet politically undecided (a young female protagonist sometimes becomes the girlfriend of the mature protagonist). The Communist Party secretary or the security force officer performs the role of a good and understanding yet vigilant father who, thanks to his political instinct, is able to detect a class enemy. As proselytizing vehicles, these films are about the acquisition of consciousness; wise party workers are only too willing to convert another nonbeliever into a devoted communist.

The positive hero is portrayed as a "soldier of the new." This romantic characterization is usually reserved in Polish mythology for fighters of national freedom, not heroes of socialist work. Such a hero always remains a part of the community. For example, in *Not Far from Warsaw*, the father of a female protagonist, himself an old, prewar communist who has "lost his revolutionary consciousness," is told that his daughter was raised not by him, but by the working class and the steelworks—in other words, by the community.

The communist authorities on the screen are always presented as the embodiment of the new: young, handsome, wise, and fatherly. They also have answers to all kinds of problems. They speak slowly, accentuating each word, because every single word matters—the Communist Party speaks through them. When a handsome, young security force colonel in *Not Far from Warsaw* tells the female protagonist "I trust you," and looks right into her eyes, she immediately regains her ideological confidence and is ready to face the enemies of the new.

To monumentalize the positive hero, filmmakers relied heavily on low-angle shots, usually medium shots. Afraid of being accused of "psychologization" and "formalism," they tended to avoid close-ups and used simple, nonexperimental narratives. Kazimierz Sobotka says that the growing importance of dialogue (which was easier to censor than images) caused the "theatricalization of films" and, consequently, the dominance of shots characteristic of dialogue. For example, 50 percent of all shots in Maria Kaniewska's *Not Far from Warsaw* are medium shots.[21]

Frequently, the protagonists of Polish socialist realist films are "new women" working in fields traditionally reserved for men, such as heavy industry and construction sites. Their career choices are opposed by their families (husbands and fathers) and, sometimes, by their male superiors, who clearly lack "the revolutionary consciousness." The "new women," however, are able to win acceptance and gain new friends. For example, in *An Adventure at Marienstadt*, an older, conservative work leader, Ciepielewski (Adam Mikołajewski), claims that women should stay at home, as his wife does. In the final scene, however, he voluntarily joins the work initiated by the young female brigade (older, tired women do not appear in filmic factories).

Conflicts between generations (old versus new) are very important in these films. Films like *Trudna miłość* (*Difficult Love*, 1954, Stanisław Różewicz) or *Not Far from Warsaw* often have a primary conflict in which a young protagonist has to choose between "reactionary" parents and a vision of a communist paradise on earth. The young workers/protagonists have to convince the older workers, who are used to prewar ways of production, that the only good methods are the Soviet ones.

The positive heroes are contrasted to those who oppose the road to communism. The "enemy of the people" or "the class enemy" is usually unmasked in the film by the vigilant hero. The role of the enemy is usually reserved for a rich miller (Polish kulak), saboteur, or spy. The class enemy lacks the human qualities displayed by the positive protagonist. Foreign (Western) spies hide in the dark like cowards, waiting for the right moment to strike, while saboteurs attempt (needless to say, without success) to interrupt the Stakhanovite work competition in factories and construction sites. Their appearance betrays them—they are sometimes elegant yet sinister, too well dressed, arrogant, "not ours," silent. Since they do not work (they only manipulate and exploit the masses), they are isolated from the community and surrounded by only a small number of other "enemies of the people" (this is always just a small number, because, the films say, the majority support the communist authorities). In *Not Far from Warsaw*, a simple woman detects the class enemy sent (of course) by American imperialists to destroy the prosperous (thanks to the Soviets' help) steelworks. She describes him in the following way: "He says little, as if he was afraid of every single word. Not ours, not foreign."

* * * *

Gender relations are also unique in socialist realist films. Rafał Marszałek discusses "women in kerchiefs," the communist model, and "women in hats," the model desired by the masses.[22] The communist model propagates the masculinization of "new women" (women driving tractors, working in coal mines, etc.). There is no time for family, "for hats," these films seem to say, when the enemy is everywhere, when the battle for the future is the most pressing problem. There is no time for privacy, intimacy, and love. "Coquetry is killed in embryo, for it would point out the relationship with the old order," writes Marszałek.[23]

The puritan communist system promotes the emancipation of women, yet films of the Stalinist era show the rough treatment of women by male heroes. Male protagonists seem to be afraid of bourgeois domesticity, and view women as an obstacle to higher production. Sobotka writes that "the male worker does not highly value his wife. More than love, he values friendship and sings songs about it. A woman can get his friendship, and respect only when she achieves professional advancement."[24] For instance, in *An Adventure at Marienstadt*, the understanding party secretary helps the young work leaders to overcome problems in their relationship. Hanka can conquer the heart of her stubborn man only after she has proved that she can be a good bricklayer. As soon as he learns that Hanka's female brigade has accomplished a record amount of work, he wants to see her.[25]

In the world of ascetic socialist realist films, in which female characters can only be with an ideologically correct man, there is no place for love, not to mention sex. A Polish scholar noted that the first kiss in Polish postwar cinema occurred as late as 1954 in *Difficult Love*.[26] In socialist realist films, enhanced production equals private success; professional advancement, "class instinct," and strong belief in the new ideology can secure somebody's love. For example, in *Autobus odjeżdża 6.20* (*The Bus Leaves at 6:20*, 1954, Jan Rybkowski), Krystyna (Aleksandra Śląska) wins her husband's love only after she leaves him and moves to Silesia, where she becomes a successful industrial worker.

The Decline of the Doctrine

In the mid-1950s, some Polish filmmakers managed to retreat from the socialist realist dogma and make realistic films in the spirit of Italian neorealism. These films, however, were still set within the thematic preoccupations characteristic of socialist realism.

Though criticized by party authorities for its "bourgeois approach" to realism, the Italian neorealist movement had a great impact on Polish cinema. This impact is discernible, for instance, in Aleksander Ford's *Piątka z ulicy Barskiej* (*Five Boys from Barska Street*, 1954) and Jerzy Kawalerowicz's epic diptych, *Celuloza* (*A Night of Remembrance*) and *Pod gwiazdą frygijską* (*Under the Phrygian Star*), both made in 1954. Besides neorealist inspirations, these films were also influenced by classic Soviet biographical films, chiefly Grigori Kozintsev and Leonid Trauberg's "Maxim Trilogy" (1935–1939) and another trilogy, Mark Donskoi's biography of Maxim Gorki (1938–1940).[27] The realistic treatment of events and people was well received by both the audience and the authorities. The latter were pleased to find traditional features of the socialist realist doctrine intact and, to their surprise, a multidimensional world with well-developed characters, documentary flavor, a realistic environment, an engaging story, and professionalism in every detail.

Ford's first film in color, *Five Boys from Barska Street*, deals with juvenile delinquency, a theme previously untouched in Polish cinema. The film stresses the impact of war on the psychology of its young protagonists, and shows their inability to change a lifestyle that results in crime, including murder. The five boys from a gang on Barska Street are introduced in a courtroom, where they are put under the guardianship of a bricklayer. He tries to help them with their lives, but the dangers of sinking back into crime are real. Ford's film ends with an appeal to help the troubled youth, to offer them a chance to live normal lives. Ford won the Best Director award for this film at the Cannes Film Festival. The film is notable for another reason: Andrzej Wajda's debut as Ford's assistant. Soon after, Wajda would make his first feature film, *A Generation*, with several people involved in the production of *Five Boys from Barska Street*, including assistant cinematographer Jerzy Lipman and two young actors, Tadeusz Janczar and Tadeusz Łomnicki.

Certainly, the most accomplished work of that period remains the epic diptych, *Night of Remembrance* and *Under the Phrygian Star*, by one of the masters of Polish cinema, Jerzy Kawalerowicz. Kawalerowicz started his career as an assistant director of the first postwar Polish film, *Forbidden Songs*. After his much criticized feature debut, *The Village Mill*, he made the acclaimed diptych, which owes a lot to its rich literary source, Igor Neverly's novel *Pamiątka z Celulozy* (*Recollection from Cellulose*, 1952). Kawalerowicz portrays in flashbacks a coming-of-age story about a peasant's son, Szczęsny (Józef Nowak), who moves to town and learns about life. The film, set in the 1930s, gives a vast panorama of prewar Poland. The second part of the diptych follows the same protagonist as he works in a cellulose factory, matures, gains "class consciousness," and becomes a communist activist. Facing arrest for his illegal activities, Szczęsny escapes to Spain to join other members of the political left in the struggles against Franco's regime.

Thematically in line with other socialist realist biographical features, the film is characterized by its novel treatment of the positive hero: it is devoid of clichés, abounds with psychological characterization, stresses the role of individual and social forces, provides a panoramic scope, and depicts realistically various social strata. One Polish critic noted: "Generally, the film

Figure 4.2 Józef Nowak and Lucyna Winnicka in *Under the Phrygian Star* (1954, Jerzy Kawalerowicz)

got rid of the unbearably vulgar automatism controlling the lives of characters."[28] Kawalerowicz's film, however, was clearly made too late, when the principles of socialist realism were already being questioned. Had it been made earlier, it would have been an exemplary illustration of how to make a politically correct picture that succeeds artistically.

Kawalerowicz is known for his unorthodox artistic choices. His next film, *Cień* (*Shadow*, 1956), written by Aleksander Ścibor-Rylski, was an unusual, suspenseful story set in the postwar Polish political climate. The Hitchcock-like narrative structure and composition of *Shadow* and its sophisticated camerawork (by Jerzy Lipman) can be viewed almost as a mockery of the central concerns of socialist realist tenets. Thematically, however, the film was behind the times, made during the post-Stalinist thaw, and, as a result, was neglected by the audience and by the critics, who always favored current political content and context over style.

"Settlement of Accounts"

The socialist realist period ended in October 1956,[29] but its thematics, as well as its way of presenting the world, reappeared later in a number of Polish films, some of them artistically accomplished works and not just blatant propaganda. During the Polish School period, several films referred to the previous thematics, including such prominent works as *Człowiek na torze* (*Man on the Track*, 1957), by Andrzej Munk; *Zagubione uczucia* (*Lost Feelings*, 1957), by Jerzy Zarzycki;[30] and *Baza ludzi umartych* (*Damned Roads*, 1959), by Czesław Petelski. The directors of these "settlement of accounts films" (*filmy rozrachunkowe*) questioned the previous screen poetics and attempted to make the theme of work more attractive. The political motivation for work disappears in their films; what matters is money or professionalism. Problems arising at work or in everyday life are not blamed on foreign spies or class enemies, but on bureaucracy, incompetence, or crime.

Zarzycki's *Lost Feelings*, for example, presents an unflattering picture of harsh conditions and rampant hooliganism at the Nowa Huta steelworks, the pride of the communists. This film's story line also radically departs from previous, optimistic stories. A husband leaves his wife and four children to pursue his career as a union activist. The woman, a tired heroine of the socialist work force (she is a model worker at the steelworks), cannot cope with the situation. Her teenage son, who helps her to take care of his siblings, rebels, leaves home, and joins the hooligans.

Lost Feelings, neorealist in spirit, demythologizes the sugarcoated communist vision of reality. It questions the material advancement of the working class by showing nightmarish apartment buildings, tough working conditions, and a destitute landscape stripped of optimism. Zarzycki's film destroys the idealistic communist vision of the city of the future, Nowa Huta, exposing it to be a claustrophobic world of concrete and mud. *Lost Feelings* is photographed as an American *film noir*: it shows the world deprived of sun (low-key lighting and night for night shooting), characters at the mercy of their hostile environment, ever present disillusionment and pessimism.

According to Ewelina Nurczyńska-Fidelska, the author of the Polish book on Andrzej Munk, Munk's *Man on the Track* became the only film to overcome the shortcomings of socialist realism; it was a conscious attempt to blow up the doctrine itself from the inside.[31] The premiere of Munk's film took place on 17 January 1957, only three months after the events of the Polish October. Munk commented: "[B]y making this film we wanted to continue a certain discussion which, at the moment of its premiere, already appeared out of date."[32] For Jerzy Płażewski, however, *Man on the Track* became "the first film of the Polish October."[33]

Man on the Track tells the story of a retired train engineer, Orzechowski (Kazimierz Opaliński), who dies under mysterious circumstances while attempting to stop a train, and whose death saves the passengers of the train. The film opens in the manner of *Citizen Kane* and *Rashomon* (1950), films revered by young Polish filmmakers, by introducing the mystery. The rest of the film becomes a search for (unattainable) truth—for the identity of a dead man and the motivations of his actions (there are suspicions of sabotage)—and a psychological portrait of the old man. The film offers three different perspectives of the event; three different narrators complement each other and provide contradictory versions of what happened. The omniscient socialist realist narrator is replaced in *Man on the Track* by several narrators whose truthfulness viewers can question. The opened composition of the film forces the viewer to doubt, to be active, to engage.

The first narrator, Orzechowski's superior, accuses him of attempting to cause the accident to avenge his unwanted early retirement. The first retrospective closely resembles socialist realist narratives; Orzechowski is pictured as a classic negative character, the enemy of the new. The next retrospective belongs to Orzechowski's young apprentice, a member of the communist youth organization, and a person spying on the train engineer. However, instead of an expected simplistic portrayal of the struggle between the old and the new, the viewer learns about the psychological complexities of the dead man. The narrator himself has doubts concerning Orzechowski, and the viewer can sense his affinities with the dead man: they share the same attitude toward work. The third version of the events adds information concerning Orzechowski's life after retirement, and explains the mystery of his death to the viewers (yet not to the judging committee, which has to rely on the third narrator's biased account). The party representative, portrayed in the manner of classic Stalinist films,

Figure 4.3 Kazimierz Opaliński in Andrzej Munk's *Man on the Track* (1957)

summarizes the events. The silence that follows is interrupted by one of the narrators. "It is stuffy here," he says, opening the window. That symbolic gesture and the words spoken may be seen to summarize the whole political atmosphere around the Polish October of 1956.

Man on the Track deals with a number of typical socialist realist issues (struggles between old and new, and the enhancement of work productivity) and presents some stock characters (the wise, prudently speaking party secretary; young Orzechowski's apprentice; and Orzechowski himself as a possible villain). The focus is, however, on people and their complexities, and that makes easy generalizations impossible. The camera work supports the story. Nurczyńska-Fidelska points out that in Munk's film the use of deep-focus photography and a panning camera replaces the dynamic montage that is present in Munk's early works.[34] Munk rejects one directorial point of view, and avoids imposing meaning on reality. He uses montage sequences during the committee's meeting, while portraying the "judges" of Orzechowski. However, when the three narrators take the stand, the camera moves and pans, thus helping the viewer to be involved in the story, and stressing the intricacy of the judged man and the different perspectives in any one man's life. In the spirit of neorealism, Munk paid attention to realistic details.[35] He shot on location, chose lesser known actors/types to facilitate realism, used down-to-earth dialogue (the beginning of his collaboration with Jerzy Stefan Stawiński, the "Polish School's" major scriptwriter), used only natural noises on the soundtrack, and avoided banality and sentimentality in the portrayal of the old man.

Conclusion

The recurrent themes and stereotypes existing in Polish cinema of the Stalinist period do not reflect the attitudes of Polish society, but rather the perspective of the communist authorities. Rarely mentioned today, and if so, with profound shame, the Stalinist films ended up on a garbage heap of history—objects of ridicule for a younger generation of viewers and critics, a millstone for the older generation, especially those involved in promoting the communist ideology.

A typical Polish socialist realist film resembles a poorly told fairy tale. It is predictable and didactic, uses the Orwellian "newspeak" instead of Aesopian language, and presents a simplistic vision of the world: good versus bad, new versus old, progressive forces versus reactionary forces, bright fields versus dark fields. The end of a film brings back the desired norm: the saboteurs are captured and punished, the young protagonists are (re)united, the factory production goes on undisturbed by the enemy of the people. Happiness prevails—or rather, a colorized version of the gray reality.

Films made in Poland during the Stalinist years have many elements in common and do not exhibit many individual traits. They are conventional, ritualistic, and clichéd; resemble one another; and, as a consequence, are boring. The socialist realist authors subdued their distinctive personalities. Wojciech Włodarczyk, in his book on Polish art between 1950 and 1954, writes that Stalinist art has no authors in the traditional sense; the author is the state.[36] Another Polish scholar and critic, Tadeusz Lubelski, rightly points out that it was a part of the game between the state, the filmmakers, and the viewers. To the state, neither the quality of the work nor the type of contact between authors and viewers was of overriding importance. What was important was that an ideologically correct communication was produced and "dedicated" to the political authorities. For Lubelski, this was "a ritual of perverted culture."[37]

Notes

1. Quoted from Michał Głowiński, *Rytuał i demagogia. Trzynaście szkiców o sztuce zdegradowanej* (Warszawa: Open, 1992), 28.
2. For instance, in 1949 Konstanty Rokossowski, a Soviet general of partial Polish origin, had been appointed marshal of Poland, the Polish minister of defense, commander in chief of the Polish armed forces, and a politburo member of the Polish United Workers Party (PZPR).
3. Włodzimierz Sokorski, "Polityka kulturalna 1944–1949," *Miesięcznik Literacki* 3 (1977): 106. Also discussed by Kazimierz Sobotka, "Robotnik na ekranie, czyli o tak zwanym 'filmie produkcyjnym,'" in *Szkice o filmie polskim*, ed. Bronisława Stolarska (Łódź: Łódzki Dom Kultury, 1985), 27.
4. Discussed by Jolanta Lemann, "Czy istniała wymuszona estetyka? (kilka uwag o filmie polskim wczesnych lat pięćdziesiątych)," *Film na Świecie* 320–321 (1985): 87–89.
5. Jakub Berman, "Pokażcie wielkość naszych czasów," *Nowa Kultura* 45 (1951). Quoted from Tadeusz Lubelski, *Strategie autorskie w polskim filmie fabularnym lat 1945–1961* (Cracow: Wydawnictwo Uniwersytetu Jagiellońskiego, 1992), 93.
6. Alina Madej, "100 lat kina w Polsce: 1949–1954," *Kino* 6 (1998): 47.
7. Ewa Gębicka, "Sieć kin i rozpowszechnianie filmów," in *Encyklopedia kultury polskiej XX wieku*, ed. Edward Zajíček (Warsaw: Instytut Kultury and Komitet Kinematografii, 1994), 433.
8. Grażyna Stachówna, "Równanie szeregów. Bohaterowie filmów socrealistycznych (1949–1955)," *Człowiek z ekranu. Z antropologii postaci filmowej*, ed. Mariola Jankun-Dopartowa and Mirosław Przylipiak (Cracow: Arcana, 1996), 15.
9. Włodzimierz Sokorski, *Sztuka w walce o socjalizm* (Warsaw: Państwowy Instytut Wydawniczy, 1950), 203 and 239.
10. Jerzy Płażewski, "Film zagraniczny w Polsce," in Zajíček, *Encyklopedia kultury polskiej XX wieku*, 335.
11. Mira Liehm and Antonín J. Liehm, *The Most Important Art: Soviet and Eastern European Film After 1945* (Berkeley: University of California Press, 1977), 117.
12. Stakhanov was a Soviet Ukrainian model worker who greatly surpassed his production quota. The term "Stakhanovism" applied to all "leaders of socialist work" (Stakhanovites).
13. Lubelski, *Strategie autorskie*, 51.
14. Discussed by Stachówna, "Równanie szeregów," 16–17. The makers of *Not Far from Warsaw* (Maria Kaniewska and Adam Ważyk, the bard of socialist realist poetry) were not credited in the film. They blamed the Film Polski authorities for this film's failure. Adam Ważyk, one of the foremost representatives of Stalinist literature at that

time, is better known for his 1955 "Poemat dla dorosłych" [Poem for Adults], published in *Nowa Kultura*, in which he bitterly denounces Stalinism and his former political convictions.

15. Polish writer Leopold Tyrmand's comment, quoted by Madej, "100 lat kina w Polsce: 1949–1954," 49.

16. Quoted from Lubelski, *Strategie autorskie*, 111. It has to be noted that the Polish box office differed from the Western. The box office of certain films, including *An Adventure at Marienstadt*, was helped by the distribution of cheap (sometimes free) tickets to factories and schools. The practice continued until the late 1970s.

17. General Świerczewski, a colorful figure, was a Polish communist living in the Soviet Union and a general in the Red Army. He fought in Spain in 1936 and during World War II. He commanded the Polish troops fighting alongside the Soviets. His assassination in 1947 was blamed on the Ukrainian Insurgent Army (UPA). Michałek and Turaj justly label *Soldier of Victory* "an aesthetic travesty" and "cinematic fiasco." Bolesław Michałek and Frank Turaj, *The Modern Cinema of Poland* (Bloomington: Indiana University Press, 1988), 13.

18. Discussed in an interview with Wanda Jakubowska by Tadeusz Lubelski, "Generalissimus płakał," *Film* 18–19 (1990). Also quoted in Lubelski, *Strategie autorskie*, 95–96. Jakubowska has always been a communist close to the official party circles.

19. *The Youth of Chopin*, treated by Polish film critics as a masterpiece and a model film to be emulated by others, was awarded in Karlove Vary (1952) and Ferrara (1959). Ford's film, however, was not the first postwar work to deal with Polish history and historical biographies. The year before, Jan Rybkowski produced *Warszawska premiera* (*Warsaw Premiere*), a film on another Polish composer, Stanisław Moniuszko. Jerzy Toeplitz, ed., *Historia filmu polskiego*, vol. 3 (Warsaw: Wydawnictwa Artystyczne i Filmowe, 1974), 246.

20. Discussed by, among others, Peter Kenez in his *Cinema and Soviet Society, 1917–1953* (Cambridge: Cambridge University Press, 1992), and idem, *The Birth of the Propaganda State: Soviet Methods of Mass Mobilization, 1917–1929* (Cambridge: Cambridge University Press, 1985). Also analyzed in Richard Taylor's *Film Propaganda: Soviet Russia and Nazi Germany* (London: Croom Helm, 1979).

21. Sobotka, "Robotnik na ekranie," 52.

22. Rafał Marszałek, "Kapelusz i chustka," in *Film i kontekst*, ed. Danuta Palczewska and Zbigniew Benedyktynowicz (Wrocław: Ossolineum, 1988), 35–55.

23. Ibid., 48.

24. Sobotka, "Robotnik na ekranie," 46.

25. In his psychoanalytic interpretation of *An Adventure at Marienstadt*, Wiesław Godzic writes that the film tells the story of a young woman in search of her sexual identity. Wiesław Godzic, *Film i psychoanaliza: problem widza* (Cracow: Wydawnictwo Uniwersytetu Jagiellońskiego, 1991), 120–128.

26. Stachówna, "Równanie szeregów," 21. The year 1954 was the "year of kisses" in Polish cinema. Earlier, before *Difficult Love* (released in April), a kiss appeared in *An Adventure at Marienstadt* (released in January).

27. The "Maxim Trilogy" consists of *Yunost Maksima* (*The Youth of Maxim*, 1935), *Vozvrashchenie Maksima* (*The Return of Maxim*, 1937), and *Vyborgskaia storona* (*The Vyborg Country*, 1939). Donskoi adapted Gorki's autobiography as *Detstvo Gorkogo* (*The Childhood of Maxim Gorki*, 1938), *V liudiakh* (*My Apprenticeship*, 1939), and *Moi universitety* (*My Universities*, 1940).

28. Krzysztof Teodor Toeplitz in *Nowa Kultura* 18 (1954). Quoted from Michałek and Turaj, *The Modern Cinema of Poland*, 97.

29. Following Khrushchev's famous speech in which he disclosed and condemned Stalin's crimes, Poland was ready to retreat from Stalinism. In October 1956, Władysław Gomułka, recently released from prison, returned to power as the First Secretary of the Communist Party (PZPR), ending some of the Stalinist practices (e.g., the collectivization of farms), making gestures toward the Catholic Church (e.g., releasing the Polish primate, Stefan Wyszyński, from prison), and making some conciliatory gestures

toward the members of the noncommunist opposition against the Germans (toward the members of the Home Army).

30. Jerzy Zarzycki (1911–1971) belongs to the generation of START members. He began his career before the war, directing the much praised *The People of the Vistula* (1938, with Aleksander Ford).
31. Ewelina Nurczyńska-Fidelska, *Andrzej Munk* (Cracow: Wydawnictwo Literackie, 1982), 38.
32. Ibid., 37.
33. Jerzy Płażewski, "Andrzej Munk, urzędnik śledczy rzeczywistości," *Życie Literackie* 5 (1975): 9.
34. Nurczyńska-Fidelska, *Andrzej Munk*, 51–52.
35. Munk was familiar with the world portrayed. Earlier, he had made a documentary, *Kolejarskie słowo* (*Railwayman's Pledge*, 1953), in the same milieu.
36. Wojciech Włodarczyk, *Sztuka polska w latach 1950–1954* (Paryż: Libella, 1986), 112.
37. Lubelski, *Strategie autorskie*, 95–96.

5

The Polish School Revisited

> The real weakness of the Polish School of the 1950s, and the reason for its inevitable disappearance, was that its films presented heroes who were more stupid than History. To my mind, it's wrong to stand on the side of History instead of on the side of your hero.
>
> *Andrzej Wajda*[1]

The true birth of postwar Polish cinema had been anticipated long before the canonical films of Kazimierz Kutz, Andrzej Munk, Andrzej Wajda, and others. The term "Polish School" was coined as early as 1954 by the film critic and scholar Aleksander Jackiewicz, who expressed his desire to see a Polish School of filmmaking worthy of the great tradition of Polish art. Jackiewicz wanted to see Polish films that confronted local history and addressed social and moral problems. A filmmaker and an influential professor at the Łódź Film School, Antoni Bohdziewicz later employed the name "Polish School" when referring to Andrzej Wajda's debut film, *A Generation*.[2]

The dramatic political events of 1956 in Central Europe[3] prompted changes in Polish arts. After the workers' riots in Poznań against the communist regime in June 1956 and Władysław Gomułka's return to power in October of the same year,[4] the impatience and the desire to see the effects of the Polish October were overwhelming. Some of the writers who had produced ghastly Stalinist works emerged reborn as the champions of the new, the first to unmask the atrocities of Stalinism. The disappointment with the Stalinist period, the urge to represent reality's complex nature, and the desire to confront issues that had functioned as taboos in the Polish political as well as cultural life created a stimulating atmosphere for young filmmakers. Their works were expected to play an important role in the political changes introduced after the October of 1956. The new era was eagerly awaiting its debut in films.

The Polish School Phenomenon

The eruption of artistic energy and the emergence of the new wave of filmmakers in Poland after 1956 is usually described as the Polish School phenomenon. When discussing particular national schools of filmmaking or film movements, critics customarily look for works that were produced within a given period by a group of filmmakers who shared the same generational experiences, and whose films embrace a number of thematic and stylistic similarities. Is this the case of the Polish School phenomenon?

Stanisław Ozimek, a Polish film historian, states in his seminal work that the Polish School "was the first discernible ideological and artistic formation in the history of national cinema."[5] He meticulously enumerates the characteristic tendencies within the school, and proposes the following periods to describe the phenomenon: (1) the initial period (1955–1956), in which the new tendencies are only indicated, hidden under the crust of socialist realist poetics; (2) the proper period (1957–1959), during which filmmakers mostly focus on the themes of war and occupation, and situate their works within the context of the Polish romantic tradition; (3) the phase of crisis (1960–1961), characterized by the classic style and the personalization of presented themes (the importance of the plebeian protagonist); (4) the final stage (1962–1965), distinguished by superficial references to the school's poetics, as well as by the polemic concerning the school's thematic obsessions.[6] A number of scholars tend to agree about the period of the origins of the school, situating it either in 1955 (the release of Wajda's *A Generation*) or in 1956 (the Polish October). There is no agreement, however, concerning the decline of the school. The majority of scholars locate the end of the Polish School phenomenon earlier than Ozimek, in 1961,[7] 1962,[8] or 1963.[9]

Traditionally, scholars deal with a multiplicity of styles. During the Polish School period, they catalogued the major thematic and stylistic properties present during this outburst of authorial expressions. Stanisław Ozimek, for instance, distinguishes the "romantic-expressive" tendency represented at its best in the films of Andrzej Wajda, *Kanał* (*Kanal*, 1957), *Ashes and Diamonds* (1958), and *Lotna* (1959); the "rationalistic" tendency embodied in the films by Andrzej Munk, *Eroica* (1958) and *Zezowate szczęście* (*Bad Luck*, 1960); and the "psychological-existential" trend present in the films of Wojciech J. Has, Stanisław Lenartowicz, and Jerzy Kawalerowicz.[10] Another scholar, Aleksander Jackiewicz, differentiates between the romantic and plebeian traditions in Polish cinema. The first is represented by Wajda and Munk, the second by Kazimierz Kutz and other Polish filmmakers.[11]

As evidenced by the number of categories listed above, it is difficult to discuss the Polish School phenomenon in terms of thematic and stylistic similarities. Unlike the tedious era of Stalinist cinema, the Polish School period is characterized by differing themes, incompatible poetics, edginess in terms of style and ideology, as well as sheer entertainment value.

The multiplicity of aesthetic tendencies, the various authorial expressions, and the open character of the school make defining or summarizing it an arduous task. One has to take into account films set during or immediately after the war, which debate the Polish romantic mythology, and works that belong to different realms: historical epic (e.g., *Krzyżacy* [*Teutonic Knights*, 1960, Aleksander Ford]), comedy (e.g., *Ewa chce spać* [*Ewa Wants to Sleep*, 1958, Tadeusz Chmielewski]), war drama (e.g., *Wolne miasto* [*Free City*, 1958, Stanisław Różewicz]), psychological drama (e.g., *Prawdziwy koniec wielkiej wojny* [*The True End of the Great War*, 1957, Jerzy Kawalerowicz]), metaphysical drama (e.g., *Matka Joanna od Aniołów* [*Mother Joan of the Angels*, 1961, Kawalerowicz]), Holocaust drama (e.g., *Biały niedźwiedź* [*White Bear*, 1959, Jerzy Zarzycki]), the "new wave experiments" (e.g., *Ostatni dzień lata* [*The Last Day of Summer*, 1958, Tadeusz Konwicki]), black comedy (e.g., Munk's *Bad Luck*), eastern (e.g., *Rancho Texas* [1959, Wadim Berestowski]), and others. The different, sometimes contradictory, approaches are discernible even if one analyzes films made by the same director. Films such as the neorealist *Krzyż Walecznych* (*Cross of Valor*, 1959) and the new wave (in spirit) *Nikt nie woła* (*Nobody Is Calling*, 1960), both directed by Kazimierz Kutz, or the expressionistic *Zimowy zmierzch* (*Winter Twilight*, 1957) and the war drama *Pigułki dla Aurelii* (*Pills for Aurelia*, 1958), both directed by Stanisław Lenartowicz, belong to different realms and represent disparate film poetics.

The ambiguous criteria pertaining to the Polish School and the lack of an aesthetic program articulated by the young filmmakers allow scholars either to limit the number of films to a small group of selected examples or to consider all of the films made during the period in question. Opting for the former approach, Tadeusz Miczka writes arbitrarily that out of 138 feature films released between 1957 and 1963, only 30 belong to the Polish School. According to Miczka, they are distinguished by the "strategy of the psychotherapist" employed by their makers, chiefly Munk and Wajda, who "deeply influenced the social consciousness since they helped to free the national mythology from mystification and lies, permeating the socialist realist poetics."[12] Other scholars, myself included, are more cautious, and choose to depart from the narrow interpretation, preferring instead to observe the complexity of the phenomenon and analyze the various means of expression that appeared during the Polish School period. Marek Hendrykowski discusses not "the school" but "the artistic formation," and stresses that "the term Polish School has been treated ahistorically so far, that it is eliminating by definition, firstly, the moment of internal evolution of the formation and, secondly, the multiplicity of tendencies and styles of its artistic explorations."[13] Hendrykowski asserts that the artistic formation known as the Polish School was open, multifaceted, evolutionary, polyphonic, and dialogic, and was created by many authors (including directors, scriptwriters, cinematographers, actors, composers, and set designers).[14] Another scholar, Ewelina Nurczyńska-Fidelska, theorizes that the Polish School, as a uniform cultural marvel, did not exist; instead, we are dealing with the emergence of *auteurs* who initiated a serious artistic and intellectual dialogue with their viewers, and who reflected the spirit of the times in their works.[15]

Undoubtedly, it is more feasible to discuss the Polish School period in terms of its authors and the generational change of guard. The Polish School had been created primarily by a new generation of filmmakers— the so-called "generation of Columbuses" (*Kolumbowie*)—born in the 1920s and embodied by the two young poets Krzysztof Kamil Baczyński and Tadeusz Gajcy, who died a soldier's death during the Warsaw Uprising of August to October 1944.[16] Maria Janion, a Polish expert on romanticism, states that this was "the generation marked by the trauma of war and death ... born under the unhappy, perhaps cursed star."[17] The young filmmakers were united in their disenchantment with the socialist realist dogma and the simplistic aesthetics of their older colleagues. They were attempting to break with their teachers, mostly prewar left-wing filmmakers and activists whom they interestingly never acknowledged, and trying to forget their own film initiation under the auspices of socialist realism. They turned to recent history, to World War II and the postwar situation, leaving the Stalinist period virtually untouched.[18] The images of Polish history and present-day reality that they produced for the screen disturbed the Polish communist authorities.

The political changes introduced after the Polish October enabled the young filmmakers to move away from socialist realism and, to a large extent, to build their films around their own experiences. Polish literature, traditionally the source for almost half of Polish films, played an even more important role in the late 1950s and at the beginning of the 1960s.[19] Unlike the prewar period, which favored adaptations of literary classics, the Polish School filmmakers preferred novels and short stories published after 1946 by their contemporaries: Jerzy Andrzejewski, Kazimierz Brandys, Bohdan Czeszko, Józef Hen, Marek Hłasko, Jerzy Stefan Stawiński, and others.[20] For example, some of the canonical works by Andrzej Wajda and Andrzej Munk, *Man on the Track*, *Kanal*, *Eroica*, and *Bad Luck*, are based on scripts by Jerzy Stefan Stawiński. This coauthor of the Polish School's success drew on his firsthand experiences as a soldier in the September campaign of 1939 against the invading Germans. He spent time in a POW camp, from which he successfully escaped, committed himself to underground political activities, participated in the Warsaw Uprising, and, after its collapse, was interred in another POW camp. Reflecting Stawiński's personal experiences, the films made by the Polish School generation bring to light the unrepresented fate of the Home Army members—the truly national resistance against both German and Soviet occupying forces—which fought under the command of the Polish government-in-exile based in London. These films also portray the humiliating military defeat in 1939, the occupation, the Warsaw Uprising, the futility of the armed struggle, and the Polish romantic mythology.

Organizational Changes

The revival of Polish cinema in the late 1950s was helped by a number of organizational changes that had already begun before the Polish October. Starting in May 1955, the film industry in Poland was based on a film units (*Zespoły Filmowe*) system, a new and efficient way of managing film production.[21] Each film unit was composed of film directors, scriptwriters, and producers (along with their collaborators and assistants), and was supervised by an artistic director, with the help of a literary director and a production manager. Film units were considered state enterprises yet had some rudimentary freedoms; thanks to them, a number of the Łódź Film School graduates quickly achieved strong positions in the national film industry.

In 1957 there were eight such film companies in operation, among them the film unit Kadr, which was instrumental in developing the Polish School phenomenon. Kadr was headed by Jerzy Kawalerowicz, with Krzysztof Teodor Toeplitz (until 1957) and (later) Tadeusz Konwicki as literary directors, and Ludwik Hager as a production manager. Among its members were Andrzej Wajda, Andrzej Munk, Janusz Morgenstern, and Kazimierz Kutz. Other film units included Ludwik Starski's Iluzjon (with directors such as Wojciech Jerzy Has, Sylwester Chęciński, and Jerzy Passendorfer), Jan Rybkowski's Rytm (Stanisław Lenartowicz, Stanisław Różewicz), Aleksander Ford's Studio (Ewa and Czesław Petelski, Janusz Nasfeter), Wanda Jakubowska's Start (Jan Batory, Maria Kaniewska), Jerzy Zarzycki's Syrena, Jerzy Bossak's Kamera (formerly known as "57"), and Antoni Bohdziewicz's Droga. The literary directors included some of the most prominent writers: Anatol Stern, Stanisław Dygat, Tadeusz Konwicki (himself a renowned filmmaker), Jerzy Stefan Stawiński, Roman Bratny, and Jerzy Andrzejewski.[22]

The year 1955 also marked the creation of the Central Film Archives (Centralne Archiwum Filmowe) in Warsaw, known today as the National Film Archives (Filmoteka Narodowa). In 1956 the Central Office of Cinema (Centralny Urząd Kinematografii; established in 1952) was replaced by the Chief Board of Cinema (Naczelny Zarząd Kinematografii), part of the Polish Ministry of Culture.

The new policy affected the distribution of films as well. Since April 1958, Polish movie theaters were obliged to screen short films (animated, documentary, or educational) before the main feature, a factor of great consequence for the future of Polish short films.[23] In 1956 there were 2,881 cinemas in operation. Between 1957 and 1961, this number increased significantly (by almost 20 percent), and by 1961 Poland had 1,490 cinemas in the cities, 1,709 in rural areas, and 333 mobile cinemas. This period also marked the appearance of the first cine-clubs (as many as 170 in 1961), which played a vital role in promoting international art cinema in Poland; they often screened films not distributed in mainstream cinemas due to political censorship.[24]

Political events in the mid-1950s—the post-Stalinist thaw and its after-math—also affected film distribution. Comparatively liberal politics allowed the Polish film industry to produce and import genre cinema and entertainment films from Western Europe and America. The Film Repertoire Council (Filmowa Rada Repertuarowa), an advisory body initially headed by Jerzy Toeplitz, was founded in 1957. This council was responsible for recommending foreign films. During the late 1950s, the number of films imported from the West increased at the expense of films from the communist countries; between 170 and 180 films from twenty-two countries were released in Poland annually, with local films making up 12 percent of the market.[25]

The new repertoire policy was characterized by its careful balance between art cinema and popular cinema. The times also required a careful geopolitical equilibrium—half of the films had to come from Soviet bloc countries. For example, the films shown on Polish screens in 1960 consisted of 42 Soviet, 27 French, 21 American, 20 Polish, 18 English, 17 Czechoslovak, 9 Italian, 6 East German, 5 Swedish, and 5 Yugoslavian films. The rest were films from Japan, West Germany, Mexico, Hungary, Romania, Bulgaria, Austria, Argentina, Denmark, Finland, the Netherlands, China, and North Korea.[26] In spite of the dominance of Soviet films (almost half of the Soviet annual production was present on Polish screens), the repertoire was rich and included the most interesting aspects of world cinema.

Immediately after World War II, the appearance of every Polish film constituted a cultural event. Local films had an average audience of about 4.7 million viewers. Between 1950 and 1955, however, the average attendance at Polish films dropped to 2.6 million. In the second part of the 1950s, Polish films regained their popularity, and although attendance was never as high as immediately after the war, they drew more than 3 million viewers per film.[27] Total annual cinema attendance was the highest immediately after the 1956 Polish October, with 231 million viewers. Later, despite the number of successful Polish films, the diversity of imported films, and the increased number of cinema theaters, there was a slow decline of cinema attendance: 205 million viewers in 1958, 195.5 in 1959, 186 in 1960, and 179.6 in 1961. As in other European countries, the increasing impact of television was partly to blame for the declining numbers. In 1957, for example, there were 22,000 television sets in Poland; only four years late, there were as many as 959,000.[28]

Polish films, always popular with local audiences, were starting to receive international acclaim, and were winning a number of awards at various films festivals. The awards include two Silver Palms at Cannes for *Kanal* and *Mother Joan of the Angels*, Grand Prix for *Ewa Wants to Sleep* at San Sebastian, FIPRESCI award for *Ashes and Diamonds* at Venice, Golden Lion at Venice for *Świadectwo urodzenia* (*The Birth Certificate*, 1961, Stanisław Różewicz), FIPRESCI award at Venice for *Nóż w wodzie* (*Knife in the Water*, 1962, Roman Polański), and Grand Prix at San Francisco for *Jak być kochaną* (*How to Be Loved*, 1963, Wojciech J. Has). During the same period, Polish documentary filmmakers (e.g., Kazimierz Karabasz) and filmmakers specializing in animation (e.g., Witold Giersz, Walerian Borowczyk, and Jan Lenica) were also being recognized abroad and winning awards at numerous film festivals.

Influences

Starting in the mid-1950s, a split developed between young emerging filmmakers, trained at the Łódź Film School, who believed in a genuine depiction of vital national themes, and older filmmakers, including Aleksander Ford and Wanda Jakubowska, who opted for cinema imitating the Soviet epic models. The young filmmakers clearly favored the Italian neorealist approach, which offered them a chance to break with their predecessors and reflect the spirit of the de-Stalinization period. Reproached by the communist authorities during the time of the reigning socialist realism, Italian neorealism became the alternative to the portrayal of falsified reality. Although often absent on Polish screens, major works of neorealist cinema were shown during closed screenings at the Łódź Film School.[29]

Neorealist influences are already discernible in some of the films made in 1954 (discussed in the previous chapter): *Five Boys from Barska Street, A Night of Remembrance,* and *Under the Phrygian Star.* Wajda's *A Generation* heralds the Polish School phenomenon, and remains an example of a transitional work fusing the poetics of socialist realist films with neorealist observation. The film tells a "coming-of-age" story set during the war. Its protagonist, an ordinary streetwise character from a poor district of Warsaw, Stach (Tadeusz Łomnicki), joins the communist resistance when he meets and falls in love with an underground communist courier, Dorota (Urszula Modrzyńska). In the film's finale, Stach leads the underground unit after Dorota is arrested.

A Generation, based on Bohdan Czeszko's novel about Gwardia Ludowa (People's Guard), the communist military resistance formed in 1942, is a work tainted by political compromise. It remains, by and large, a socialist realist film influenced by the neorealist style. Like Czeszko's novel, Wajda's film is heavily stereotyped and rewrites recent Polish history from the communist perspective. It contains a distorted picture of the occupation in Poland with its black-and-white portrayal of the different factions of the underground—the nationalist Home Army members are stereotyped as "collaborators" and "pseudopatriots," and the communist People's Guard members are vaunted as the "true patriots." The film also reverses the proportions of the Polish underground: the role of the communist underground is exaggerated at the expense of the Home Army. Like other socialist realist works, Wajda's film also has its "positive" working-class hero in the center, who acquires the correct (Marxist-Leninist) knowledge about history thanks to the guidance of the experienced communist activists. *A Generation* is less schematic than classic socialist realist films: "It successfully combines an expression of an acceptably optimistic social and political position with true lyricism, an idealization of personal experience, of remembered attitudes," rightly observes Bolesław Sulik.[30]

The straightforward story of *A Generation*, set in the working-class milieu, was shot mostly on location with young, unknown actors, who were to become familiar faces of the Polish School cinema: Tadeusz Janczar (1926–1997), Zbigniew Cybulski (1927–1967), Tadeusz Łomnicki (1927–1992), and Roman Polański (b. 1933). The opening tracking shot of the film introduces a familiar setting from a number of Italian neorealist films: an impoverished Warsaw suburb with shacks and barren industrial buildings. The viewer sides with the most complex character in this film, Janek Krone (Tadeusz Janczar), the prototype of Wajda's heroic protagonist: doubtful, troubled, and tragic. At first, the character of Janek appears to provide a contrast to the socialist realist hero, Stach. But Janek is multidimensional and ambiguous, and ends up dying an unnecessary, "absurdly heroic death."[31] This type of character anticipates other film personae such as Maciek Chełmicki in *Ashes and Diamonds*.

The realistic depiction of the war and the postwar reality was a natural reaction against the sugarcoated poetics of socialist realism. There were both stylistic and ideological oppositions created by the Łódź Film School graduates, who wanted to manifest a personal, auteurist approach after the Stalinist period during which the author had been silenced and only the system had a voice. The dose of realism, enormous by Polish standards in the mid-1950s, was often unbearable for the censors, who reacted in several cases; they were harsher toward contemporary realistic films than films dealing with recent history. Jerzy Zarzycki's *Lost Feelings*, for example, was withdrawn from the screens soon after its release. The premieres of two other, lesser known films, *Koniec nocy* (*The End of the Night*) and *Miasteczko* (*Small Town*), both collectively directed, were delayed. The former, made in 1956, was released in December 1957; the latter, produced in 1958, premiered in March 1960.[32]

The End of the Night,[33] *Lunatycy* (*Sleepwalkers*, 1960, Bohdan Poręba), and *Lost Feelings* all deal with the themes of juvenile delinquency and hooliganism, which were "discovered" approximately at the same time by Polish documentary filmmakers. From 1956 to 1959, about twenty films of the so-called "black series" were made, beginning with Jerzy Hoffman and Edward Skórzewski's *Uwaga, chuligani* (*Attention, Hooligans*, 1955). In contrast to the socialist realist mode of representation, this and other documentary films portrayed the negative aspects of life as well. These facets—hooliganism, prostitution, and alcoholism—were never mentioned in the previous era. Particularly known are documentaries by Kazimierz Karabasz and Władysław Ślesicki, *Gdzie diabeł mówi dobranoc* (*Where the Devil Says Good Night*, 1957), and *Ludzie z pustego obszaru* (*People from Nowhere*, 1957). The title of the latter became a description of the criminal sphere of life.

Ewelina Nurczyńska-Fidelska applies the term *czarny realizm* (literally, "black realism") to a group of realistic, yet stylistically different, films including *The End of the Night, Small Town, Lost Feelings, Sleepwalkers, Winter Twilight, Damned Roads,* and *Pętla* (*Noose,* 1958, Wojciech J. Has).[34] They formed the Polish version of Italian neorealism and, as Nurczyńska-Fidelska suggests, were characterized by a dark presentation of reality and stylistic as well as thematic borrowings from American *film noir*. In the context of Polish politics during the 1950s, every attempt at representing the darker side of everyday life became explicitly a political act. Hooliganism, for instance, was not portrayed exclusively as a social malady; instead, it was presented as an indirect accusation of the communist system.[35]

Damned Roads, directed by Czesław Petelski and based on Marek Hłasko's short story, frequently and deservedly appears in Polish critical works as the main example of "black realism." The film, set after the war in the sparsely populated Bieszczady Mountains (in southeastern Poland), deals with a group of brutal, rootless men working as logging truck drivers. *Damned Roads* also serves as an example of a socialist realist film about production à *rebours*. It lacks the didacticism of the previous era. The characters populating the screen (played by Emil Karewicz, Leon Niemczyk, Roman Kłosowski, and others) are clearly anti-model workers—daredevils known only through their pseudonyms, shipwrecked people driving old rickety trucks.[36] Although there is one Communist Party member among them, Zabawa (Zygmunt Kęstowicz), sent there to supervise the production plan, he has nothing to do with the Stalinist heroes. His wife Wanda (Teresa Iżewska), the only female in this male-oriented world, the equivalent of a *film noir* femme fatale, dreams of escaping from this god-forsaken place with any willing man from the base.

Kurt Weber's cinematography aptly captures the gloomy scenery of the portrayed reality and stresses its fatalistic and claustrophobic aspects. Even the optimistic ending, which features new trucks coming to the base for the two remaining truck drivers, does not weaken this film's overwhelmingly pessimistic tone. Criticized in 1959 by some film reviewers for its dark portrayal of an animal-like existence, and by Hłasko himself for the addition of a happy ending that is not present in his short story (he withdrew his name from the credits), *Damned Roads* remains to this day one of the darkest pictures of the "bright communist reality."

A number of filmmakers adopted influences apart from neorealism in order to free themselves from the stiff corset of socialist realist poetics. For instance, *Winter Twilight* and *Noose,* labeled as "black realist" films, situate themselves on the margin of mainstream Polish cinema by relying on expressionistic devices and mood. *Winter Twilight* portrays a small town somewhere in the eastern part of Poland. Its episodic narrative structure (Tadeusz Konwicki's script) focuses on an old railwayman, Rumsza (Włodzimierz Ziembiński), who is disappointed with his son Józek's choice of a wife. Józek (Bogusz Bilewski) marries a woman from outside the small community after finishing his military service. The film's plot is suggested rather than developed; the atmosphere remains more important than the action. With the help of Mieczysław Jahoda's cinematography, Stanisław Lenartowicz (b. 1921) creates delicate mood and intimacy. The reliance on stylized flashbacks into the prewar period, the use of symbolism and expressionistic imagery, the observation of local customs and rituals produce a place that did not exist previously in the socialist realist world. Film critic Stanisław Grzelecki notes that "on the rubble of socialist realism spins what was cursed before: metaphors and symbols, moods and half-tones, dreams and fogs … indistinct life at small railroad stations."[37] This film's symbolism and expressionist devices, however, were criticized by the majority of Polish critics. Interestingly, Lenartowicz objected to the labeling of his film as "expressionistic," considering expressionism as a distinct and closed period in film history.[38]

Noose, another expressionistic film, deals with alcoholism and portrays a single day in the life of an alcoholic young man, Kuba (Gustaw Holoubek). It is a film about the impossibility of escaping fate, about a reckless drive to destruction that ends in suicide. The action of *Noose* is limited to the protagonist's room and several streets that resemble a nightmarish landscape peopled by weird characters. The city serves as a reflection of Kuba's anxieties and his state of mind, which is on the verge of collapse. As in other films by Has, small objects, such as the clock and the black telephone, have important roles and virtually become characters in this film.

In *Noose* and his other works, Wojciech J. Has ignores history and politics, that fateful fascination of Polish cinema; he does not take political stands, and trusts his own imagination. He has always been unreceptive to artistic and political fads and the current polemics surrounding Polish film. He looks for universal themes and universal settings. "I reject matters, ideas, themes only significant for the present day. Art film dies in an atmosphere of fascination with the present," declares Has in a 1981 *Kino* interview.[39] Like Wajda's, Has's scripts are based on well-known works of literature, yet he always transforms them with his easily recognizable visual style. In his works made during the Polish School period—*Noose*, *Pożegnania* (*Farewells*, 1958), *Wspólny pokój* (*Shared Room*, 1960), *Złoto* (*Gold*, 1961), and *How to Be Loved*—Has does not present typical Polish romantic heroes. His characters do not rebel or fight, and history seems to ignore them. The world they inhabit is built of their own dreams, fantasies, and fears. They live as if outside of history and time, trapped in a surreal reality. "The protagonists remain paralyzed by internal defeat; their world passes with cruelty, madness, and beauty, but this is a simulated movement, a simulated time," explains Piotr Wojciechowski.[40] *How to Be Loved*, Has's classic film based on Kazimierz Brandys's story, is slightly different. It offers a female perspective on the war. The protagonist Felicja (Barbara Krafftówna) finds love more important than national duty, and she pays a heavy price for it.

Figure 5.1 Barbara Krafftówna and Artur Młodnicki in *How to Be Loved* (1963, Wojciech J. Has)

World War II

Realistic depictions of the post-Stalinist reality did not constitute the main trend during the Polish School period. The primary concern remained history, World War II in particular. For the filmmakers, the "point of reference is not the historical reality," says Andrzej Werner, "but the notions that surround it, those mythologized forms of comprehension."[41] The Polish School filmmakers did not introduce just a single perspective on recent Polish history. Instead, they offered polemic voices and a variety of cinematic styles. The atmosphere of the post-Stalinist thaw enabled them to deal with several taboo topics, such as the Warsaw Uprising of 1944 and the fate of the Home Army fighters.

The differences in the treatment of history can be seen in a number of films polemic to the then official version of history and to each other. For example, two films dealing with the Warsaw Uprising, Andrzej Wajda's *Kanał* and Andrzej Munk's *Eroica*, both scripted by Jerzy Stefan Stawiński, portray two visions of this both cherished and criticized moment in the Polish past.[42] The majority of Polish scholars discuss these and other films in the context of the local romantic tradition as the works inspired by and debating this legacy. Scholars frequently juxtapose Wajda's romanticism and Munk's rationalism, comparing Wajda's dramatic characters, torn between their sense of duty to the nation and their personal happiness, to Munk's commonsensical, pragmatic protagonists.[43]

Andrzej Wajda, a proponent of the Polish romantic tradition, deals with the national history in his most important works made during the Polish School period. "Wajda's films are pervaded with the intention of interpreting the manifestations, the features and the social functions of the national mythology," writes Ewelina Nurczyńska-Fidelska.[44] His protagonists are caught by the oppressive forces of history and function as its unfortunate victims. Wajda's breakthrough film, *Kanal*, concerns the final stage of the Warsaw Uprising. It narrates the story of a Home Army unit that manages to escape German troops via the only route left—the city sewers.[45] From its opening sequence, *Kanal* depicts a bleak vision of defeat. The voice-over narration introduces the leading character-insurgents, offers laconic comments on them, and tells the viewers that they are watching the last hours of the characters' lives. Since the viewer is told that there is no hope for the protagonists, the film's dramaturgy relies on "how" rather than "what." The main part of the film is set in the Warsaw city sewers, in which the majority of the fighters meet their deaths. The choice of this unusual environment largely explains the use of expressionistic lighting and claustrophobic camera angles, as well as the darkness of the set. The setting of the action, expressionistic in style, is also surrealist in spirit. It is a nightmarish underworld permeated by madness, death, and despair—full of dead bodies, German booby traps, and excrement.

Figure 5.2 Tadeusz Janczar and Teresa Iżewska in Andrzej Wajda's *Kanal* (1957)

Kanal offers an allegory on the agony of the city and the annihilation of its inhabitants. From a contemporary perspective, however, it is easy to point out the film's historical inaccuracies, for example, that the Red Army was watching on the other bank of the Vistula River when the uprising was suppressed by the Germans. In a defensive comment, Wajda explains:

> the only thing that may strike one is the absence of one element, namely "force of circumstances" (let us leave it at that, in inverted commas) which precipitated the drama; but I can see no way of presenting this on the screen until the problem has first been sorted out by the historians on the basis of the evidence. Anything that I might suggest going on my own conjectures would be merely nebulous hypothesis.[46]

The Warsaw Uprising is a controversial subject in Poland to this day, and the release of *Kanal*, the first film to portray the legendary uprising, sparked passionate debates. In the film, Wajda neither glorifies the uprising, as was expected by the majority of his countrymen in 1957, nor does he criticize the official communist stand on the "liberation" of Warsaw by the Soviet troops. Instead, he stresses the patriotism of the Home Army soldiers, their sense of duty, and their heroic yet futile effort. They gain sympathy as ill-fated casualties of the war and the victims of political manipulations. Certainly, *Kanal* is not a paean to the Home Army heroes, but rather a film demythologizing Polish-style heroism. The commanding officer of the company of insurgents, Lieutenant Zadra (Wieńczysław Gliński), voices his doubts: "With small arms and hand grenades against tanks and planes. We'll never learn." His second-in-command, Lieutenant Mądry (Emil Karewicz) responds: "Orders are orders. Stop rationalizing."[47] Earlier in the film, after listening to an officer say "we'll be hailed by posterity. They won't take us alive," Zadra bitterly responds: "That's right, the Polish way!"

The Warsaw Uprising is also the central focus of the first part of Andrzej Munk's *Eroica: Scherzo alla Polacca*, released eight months after *Kanal*.[48] It is a tragic-grotesque film that depicts a different, everyday face of Polish heroism stripped of romantic myths. The film introduces an unusual (by Polish standards) wartime antihero, Dzidziuś Górkiewicz (Edward Dziewoński). He is an opportunist, a black-market dealer, and an accidental hero of the uprising. This protagonist is not a brave, doomed soldier as one might expect, but rather a suspicious civilian. Acting as a mediator between the Home Army command in Warsaw and the Hungarian army unit, which is stationed near his house at the outskirts of Warsaw, Munk's protagonist serves the uprising. But his motivations are not ones cultivated by the Polish romantic tradition.

Rafał Marszałek writes that Poles learned the ideals of sacrifice and martyrdom from their tragic eighteenth- and nineteenth-century history, which resulted in the standardization of the national past. This history has affected Polish "patriotic art," which is characterized by a combination of idealism and naturalism, and by a reliance on pathos, national symbols,

Figure 5.3 (From the left) Barbara Połomska, Edward Dziewoński, and Leon Niemczyk in Andrzej Munk's *Eroica* (1958)

and allegories.[49] Munk's film introduces characters facing the same problems as Wajda's insurgents, yet their actions are devoid of the romantic aura. The director clearly separates himself from the dominant national mythology, and offers a bitter satire on Polish-style heroism—pejoratively known in Polish as *bohaterszczyzna* (heroism for the sake of it).

Munk's film *Zezowate szczęście* (*Bad Luck*, aka *Cockeyed Luck*, 1960), also scripted by Jerzy Stefan Stawiński, belongs to the same tradition. Set between the 1930s and the 1950s, it introduces another perspective on history that is atypical for Polish cinema. The film's protagonist, Jan Piszczyk (Bogumił Kobiela), is a Polish Everyman who desperately wants to play an important role in the course of events, yet, with no luck on his side, becomes another victim of history.[50] Piszczyk is an antihero—a moronic opportunist and an unreliable narrator who relates the sad story of his life. In six flashbacks he presents himself as "the eternal plaything of history whose pranks he subjectively interprets as 'bad luck.'"[51] The mixture of generic conventions (from burlesque to political satire) helps Munk to portray Piszczyk as the victim of political circumstances—totalitarian systems (communism and fascism) and the war—and an oppressive childhood. Munk's tale about the failure of political mimicry may be perceived as a very Central European story. This model had an impact on other films, for example, Péter Bacsó's *A tanú* (*The Witness*, produced in 1969, released in 1978), a Hungarian film set during the Stalinist years that introduces another hapless opportunist clashing with political circumstances beyond his understanding.

* * * *

The discourse on recent Polish history permeates a number of other films made during the Polish School period. Andrzej Wajda's *Ashes and Diamonds* and Kazimierz Kutz's *Nobody Is Calling* deal with the fate of the Home Army soldiers at a time when World War II was practically over, but fighting continued between the Soviet-imposed communists and the nationalist Home Army, the two warring factions in Poland. Both films explore similar themes, yet present them in a disparate manner.

Ashes and Diamonds is generally regarded as the climax of the Polish School. It is considered the world cinema classic that "tamed communist Poland for the Western viewer, rendering it palatable, acceptable."[52] But when this film was made, it was attacked by the communist establishment and by Aleksander Ford, who contested its alleged "counterrevolutionary nature." The film was poorly received at the official state meeting of the film commission. It was only because of another screening organized for Communist Party intellectuals by the author of the adapted book, Jerzy Andrzejewski, that the film's release had any success.[53]

The film takes place in a small provincial town "somewhere in Poland" with its action beginning on 8 May 1945, a date that symbolically signals the end of the war. Its action is largely confined to the Monopol Hotel, where the official preparations to celebrate the end of the war are being made by the authorities. Because of the unity of place and time (the bulk of the film is set at night) and the thespian conflict of choices, the film can be considered a classical drama. The story concerns the Home Army fighter Maciek Chełmicki (Zbigniew Cybulski), who carries out his superiors' orders and assassinates the new district secretary of the Communist Party, Szczuka (Wacław Zastrzeżyński). *Ashes and Diamonds*, however, does not portray a personal conflict, but rather a conflict of opposing political forces ("The fight for Poland, the fight for what sort of country it's going to be, has only just started," explains Szczuka at the beginning of the film). The "new Poland" is represented by the Polish communists, the security force officers, the small-town political opportunists, and the Polish and Soviet troops on the city streets. The "old Poland" is embodied by the isolated Home Army fighters and their officers, and by the anachronistic remnants of the prewar nobility and intelligentsia who are ridiculed in the film. Given the political circumstances, Maciek's death is inevitable: Polish soldiers shoot him, and he lies in convulsions in a fetus-like position as death overtakes him on the enormous city garbage heap (perhaps the Hegelian rubbish heap of history).

Maciek serves as another tragic romantic hero torn between duty to the national cause and the yearning for a normal life. The Polish romantic protagonist always solves such a dilemma by considering national matters as having topmost priority; he knows that he has to sacrifice his private happiness at the altar of national needs. Like other Polish romantic characters, Maciek is a prisoner of a fate that he is powerless to escape. By killing Szczuka, he expects to fulfill his duties to the underground Home Army and to free himself from the war. The girl he meets and falls in love with, Krystyna (Ewa Krzyżewska), offers him a chance to lead a normal life. This is, however, an illusory prospect, since the postwar Polish reality did not welcome people with Maciek's past. In Wajda's film, the Home Army Major Waga (Ignacy Machowski) elaborates on this in his comments to Andrzej (Adam Pawlikowski), Maciek's commanding officer: "And what have you been fighting for? For a free Poland, wasn't it? But was this how you imagined it? You must be aware, lieutenant, that in Poland as it is, the only chance for you and thousands like you is to fight on. Where can you go with your record? In this country everything is closed to you. Except prison."

Ashes and Diamonds depicts a cross-section of Polish society. Unlike the one-dimensional archetype of socialist realist characters, Wajda's protagonists are multilayered and open to interpretation. According to his trademark formula, "lyric protagonists in dramatic situations,"[54] Wajda makes the anticommunist Maciek a seductive hero who contemplates the "to kill or not to kill" dilemma. The director contrasts the stylized acting

Figure 5.4 Zbigniew Cybulski (left) and Adam Pawlikowski in Andrzej Wajda's *Ashes and Diamonds* (1958)

of Cybulski (Maciek) with the restrained acting of Pawlikowski (Andrzej). Furthermore, Maciek's political enemy, Szczuka, the new party secretary, an ex-soldier of the Spanish Civil War who has just returned from the Soviet Union, is portrayed as a leader with human qualities, not a poster-like exemplar at all: he is aging, fatherly, and tired. In the opening sequence, when Szczuka meets the workers after the first failed attempt on his life, the camera portrays him in the manner typical of socialist realist films, with low-angle shots of him standing in front of the workers who are portrayed, also typically, as a group. Other diverse characters in supporting roles include the opportunist Drewnowski, the apparatchik Święcki, the alcoholic journalist Pieniążek, and Szczuka's teenage son, Marek, a Home Army soldier captured by the security forces (this story element is not present in the literary source).

Wajda comments on the tragic fate of his protagonist: "The source of his tragedy is that this boy does not accept reality, does not accept history as it is, but history as he has dreamt of it. Precisely speaking, thinking about life, about history, about the country, he uses notions he received as an inheritance from the romantic stream of Polish literature."[55] Wearing dark glasses ("during the uprising, I stayed too long in the sewers," he explains to Krystyna) and clothing that do not represent the postwar reality, Maciek serves as an exemplary hero of the late 1950s. Polish writer and filmmaker Tadeusz Konwicki writes on Cybulski's rendition of Maciek:

> I didn't like him as Maciek in *Ashes and Diamonds* because he reminded me too much of the American actors in fashion at that time—James Dean, Montgomery Clift.... But Home Army bumpkin that I am, it [the film] stuck in my throat. Yes, we had our fashions, fads, modes. But our fashions did not include blue jeans, sunglasses, excessive drinking, neurotic kicks, hysterical sobbing, and short-term love affairs.... We were coarse, common; we wore knickers; we were punctual, reliable, restrained, embarrassed, hungry for death, afraid of one another, mistrustful of the elite, and timid in our feelings, gestures and words. We were simply different, we were simply genuine because we had not yet been reflected in the mirror of art.[56]

Although Cybulski has been frequently compared by Polish critics to Dean, the similarities between the two actors seem superficial. When asked about it, Cybulski said, "Dean had such great individuality that copying him is an unattainable dream. One can copy him in a satirical program, but not in a two-hour film. Besides, I acted in a similar manner in *A Generation*, and I did not know that he existed and I couldn't have known, because his films, as we all know, were made in 1955 and 1956. Comparisons are made because I employ the same acting method...."[57]

Ashes and Diamonds is known for its romantic celebration of doomed heroes and its flamboyant style ("baroque" is the frequently ill-used word in film criticism). Striking visual effects, references to Polish national symbolism, and the ambivalent use of religious imagery characterize the film. The motif of fire in particular, here associated with death, plays an important role in Wajda's film. In the opening sequence, Maciek's victim is shot in the back, and he catches fire as he collapses against church doors that open, revealing the altar. In another celebrated example, Maciek and Andrzej recall (while at the hotel bar) the years of fighting, during which ideological distinctions were clear. They drink to the memory of their dead companions, lighting glasses of alcohol as blazing memorials to their fallen friends. In the final sequence, the killer and his victim embrace in a grim dance of death, with fireworks bursting suddenly behind them. The fire of Maciek's gun and the festivity's fireworks marking the end of the war provide an ironic and bitter comment on the illusory nature of peace. Wajda also employs symbols taken from Polish art iconography. Some of them border on surreal touches, for example, an upside-down crucifix in a destroyed church that separates the two lovers, Maciek and Krystyna; the presence of a white horse; and the final scene with the Ogiński polonaise played off key. The accumulation of some religious symbols in *Ashes and Diamonds* and the treatment of religion in general are seen by Paul Coates as Buñuelian in spirit.[58]

Unlike Wajda, Kutz portrays surviving heroes who give up their romantic gestures; he is interested in their isolation and loneliness, which is stressed through the composition of frame and the use of the landscape. Although sometimes classified with Munk as representative of the demythologizing trend in Polish cinema, Kutz focuses not on the national mythology but on the everyday, the unheroic, and the plebeian. He is interested not in symbols of national importance but in concrete situations, not in history and the fate of Poles but in detailed observations of human psychology. This treatment of common protagonists is already present in Kutz's well-received debut, *Krzyż Walecznych* (*Cross of Valor*, 1959), which consists of three novellas dealing with ordinary soldiers in ordinary situations. The first one, *Krzyż* (*Cross*), narrates the story of Socha (Jerzy Turek), a soldier from a village who returns home only to find it destroyed. In this new situation, his medals and bravery make no sense. In the second part, *Pies* (*Dog*), a group of Polish soldiers cannot carry out an order to shoot a German shepherd dog, although they have learned that it was used in a concentration camp. The third novella, *Wdowa* (*Widow*), which deals with maintaining myths at all costs, tells the story of ex-soldiers who, after the war, settle in a small town. There they keep alive the mythic presence of their dead military commander, imposing this cult onto his unhappy, young, and beautiful widow.

One of the most original, yet for a long time critically neglected, films made during the Polish School period is Kutz's *Nobody Is Calling*, scripted by Józef Hen and loosely based on his novel.[59] Kutz admits that his intention was to make a film polemic with *Ashes and Diamonds* since, as he puts it, the protagonist of Andrzejewski and Wajda serves as an example of the very Polish form of stupidity that places the romantic gesture above one's own life.[60] Maciek's alter ego in *Nobody Is Calling*, Bożek (Henryk Bouko-łowski), is a Home Army fighter who is hunted by his former colleagues

Figure 5.5 Jerzy Turek in Kazimierz Kutz's *Cross of Valor* (1959)

for an act of military disobedience: his refusal to carry out the death sentence on a communist. He hides after the war in a small town in Poland's western territories (the so-called "Regained Lands"). Among other displaced people, wounded by war and with complex backgrounds, he meets Lucyna (Zofia Marcinkowska) and falls in love with her.

After working together on *Cross of Valor*, Kutz and his cinematographer Jerzy Wójcik (also the cinematographer of *Ashes and Diamonds*) strove to challenge the prevailing aesthetics of Polish films. The episodic, slow-paced story of *Nobody Is Calling* is maintained by means of the ascetic, frequently static black-and-white images. The youth and the physical attraction of the two lovers clash with the gloomy atmosphere of the city, as if to stress that love has been born against the environment or in spite of it. In the course of the love affair, there are fewer and fewer objects within the frame, probably to present the perspective of the lovers, who are completely obsessed with each other and shut out the world. The images of dilapidated walls, empty streets and apartments, decaying window frames, and the devastated postwar landscape register the feelings of the two protagonists and function as their psychological landscape.

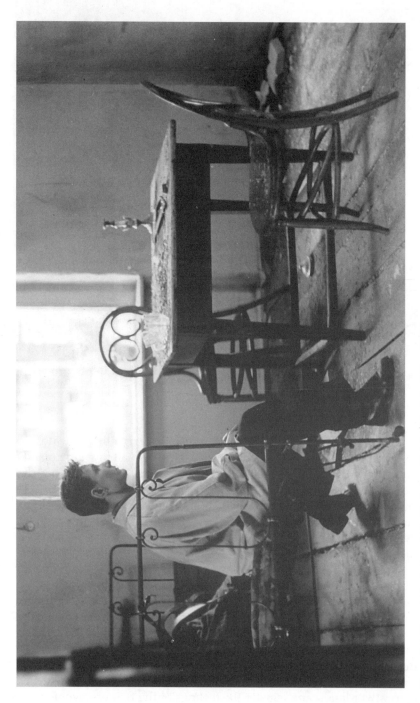

Figure 5.6 Henryk Boukołowski in Kazimierz Kutz's *Nobody Is Calling* (1960)

The meticulous composition of frame, the scarcity and repetitiveness of dialogue that is supplemented by Bożek's voice-over narration, Wojciech Kilar's original music (his debut as a composer), and the contrasting acting personalities of Marcinkowska and Boukołowski help to create the new wave-like style of the film. Like Stanisław Lenartowicz in *Winter Twilight* and Tadeusz Konwicki in *The Last Day of Summer*, Kutz searches for a new style and a new language of cinema. *Nobody Is Calling* bears similarities to the later new wave films, chiefly works by Michelangelo Antonioni. In the context of highly politicized Polish cinema, its formalist poetics, bordering on aesthetic provocation, caused consternation among film critics and the disapproval of the film authorities. As a result, voice-over narration that clarifies the action was added, but the shortened film had to wait several years to be recognized as a work of art.[61]

Kutz's return to the realistic depiction of World War II with *Ludzie z pociągu* (*People from the Train*, 1961) was greeted with a sigh of relief by Polish critics. The film, set in a small provincial railway station during the war, portrays an "average" day during the occupation, with the familiar psychology of the crowd and accidental heroism. While presenting the mosaic of intertwined incidents and the broad spectrum of Polish society, Kutz depicts gestures devoid of pathos, and relies on detailed observations that may foreshadow the "small realism" of the Czechoslovak cinema in the 1960s. Unlike Wajda, he deheroicizes the protagonists (Kutz's trademark throughout his career) and narrates their stories in a realistic manner, eschewing symbols and metaphors.

The themes of the war and the occupation return in a number of films, not necessarily works entangled in the national debate about the Polish romantic legacy. Frequently, these are reconstructions of well-known military actions that do not refer to the national discussions usually accompanying the portrayal of the armed struggle. Stanisław Lenartowicz, in *Pills for Aurelia*, and Jerzy Passendorfer (b. 1922), in *Zamach* (*Answer to Violence*, 1959), focus on the sensational aspect of the occupation and portray the Home Army actions in the manner of action suspense cinema. For example, the latter film, popular with Polish audiences, reconstructs the actual February 1944 assassination of Franz Kutschera, the commander of the SS and police forces in occupied Warsaw.

The war also features prominently in the films directed by Witold Lesiewicz (b. 1922). *Dezerter* (*The Deserter*, 1958), set during the war in Upper Silesia, concerns the fate of young Poles living in the territories annexed by the Reich who are forced to join the German army. The film is known for its well-used setting of a coal mine, where the main part of the action takes place, and the suspenseful chase sequence in the mine's labyrinths. Lesiewicz's next film, *Rok pierwszy* (*First Year*, 1960), narrates the story of Otryna (Stanisław Zaczyk), a communist sergeant left behind the front line who, in the fall of 1944, tries to implement communist rule in a small Polish town. At the militia station, however, the sergeant encounters members of the Home Army, led by the corporal Dunajec

(Leszek Herdegen), who do not support his plans and who are his political opponents. Otryna is unable to convince them to join the new political order, and is powerless to prevent six of them from joining the anticommunist partisans. The conflict in *First Year* is presented as a drama of choices; the personal conflict is related without resorting to black-and-white schematas. A similar portrayal of the psychology of varied characters can be seen in Lesiewicz's subsequent film, *Kwiecień* (*April*, 1961), a story concerning the soldiers of the Second Polish Army during the final stages of the war (April 1945). Although known chiefly for its epic portrayal of the war, *April* pays tribute to the common soldier, the plebeian soldier introduced by Kutz in his *Cross of Valor*.

Another common character-soldier appears in *Ogniomistrz Kaleń* (*Sergeant-Major Kaleń*, 1961), directed by Ewa and Czesław Petelski.[62] The film, set in 1946 in the Bieszczady Mountains (in southeast Poland), describes the bloody postwar conflict involving Ukrainian nationalists of the Ukrainian Insurgent Army (UPA), remnants of the Polish underground fighting the communist government, and regular Polish troops. The protagonist of this "cruel ballad,"[63] Kaleń (Wiesław Gołas), is portrayed almost as a folk hero. Not a typical heroic soldier, he experiences torture, betrayal, and the ferocious death of his comrades. The scene of their death at the minefield, where they are pushed by the encircling Ukrainian unit, is one of the strongest scenes in Polish cinema. The setting of the film in the Polish "wild east," its lively action filled with chases and escapes, and its individualistic hero prompted some Polish critics to look for parallels with the American Western genre. The Western conventions, however, seem to be of lesser importance in *Sergeant-Major Kaleń* than those of the Soviet "action film classics," such as the Vasilievs' *Chapaev* (1934).[64]

In Polish history September 1939 symbolizes defeat and betrayal. It also marks the end of an era harshly criticized in postwar Poland. A small group of works set at the outbreak of war include Leonard Buczkowski's *Orzeł* (*The Submarine "Eagle,"* 1959), a film about the escape of an interned submarine; Stanisław Różewicz's *Free City*, the story of the heroism of the Polish postal workers on the first day of war in Gdańsk (Danzig); and the same director's first novella in his three-part *Birth Certificate*. The last portrays September 1939 through the perspective of a child, and introduces an almost archetypal character in Polish cinema, played by Wojciech Siemion: a simple soldier entangled in the meshes of history.[65]

The release of another film, Andrzej Wajda's *Lotna*, stirred a heated national debate in Poland about the representation of the military effort in 1939. Wajda's solemn treatment of vital national concerns sometimes works against his films. The accumulation of national symbols and nostalgic images associated with prewar Poland in *Lotna*—Wajda's farewell to the Polish romantic mythology—appears almost as a mockery of Polish romantic concerns. Wajda's first film in color narrates the story of a mare, Lotna, that passes from one ulan to another during the September campaign. The film also features one of the most discussed scenes in Polish cinema: the symbolic attack on the German panzer troops undertaken by the Polish cavalry. Especially powerful is an image of an ulan hitting the barrel of a German tank with a sabre in an act of desperation.

Made twenty years after the September campaign of 1939, *Lotna* is saturated with images that refer to the national iconography. It resembles a "national chromolithograph" peopled not by full-blooded characters, but rather by clichéd figures performing anachronistic rituals. Wajda's film refers to the patriotic paintings by Artur Grottger and Wojciech Kossak, and employs the stereotypical, almost kitschy, emblems of the "old Poland": an old country manor and an equally stereotypical image of a village; a girl from the manor bidding farewell to her soldier; picturesque ulans parading to face their death; the typical Polish countryside bathed in gold and green. The film features ulans, relics of the Polish romantic myth, and symbols of the Polish soldier up until World War II. Commenting on the importance of the mythology of ulans in Poland, Marian Ursel writes: "The apotheosis of the ulanship and its features led to the almost mythical cult of this formation. The ulan himself became the model to be emulated. The year 1939 caused this myth to be turned into ashes by the steel caterpillar treads of German tanks."[66]

The war also serves as a point of departure for films focusing on the psychology of their characters. This is especially evident in some of the films of Stanisław Różewicz, Jerzy Kawalerowicz, and Tadeusz Konwicki. Różewicz's *Trzy kobiety* (*Three Women*, 1957) could be considered the continuation of Jakubowska's *The Last Stage*.[67] It is the story of a group of women who are liberated from a prison camp and settle in a small town in the Polish "Regained Lands." This realistic film is about the friendships that survived the war, but are now tested by everyday life.

Psychological war dramas usually narrate their stories with two planes of action. Set in the present, they stress the effects of the war, the inability to communicate and love because of the war. Memories of the war return as nightmarish flashbacks and prevent burned-out protagonists from completely returning to life. Jerzy Kawalerowicz's *The True End of the Great War* serves as a good example of this narrative strategy. It is a psychological study of a woman, Róża (Lucyna Winnicka), and the two men in her life—her emotionally disturbed husband, a concentration camp survivor, and the man she turned to when she thought that her husband was dead. Róża no longer loves her husband, yet she tries to take care of him out of pure compassion. This situation, hopeless for her and the two men involved, ends with her husband's suicide.

Kawalerowicz's intimate film, made in the spirit of the post-October thaw, breaks with the stylistic monotony of socialist realist works, and relies heavily on the use of subjective camera. "The camera seems omnipresent, all knowing, taking often the point of view of one of the characters; the consistently maintained depth of focus gives it an opportunity to display its potential," writes Alicja Helman.[68] Kawalerowicz explains that he "wanted to give the film a slow, hopeless rhythm which is the rhythm of the protagonists' lives."[69] The realistic scenes, set in the postwar conditions, are interrupted by flashbacks into the past, done in an almost expressionistic manner. In the opening sequence, Róża's reminiscences of a happier past are juxtaposed by her husband's recollections of the death camp. The reality of the camp, portrayed from his point of view, is nightmarish and deformed—a reflection of his suffering as well as his psychological and physical disintegration.

Tadeusz Konwicki's films also move between the present and the past. He attracted the attention of critics and readers when he detached himself from the socialist realist dogma with his 1956 novel *Rojsty* (*Marshes*), which told the story of the Home Army unit who fights the Germans then the Soviets. Konwicki's 1958 experimental film, *The Last Day of Summer*, intimate and ascetic in style, deals with his favorite themes: evocations of past times, and the impossibility of overcoming the burden of war. Although the war is not shown directly in this film, it overshadows the action of two characters who meet by chance on an empty Baltic beach. In his next film, *Zaduszki* (*All Souls Day*, 1961), Konwicki discontinues the realistic narrative by including four lengthy flashbacks that deal with the past war. The obsessive memories of Michał (Edmund Fetting) and Wala (Ewa Krzyżewska) are nearly independent filmic novellas within this film. The two protagonists, who are crippled by war experiences, are incapable of forgetting and unable to live in the present. They cannot free themselves from the war, portrayed as a destroyer of happiness, which hangs over them and meddles with their current affairs. In Michał's recollections of the past, a beautiful female lieutenant, Listek (Elżbieta Czyżewska), appears. She is antiheroic, fragile (emphasized by her oversized uniform and a delicate voice when she makes patriotic speeches), and protected by the whole partisan unit, which is in love with her. When Listek dies an absurd death, she is mourned as a saint or, perhaps, the symbol of a better world.

Beyond the War

To limit the Polish School to films dealing with World War II and realistic works portraying Poland during the de-Stalinization period (the narrow definition of the Polish School) is to neglect the most important aspect of the post-October cinema in Poland: its diversity. This period introduced animators who achieved international success in the world of animated films: Walerian Borowczyk, Jan Lenica, Mirosław Kijowicz, Witold Giersz, and Daniel Szczechura, among others. Children's films that also targeted adult audiences—such as Janusz Nasfeter's *Małe dramaty* (*Small Dramas*, 1960) and *Kolorowe pończochy* (*Colored Stockings*, 1960), and Jan Batory's *Odwiedziny prezydenta* (*The Visit of the President*, 1962)—were noticed by Polish critics and received awards at international festivals. Also, there were the first films about the young generation that did not refer directly to politics or social problems: *Do widzenia, do jutra* (*See You Tomorrow,* 1960), by Janusz Morgenstern, and *Niewinni czarodzieje* (*Innocent Sorcerers,* 1960), by Andrzej Wajda. Both featured jazz scores by Krzysztof Komeda, and tried to introduce new lyrical tone to contemporary films. Another film, *Rancho Texas,* by Wadim Berestowski, was an unsuccessful attempt to produce a Polish version of the American Western.

The year 1960 marked the production of the first postwar historical epic and the most popular Polish film—an adaptation of Henryk Sienkiewicz's *Teutonic Knights* by Aleksander Ford. This widescreen film in Eastmancolor, the first of its kind in Poland, had 14 million viewers in the first four years of its release, and was exported to forty-six countries.[70] According to figures from 1987, *Teutonic Knights* remains the most popular film screened in Poland, with almost 32 million viewers, ahead of two other Sienkiewicz adaptations—the children's film *W pustyni i w puszczy* (*In Desert and Wilderness,* 1973, Władysław Ślesicki), with 30.6 million viewers, and another historical epic, *Potop* (*The Deluge,* 1974, Jerzy Hoffman), with 27.5 million viewers.[71]

The epic character of Ford's *Teutonic Knights* was seen, according to one of the local reviewers, as "the crowning of our achievements to develop the Polish film industry, the evidence of a certain maturity in the sphere of production and organization."[72] At the center of Ford's film is the historical defeat of the Order of Teutonic Knights by the combined Polish-Lithuanian forces at the battle of Grunwald in 1410. The making of this film 550 years after the battle, and almost one thousand years after the baptism of Poland (the year 966), certainly had major political relevance. Like Sienkiewicz's novel, it reinforced the images of the heroic past and functioned as "the national remedy in all colors."[73]

Another film, *Ewa Wants to Sleep,* by Tadeusz Chmielewski (b. 1927) became the second successful Polish postwar comedy after *Treasure.* Unlike *Treasure, Ewa Wants to Sleep* offers absurdist, grotesque, situational humor and lyricism in the spirit of René Clair, a director highly regarded in Poland. The influence of Clair's early sound period films (for example, *Le Million,* 1931) is visible in Chmielewski's balancing of fantasy and fact, and in his light and witty treatment of situations and protagonists. The simple story concerns a young woman, Ewa (Barbara Kwiatkowska), who comes to a strange town where the whole population seems to be either policemen or thieves, and are busy playing their games. This surreal town offers Ewa no place to sleep, and this problem of not having a place to spend the night is at the center of Chmielewski's comedy. Although saturated with thinly veiled references to Polish reality, this film belongs to a group of the first postwar Polish pictures that were produced for pure entertainment. Others include later comedies by Chmielewski, and a series of films starring Tadeusz Fijewski as Anatol, beginning with *Kapelusz pana Anatola* (*The Hat of Mr. Anatol,* 1957, Jan Rybkowski).[74]

During the Polish School period, Jerzy Kawalerowicz also produced two stylistically refined films: *Pociąg* (*Night Train;* aka *Baltic Express,* 1959)

Figure 5.7 A scene from Aleksander Ford's *Teutonic Knights* (1960)

and, two years later, *Mother Joan of the Angels*. These two internationally known films place themselves outside of mainstream Polish cinema, at least the kind of cinema praised by local critics during the Polish School period. Both films received numerous awards, including the Georges Méliès award, and Lucyna Winnicka received the Best Actress award at the 1959 Venice Film Festival for her role in *Night Train*. Kawalerowicz also won a Silver Palm at the 1961 Cannes Film Festival for *Mother Joan of the Angels*.

The protagonists of *Night Train*, Marta (Lucyna Winnicka) and Jerzy (Leon Niemczyk), are forced to share a compartment in an overnight train heading for a Baltic resort. Both characters are confused and feeling lonely: Marta wants to break up with her lover (Zbigniew Cybulski), who follows her onto the train; Jerzy is a surgeon who blames himself for the death of one of his patients on an operating table. The film becomes a murder mystery when an afternoon paper reports the case of a wife murdered by her husband; Jerzy's nervousness makes him a possible suspect. The action of the film, mostly restricted to a train compartment, develops slowly until the police board the train to search for the suspected murderer. The chase sequence, as police and passengers try to apprehend the murderer, interrupts the rhythm of the film, and temporarily moves the action out of the train. The capture of the terrified murderer (which clears Jerzy from suspicion) is neither the climax nor the finale of the film. The train continues its unhurried journey and stops at its destination without any major dramatic shift. The trip ends as it began—in normality.

Kawalerowicz's film defies simple interpretations. Its narrative barely sketches the characters' psychology (similar to one's actual knowledge in comparable circumstances), yet the characters are intriguing and the story involving, almost suspenseful. *Night Train* is a film with Hitchcockian overtones. With the help of his cinematographer Jan Laskowski, Kawalerowicz fills the story with tension and nuance—mostly, with his careful composition of frame. "Through setting, rhythm, pace, lighting, physicality, in short, with his mise en scène Kawalerowicz placed himself among the great directors of Europe," write Michałek and Turaj.[75] The limited space of the action does not pose problems for him. While the background is moving (images behind the train windows), the center of the action remains comparatively motionless. The camera captures the gestures and behaviors of the two main characters and other passengers on the crowded train. Kawalerowicz explains: "In *Night Train* I split, if I can say so, the story of one melodrama onto several characters; the yearning for feelings was granted to all the characters in the film."[76] Their expectations and unstated desires are matched by the rhythm of the moving train, the opening and closing of compartment doors, the overall monotony of the travel.

According to Alicja Helman, *Night Train* introduced the "motif of a woman who feels foreign in a world ruled by men, a woman who is not understood, and who attempts to slip away from men's hates and loves, both of which are painful."[77] This motif, prominent in Kawalerowicz's later work, is also discernible in *Mother Joan of the Angels*. This film is loosely based on the well-known story about the possessed nuns at the seventeenth-century monastery in Loudun, France—also the subject of Ken Russell's film *The Devils* (1971). Kawalerowicz's work is an adaptation of Jarosław Iwaszkiewicz's short story set in eighteenth-century eastern Poland. This classic tale about demonic possession presents two main characters: Mother Joan (Lucyna Winnicka), the supposedly possessed mother superior, and Father Suryn (Mieczysław Voit), a young ascetic and devout exorcist. The latter is sent to the convent after one of his predecessors was burned at the stake for his involvement with Mother Joan. Others unsuccessfully try to free Mother Joan from her demons (she admits to being possessed by several demons, and she can even name them). To understand the nature of evil, Suryn visits the rabbi (also played by Voit). The manner of portraying this encounter indicates Suryn's journey into the self.[78] The exorcist is unable to free Mother Joan and the possessed nuns from demons. In the course of time, the psychological tension, and perhaps a physical attraction, develops between Joan and Suryn. When Father Suryn exhausts the traditional methods (prescribed rituals, prayers, self-flagellation), he consciously commits a horrid crime (the killing of two stable boys) to liberate Mother Joan and the convent's sisters from demons and place them under his care.

The ascetic mise en scène of Kawalerowicz's film indicates the characters' psychology. Jerzy Wójcik's photography, with clear contrast between black and white elements within the frame, portrays a barren, inhospitable landscape with only four buildings. The bright convent on the hill and the dark inn at its bottom play a crucial role in the film's concept. The convent is inhabited by the white figures of the nuns, whirling during the devil's activities, their robes flowing in a carefully choreographed manner. The whiteness of the nuns' robes is juxtaposed with the dark robes of the exorcists and the black or shadowy background. The carefully composed static images, with the occasional vertical and horizontal movement of the camera, capture the characters in the center of the frame.[79]

The first feature-length film by Roman Polański, *Knife in the Water*, which was released exactly one year after the premiere of *Mother Joan of the Angels*, offended political leaders and the film authorities because of its "cosmopolitan" and apolitical nature.[80] Like Kawalerowicz in *Night Train*, Polański employs elements of the thriller genre, avoids political or social commitment, and defies the typical communist expectations of a work of art. The film's success in the West (including the first Polish nomination for the Academy Award in 1963) was treated with suspicion in Poland, and only increased the hostility toward its maker.[81] A number of Polish critics looked at Polański's film through the prism of the director's personality and biographical legend, which later became a critical pattern in the West, with the release of Polański's subsequent films.[82]

After his early series of surrealistic and grotesque short films, including the best-known *Dwaj ludzie z szafą* (*Two Men and a Wardrobe*, 1958),

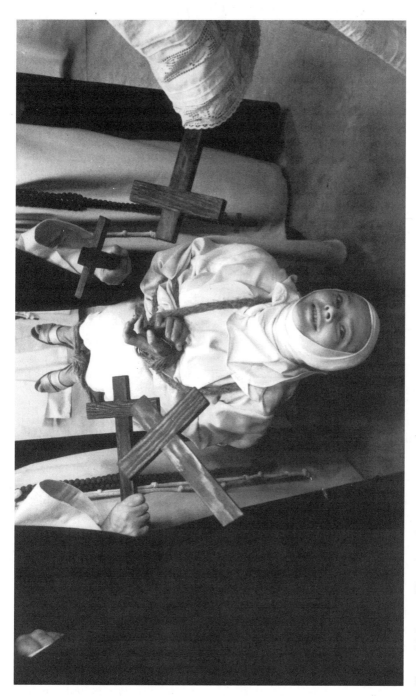

Figure 5.8 Lucyna Winnicka in Jerzy Kawalerowicz's *Mother Joan of the Angels* (1961)

Polański strove with *Knife in the Water* to make a film "rigorously cerebral, precisely engineered, almost formalist." As he further recalls in his biography, *Roman*, "It started out as a straightforward thriller: a couple aboard a small yacht take on a passenger who disappears in mysterious circumstances. From the first, the story concerned the interplay of antagonistic personalities within a confined space."[83] The story, limited to three characters, concerns a well-to-do Warsaw sports journalist, Andrzej (Leon Niemczyk), and his younger wife, Krystyna (Jolanta Umecka), who invite a young hitchhiker (Zygmunt Malanowicz) for a yachting weekend. The bulk of the film's action is then confined to a small boat in the Mazurian lakes, where a fierce rivalry develops between the worldly journalist and the insecure hitchhiker who challenges him. Often framed between the two men, Krystyna serves as their "prize," and is perfectly aware of her role in the conflict. The jazz score of Krzysztof Komeda, who also worked on Polański's short films, and the photography of Jerzy Lipman help to create the vibrating, jazzy tempo and mood; Marek Hendrykowski compares the composition of Polański's film to modern jazz compositions.[84]

The End of the Formation

A number of voices in recent Polish scholarship favor the assertion that the decline of the Polish School was not "natural," that it was not related to the exhaustion of its themes and the manner in which they were presented, but rather that it had to do with the pressure of politics and the increasing conflict between the filmmakers and the communist regime.[85] The demands for greater independence for the film units and softer censorship were incompatible with the attempts of the Communist Party to regain total control over the filmmaking process, which had been characteristic of the pre-October period.

Toward the end of the 1950s, the communist authorities had been sending many signals that the relative freedom of expression would no longer be tolerated. The party was disappointed with the messages and themes permeating Polish films, and with the "westernization" of Polish filmmakers. As a result, the autonomy of the film units was gradually limited, and stricter control of films was administratively implemented. Although the Main Office for Control of the Press, Publications, and Public Performances (Główny Urząd Kontroli Prasy, Publikacji i Widowisk) was responsible for media censorship in general, censorship was frequently much harsher at the film units level. The Committee for Evaluation of Scripts (Komisja Ocen Scenariuszy) was the first major obstacle for a film project to be approved.

The restrictive policy of the Communist Party can be observed toward some of the representative films of the Polish School. The most frequent way to punish the makers of "unwanted films" was the limited distribution of their works (as in the case of *Nobody Is Calling*, *Winter Twilight*, and

The End of the Night). Another form of punishment was delaying the premiere of some films, and in extreme instances even banning them, as was the case with *Ósmy dzień tygodnia* (*Eighth Day of the Week*), directed by Aleksander Ford. This Polish/West-German production, based on Marek Hłasko's story and starring Zbigniew Cybulski and Sonia Ziemann (the German actress), was made in 1958 and distributed in Germany (as *Der Achte Wochentag*); it did not premiere in Poland until as late as 1983.[86] The third practice, which reflects the suspicion, as well as the aversion, of the communist leaders toward some of the films, was the reluctance to send some of them to international film festivals.[87]

The Resolution of the Central Committee Secretariat of the Polish United Workers' Party, issued in June 1960, marked the actual end of the Polish School.[88] In this document, the communist authorities objected *expressis verbis* to the pessimism of a number of Polish films, their lack of compliance with the party line, and the strong role played by Western cinema in Poland. As a remedy, the resolution imposed stricter limits and more rigorous criteria on imported films from the West. It also postulated that films purchased from other socialist countries, chiefly from the Soviet Union, should be privileged. As a result, between 1961 and 1969, the number of films from the Soviet bloc countries increased to 57 percent (for 35mm films) and 75 percent (for 16mm films).[89] This same party document also postulated making political and educational films needed in the process of "building socialism," films that reflected current problems from the socialist perspective, and works inspired by the "progressive tendencies" in Polish history. The document also referred to the role of "socialist film criticism." It recommended increasing the number of pro-party writers and party functionaries in the processes of scriptwriting and script approval, and proposed to develop "socialist entertainment films." The intentions behind the latter directive, which were fully implemented in the 1960s, were twofold: to neutralize the popularity of foreign "bourgeois" films, and to turn away the attention of Polish society from the pressing economic problems experienced under Władysław Gomułka's regime.

The Polish School began to lose its impetus at the beginning of the 1960s. Although political developments once again defined the Polish cinema, there were also nonpolitical reasons that contributed to this decline. In September 1961, Andrzej Munk died tragically while making his *Pasażerka* (*The Passenger*, finished by Witold Lesiewicz, with a premiere in 1963). At the beginning of the 1960s, Andrzej Wajda began making films abroad: in 1962 *Sibirska Ledi Makbet* (*Siberian Lady Macbeth*, aka *Fury Is a Woman*), produced in Yugoslavia; an episode in France for *Love at Twenty*; then, in 1967, *Gates to Paradise* in England.[90] During the early 1960s a group of young filmmakers emerged for whom the point of reference was no longer local history or other concerns associated with the Polish School. For example, the first films by Roman Polański and Jerzy Skolimowski were similar to current international cinema and influenced by their own personal experiences. Polański migrated to France after making *Knife in the Water*, his only full-length film made in Poland.[91]

Several films made in the mid-1960s, however, returned to Polish history and the moral dilemmas of World War II. These films, including Tadeusz Konwicki's *Salto* (*Somersault*, 1965), debunk the Polish war mythology and focus on the impossibility of freeing oneself from the shadow of the war, as in Wojciech J. Has's *Szyfry* (*Cyphers*, 1966) and Stanisław Jędryka's *Powrót na ziemię* (*Return to Earth*, 1967). Another prominent group of films refers directly to the war: the Holocaust in *Naganiacz* (*The Beater*, 1964), directed by Ewa and Czesław Petelski; moral dilemmas of the underground fighters in *Stajnia na Salwatorze* (*The Barn at Salvator*, 1967), by Paweł Komorowski; and the tragedy of September 1939 in *Westerplatte* (1967), by Stanisław Różewicz. The main preoccupations of the Polish School also return in some of the films made in the 1970s, for instance, in the film *Hubal* (1973) by Bohdan Poręba. The real end of the Polish School, and the farewell to its poetics, is probably marked by Andrzej Wajda's *Pierścionek z orłem w koronie* (*The Ring with a Crowned Eagle*, 1992), a film that examines issues first explored in *Ashes and Diamonds*.[92]

Notes

1. Andrzej Wajda, quoted in Peter Cowie, "Wajda Redux," *Sight and Sound* 49, no. 1 (1979–1980): 32.
2. Aleksander Jackiewicz, "Prawo do eksperymentu," *Przegląd Kulturalny* 51/52 (1954); Antoni Bohdziewicz, "Czyżby cyprysy i pinie na Powiślu?" *Łódź Literacka* 2–3 (1955). Quoted from Stanisław Ozimek, "Konfrontacje z Wielką Wojną," in *Historia filmu polskiego 1957–1961*, vol. 4, ed. Jerzy Toeplitz (Warsaw: Wydawnictwa Artystyczne i Filmowe), 14.
3. October 1956 marks the uprising against the communist regime in Hungary, which was brutally crushed by the invading Soviet troops at the beginning of November.
4. On 20 October 1956, the newly elected leader (First Secretary) of the Polish United Workers' Party, Władysław Gomułka, summarized the Stalinist period by saying: "The system of the years past broke human characters and consciences, trod on people, spat on their honor. The instrument of power was slander, falsehood, and even provocation. Tragic missteps were committed, innocent people were sent to their deaths. Others were imprisoned, many for long years. Some of them were Communists. Many people were bestially tortured. Fear and demoralization reigned. We have finished with this system, or better said, we shall finish with it once and forever." Quoted from Mira Liehm and Antonin J. Liehm, *The Most Important Art: Soviet and Eastern European Film after 1945* (Berkeley: University of California Press, 1977), 176. In spite of his denouncement of Stalinism, Gomułka was by no means a liberal leader. The Polish October was an eruption of patriotic feelings and hopes that were quickly suppressed by the Communist Party.
5. Stanisław Ozimek, "Spojrzenie na 'szkołę polską,'" in Toeplitz, *Historia filmu polskiego 1957–1961*, 201.
6. Ibid., 206–207.
7. Tadeusz Lubelski, *Strategie autorskie w polskim filmie fabularnym lat 1945–1961* (Cracow: Wydawnictwo Uniwersytetu Jagiellońskiego, 1992), 113–193.

8. Bolesław Michałek and Frank Turaj, *The Modern Cinema of Poland* (Bloomington: Indiana University Press, 1988), 19–34.
9. Liehm and Liehm, *The Most Important Art*, 174–198; David A. Cook, *A History of Narrative Film* (New York: Norton, 1996), 684.
10. Ozimek, "Spojrzenie na 'szkołę polską,'" 205–206.
11. Aleksander Jackiewicz, "Kordianowskie i plebejskie tradycje w filmie polskim," *Kino* 11 (1969): 2–11. Also discussed in his "Powrót Kordiana. Tradycja romantyczna w filmie polskim," *Kwartalnik Filmowy* 4 (1961): 23–37.
12. Tadeusz Miczka, "Cinema under Political Pressure: A Brief Outline of Authorial Roles in Polish Post-War Feature Film 1945–1995," *Kinema* 4 (1995): 37. The term "psychotherapy" had been also used consciously by some of the filmmakers, for instance, by Wajda, who stated that Polish filmmakers "approach their work seriously, as a kind of psychotherapy." Stanisław Janicki, *Polscy twórcy filmowi o sobie* (Warsaw: Wydawnictwa Artystyczne i Filmowe, 1962), 84.
13. Marek Hendrykowski, "'Polska szkoła filmowa' jako formacja artystyczna," in *Szkoła polska – powroty*, eds. Ewelina Nurczyńska-Fidelska and Bronisława Stolarska (Łódź: Wydawnictwo Uniwersytetu Łódzkiego, 1998), 9.
14. Ibid., 10–11.
15. Ewelina Nurczyńska-Fidelska, "'Szkoła' czy autorzy? Uwagi na marginesie doświadczeń polskiej historii filmu," in Nurczyńska-Fidelska and Stolarska, *Szkoła polska – powroty*, 30–31.
16. Andrzej Munk and the scriptwriter Jerzy Stefan Stawiński were born in 1921, Jerzy Kawalerowicz in 1922, Stanisław Różewicz in 1924, Wojciech J. Has in 1925, Tadeusz Konwicki and Andrzej Wajda in 1926, and Kazimierz Kutz in 1929. The term *Kolumbowie* (Columbuses) comes from the celebrated novel by Roman Bratny, *Kolumbowie rocznik 20* [*Columbuses Born in 1920*], published for the first time in Warsaw in 1957. The novel was adapted in 1970 as a popular television series, *Kolumbowie* (five episodes), directed by Janusz Morgenstern (b. 1922).
17. Maria Janion, "Jeruzalem Słoneczna i Zaklęty Krąg," *Kwartalnik Filmowy* 17 (1997): 5.
18. Stalinism was unavailable to filmmakers because of censorship. One may speculate that perhaps another reason was the involvement of some of the filmmakers with the socialist realist dogma—they would have to deal with their own fascination with Stalinism. For instance, Andrzej Munk, who later made seminal Polish School films, started his career at the beginning of the 1950s with a number of documentary films made in the spirit of socialist realism. They include, among others, *Zaczęło się w Hiszpanii* (*It Started in Spain*, 1950), *Kierunek Nowa Huta* (*Direction: Nowa Huta*, 1951), and *Pamiętniki chłopów* (*Peasant Diaries*, 1953).
19. The importance of Polish literature as a source for Polish films is discussed in the context of postwar cinema by, among others, Marek Hendrykowski, "Zagadnienie kontekstu literackiego filmu na przykadzie polskiej szkoły filmowej," in *Film polski wobec innych sztuk*, ed. Alicja Helman and Alina Madej (Katowice: Wydawnictwo Uniwersytetu Śląskiego, 1979), 44–60; Wojciech Soliński, "Podłoże literackie filmów szkoły polskiej," in *Polska Szkoła Filmowa. Poetyka i tradycja*, ed. Jan Trzynadlowski (Wrocław: Ossolineum, 1976), 31–39; Maryla Hopfinger, "Adaptacje utworów literackich w polskim filmie okresu powojennego," in *Problemy socjologii literatury*, ed. Janusz Sławiński (Wrocław: Ossolineum, 1971), 467–489.
20. However, to my knowledge, the term "Polish School of literature" has never been used in Poland to describe the works written by these writers.
21. The concept of film units goes back to the ideas propagated before the war by the Society for the Promotion of Film Art START. Before 1955 there were unsuccessful attempts to create film units. For example, in 1948 three such units were founded in order to stimulate film production: Blok, managed by Aleksander Ford; Zespół Autorów Filmowych (ZAF), by Wanda Jakubowska; and Warszawa, by Ludwik Starski. They were disbanded in 1949.
22. I refer to Edward Zajíček's data in his *Poza ekranem: Kinematografia polska 1918-1991* (Warsaw: Filmoteka Narodowa and Wydawnictwa Artystyczne i Filmowe, 1992), 142 and 202.

23. Jerzy Toeplitz, "Drogi rozwoju kinematografii," in Toeplitz, *Historia filmu polskiego 1957–1961*, 383.

24. Ibid., 381 and 388.

25. Ewa Gębicka, "Sieć kin i rozpowszechnianie filmów," in *Encyklopedia kultury polskiej XX wieku: Film i kinematografia*, ed. Edward Zajiček (Warsaw: Instytut Kultury and Komitet Kinematografii, 1994), 436.

26. Jerzy Płażewski, "Film zagraniczny w Polsce," in Zajiček, *Encyklopedia kultury polskiej XX wieku*, 341.

27. Edward Zajiček, "Szkoła polska. Uwarunkowania organizacyjne i gospodarcze," in Nurczyńska-Fidelska and Stolarska, eds., *"Szkoła polska" – powroty*, 177 and 180. For example, *Ewa Wants to Sleep* had 3.6 million viewers; *Answer to Violence*, 3.8 million; and *Ashes and Diamonds*, 3.4 million.

28. Toeplitz, "Drogi rozwoju kinematografii," 388 and 417.

29. Bolesław Michałek, "Polska przygoda neorealizmu," *Kino* 1 (1975): 30.

30. Bolesław Sulik, Introduction, *Andrzej Wajda: Three Films* (London: Lorrimer, 1973), 12.

31. Ibid., 13.

32. Aleksander Jackiewicz, in a review of *The End of the Night* titled "Neorealizm polski" (Polish Neorealism), states that this modest film fully implements the neorealist tenets for the first time in Polish cinema. Another critic, Juliusz Kydryński, compares this film with *Blackboard Jungle* (1955), by Richard Brooks, then not shown in Poland. Quoted from Lubelski, *Strategie autorskie*, 123.

33. *The End of the Night* is truly a cooperative, almost a student, effort. Apart from the three directors (Julian Dziedzina, Paweł Komorowski, and Walentyna Uszycka), it has six scriptwriters (including Professor Antoni Bohdziewicz of the Łódź Film School and writer Marek Hłasko—the symbol of the post-October Polish literature), and three cinematographers (including Jerzy Wójcik, the cinematographer of *Ashes and Diamonds*, *Nobody Is Calling*, and *Mother Joan of the Angels*).

34. Ewelina Nurczyńska-Fidelska, "Czarny realizm. O stylu i jego funkcji w filmach nurtu współczesnego," in Nurczyńska-Fidelska and Stolarska, *Szkoła polska – powroty*, 33–47.

35. Ibid., 38.

36. The film's thematics were often compared to Henri-George Clouzot's *The Wages of Fear* (1953), popular on Polish screens since its 1955 premiere.

37. Stanisław Ozimek, "Od wojny w dzień powszedni," in *Historia filmu polskiego 1957–1961*, vol. 4, ed. Jerzy Toeplitz (Warsaw: Wydawnictwa Artystyczne i Filmowe, 1980), 139.

38. Janicki, *Polscy twórcy filmowi o sobie*, 50.

39. Piotr Wojciechowski, "Prorok naszych snów," *Kino* 4 (1995): 20.

40. Ibid., 20.

41. Andrzej Werner, "Film fabularny," in *Historia filmu polskiego 1962–1967*, vol. 5, ed. Rafał Marszałek (Warsaw: Wydawnictwa Artystyczne i Filmowe, 1985), 21.

42. Another film set during the Warsaw Uprising, *Kamienne niebo* (*A Sky of Stone*, 1959), directed by Ewa and Czesław Petelski, deals with the fate of a group of Warsaw dwellers buried in a cellar of the collapsed building.

43. For example, the difference is already stressed in the table of contents of Michałek and Turaj's *The Modern Cinema of Poland*: "Andrzej Munk: The Perspective of a Sceptic" and "Andrzej Wajda: The Essential Pole."

44. Ewelina Nurczyńska-Fidelska, "Romanticism and History: A Sketch of the Creative Output of Andrzej Wajda," in *Polish Cinema in Ten Takes*, ed. Ewelina Nurczyńska-Fidelska and Zbigniew Batko (Łódź: Łódzkie Towarzystwo Naukowe, 1995), 9.

45. The Polish title of the film, *Kanał*, literally means "sewer."

46. In Bolesław Michałek, *The Cinema of Andrzej Wajda* (London: Tantivy Press, 1973), 32.

47. All of the Home Army fighters' names are pseudonyms, for example, "Zadra" means "splinter," "Mądry" means "wise."

48. The second part, *Ostinato Lugubre*, which narrates the story of Polish prisoners of war in a German camp, is a satire on heroism and the anachronistically understood "soldier's honor." The third segment, *Con bravura*, different in spirit since it utilizes the Polish

romantic legend, deals with the experiences of the wartime couriers crossing the Tatra Mountains. Munk decided to drop *Con bravura* from the final version of his film; it premiered in 1972 on Polish television. The "musical titles" are obviously of parodic nature, but they also testify to Munk's interest in music. See, for example, his 1958 short film *Spacerek staromiejski* (*A Walk in the Old Town*).

49. Rafał Marszałek, *Filmowa pop-historia* (Cracow: Wydawnictwo Literackie, 1984), 344.

50. In the *Scherzo alla Polacca* part of *Eroica*, as well as in *Bad Luck* and later in *The Passenger*, Andrzej Munk introduces the perspective of characters with whom the viewer cannot identify—that of the sly dog, the opportunist, and the German female officer from the concentration camp, respectively. Munk's merciless satire on opportunism and bureaucracy, *Bad Luck*, is continued by Andrzej Kotkowski in *Obywatel Piszczyk* (*Citizen P.*, 1989), and by Kazimierz Kutz in *Straszny sen Dzidziusia Górkiewicza* (*The Terrible Dream of Dzidziuś Górkiewicz*, 1993), both scripted by Jerzy Stefan Stawiński.

51. Alicja Helman, "Andrzej Munk: *Cockeyed Luck*," *MovEast* 2 (1992): 101.

52. Tadeusz Konwicki, *Moonrise, Moonset*, trans. Richard Lourie (New York: Farrar, Straus, and Giroux, 1987), 56.

53. See Lubelski, *Strategie autorskie*, 154. The title of the film—and its literary source, Jerzy Andrzejewski's novel—comes from a metaphor drawn from a nineteenth-century poem, "Za kulisami," by Cyprian Kamil Norwid. Its lines are recited in the film.

54. Wajda's comment, originally published in *Przegląd Kulturalny* 15 (1959). Quoted from Marian Ursel, "Legenda romantyczna w polskiej szkole filmowej," in Trzynadlowski, *Polska Szkoła Filmowa*, 83.

55. Bolesław Michałek, "Mówi Andrzej Wajda" [interview with Wajda], *Kino* 1 (1968): 42.

56. Konwicki, *Moonrise, Moonset*, 56–57.

57. Konrad Eberhardt, *Zbigniew Cybulski* (Warsaw: Wydawnictwa Artystyczne i Filmowe, 1976), 59.

58. Paul Coates, "Forms of the Polish Intellectual's Self-Criticism: Revisiting *Ashes and Diamonds* with Andrzejewski and Wajda," *Canadian Slavonic Papers* 38, nos. 3–4 (1996): 294–296. The scene with the inverted crucifix that separates the two lovers may be understood as a symbol of the overthrown values, "mordantly fuses the Wellesian and the Buñuelian," according to Coates (p. 294).

59. Tadeusz Lubelski provides a detailed analysis of the adaptation of Hen's novel into film. Hen's novel dealt with a taboo topic: the fate of the Polish citizens in the Soviet Union after the outbreak of World War II and the annexation of the eastern Polish provinces by the Soviets. Banned for almost forty years, the book was not published until 1990. Tadeusz Lubelski, "Z Samarkandy do Bystrzycy, czyli o perypetiach filmu *Nikt nie woła*," in Nurczyńska-Fidelska and Stolarska, *Szkoła polska – powroty*, 81–97.

60. Elżbieta Baniewicz, *Kazimierz Kutz: Z dołu widać inaczej* (Warsaw: Wydawnictwa Artystyczne i Filmowe, 1994), 152.

61. Lubelski, "Z Samarkandy do Bystrzycy," 93–95.

62. Ewa (b. 1920) and Czesław (1922–1996) Petelski, the married couple working together on the majority of their films.

63. Ozimek, "Konfrontacje z Wielką Wojną," 121.

64. Ibid., 120–121. Stanisław Ozimek quotes the 1974 interview with the Petelskis in which they stress that their Łódź Film School generation was educated on *Chapaev*, and that the ending of *Sergeant-Major Kaleń* (the death of the protagonist) testifies to this inspiration.

65. Wojciech Siemion (b. 1928) almost repeated his role from *Birth Certificate* in Jerzy Passendorfer's films, chiefly in *Kierunek Berlin* (*Direction Berlin*, 1969) and its sequel, *Ostatnie dni* (*Last Days*, 1969).

66. Ursel, "Legenda romantyczna w polskiej szkole filmowej," 74.

67. Aleksander Jackiewicz stresses this aspect in his review of Różewicz's film, "*Ostatniego etapu ciąg dalszy*" [*The Last Stage* Continues] reprinted in his *Moja filmoteka: kino polskie* (Warsaw: Wydawnictwa Artystyczne i Filmowe, 1983), 196.

68. Alicja Helman, "Jerzy Kawalerowicz: A Virtuoso of the Camera," in Nurczyńska-Fidelska and Batko, *Polish Cinema in Ten Takes*, 53–54.

69. Ozimek, "Konfrontacje z Wielką Wojną," 82.
70. Stanisław Janicki, *Aleksander Ford* (Warsaw: Wydawnictwa Artystyczne i Filmowe, 1967), 81.
71. Quoted from Małgorzata Hendrykowska, *Kronika kinematografii polskiej 1895–1997* (Poznań: Ars Nova, 1999), 427. The figures clearly show the preference for local films, mostly adaptations of national literary canon; out of twenty films listed, as many as thirteen are Polish productions.
72. Jerzy Pelc, "Krzyżacy," *Film* 36 (1960): 5.
73. The title of Zygmunt Kałużyński's review, "Lekarstwo narodowe we wszystkich kolorach [National remedy in all colors]. Quoted from Ozimek, "Od wojny w dzień powszedni," 187.
74. Its continuations were made in 1959: *Pan Anatol szuka miliona* (*Mr. Anatol Is Looking for a Million*), and *Inspekcja pana Anatola* (*The Inspection of Mr. Anatol*), both also directed by Jan Rybkowski.
75. Michałek and Turaj, *The Modern Cinema of Poland*, 101.
76. Janicki, *Polscy twórcy filmowi o sobie*, 35.
77. Helman, "Jerzy Kawalerowicz," 55. The emergence of the new protagonists during the Polish School period, both men and women, deserves a separate publication. Unlike the socialist realist characters, who were immune to sex and unwilling to give up production for love, the new protagonists are multidimensional, are torn between duty to the nation and private aspirations, and are frequently interested only in personal issues. For example, Urszula Modrzyńska, the socialist realist star in *Not Far from Warsaw* and *A Generation*, displays different qualities in Leonard Buczkowski's *Deszczowy lipiec* (*Rainy July*, 1958). Lucyna Winnicka in *Night Train*, the female insurgent Stokrotka (Teresa Iżewska) in *Kanal*, and other female characters are experienced, strong, sexual, and in charge of men. The issue of the representation of female characters by the Polish School filmmakers is discussed by Joanna Pyszny, "Kobieta w filmach szkoły polskiej," in Trzynadlowski, *Polska Szkoła Filmowa*, 91–101.
78. Seweryn Kuśmierczyk, "*Matka Joanna of Aniołów*: Szkic antropologiczny," *Kwartalnik Filmowy* 17 (1977): 82–83.
79. Michałek and Turaj, *The Modern Cinema of Poland*, 104.
80. Władysław Gomułka, the First Secretary of the Polish United Workers' Party, officially condemned the film in August 1963 at the plenary assembly of the Central Committee. Grażyna Stachówna, *Roman Polański i jego filmy* (Warsaw, Łódź: Wydawnictwo Naukowe PWN, 1994), 42.
81. I am writing here about the "official hostility" toward Polański's film in Poland. *Knife in the Water* won the "Złota Kaczka" [Golden Duck] award for the best Polish film of 1962 in the popular plebiscite organized by the magazine *Film*.
82. Roman Polański's life often overshadows his films. His films are (pop) psychoanalyzed to excess. The number of books on Polański does not match their quality. These are mostly biographies, sometimes scandalizing ones, that cannibalize Polański's much publicized "private" life. Fine texts, such as Herbert Eagle's chapter on Polański, are rather infrequent. Herbert Eagle, "Polanski," in Daniel J. Goulding, ed., *Five Filmmakers* (Bloomington and Indianapolis: Indiana University Press, 1994), 92–155.
83. Roman Polanski, *Roman* (New York: William Morrow, 1984), 156–157.
84. Marek Hendrykowski, "*Nóż w wodzie*: Modern Jazz," *Kwartalnik Filmowy* 17 (1997): 86–96.
85. For example, Ewa Gębicka, "Partia i państwo a kino. Przypadek 'szkoły polskiej.' O ideologicznym stylu odbioru filmów i jego konsekwencjach," in Nurczyńska-Fidelska and Stolarska, *Szkoła polska – powroty*, 129–144; Alina Madej, "Bohaterowie byli zmęczeni?" in *Syndrom konformizmu? Kino polskie lat sześćdziesiątych*, ed. Tadeusz Miczka, assistant ed. Alina Madej (Katowice: Wydawnictwo Uniwersytetu Śląskiego, 1994), 10–26.
86. The dark picture of Polish reality portrayed in *Eighth Day of the Week* was unacceptable for the Communist Party authorities. The banning of Ford's film served as a clear signal that nobody was exempted from communist censorship. Ford "was the Film Polski" for

a number of years, and still an influential and well-connected person in the late 1950s. Problems experienced with *Eighth Day of the Week*, however, did not prevent Ford from making the epic superproduction *Teutonic Knights* just two years later.

87. This is the case of *Ashes and Diamonds*. Wajda's film had not been sent to Cannes because, in Aleksander Ford's words, it had "ambiguous political meaning." Quoted from Madej, "Bohaterowie byli zmęczeni?" 15.

88. "Uchwała Sekretariatu KC w sprawie kinematografii," National Film Archives in Warsaw (no. 130). Reprinted in Miczka and Madej, *Syndrom konformizmu?* 27–34.

89. Ewa Gębicka, "Obcinanie kantów, czyli polityka PZPR i państwa wobec kinematografii lat sześćdziesiątych," in Miczka and Madej, *Syndrom konformizmu?* 42.

90. Wajda's *Gates to Paradise* has never been released in cinema theaters.

91. Roman Polański's films made outside of Poland include works made in England, France, and the United States. Polański directed *Repulsion* (1965), *Cul-de-sac* (1966), *The Fearless Vampire Killers* (1967), *Rosemary's Baby* (1968), *The Tragedy of Macbeth* (1971) *Che? (What?* 1973) *Chinatown* (1974), *Le Locataire* (*The Tenant*, 1976), *Tess* (1979), *Pirates* (1986), *Frantic* (1988), *Bitter Moon* (1992), and *The Ninth Gate* (2000). Polański's artistic output, because of its diversity, manipulation of the genres' rules, and cosmopolitan nature, is not easily defined. There is, presumably, nothing Polish about his films, unless we take a tendency toward the bizarre and the grotesque as a typical Polish feature. In spite of their diversity and genre-oriented nature, Polański's films break conventional formulae and are characterized by the strong presence of the authorial self. The films exhibit the director's highly visual style, his personal thematic obsessions, prevailing images of the violent and the grotesque, and an adept mastery of manipulating the viewer's emotions.

92. As described by Andrzej Wajda. See Bożena Janicka, "Żegnaj, szkoło polska" [Farewell, the Polish School] *Film* 4 (1993): 2–3. Paul Coates writes: "It is tempting to describe *The Ring with a Crowned Eagle* as frustrated dreamwork upon *Ashes and Diamonds*." Coates, "Forms of the Polish Intellectual's Self-Criticism," 300.

6

Adaptations, Personal Style, and Popular Cinema between 1965 and 1976

The spirit of the 1956 Polish October was short-lived and gave way to a period commonly known in Poland as the 1960s "small stabilization." The term "small stabilization" was adopted from the title of the play *Świadkowie albo nasza mała stabilizacja* (*Witnesses or Our Small Stabilization*, 1962), written by a distinguished modern Polish playwright, Tadeusz Różewicz. This expression serves as an ironic comment on the period of Władysław Gomułka—the Communist Party leader between 1956 and 1970. The term does not refer to socialist prosperity, as one might expect, but calls for tougher measures in politics, boredom, and empty rituals.

By and large, Polish films of the 1960s do not reveal disenchantment with the state of affairs, that is, the fiasco of the limited democratization introduced for a brief period during the October events of 1956. Due to harsh communist censorship, Polish filmmakers were unable to voice their real concerns regarding recent national history, politics, and social issues. Rather, they retreated to safer adaptations of the national literary canon and popular cinema. "The cinema of small stabilization created an image of the non-existent country," aptly writes Krzysztof Kornacki, who adds that this cinema reflected the personal stabilization of Polish filmmakers rather than the economic and political stabilization of the country.[1]

Political developments once again contributed to the state of the Polish film industry. The filmmaking was affected by the events of 1968: brutally crushed student demonstrations in Warsaw (the March Events), and the anti-Semitic campaign orchestrated by a nationalistic faction of the Communist Party in order to remove some seasoned party and security force members, many of whom were Jewish, from their privileged positions. The film industry in Poland was heavily affected by the emigration of a number of filmmakers of Jewish origin, among them director Aleksander Ford,[2] cinematographer Jerzy Lipman, and a large group of experienced production managers, including Ludwik Hager.

After 1968, the communist authorities tightened censorship, criticized "commercialism," and called for films reflecting the true spirit of socialism. They also reorganized the existing film units to introduce a more centralized organization of the film industry. In 1969 the following six film units were in operation: Iluzjon, Kraj, Nike, Plan, Tor, and Wektor. Founded in 1967, film unit Tor, managed by Stanisław Różewicz, drew such prominent directors as Andrzej Wajda, Krzysztof Zanussi, and Janusz Majewski. Kazimierz Kutz, Jerzy Hoffman, Jerzy Skolimowski, and Andrzej Żuławski worked for another unit, Wektor, headed by Jerzy Jesionowski. The third important unit, Ryszard Kosiński and Stanisław Zieliński's Plan, employed, among others, Tadeusz Chmielewski, Wojciech J. Has, Jerzy Kawalerowicz, and Jan Rybkowski.

The December 1970 workers' strikes in the Baltic ports, which were violently suppressed by the communist authorities, led to the downfall of Gomułka. The more pragmatic Edward Gierek became the new party leader, and introduced some minor economic reforms. With the help of foreign loans, he focused on economic investments and consumer goods. The first part of the 1970s also brought changes to film practice in Poland. Another reorganization of the film units granted them more artistic freedom. As Michałek and Turaj write, "Top management was composed of—miracle of miracles in any country or field—people of genuine professional accomplishment, who enjoyed the confidence of the cinema community. This was indeed why the seventies became such a thoroughly successful time for Polish film...."[3] In 1972 there were seven film units: Stanisław Różewicz's Tor, Czesław Petelski's Iluzjon, Jerzy Kawalerowicz's Kadr, Jerzy Passendorfer's Panorama, Aleksander Ścibor-Rylski's Pryzmat, Andrzej Wajda's X, and the only unit established outside of Warsaw—Kazimierz Kutz's Silesia in Katowice.

This period of relative prosperity, heightened by the "propaganda of success" in Poland, ended in the late 1970s. Workers' protests in 1976 (caused by food price increases) spotlighted the growing problems of the Gierek administration: mismanagement of foreign credits, corruption, and the deepening economic crisis barely masked by the triumphant propaganda.

Although in the second part of the 1960s the repertoire of Polish cinema theaters was dominated by European art films and selected American films (usually the best), the most popular fare among Polish audiences remained commercially oriented productions, for example, *Vinnetou* (1964–1965, Harald Reinl) released in 1968 (4.7 million viewers), and *Cleopatra* (1963, Joseph L. Mankiewicz), which premiered in 1970 (5.7 million viewers).[4] Polish films, mostly adaptations of the Polish literary canon, successfully competed with foreign products. For example, Jerzy Hoffman's version of Henryk Sienkiewicz's classic, *Pan Wołodyjowski* (*Pan*

Michael, aka *Colonel Wolodyjowski*, 1969), had nearly 10 million viewers. Another film, Jerzy Kawalerowicz's *Faraon* (*The Pharaoh*, 1966), based on Bolesław Prus's novel, had 8.5 million viewers.[5]

In 1965 Poland had the highest number of cinema theaters in its history—3,935, including 381 mobile cinemas, with 732,000 seats. Later, until the mid-1970s, this number was drastically reduced by 1,296 cinemas and almost 180,000 seats. During the 1970s, Albania was the only European country with fewer cinema seats per number of inhabitants than Poland.[6] Cheap admissions, the deterioration of the remaining cinemas, the disregard for genre cinema, fewer imports from the West, and the continuous preference for films from Soviet bloc countries contributed to the growing financial deficit and the decreasing number of cinema theaters. In the course of time, only art house theaters and cine-clubs were offering a variety of films from the West, and their number was increasing. For example, the number of cine-clubs reached 241 in 1968, with as many as 351 in 1972.[7]

As elsewhere in Europe, the decline in cinema attendance can be attributed to the popularity of television. The number of television sets grew from 3,389,000 in 1968 to 5,200,000 in 1972.[8] The most popular films were television productions, such as *Czterej pancerni i pies* (*Four Tankmen and a Dog*, 21 episodes, 1966–1967), directed by Konrad Nałęcki, and *Stawka większa niż życie* (*Stake Higher Than Life*, 18 episodes, 1967–1968), directed by Janusz Morgenstern and Andrzej Konic. The former, based on Janusz Przymanowski's novel (also the co-scriptwriter of the film), is an adventure war film featuring the tank "Rudy" and its crew on their road to Poland from the Soviet Union. The latter, also set during the war, offers an equally cartoonish, simplified, and stereotypical version of history. The film narrates the story of Hans Kloss (Stanisław Mikulski), a Polish superspy dressed in a German uniform. Because of this role, Mikulski became one of the most popular Polish actors of the day. The popularity of these two television series prompted their makers to release theatrical versions in 1968 and 1969. Subsequent television series, for example *Chłopi* (*Peasants*, 1973, Jan Rybkowski) were frequently made with the theatrical release in mind. This was a practice first begun by Jerzy Antczak, the maker of a historical film *Hrabina Cosel* (*Countess Cosel*, 1968).

In the late 1960s, Polish television films were produced by established filmmakers and recent graduates of the Łódź Film School. The latter often started their careers by producing medium-length television films. For example, Krzysztof Zanussi attracted international attention with his diploma film, *Śmierć Prowincjała* (*Death of a Provincial*, 1966), which won awards at the Venice and Mannheim film festivals, and two television films made in 1968, *Twarzą w twarz* (*Face to Face*) and *Zaliczenie* (*Pass Mark*). Television became a training ground for a number of young filmmakers as well as a venue for documentary films. The best-known examples of documentary cinema made at the beginning of the 1960s dealt with the war and the Holocaust: *Powszedni dzień gestapowca Szmidta* (*An Ordinary Day of Szmidt, the Gestapo Man*, 1963) by Jerzy Ziarnik, and *Requiem dla 500 000* (*Requiem for 500,000*, 1963) by Jerzy Bossak and Wacław Kaźmierczak. The most influential, however, became the classic examples of sociological documentary produced by Kazimierz Karabasz: *Muzykanci* (*The Sunday Musicians*, 1960), and *Rok Franka W.* (*The Year of Franek W.*, 1967).

Adaptations

Film adaptations of the national literary canon had the most successful ticket sales in Polish cinema during the mid-1960s. They were also well received by Polish critics. The majority of adaptations stirred heated national debates, usually dealing with historical and political issues surrounding the films, rather than the films themselves. Some were also received as historically distant parables on contemporary Poland. This way of reading films was an established tradition in Poland; it became even more prominent in the late 1970s and after the introduction of martial law in December 1981. Acclaimed Polish writer Ryszard Kapuściński aptly describes the peculiar situation under communist rule:

> In Poland every text is read as allusive, every written situation—even the most distant in space and time—is immediately, without hesitation, applied to the situation in Poland. In this way, every text is a double text, and between the printed lines we search for sympathetic messages written in invisible ink, and the hidden message we find is treated as the most valid, the only real one. The result stems not only from the difficulty of open speech, the language of truth. It is also because this country of ours has suffered every possible experience in the world, and is still exposed to dozens of different trials, so that now in the normal course of things every Pole sees in histories that are not ours, connections with his own life.[9]

Andrzej Wajda's *Popioły* (*Ashes*, 1965), an adaptation of Stefan Żeromski's novel, serves as a good example here. This almost four-hour-long black-and-white film generated one of the most intense debates in Poland; its filmic aspects were of secondary importance in this discussion.[10] Set in the Napoleonic times and portraying the fate of the young Polish legionnaires, *Ashes* is "not a straightforward historical novel in the Dumas genre, but a giant historical and historico-philosophical fresco which resembles, if anything, Stendhal and Tolstoy."[11] The film covers the public disillusionment with Napoleon and the loss of hope that he will restore the Polish state. Discussions about Wajda's film, as always, touch on the issue of faithfulness to the literary source, and emphasize parallels between Wajda's generation of Columbuses and the young generation of Polish legionnaires, both outsmarted by "the forces of history." Tadeusz Sobolewski expresses the issue as follows: "*Ashes* opposed the propaganda, which stated that the Polish People's Republic was crowning the dreams of independence, by portraying history as a cemetery of Polish hopes."[12] In spite of its ambitious theme, an epic scope, and painterly black-and-white photography (Jerzy Lipman), *Ashes* does not belong to Wajda's successful works. Its incoherent narrative, superfluous plots, and multitude of characters, with whom a viewer cannot identify, weaken the impact of this film.

One of the best Polish historical films, Jerzy Kawalerowicz's epic production *The Pharaoh*, was given the same political reading as its contemporaries. The script by Kawalerowicz and Tadeusz Konwicki follows Bolesław Prus's celebrated novel about a young pharaoh, Rameses XIII, who tries to modernize Egypt but is defeated by his antagonists—the priests led by the archpriest Herhor. Faithful to the literary source, Kawalerowicz's film narrates the story of a young, impatient, and impulsive heir to the throne in ancient Egypt (Jerzy Zelnik), who is eager to limit the priests' impact on politics. When Rameses XIII becomes pharaoh after the death of his father, he attempts to reform the country with the help of treasures held by the priests. Since he cannot count on popular support, he decides to use force to take the labyrinth where the treasures are kept. The knowledgeable priests use the eclipse of the sun, which coincides with the attack, to threaten the soldiers, who consequently flee in panic. Rameses XIII later dies at the hand of his double, Lykon (also played by Jerzy Zelnik), who has been prepared by the priests to replace the young pharaoh.

Since the year 1966 marked the height of the ideological battle between the Polish Roman Catholic Church and the communist regime,[13] Kawalerowicz's film was used in this conflict. The story of a young heir unable to reform the country, the struggle for power between the church and the secular rulers, the role of "progressive" priests supporting the ruler, and the impact of religion happened to be very close to the complexities of modern Polish politics. Today, however, Kawalerowicz's historical epic, enormous by Polish standards, is absorbing not only for its theme, but chiefly for its grand formal beauty. Eisensteinian compositions of frame (cinematography by Jerzy Wójcik), stylized gestures and movements of actors, creative design by Jerzy Skrzepiński, and original, subjective shots (for example, the battle between Egypt and Assyria is seen from the point of view of a common soldier) make this film intriguing to audiences. In spite of its anti-Hollywood treatment of history, *The Pharaoh* received an Oscar nomination in 1967 in the Best Foreign Film category.

In the mid-1960s, Wojciech J. Has changed the intimate style that is characteristic of his films made during the Polish School period, and moved to the realm of historical spectaculars based on great literary works. His 1965 black-and-white *Rękopis znaleziony w Saragossie* (*The Saragossa Manuscript*) was adapted from the novel, published in French in 1813, by a writer of the European Enlightenment, Count Jan Potocki. Like the novel, Has's film offers a complex, labyrinth-like narrative structure that is open to interpretation. The viewer follows Captain Alfons von Worden (Zbigniew Cybulski) and his improbable voyages across eighteenth-century Spain. His surreal journey is governed by the logic of dreams. The oneiric dimension

Figure 6.1 Jerzy Zelnik as the young pharaoh (in the middle) in Jerzy Kawalerowicz's *The Pharaoh* (1966)

of this travel, the motif of a journey into one's past, and the appearances of characters who emerge from the realm of dreams or memories also characterize some of Has's later films, including *Sanatorium pod Klepsydrą* (*Hospital under the Hourglass*, 1973). This adaptation of Bruno Schulz's prose deals with the theme of childhood recollections. The film's protagonist, Józef (Jan Nowicki), travels in time; painterly dreamlike and surrealist images accompany his voyage.

Has adapted Bolesław Prus's novel *Lalka* (*The Doll*, 1968) in a more conventional manner. Set in the late nineteenth century, *The Doll* tells a love story between an impoverished aristocratic young lady, countess Izabella Łęcka (Beata Tyszkiewicz), and a rich merchant, Stanisław Wokulski (Mariusz Dmochowski). *The Doll* centers around two worlds of conflict: the emerging Polish capitalism, represented by Wokulski and his class, and the old Polish romantic tradition, represented by Łęcka, her family, and Wokulski's shop assistant Rzecki (Tadeusz Fijewski). This film's vast panorama of Polish society after the failed January Uprising of 1863–1864 against Russia greatly contributed to its critical and box-office success.[14]

Vast panoramas, epic scopes, historical adventure stories utilizing Polish history, and, above all, Henryk Sienkiewicz's name proved to be enough to attract millions to *Pan Michael* and *The Deluge*, both directed by Jerzy

Figure 6.2 Jan Nowicki (left) and Ludwik Benoit in *Hospital under the Hourglass* (1973, Wojciech J. Has)

Hoffman (b. 1932). Like the earlier popular success, Aleksander Ford's *Teutonic Knights*, adaptations of Sienkiewicz were eagerly awaited by Polish audiences for whom this writer and the characters populating his historical novels are household names. *Pan Michael* deals with the seventeenth-century defense of Christianity against the Islamic Turks. It is a generic adventure film, almost a "cloak and dagger" with elements of romance, set in an environment that is a stereotype of Polish history. This film's likeable protagonists, Michał Wołodyjowski (Tadeusz Łomnicki) and his beloved Basia (Magdalena Zawadzka), and the straightforward, colorful version of the not-so-colorful past generated success with local as well as foreign audiences; between 1969 and 1986, the film was sold to twenty-eight countries.[15]

The two-part, five-hour-long epic *The Deluge* is also set in the turbulent mid-seventeenth century, during the Swedish invasion of Poland known as the "Swedish Deluge."[16] Hoffman's film narrates a melodramatic love story between a color sergeant, Andrzej Kmicic (Daniel Olbrychski) and Oleńka Billewiczówna (Małgorzata Braunek). Kmicic swears an allegiance to the Lithuanian prince Janusz Radziwiłł, who later betrays the Polish· king to the Swedish invaders. Torn between his loyalty to Radziwiłł and a sense of patriotism, Kmicic changes sides. He defends the holy monastery at Częstochowa under a different name. Thanks to his heroic deeds, he is pardoned by the Polish king for his treason and later reconciled with Oleńka. The transformation of a fun-loving, irresponsible young man into a national hero is at the structural center of this film. Another adaptation of Sienkiewicz, Władysław Ślesicki's *In Desert and Wilderness*, 1973), proved to be the most popular film for children and one of the most popular films in Polish history.

Noce i dnie (*Nights and Days*, 1975), Jerzy Antczak's (b. 1929) faithful adaptation of Maria Dąbrowska's revered novel, also belongs to a group of Polish box-office successes.[17] This epic melodramatic account of love between emotional and ambitious Barbara (Jadwiga Barańska) and down-to-earth Bogumił (Jerzy Bińczycki) covers almost forty years, beginning in 1874. The film deals with Barbara's reminiscences of her life, and the theme of long-lasting love against all odds. Like Dąbrowska's family saga, it offers a nostalgic tour into the past. The film begins and ends with the outbreak of World War I, which destroys the tranquillity experienced in the past. Jan Rybkowski's *Peasants*, based on the novel written by another Polish Nobel Prize winner for literature, Władysław Stanisław Reymont, introduces a different reality: the colorful late-nineteenth-century peasant culture. Another popular adaptation was made by Walerian Borowczyk (b. 1923), a Polish filmmaker living in France, who returned to Poland in 1975 to produce *Dzieje grzechu* (*The Story of Sin*, 1975), the third adaptation of Stefan Żeromski's novel.[18] This stylish, erotic drama—a style which could be expected from the maker of *Blanche* (1972) and *Contes immoraux* (*Immoral Stories*, 1974)—tells the story of the unhappy life of Ewa (Grażyna Długołęcka) and her descent into prostitution and crime.

Andrzej Wajda's Films: 1969–1976

In 1969 Andrzej Wajda released his most personal film, *Wszystko na sprzedaż* (*Everything for Sale*), following the tragic death of his *Ashes and Diamonds* star, Zbigniew Cybulski (1927–1967). Although Cybulski's name is not mentioned, the film deals with Cybulski's legend—and what is left of it after the hero's death. By 1969 Wajda's films had become identifiable by certain themes and by his well-developed and personal visual style. As Bolesław Michałek suggests, the director may have become "a prisoner of his themes and his obsessions with national cross-purposes."[19] If an artist wants to develop his art, the title of the film suggests, it is necessary for him to put everything up for sale.

Everything for Sale, though, is not so much a film about Cybulski, as it is about Wajda, his actors, his other films, and the uncertainty of the future of his artistic career. The main protagonist, a film director Andrzej (Andrzej Łapicki), clearly serves as Wajda's alter ego. "How could he do this to me," he speaks of the deceased actor. The enactment of Cybulski's life and death constitutes the narrative axis of the film. The film is cast with real-life characters, friends of Cybulski and Wajda who appear under their own names: Beata Tyszkiewicz as Beata, Elżbieta Czyżewska as Ela, Bogumił Kobiela as Bobek, and Daniel Olbrychski as the rising new star Daniel, who replaces the dead actor. Wajda's film tries to discover Cybulski through memories of those who knew him and ultimately remarks on the impossibility of re-creating a true picture. Konrad Eberhardt comments that "Wajda made a ballet of forms and ostentatiously bright colors. His film is nervous, breathless, and has a rhythm of a chase. In it there is a search for the film's idea, and also for the shadow of a person who has passed away."[20]

Every aspect of life, including death or an artistic crisis, can be turned into art. Like Federico Fellini's *Otto e mezzo* (*8 1/2*, 1963) and François Truffaut's *La nuit américaine* (*Day for Night*, 1973), *Everything for Sale* is a self-reflective, exhibitionist film about a creative process—a film within a film. During the last scene of Wajda's film, the camera focuses on Olbrychski. He is "Wajda's new-found symbol of the Polish consciousness," remarks Paul Coates. He goes on to say: "The camera turns away from the railway tracks that recall the death of Cybulski. One may almost feel it licking its lips at the prospect of filming Olbrychski in later works."[21] Daniel Olbrychski (b. 1945), who in the film rejects the identification with Cybulski, became the most popular Polish actor in the early 1970s. He debuted in 1964 in *Ranny w lesie* (*Wounded in the Forest*, Janusz Nasfeter), then starred in Wajda's *Ashes* and several other films in the late 1960s. Olbrychski sealed his popularity in Jerzy Hoffman's adaptations of Henryk Sienkiewicz. The role of Kmicic in *The Deluge* was the pinnacle of his career.

The majority of Andrzej Wajda's films constitute adaptations of the Polish national literary canon. At the beginning of the 1970s, Wajda produced a number of important adaptations revolving around the characters' psychology rather than the historical and political contexts. They include: *Krajobraz po bitwie* (*Landscape after Battle*, 1970), based on Tadeusz Borowski's short stories; *Brzezina* (*Birchwood*, 1970), an adaptation of Jarosław Iwaszkiewicz's short story; *Wesele* (*The Wedding*, 1973), an adaptation of the canonical Polish drama by Stanisław Wyspiański; *Ziemia Obiecana* (*The Land of Promise*, 1975),[22] based on Władysław Stanisław Reymont's novel about the birth of Polish capitalism in Łódź; and *Smuga cienia* (*The Shadow Line*, 1976), a lesser known adaptation of Joseph Conrad.[23]

Landscape after Battle opens with a memorable sequence that sets the tone for the whole film—the liberation of a German concentration camp by American troops. Lacking dialogue and accompanied by Antonio Vivaldi's *Four Seasons*, the sequence portrays the first minutes of freedom. The prisoners in their striped camp clothing run through a snow-covered field, finally encountering a barbed-wire fence. They wait, confused and tired, before one of them (Mieczysław Stoor) touches it and discovers that it is not electrified. A sharp contrast follows when the prisoners avenge their misery by killing a *kapo* (a prisoner who was granted authority to control other prisoners). They literally stamp him into the dirt after the lofty speech of an American officer-liberator. The camera then introduces the film's protagonist, writer Tadeusz (Daniel Olbrychski), who has the

Figure 6.3 Stanisława Celińska and Daniel Olbrychski in *Landscape after Battle* (1970, Andrzej Wajda)

low number "105" tattooed on his arm, indicating a long stay in the camp. He appears to be an almost stereotypical young intellectual: wearing wire-rimmed glasses, absent-minded, and rescuing books from fire while others search for food and clothing.

The film's action then moves to a displaced persons camp, organized in a former SS barracks. The concentration camp prisoners, POWs, Polish refugees, and survivors from other camps live in this place under the guard of American soldiers before being sent home. Although Wajda portrays political differences among the Poles, he is primarily concerned with the love that surfaces between two survivors: Tadeusz and Nina (Stanisława Celińska), Jewish refugee from Poland. As it often happens in Wajda's films, the sudden manifestation of love serves only as a romantic interlude before death. Ironically, while returning with Tadeusz to the camp, Nina is accidentally killed by an American guard. As in Wajda's later film *Birchwood*, the death of a loved one enables the protagonist to awaken psychologically and regain some human emotions. In the film's finale, Tadeusz boards a train to Poland with numerous other refugees.

In 1970 Wajda paired once again with his cinematographer Zygmunt Samosiuk to produce *Birchwood*, a modest television film (first distributed theatrically) that was of great importance for Wajda. The story, set in the 1930s, concerns the relationship between two brothers. The older, Bolesław (Daniel Olbrychski), is a widower who works as a forest warden and lives with his daughter Ola. The younger brother, Stanisław (Olgierd Łukaszewicz), who is dying of tuberculosis, has just returned from a sanatorium in Switzerland to spend the last moments of his life with Bolesław. A local woman, Malina (Emilia Krakowska), serves as the very embodiment of the life force and the symbol of sexuality. The brothers become rivals when they realize that they both want this woman. When Stanisław dies, he is buried next to Bolesław's wife in the birchwood. Revitalized, Bolesław leaves both the forest and Malina, who is about to marry her village suitor.

The themes of love and death permeate the film. The Polish *art nouveau* painter Jacek Malczewski serves as the source of painterly inspirations.[24] Bolesław Michałek says: "[T]the colour is certainly eerie, ugly in its way, 'cadaverous' as it was called—a mélange of putrid yellows, greens and violets. These tones dominate the photography of human bodies with their faces splodged by sickly, sinister stains. The use of the same spectrum as Malczewski lent the film's images a disquieting, misty, but ever-present air of disease, decomposition and death."[25] The presentation of the struggle between Eros and Thanatos (love and death) in this life-affirming film is new for Wajda. As Ewelina Nurczyńska-Fidelska points out, Wajda has dealt with the themes of love and death, and with protagonists who experience love for only a short time before their deaths. This is a common theme in his films *A Generation*, *Kanal*, *Ashes and Diamonds*, *Lotna*, *Ashes*, and *Landscape after Battle*.[26] The deaths in *Landscape after Battle* and in *Birchwood*, however, are devoid of the political dimension; they are not sacrifices at the altar of national needs.

Wajda's next film, an adaptation of the stage play *The Wedding* by the multitalented fin-de-siècle artist Stanisław Wyspiański, is abundant with national symbolism and alludes to Polish mythology, history, and national complexes. Staged for the first time in Cracow in 1901, the play deals with the actual wedding of a Cracow poet, Lucjan Rydel, and a peasant girl, Jadwiga Mikołajczyk, in the village of Bronowice, just outside of Cracow. Set in 1900, *The Wedding* portrays the illusory unity of the intelligentsia and the peasants, explores the different political goals of these two groups, and stresses the impossibility of overcoming the burden of the past. Wajda's film faithfully follows the play, preserving its rhymed dialogues and emphasizing its dreamlike qualities. The director reinforces symbolism that refers to the Polish past, adds the aura of uncanniness to Wyspiański's phantoms from the nation's history, and injects a vibrating rhythm to this national psychotherapeutic drama. Similar to *Ashes and Diamonds*, the psychedelic rhythm of *The Wedding* finds its culmination in another, symbolic dance in the film's finale. Wajda's "masterpiece of cine-painting"[27] relies on familiar Polish iconography more than his other films, and draws inspirations from the local painting tradition.[28]

The painterly aspect is also important in Wajda's next film, *The Land of Promise*. Its action, set in the fast-growing industrial city of Łódź, introduces three protagonists/friends: a Pole, Karol Borowiecki (Daniel Olbrychski); a Jew, Moryc Welt (Wojciech Pszoniak); and a German, Max Baum (Andrzej Seweryn), all of whom attempt to build a textile factory. The film tells how the three young enterpreuners try to establish themselves in Łódź, yet it is essentially the story of the city: multicultural, dynamic, vulgar, and tempting. Wajda paints an almost Marxist image of the city-Moloch devouring its children. He follows Reymont's portrayal of the end of the romantic era on the Polish territories, the loss of traditional values, and the triumphant march of uncouth and dynamic nineteenth-century capitalism. Like Reymont, Wajda portrays Łódź as having energy, potential, wealth, and national/class diversity. He also deals with the plight of the remnants of the pauperized nobility, who were forced to move from their country manors—the bastions of traditionally understood Polishness—to newly developed industrial cities such as Łódź. Łódź, the land of promise for many, means destruction for others in this film, which was well received by critics and audiences alike.[29]

The War Experiences

The war still features prominently in Polish films made in the second half of the 1960s and at the beginning of the 1970s. The best-known works return to the main preoccupations and poetics of the Polish School. The events of September 1939 are depicted in *Westerplatte*, Stanisław

Różewicz's film about the defense of the Polish garrison at the Wester-platte peninsula near Gdańsk. Różewicz reconstructs the one-week battle in a realistic manner, even incorporating newsreels, and avoids romanticizing this habitually mythologized aspect of the year 1939. The garrison's commander, Major Henryk Sucharski (Zygmunt Hübner), is portrayed as a brave, well-disciplined, and pragmatic officer. He cares about his people, not history.

In *Hubal*, Bohdan Poręba (b. 1934) deals with another legend, that of Major Dobrzański, known as Hubal (portrayed by Ryszard Filipski in a memorable performance), who kept fighting the Germans after the Polish armies were defeated in September 1939, until he died in action in the spring of 1940. The film alludes to the romantic tradition in Polish arts and immortalizes Hubal, but it also stresses the practical aspect of the protagonist's actions. At first glance, the setting of Poręba's film resembles Wajda's *Lotna* (in which the cavalry men struggle with the Germans during the September campaign), but the issue of heroism is treated differently. Heroism is mixed with everyday struggle. The cavalry men turned partisans are heroic but are also tired men making a futile effort to reverse history.

A distinct group of films, epic in scope and aspirations, affirms rather than questions Polish history. These films, told from the perspective of a common soldier advancing westward with the First Polish Army, lack the dilemmas that permeate Wajda's films; their interest lies not in tragedy but in glory. *Kierunek Berlin* (*Direction Berlin*, 1969), by Jerzy Passendorfer, and *Jarzębina czerwona* (*The Rowan Tree*, 1970), by Ewa and Czesław Petelski, although made in the spirit of the Soviet epic war films, stress the everyday aspect of war and the ordinary heroism of common soldiers. Both films portray the last days of war: the storm of Berlin and the battle of Kołobrzeg (Kolberg)—one of the bloodiest combat battles fought by Polish soldiers during the war.

In 1967 two modest, realistic films were made, portraying an average day under the occupation: *The Barn at Salvator* by Paweł Komorowski (b. 1930), and *Kontrybucja* (*Contribution*) by Jan Łomnicki (b. 1929). Both examine the moral dilemmas of the underground fighters whose psychology and dramatic choices are of utmost importance. These dramas of choices have a lot of in common with Kazimierz Kutz's and Stanisław Różewicz's depiction of the war. The protagonists do not serve as personifications of different ideological stands; they are psychologically complex characters with family lives, fears, and responsibilities. In *The Barn at Salvator*, an underground soldier, Michał (Janusz Gajos), gets an order to kill a friend who, due to tortures inflicted by the Gestapo, has betrayed the organization and endangered the lives of others. *Contribution* deals with an underground fighter's attempts to free his brother-in-law, who has been captured by the Germans. He does not obey his superiors' orders, and pays the highest price for it. Both films are presented in an almost documentary tone and offer psychological landscapes rather than epic scope and action. They refrain from breakthrough moments in Polish history and concentrate on everyday experiences in order to understand history. As Aleksander Jackiewicz writes, they "reflected the time, which cannot be compared to ordinary time, although it was ordinary at the time."[30]

Other films depict the war in a different manner. For example, Andrzej Żuławski's *Trzecia część nocy* (*The Third Part of the Night*, 1972), based on the novel written by the director's father, Mirosław Żuławski, concerns human lice feeders employed by the Germans during their experiments on typhoid. The film is replete with shocking images, symbolism, stylized dialogues, and expressionistic acting. It is controversial and thought provoking, yet borders on kitsch.

The mannerism, violent imagery, exhilarating camera movement, and nonconformity of the early films of Żuławski (b. 1940) surprised and shocked both viewers and film authorities. Due to its accumulation of shocking imagery, Żuławski's *Diabeł* (*Devil*, 1972) is frequently labeled a horror film, and was not released until 1988. The two-year-long production of *Na srebrnym globie* (*On the Silver Globe*), Żuławski's lavish science fiction film, was stopped by the authorities in 1977 for going over budget; a reconstructed version of this film was premiered by the director in 1989. Żuławski decided to move permanently to France where he directed, among others, *Possession* (1981), *La femme publique* (*The Public Woman*, 1984), *L'amour braque* (*Mad Love*, 1985), *Boris Godunov* (1990), *La note bleue* (*Blue Note*, 1991), and *La fidélité* (*Faithfulness*, 2000). In 1996 Żuławski returned briefly to Poland to direct *Szamanka* (*She-Shaman*), aptly nicknamed by Polish critics as "Last Tango in Warsaw."

The divisions among the Polish underground toward the end of the war and the plight of the Home Army and other underground units after 1945 are reflected in, among others, Jerzy Passendorfer's *Barwy walki* (*Scenes of Battle*, 1965), Janusz Morgenstern's *Potem nastąpi cisza* (*Then There Will Be Silence*, 1966), Sylwester Szyszko's *Ciemna rzeka* (*Dark River*, 1974), and Kazimierz Kutz's *Znikąd donikąd* (*From Nowhere to Nowhere*, 1975). With the exception of the action-oriented *Scenes of Battle*, based on the book written by Mieczysław Moczar, minister of the interior, which celebrates the communist partisans, other films deal with the political divisions after the war, the moral aspect of the war, and the struggles between the remaining Home Army units and the regular Polish troops.

The postwar situation is also present in the embryonic Polish genre cinema. The influences of the Western genre are transparent in films such as *Prawo i pięść* (*Law and Fist*, 1964), by Jerzy Hoffman and Edward Skórzewski, and *Wilcze echa* (*Wolves' Echoes*, 1968), by Aleksander Ścibor-Rylski. The scenery of the action becomes the postwar reality in the "Regained Lands" and the Bieszczady Mountains in southeast Poland. Both films employ the motif of a lone defender of the law who clashes with gangster types. These superficial transplants of the Western genre became popular partly due to the absence of American popular cinema on Polish screens.

Figure 6.4 Ryszard Pietruski in *Law and Fist* (1964, Jerzy Hoffman and Edward Skórzewski)

Third Polish Cinema

The tendency to disregard the prewar period in Polish cinema and discuss only its postwar achievements is reflected in the term *Trzecie kino polskie* (Third Polish Cinema), coined by some Polish critics in the mid-1960s.[31] They wanted to stress another generational change occurring in Polish cinema. For them, "the third generation" consisted of filmmakers raised, sometimes even born, in postwar Poland, whose political baptism by fire was not the war and its aftermath, but rather the events of the Polish October and the Gomułka years of "small stabilization." After the "first generation," the postwar generation represented by, among others, Wanda Jakubowska and Aleksander Ford, and the "Polish School (second) generation", the late 1960s marked the emergence of filmmakers for whom national history and politics are not important. Reality and philosophical reflections on culture are of prime importance. These filmmakers are characterized by their different interests and cinematic styles; they are preoccupied with reality, skeptical about the world, suspicious of the national romantic tradition, and interested in personal cinema. Aleksander Jackiewicz observes, "Polański, Skolimowski, Majewski, and now Kluba. Maybe this is another generation of Polish cinema? After Munk, Wajda, Kawalerowicz, Has, after the Polish School, new generation? The earlier filmmakers were serious, excessive, baroque, expressionistic, naive. The latter with a distance, a smile, with tendencies to mystification and caricature. The earlier came from romanticism, surrealism, Wyspiański, Buñuel, Olivier's 'theater,' and Kurosawa. The latter from Beckett, Mrożek, Godard, and the 'new cinema.'"[32]

Rafał Marszałek states that "the third generation" not only introduced the new language of cinema, but also complicated the one-dimensional world-view that had dominated Polish cinema: "We know, that univocality was for many years the aesthetic ideal of Polish cinema. Before the war it relied on the mass audience, and after the war was subordinated mainly to educational and propagandist norms." According to Marszałek, the newcomers "proposed a different aesthetic hierarchy based on the multi-layered status of the work of art and its equivocal reading."[33]

The term "Third Polish Cinema," which also appears in books published in North America,[34] has little explanatory power. It covers disparate film poetics and distinct directorial personalities. Among the new filmmakers emerging after the Polish School period, two stand out from the rest: Jerzy Skolimowski (b. 1936) in the mid-1960s, and Krzysztof Zanussi (b. 1939) in the late 1960s and early 1970s. Both created personal films that are unique in the context of Polish cinema, and introduced characters with personal rather than political problems, moral dilemmas rather than disputes about history, and new generational experiences reflected in a refreshing style.

In his trilogy about the new generation—*Rysopis* (*Identification Marks: None*, 1965), *Walkower* (*Walkover*, 1965), and *Bariera* (*The Barrier*, 1966)—

Skolimowski introduces an outsider who searches for his own way of life, a nonconformist who refuses to accept reality. The protagonist, played in the first two films by Skolimowski, does everything to destroy any possibility of entering the mainstream of life. Although frequently analyzed in the context of European new wave cinema,[35] the protagonist is much in line with the traditional Polish romantic hero, with his rebellious, self-destructive nature.[36] Skolimowski's stylized language, full of references to Polish culture and politics and to his own biographical legend (as a poet, a scriptwriter for *Innocent Sorcerers* and *Knife in the Water*, and a boxer), attacks the post-Stalinist conformity. The protagonist's search for the new, his journey (both physical and psychological), defies the world of "small stabilization." The presence of Skolimowski on the screen and a number of autobiographical features certainly help to make the film a personal statement and to reflect on the texture of the epoch.

As stated above, Skolimowski's films have a style similar to the new wave trends in European cinema of the 1960s. His films are open, documentary-like constructs, shot on location without artificial lighting, frequently improvised on the set,[37] and characterized by their reliance on long takes (for example, there are only thirty-five cuts in *Walkover*).[38] This style was already evidenced in Skolimowski's diploma film made at the Łódź Film School, *Identification Marks: None*, which was produced from a number of student exercises, filmic etudes made since the second year of Skolimowski's studies.[39] The episodic film centers on Andrzej Leszczyc (Skolimowski), who is expelled from the university due to his own mistake, not because he supported some political causes. The protagonist does not want to live like the older generation, and attempts to prolong his youth by avoiding personal or professional commitments. Skolimowski produces the "spiritual generational biography,"[40] and offers the essence of authorial cinema: he is the director-scriptwriter-actor of the film, which features his then wife, Elżbieta Czyżewska, and his Łódź Film School friends. Skolimowski's next film, *Walkover*, continues to follow the story of Andrzej Leszczyc, now a thirty-year-old boxer, living on his modest boxing prizes. When he tries to win another boxing tournament and faces a stronger opponent, he decides not to give up. This decision signals that he wants to embrace a mature life, which requires fight and commitment.

Certainly, the most elaborate is the third part of the generational trilogy, *The Barrier*. Jan Nowicki replaces Skolimowski as a nameless outsider about to begin a new life. In the first sequence, the protagonist leaves the university campus with a suitcase containing a piggy bank won at the student hall. Convinced that ideals are meant to be lost sooner or later, he decides to speed up the process, marry a rich woman, and quickly establish himself within the society of "small stabilization." A chance meeting with a young female tram driver (Joanna Szczerbic) leads to an internal confrontation with his ideas about life.

The Barrier works against the mainstream of Polish cinema, which is obsessed with the romantic, martyrological aspect of the past, World War II in particular. By introducing some characters against a white background, with their hands held tightly behind their backs, the opening scene of *The Barrier* looks like another Polish war/partisan film. The viewer learns later that this is a part of the absurd student game. The very title of the film introduces the theme of a generational conflict—the barrier has been built between the generation of fathers, locked in their past, not in touch with the new reality, and the new generation, which was too young to be active during the war. The protagonist's alienation from the older generation as well as the grotesque aspect of the war veterans' behavior are ridiculed in a scene in which a number of male war veterans sing a patriotic song. Not understood by the protagonist (and the viewers), they sing asynchronously, sometimes not even remembering the lyrics, while the camera pans over a group of women sitting at the tables, waiting patiently. Skolimowski also mocks the exaggerated and fake wartime stories of the older generation, for example, in the encounter with a man faking his blindness and inventing his tragic war story. The protagonist compares those who helped to develop "the small stabilization" to geese: "You get fat and lose bird's ambition to fly. I understand you."

Since the film is set around Easter time, the theme of resurrection, both personal and generational, comes to the foreground. The music, composed by Krzysztof Komeda, with the Hallelujah sung by a vocal group, provides an ironic, sometimes almost tragic, comment on the action. To make *The Barrier* even more personal, the cleaning lady in the film unexpectedly begins a song to the poetry of Skolimowski. Michael Walker comments that "sequences of 'pure fantasy' are blended with stylised visualisations of reality, creating a richly poetic (*and* homogeneous) texture."[41] The poetic stylization and ornate symbolism in the film refer to Polish history and culture. Carrying his father's saber, the protagonist wanders through an artificial space that is frequently only a white, dreamlike, and surrealist landscape.

The Barrier proved to be the last film Skolimowski was able to produce and release in the 1960s in Poland. His next project, *Ręce do góry* (*Hands Up*), about the postwar generation that quickly gave up its ideals and turned to a middle-class existence and middle-class aspirations, was completed in 1967, but released as late as 1985. This film, one of the first to deal with the Stalinist years, was too difficult for communist authorities to take. Unable to continue his career in Poland, Skolimowski left the country. He went on to make a number of films in the West, including *The Shout* (1978, U.K.), *Moonlighting* (1982, U.K.), *Success Is the Best Revenge* (1984, U.K.), *The Lightship* (1985, U.S.), and *Torrents of Spring* (1989, France/Italy). In 1991 Skolimowski directed *Ferdydurke* (*30 Door Key*), a Polish-English-French coproduction based on a novel by the celebrated Polish writer Witold Gombrowicz.

Krzysztof Zanussi's unusual road to filmmaking is clearly reflected in his films. After years of studying physics and philosophy, and making amateur films, he enrolled at the Łódź Film School. He attracted international attention in 1966 with his medium-length diploma film, *Death of a Provincial*, and two television films made in 1968, *Face to Face* and *Pass Mark*. These films contain a number of thematic features characteristic of his later films: the mystery of death, the conflict between the individual and the society, existential problems, and moral choices. Zanussi's Bergmanian themes and his austere, noncommittal style became his trademark. Usually, Zanussi avoids films that make a social commitment, that refer to the romantic roots of Polish culture. He prefers multidimensional and detailed realistic observation. Paul Coates aptly writes: "Not until the arrival of Zanussi was a new style created that other directors could assimilate: that of the low-key television drama. Zanussi replaced the pathos-laden style of the Polish school with scrupulous attention to the everyday.... The bad faith of faithful reconstruction of irrelevant pasts gave way to a careful examination of the present."[42] Zanussi's realism refers less to the social and more to the psychological and philosophical reality; therefore, the terms "intellectual cinema" and "artist-intellectual" are frequently applied to his works.[43]

Zanussi's full-length films, beginning with *Struktura kryształu* (*The Structure of Crystals*, 1969), created his reputation as an *auteur* interested in specific characters, known as "Zanussoids"—young intellectuals questioning the corrupt world.[44] Several young members of the Polish intelligentsia identified with the protagonist of *Iluminacja* (*Illumination*, 1973), and later praised the parable on politics presented in *Barwy ochronne* (*Camouflage*,

Figure 6.5 Barbara Wrzesińska (Anna) and Andrzej Żarnecki (Marek) in Krzysztof Zanussi's *The Structure of Crystals* (1969)

1977). Zanussi started to function as the representative of "intellectual cinema," a cosmopolitan Pole at home everywhere, a cultural ambassador of the Catholic Poland.

Aleksander Jackiewicz commented: "With *The Structure of Crystals*, a long-awaited personality in Polish cinema has been born."[45] Zanussi's film was also the start of a permanent collaboration with the composer Wojciech Kilar. This modest black-and-white film, made during the era of big-budget historical adaptations, was shot entirely on location. It is very authentic, resembling a documentary film, and is addressed to sophisticated viewers. "For the first time we get into a filmic reality that is not simulated," states Rafał Marszałek.[46] Scripted by Zanussi, who scriptwrites or co-scriptwrites all of his films, *The Structure of Crystals* depicts young intellectuals and their moral choices and ethical problems. The story concerns the meeting of two physicists, former university friends. The worldly Marek (Andrzej Żarnecki) lives in Warsaw, and has just returned from a fellowship in the West; Jan (Jan Mysłowicz) works at a provincial meteorological station and lives with his wife Anna (Barbara Wrzesińska) in a remote village. Marek tries to convince Jan to return to the university, and gradually learns the reasons behind his friend's decision to live a quiet life. The film introduces two personalities and two ways to succeed in life: dynamic expansion and professional success versus calmness and independence—the narrow approach (Marek specializes in the structure of crystals) versus the broad, humanistic outlook. Zanussi grants virtues evenly to both protagonists, and does not offer easy solutions in the choice between *vita activa* and *vita contemplativa*.

In the psychological drama *Życie rodzinne* (*Family Life*, 1971), Zanussi introduces another conflict between differing philosophies of life and moral issues. The director queries whether one has the right to get rid of one's roots if they prove to be an obstacle to living a desired life. He narrates the conflict between the father (Jan Kreczmar), the prewar factory owner out of touch with the new reality, and the son, Wit (Daniel Olbrychski), who loosens his ties to his family. Zanussi's favorite actress, Maja Komorowska (b. 1937), appears for the first time in *Family Life* as Wit's sister, Bella. She had begun her long collaboration with Zanussi the year before, appearing in the television film *Góry o zmierzchu* (*Mountains at Dusk*). Her next television film for Zanussi, *Za ścianą* (*Next Door*, 1971), fully demonstrated her ability to convey the uneasiness and psychological torment of her characters. Both she and another prototypical "Zanussian actor," Zbigniew Zapasiewicz (b. 1934) as a reserved docent (associate professor), greatly contributed to the success of this classic Polish television production.

Bilans kwartalny (*Balance Sheet*, aka *A Woman's Decision*, 1975), one of Zanussi's finest films, also stars Maja Komorowska as Marta, an altruistic accountant who is always thinking of others yet is bored with her own life. She has a short-lived extramarital affair with Jacek (played by a director, Marek Piwowski), a free-spirited man not preoccupied with the material aspects of life. In this story of a marital triangle, Marta's husband Janek (Piotr Fronczewski) is portrayed as a person obsessed with work and unable to show his true emotions. The whole affair is depicted in an observational manner, with a lot of attention paid to everyday details, to the Polish reality of the 1970s. The linear, slow-paced narrative of this well-received, internationally known film is devoid of the structural complexities of Zanussi's previous film, *Illumination* (1973).

Illumination is a philosophical essay unusual in Polish cinema. The film links an episodic, fictional narrative with documentary fragments (newsreels, interviews with noted Polish scientists, and fragments of their lectures). It begins with an explanation of the film's title delivered by a prominent Polish philosopher, Władysław Tatarkiewicz. *Iluminatio* (illumination), a medieval philosophical term introduced by St. Augustine, stands for an intellectual and spiritual enlightenment gained through intellectual hardship and purity of heart.[47] The narrative of Zanussi's film concerns ten years in the life of a young physicist, Franciszek Retman (Stanisław Latałło). The camera follows him from his matriculation in a small-town school, through his studies in physics, his first sexual experience with an older woman, his marriage to Małgosia (Małgorzata Pritulak), the birth of their child, work, the death of a friend, personal crisis, the search for answers at the Cameldolite monastery, the return to his family, and the acceptance of his fate. Zanussi admits that he uses the term "illumination" in a bitter sense.[48] Although convinced that truth can

Figure 6.6 Stanisław Latałło as Franciszek Retman in Krzysztof Zanussi's *Illumination* (1973)

be fathomed rationally, the film's protagonist gains illumination through his life experience. Zanussi employs real scientists, nonprofessional actors (such as Latałło, a film operator), and the form of a filmic essay to tell the story of a typical individual almost in the manner of a clinical case. "Zanussi's film belongs to those rare moments in film history," writes Aleksander Jackiewicz, "when a film seems to be granted the grace of illumination."[49]

* * * *

Among the newly emerging filmmakers, Edward Żebrowski's films thematically and stylistically resemble the cinema of Zanussi. A collaborator with Zanussi (the co-scriptwriter of several of Zanussi's films), Żebrowski (b. 1935) started his career with *Ocalenie* (*Deliverance*, 1972). The film deals with a scientist (Zbigniew Zapasiewicz) whose busy routine is interrupted when he contracts a fatal illness, forcing him to reflect on his life. In *Szpital Przemienienia* (*The Hospital of Transfiguration*, 1979), Żebrowski continues his examination of a character facing dramatic choices. Set in September 1939, the film tells a story about the Nazi's killing of patients in a mental asylum. The director portrays the microcosm of Polish prewar society through the divisions among the hospital staff who experience the extreme situation.

Chudy i inni (*Skinny and Others*, 1967) and *Słońce wschodzi raz na dzień* (*The Sun Rises Once a Day*, 1967, released in 1972),[50] directed by Henryk Kluba (b. 1931) and scripted by Wiesław Dymny, offer different film poetics. *Skinny and Others*, a socialist realist production film *à rebours*, introduces antiheroic workers. *The Sun Rises Once a Day* focuses on the postwar reality in the Beskidy Mountains and the clash between the new communist reality and the self-governing aspirations of the mountaineers. It is a highly stylized folk ballad—with a choir of village elders commenting on the action—that portrays public distrust of the new political order.

Żywot Mateusza (*The Life of Matthew*, 1968), directed by Witold Leszczyński (b. 1933), is certainly one of the unique films of the late 1960s in Poland. The slow-paced story, divided into seven chapters, concerns the forty-year-old Matthew (played by Franciszek Pieczka), an oversensitive person who is considered mentally handicapped by his neighbors. Living with his sister Olga (Anna Milewska) in virtual isolation on the lake, Matthew develops an unusual closeness to nature. When the outside world turns on Matthew (his sister falls in love with an outsider, a woodcutter), he paddles to the middle of the lake and punches a hole in the bottom of his boat. The director introduces the psychological study of loneliness and of the relationship between man and nature. Exquisite cinematography by Andrzej Kostenko, and the skillful use of classical music by Arcangelo Corelli enhance the poetic atmosphere of the film. The co-scriptwiter of *The Life of Matthew*, Wojciech Solarz (b. 1934), one year later directed his debut film *Molo* (*Jetty*), an ingeniously narrated story dealing with the middle-age crisis of a ship designer, played by Ryszard Filipski.

Another rare film was made by one of the most independent Polish filmmakers, Grzegorz Królikiewicz (b. 1939). After a series of short films, he made an ambitious and provocative documentary-like film, *Na wylot* (*Through and Through*, aka *Clear Through*, 1973), a work based on a well-publicized murder case in prewar Poland. The Malisz couple—unemployed, alienated from the society, and desperate to change their miserable conditions—murder a postman and the elderly couple who witnessed their deed. Królikiewicz shows the ugliness and despair of the characters, played by Franciszek Trzeciak and Anna Nieborowska, and the revolting reality that surrounds them; he is not afraid to portray the repulsive physicality of the murder, an animal-like attack that shocks an unprepared viewer. Atypical camera movement, bizarre angles, merciless close-ups that disfigure the protagonists, images difficult to decipher, and bizarre sound effects help to intensify the emotional aspect of the film.

Królikiewicz is not only a scriptwriter-director, but also a film theorist who has taught at the Łódź Film School since 1977. His theoretical works, especially his examination of the off-screen space,[51] are reflected in techniques used in *Through and Through*: rudimentary dialogues, unusual camera angles, and the uncommon composition of frame. For example, in the murder scene the viewer sees one of the images upside down, with the victim's blood dropping from bottom to top of the screen. Królikiewicz also experiments with sound; he relies on sound and unusual sound effects to tell the story when the action is outside of the camera's gaze, or when the camera pans away. The search for a new cinematic language and the avoidance of psychologization later resulted in the mixed reception of Królikiewicz's films. His formal experiments were often unintelligible, even to the critics.

Slightly older than Skolimowski and Zanussi, Janusz Majewski (b. 1931) began his career in the 1960s with films in a variety of genres. Trained as an architect and later at the Łódź Film School, Majewski started out as an art director and a documentary filmmaker. His *Album Fleischera* (*Private Fleischer's Photo Album*, 1963), which portrays the war through the eyes of an ordinary German soldier, became a classic example of Polish documentary cinema. Majewski also made a number of successful television films, mostly mysteries, such as *Awatar, czyli zamiana dusz* (*Awatar, or the Exchange of Souls*, 1964), and *Ja gore* (*I Am Burning*, 1967). His range is demonstrated by another well-received television drama, the psychological study *Czarna suknia* (*The Black Dress*, 1967), with Ida Kamińska and Aleksandra Śląska.

Majewski is chiefly known for his well-crafted, stylish literary adaptations made in the late 1960s and the 1970s. He began with a black comedy, *Sublokator* (*The Lodger*, 1967), which was followed by a crime film, *Zbrodniarz, który ukradł zbrodnię* (*The Criminal Who Stole a Crime*, 1969), frequently cited as one of the best Polish crime films.[52] In *Lokis* (*The Bear*, 1970), based on Prosper Mérimée's short story, Majewski continued his fascination with the horror genre. Critical acclaim, however, allowed him to make subtle adaptations of the prewar Polish literary canon: *Zazdrość i medycyna* (*Jealousy and Medicine*, 1973), based on Michał Choromański's novel, and *Zaklęte rewiry* (*Hotel Pacific*, 1975), an adaptation of Henryk Worcell's fiction. The latter, a Polish-Czechoslovak coproduction, narrates the experiences of a young waiter (Marek Kondrat) working in an exclusive Cracow hotel in the 1930s. The film's detailed reconstruction of the past (with cinematography by Miloš Forman's collaborator, Miroslav Ondříček) is combined with a psychological observation of the power struggle and mechanisms of power in the small, hierarchic world of the restaurant.

Majewski's films made in the late 1970s were also set in the past. *Sprawa Gorgonowej* (*The Gorgon Affair*, 1977) and *Lekcja martwego języka* (*The Lesson of a Dead Language*, 1979) established his name as a filmmaker sensitive to the nuances of the past and able to capture its tone. The former, set in the 1930s, tells about the actual trial of Rita Gorgon (Ewa Dałkowska), who was accused of murdering the teenage daughter of her employer and lover. Although Gorgon maintained her innocence, she received the death sentence, which was later changed to eight years in prison. Majewski deals with the atmosphere of hysteria surrounding the trial and xenophobic attitudes toward Gorgon (she was a foreigner). *The Lesson of a Dead Language*, based on Andrzej Kuśniewicz's novel, concerns the demise of the Austro-Hungarian Empire, the end of a historical epoch. Set in 1918, the film narrates the story of the ulan lieutenant Alfred Kiekeritz (Olgierd Łukaszewicz), who is dying of tuberculosis and has been sent to a sanatorium in a small Carpathian town situated on the periphery of the monarchy. The lieutenant, a known art collector and connoisseur, awaits his death there. The motif of death, both personal (Kiekeritz) and political (the empire), permeates the film.

Unlike Majewski, a number of young emerging filmmakers at the beginning of the 1970s dealt with different aspects of contemporary life. Their equally young protagonists learn about life, experience first love, get first jobs, and follow their dreams in a conformist world. For example, in *Kardiogram* (*Cardiogram*, 1971) Roman Załuski (b. 1936) portrays the Polish province as seen through the eyes of a young physician (Tadeusz Borowski), who chooses to settle and start his career in a small town. Another physician, also played by Borowski, appears in Załuski's next film, *Zaraza* (*The Outbreak*, 1972), a psychological drama about the outbreak of black smallpox in Wrocław. In 1972 Załuski also made *Anatomia miłości* (*Anatomy of Love*, 1972), starring Jan Nowicki and Barbara Brylska, which offered a popular, contemporary love story.

Janusz Zaorski's debut film, *Uciec jak najbliżej* (*Escape as Near as Possible*, 1972), made when he was twenty-four, paints a realistic picture of the younger generation. It introduces a young man who travels across Poland on business, representing a small company that produces road signs. Zaorski portrays a typical generational character. Symbolically, the protagonist carries only road warning signs and signs that must be obeyed—no directional signs. He also comes from a town that is the geographical center of Poland. In the final scene, he enters a sports stadium where the young women are practicing gymnastics for the state holiday and searches for the girl he has just met and spent the night with. Suddenly, the women form the map of Poland, and he finds himself in its middle: undecided, confused, and without direction.

In the film, *Palec Boży* (*God's Finger*, 1973), directed by Antoni Krauze (b. 1940), the protagonist is so focused on his future profession as an actor that it becomes the source of his psychological problems. Marian Opania stars as an oversensitive, small-town dreamer whose goal of becoming an actor is unfulfilled.[53] Several films also deal with juvenile crime in a realistic manner, for example, *Trąd* (*Leprosy*, 1971) and *Zapis zbrodni* (*Record of Crime*, 1974), by Andrzej Trzos-Rastawiecki (b. 1933). *Record of Crime*, in particular, refers to an actual murder case and offers a paradocumentary examination of the sociological and psychological circumstances leading to crime.

Probably the finest film concerning the younger generation was made by the Polish School generation filmmaker Janusz Morgenstern. His *Trzeba zabić tę miłość* (*Kill That Love*, 1972), scripted by Janusz Głowacki, depicts love between two young people who did not get enough points to enter the university. They start their first jobs to support themselves and to prepare for their future studies. Jadwiga Jankowska-Cieślak as Magda, a girl dreaming about becoming a doctor, created one of the most interesting characters in Polish cinema of the 1970s. The Polish reality—a degraded world in which everybody cheats—is presented in the film as an obstacle to happiness. The protagonists' love for each other is not strong enough to survive the grotesquely portrayed socialist reality. This aspect of the film owes greatly to the scriptwriter, Głowacki, who was then known for his short stories and a column published in the weekly *Kultura*. Głowacki's feel for the propagandist's newspeak, as well as his ironic and grotesque comments, enrich Morgenstern's film. *Kill That Love* also has a subplot without dialogue that comments on the action. It concerns the warehouseman, played by Jan Himilsbach, who sells cement on the black market while he is supposed to be on guard. In the film's final scene, he wants to kill his faithful dog, who barked at his "clients," by attaching a stick of dynamite to it. The dog, however, hides in a warehouse (the place where the lovers first met), and the explosion that follows serves as an ironic reference to *Zabriskie Point* (1969), a film about youth rebellion.

Kazimierz Kutz's Silesia

In the 1960s Kazimierz Kutz made a series of realistic films set in provincial Poland that received mixed reviews from the Polish critics: *Tarpany* (*Wild Horses*, 1962), *Milczenie* (*Silence*, 1963), *Ktokolwiek wie* (*Whoever Knows*, 1966), and *Skok* (*Robbery*, 1969). As always, Kutz worked against the mainstream of Polish cinema. In the decade of epic adaptations, his films were realistic pictures, new wave narrative experiments, examinations of provincial places, simple people, and everyday rituals. The failed attempt to steal money in *Robbery* is only a pretext to portray a realistic picture of young people. *Silence* describes the small-town indifference faced by a young boy who was blinded by an accident. In *Whoever Knows* a young reporter (Edward Lubaszenko) searches for a missing girl. He discovers her background and family history, the pressure of her social circle, and her alienation. Made in the spirit of Michelangelo Antonioni's early works, Kutz's film offers no solutions; the reporter simply gives up his search.

Kutz's return to his roots, his native Upper Silesia,[54] proved to be one of the most important moments in Polish postwar cinema. He produced a trilogy of personal films that form the contemporary Polish canon: *Sól ziemi czarnej* (*Salt of the Black Earth*, 1970), *Perła w koronie* (*The Pearl in the Crown*, 1972), and *Paciorki jednego różańca* (*Beads of One Rosary*, 1980). Traditionally regarded by the Warsaw-based Polish film industry as an unglamorous, unphotogenic province of hard work, coal mines, and unfamiliar history, Silesia burst into the Polish consciousness thanks to the powerful vision of Kutz. Unlike the realistic *Beads of One Rosary*, set in the late 1970s, the first two parts of the trilogy deal with modern history and the culture of Silesia. Scripted by Kutz, and with music by Wojciech Kilar, all of these films introduce authentic places and real people with local dialects, modes of thinking, and dreams. Kutz continues his interest in "simple people" with the plebeian character that he developed during the Polish School period. He does not want to follow the filmic fashions that Polish cinema slavishly emulates. As he explains, "[I]nstead of narrating about a human being, it [Polish film] relates about the cause, mostly the patriotic one, which has to elevate that person, give him some worth, and show it in the context of Polish suffering."[55]

Salt of the Black Earth deals with the Second Polish Uprising against the German rule of Silesia during August 1920.[56] The story concerns the Basista family: the patriarchal father, the silent mother and sisters, and the seven miner-brothers. The Basista family house serves as the bastion of Polishness and traditional rituals concerning family life, work, and the love for the region. The youngest son, Gabryel (Olgierd Łukaszewicz), and his coming-of-age story remain at the center of the film. The film depicts his political and sexual initiation, his love for a German nurse, and his irresponsible behavior as an insurgent in the uprising when, in a stolen German uniform, he moves into enemy territory to see the nurse. In the final days of the uprising, the wounded Gabryel is carried to the Polish border by four young women-angels.

Although the film is set during the actual political event, surprisingly it neglects politics at the cost of creating a poetic image of the province. In folk-ballad form, Kutz shows grayish images of industrial Silesia—coal mines, piles of waste coal, steelworks, and railway tracks—contrasted with the reddish color of miners' brick houses.[57] The regional costumes, folk art, chants, everyday rituals, and customs enhance the authenticity.

Several compositions of the frame resemble medieval, perhaps naive, paintings. Rafał Marszałek justly compares the symbolism of Kutz in *Salt of the Black Earth* with that of Sergei Paradzhanov in *Sayat-nova* (*The Color of Pomegranates*, 1969, released in 1972). In both films, everyday rituals are full of symbolic meaning.[58] While agreeing with Marszałek's comment, I would also like to point out similarities with Miklós Jancsó's 1960s Hungarian films. Both filmmakers use similar rhythms, symbolism, and choreographed movements of actors. For example, in the final sequence of Kutz's film, the defeated and encircled insurgents try to break through German positions to reach the nearby Polish border. They rip off their jackets in the futile hope of running faster. The bullets strike them in the back, and their white shirts get soaked with red blood—the colors of the Polish flag. The scene, shown partly in slow motion, was filmed with a handheld camera for point-of-view shots. Finally, the street is white and red, covered by fallen insurgents. Gabryel's nurse moves among the dead and the wounded, beginning her work. In the next scene, while some insurgents lie dead in the street, their bodies arranged in an orderly manner like animals killed after the hunt, the execution of others begins. There are, obviously, numerous differences between the styles of Kutz and Jancso. Wiesław Zdort's camera in *Salt of the Black Earth* is not circling; there is no elaborate panning, lengthy take, or tracking. Unlike Jancso's solemn metaphorical imagery, Kutz's film introduces comic interludes during fights, and folk festivities between them. Kutz portrays death as an everyday phenomenon, and utilizes pointed, sometimes crude, dialogues in the Silesian dialect. The composition of frame relies primarily on long shots with distant figures of insurgents moving through the industrial landscape. The characters, however, are not alienated from this landscape; the mise en scène stresses that the characters belong there.

Kutz juxtaposes the images of industrial Silesia with the pastoral vision of Poland. For example, when Gabryel conquers a German tower, he looks through a military telescope at the idyllic landscapes of nearby Poland: the tranquil splendor of green valleys and the dangerous beauty of the mountains. Kutz also pictures the pragmatism of the Silesians, which clashes with the traditional Polish romanticism. The uprising is portrayed almost like a job that must be done, and patriotism is understood as love for the region. The Basista brothers go to the uprising without any romantic notions; when overpowered by the Germans, the commander of the insurgent unit, Erwin (Jan Englert), simply announces the end of the uprising. This pragmatic approach is contrasted sharply with the idealism of a young Polish artillery officer (Daniel Olbrychski), as handsome as a figure in a romantic chromolithograph, who helps the miners against orders and dies a clichéd, romantic death. His appearance, short participation in the uprising, and death and burial epitomize the essence of traditional Polish romantic ideals. Commenting on the differences between Silesia and Poland, Kutz observes:

Figure 6.7 A scene from Kazimierz Kutz's *Salt of the Black Earth* (1970)

Poland appears to us as a land of gentry, the nobility living in whitewashed manors, with obedient and backward peasantry dependent on them. The peasants are educated by virtuous maidens who do so because of a shortage of more useful occupations. In a sentence, this is a country where work is not the basis of existence. In my memory, there was nothing like that in Silesia. I grew up in a world of concrete work, in a harrowing landscape, and my surrounding was always the family group, generations living in the same place, and inheriting professions and the customs.[59]

The second part of the trilogy, *The Pearl in the Crown*, concerns the coal miners' strike in the 1930s, which was brought on by the closure of their mine, Zygmunt. Although this part of Silesia now belongs to Poland, the mines are administered by German owners and protected by Polish police. The miners try to prevent the flooding of their mine by occupying it. When negotiations fail, they continue with a hunger strike. The film's protagonist, Jaś (Olgierd Łukaszewicz), remains with the strikers out of solidarity, although he would rather have stayed at home with his wife Wichta (Łucja Kowolik) and their two small sons. The strikers, led by their leader, Hubert Siersza (Franciszek Pieczka), are supported by the Silesians on the ground and organized by Erwin (Jan Englert), the former insurgent in *Salt of the Black Earth*, now unemployed. The first sequences of the film portray the harsh reality of the economic crisis, the closure of the mines, and the small coal pits run by the unemployed miners.

Figure 6.8 Kazimierz Kutz's *The Pearl in the Crown* (1972). Łucja Kowolik as Wichta and Jan Englert as Erwin (in the middle)

The Pearl in the Crown provides discourses on class solidarity, family ties, tradition, love for one's family, and love for the land. The film also serves as a powerful love story: the intensity of its lyricism and eroticism is probably unparalleled in Polish cinema. As in *Salt of the Black Earth*, Kutz portrays Silesia—a region traditionally seen as colorless and almost inhuman—in a poetic, folk-ballad manner. Similarly, he glorifies the traditions and celebrates the patriarchal order with highly stylized images. Simple, everyday rituals attain a symbolic meaning. For example, the protagonist's sons always wait for him after work and escort him home, where his wife washes his feet and assists with his bath. Further links with the first part of the trilogy are established by using the same actors, such as Olgierd Łukaszewicz, Jan Englert, and the "Silesian actors"— Jerzy Cnota and Bernard Krawczyk.

In *The Pearl in the Crown*, Kutz moves further into stylization, symbolism, and mythologization of everyday rituals. He introduces authentic people playing themselves, speaking their own dialects and celebrating their own customs. Kutz claims without exaggeration that his films could be called scientific ethnographic works.[60] With the help of his cinematographer, Stanisław Loth, the director also relies on contrast, this time between the harsh reality inside the mine (blackness, hunger strike) and the colorful reality on the ground (the picturesque crowd waiting for the strikers). Kutz also shows the differences between the happiness of the protagonist's home and the brutal reality outside. In the course of the film, the juxtaposition of the gloomy underworld of the mine and the vibrant world outside gains more and more importance: "[T]he more the miners melt into a black, amorphous mass, the more replete with the bright colours of regional costume becomes the world of the surface."[61] In the final scene, the triumphant strikers—exhausted, deprived of food and oxygen, and holding each other—emerge from the shaft of the coal mine to face an almost medieval carnival in front of the mine: the colorful crowd in folk costumes, exotic animals, and a brass orchestra.

The realistic picture of Silesia portrayed in *Beads of One Rosary* is the story of a retired miner, Karol Habryka (Augustyn Halotta), who does not want to leave his old house, scheduled for demolition, and move to a new apartment building. In his house, Habryka recalls that he "has survived the two world wars, the emperor, unemployment, strikes, different debasements, Hitler, and other humiliations." The protagonist belongs to the insurgents generation (he also took part in the Silesian Uprising), yet to the authorities, his refusal to leave his home constitutes an example of antisocial behavior. Finally, recognizing his glorious past (he was also an exemplary miner), the authorities give him a modern house in which he feels completely out of place. A few months after moving, Habryka dies. His burial, and the burial of old culture, is Kutz's farewell to the old Silesia.

As in his two previous "Silesian films," Kutz elevates ordinary activities, such as having breakfast and pipe smoking, and grants them symbolic status. He also relies on nonprofessional actors from Silesia, this time casting them in the leading roles (Halotta, and Marta Straszna as Habryka's wife). Their personalities, feeling for the local dialect, peculiar humor, and behavior create the intimate atmosphere of this film.[62]

Comedies

Alicja Helman writes in 1971 that "we have cultivated an art film whose makers cannot produce popular culture."[63] After 1961, however, comedies began to play a more important role in Polish cinema. Between 1961 and 1965, twenty-four films were listed as comedies, out of the 119 produced.[64] This genre gained immediate prominence on television, as well. *Kabaret Starszych Panów* (*Cabaret of Elderly Gentlemen*), created by writer Jeremi Przybora and composer Jerzy Wasowski (the two "elderly gentlemen" of the title), featured some of the best Polish actors: Wiesław Michnikowski, Mieczysław Czechowicz, Kalina Jędrusik, Wiesław Gołas, Irena Kwiatkowska, among others. The absurdist, sophisticated, and elegant humor of Przybora and Wasowski, and their delicate mockery of the communist reality, can also be seen in the full-length comedy *Upał* (*Heat*, 1964), directed by Kazimierz Kutz, which continues with the same formula as the cabaret.

Comedies were very popular among the Polish audiences, yet rarely appreciated by the critics, who awaited the next *Ewa Wants to Sleep* or *Treasure*. The names of Tadeusz Chmielewski, Stanisław Bareja, and Sylwester Chęciński became synonymous with comedy, although these filmmakers were also working in other genres. Chmielewski's *Gdzie jest generał?* (*Where Is the General?* 1964), *Jak rozpętałem II wojnę światową* (*How I Started the Second World War*, three parts, 1970), and *Nie lubię poniedziałku* (*I Hate Mondays*, 1971), despite their popularity, never achieved the critical success of his *Ewa Wants to Sleep*. Chęciński (b. 1930) became more successful with his trilogy scripted by Andrzej Mularczyk: *Sami swoi* (*All Among Ourselves*, 1967), *Nie ma mocnych* (*Big Deal*, 1974), and *Kochaj albo rzuć* (*Love It or Leave It*, 1977). These three films are now considered classics of Polish comedy. They are structured around a feud between two families who, due to postwar politics and changing borders, were transplanted from their eastern village to the Polish western "Regained Lands." Kazimierz Pawlak (Wacław Kowalski) and Władysław Kargul (Władysław Hańcza), the two heads of the quarrelling families, seem inseparable—they fight yet they cannot live without each other. The situational humor of these comedies, their tempo, the protagonists' accent, which plays a prominent role in their witty dialogues—all contributed to the box-office success of these films.[65]

The majority of Polish comedies in the late 1960s and at the beginning of the 1970s were highly didactic. Unable to laugh openly at political and social issues, they portrayed, as Iwona Rammel notes, a "wishful thinking" reality. As she writes, the film protagonists frequently travel to the

West (a prospect unattainable for the majority of Poles), only to stress the authorities' desired message that "there is nothing like home," and that "there is no place for sincere Poles in the West." When Polish comedies feature love across the borders, for example in *Żona dla Australijczyka* (*The Wife for an Australian*, 1964, Stanisław Bareja), the love "never jeopardizes our political alliances."[66] Comedies of the 1960s and the 1970s range from situational comedies, such as *Rzeczpospolita babska* (*Women's Republic*, 1969, Hieronim Przybył), set during the postwar period and focusing on the gender relations between male and female veterans who have settled on two neighboring farms, to satires such as Andrzej Wajda's *Polowanie na muchy* (*Hunting Flies*, 1969).

Among the many attempts at comedy, one stands out from the rest: *Rejs* (*The Cruise*, 1970), directed by Marek Piwowski (b. 1935), who also scripted the film with Janusz Głowacki. The film took the Polish critics by surprise, and their opinions were initially polarized. Today, this is one of a few cult films in Poland. At first glance, Piwowski's film appears to be an amateurish production without an underlying structure due to its improvised dialogues and quasi-documentary look, and the presence of nonprofessional actors/types. *The Cruise* portrays a group of people on board the *Dzerzhinsky* during a leisurely tour on the river. The film clearly serves as a Polish parable; its situational humor and dialogues refer to the current political reality and laugh at the schizophrenic absurdities of communist Poland. Piwowski's film speaks with an idiom distinctly Polish, virtually inaccessible to a Westerner. It is a satire on communism with its references to newspeak, the Gomułka epoch, and the private and official truth. It also serves as a satire on any totalitarian system, a "bitter comedy about a collective escape from freedom."[67]

Influenced by the poetics of Jacques Tati's *Les Vacances de Monsieur Hulot* (1953), and the early films by Miloš Forman, *The Cruise* features a number of standup comedians, as well as nonprofessional and professional actors. In a memorable scene, Zdzisław Maklakiewicz as the engineer Mamoń delivers a frequently cited talk about the misery of Polish cinema: "In Polish film it is as follows: boredom … nothing happens … poor dialogues, very poor dialogues … in general, there is no action, nothing happens. One wonders why do they not copy foreign films." Maklakiewicz, paired with another actor from Piwowski's film, Jan Himilsbach, also appears in Andrzej Kondratiuk's productions: the television cult film *Wniebowzięci* (*The Ascended*, 1973), and *Jak to się robi* (*How to Do It*, 1974).

* * * *

Polish cinema of the 1960s and 1970s was also shaped by other filmmakers who were determined to continue their personal style. For example, Tadeusz Konwicki's *Jak daleko stąd, jak blisko* (*How Far from Here, Yet How Near*, 1972) is, like his novels, a filmic essay replete with autobiographical features, an "illogical" film narrative that is "governed by laws of dream."[68]

The oneiric narrative of Konwicki mixes different genres and styles. Basically a poetic evocation of times past, it contains thinly veiled political observations, references to history, and the new wave narrative devices.

In the 1970s, Janusz Nasfeter (1920–1998) continued to make important films, which were primarily addressed to children but had universal meaning, such as *Abel, twój brat* (*Abel, Your Brother*, 1970), and *Motyle* (*Butterflies*, 1973). A versatile filmmaker, he also succeeded in making a psychological war drama, *Weekend z dziewczyną* (*Weekend with a Girl*, 1968), as well as a crime film, *Zbrodniarz i panna* (*The Criminal and the Maiden*, 1963), starring Ewa Krzyżewska and Zbigniew Cybulski. One of his most interesting works, however, remains *Niekochana* (*Unloved*, 1966), based on Adolf Rudnicki's short story. It deals with the unhappy, obsessive and damaging love of a Jewess, Noemi (Elżbieta Czyżewska), for a Polish fine arts student, Kamil (Janusz Guttner). Taking place before the war, the film portrays the story of their separations and reunions, and her mental breakdown, set against the background of claustrophobic corridors, streets, and unappealing rooms. Noemi's love destroys her life; in the last scene of the film, she faces the outbreak of the war alone and depressed.

In the mid-1970s, a growing number of filmmakers became interested in recording reality and favored the style of documentary cinema. Television films such as Krzysztof Kieślowski's *Personel* (*Personnel*, 1975) and Wojciech Wiszniewski's *Historia pewnej miłości* (*The Story of a Certain Love*, 1974, released in 1982) heralded the tone and the thematic preoccupations of a group of films called the "Cinema of Moral Concern."

Notes

1. Krzysztof Kornacki, "Bohater w przydeptanych kapciach," in *Człowiek z ekranu. Z antropologii postaci filmowej*, ed. Mariola Jankun-Dopartowa and Mirosław Przylipiak (Cracow: Arcana, 1996), 77.
2. After leaving Poland in 1969, Aleksander Ford tried to continue his career in West Germany, Denmark, and the United States. He directed *Sie Sind Frei, Dr. Korczak* (*Dr. Korczak, the Martyr*, 1974, West Germany-Israel). In 1980 Ford committed suicide.
3. Bolesław Michałek and Frank Turaj, *The Modern Cinema of Poland* (Bloomington: Indiana University Press, 1988), 50.
4. Ryszard Koniczek, "Kultura filmowa, polityka repertuarowa i produkcyjna," in *Historia filmu polskiego 1968–1972*, vol. 6, ed. Rafał Marszałek (Warsaw: Wydawnictwa Artystyczne i Filmowe, 1994), 486.
5. Edward Zajiček, *Poza ekranem. Kinematografia polska 1918–1991* (Warsaw: Filmoteka Narodowa and Wydawnictwa Artystyczne i Filmowe, 1992), 190.
6. In the 1970s, Poland had only 21.1 cinema seats per one thousand inhabitants. Ewa Gębicka, "Sieć kin i rozpowszechnianie filmów," in *Encyklopedia kultury polskiej XX wieku: Film i kinematografia*, ed. Edward Zajiček (Warsaw: Instytut Kultury and Komitet Kinematografii, 1994), 440–441.
7. Koniczek, "Kultura filmowa," 489.
8. Ibid., 478.

9. Ryszard Kapuściński, *Lapidarium* (Warsaw: Czytelnik, 1990), 39. Quoted from Carl Tighe, "Ryszard Kapuściński and *The Emperor*," *The Modern Language Review* 91, no. 4 (1996): 933–934.
10. Tadeusz Miczka discusses the political and cultural context of Wajda's *Ashes* in his "Tekst jako 'ofiara' kontekstu," in *Syndrom konformizmu? Kino polskie lat sześćdziesiątych*, ed. Tadeusz Miczka, assistant ed. Alina Madej (Katowice: Wydawnictwo Uniwersytetu Śląskiego, 1994), 147–166. The Polish reception of *Ashes* is discussed by Andrzej Werner, "Film fabularny," in *Historia filmu polskiego 1962–1967*, vol. 5, ed. Rafał Marszałek (Warsaw: Wydawnictwa Artystyczne i Filmowe, 1985), 28–33.
11. Bolesław Michałek, *The Cinema of Andrzej Wajda* (London: Tantivy Press, 1973), 82.
12. Tadeusz Sobolewski, "100 lat kina w Polsce: 1965–1966," *Kino* 1 (1999): 52.
13. Polish ruler Mieszko I of the Piast dynasty was baptized in the year 966. Celebrations of the millennium of Poland's baptism were held in 1966.
14. *The Doll* was adapted once again in 1977, this time by Ryszard Ber for television (nine episodes).
15. Rafał Marszałek, "Film Fabularny," in Marszałek,*Historia filmu polskiego 1968–1972*, 71 .
16. The Polish-Swedish war is also portrayed in the interwar popular success *Abbot Kordecki: The Defender of Częstochowa* (1934).
17. In 1987 a list was created of the twenty films, both local and foreign, that had the most viewers in Poland. *Nights and Days* is ranked fifth with 22.3 million viewers. Figures from Małgorzata Hendrykowska, *Kronika kinematografii polskiej 1895–1997* (Poznań: Arcana, 1999), 427. Jerzy Antczak also produced a television series of *Nights and Days* (thirteen episodes), which premiered on Polish television after the theatrical release of the film.
18. The first version of Żeromski's *The Story of Sin* was made in 1911 by Antoni Bednarczyk (the film is lost). The second adaptation was produced in 1933 by Henryk Szaro.
19. Michałek, *The Cinema of Andrzej Wajda*, 99.
20. Konrad Eberhardt, "Wajda – epoka błękitna," *Ekran* 6 (1969). Quoted from Marszałek, *Historia filmu polskiego 1968–1972*, 361.
21. Paul Coates, *The Story of the Lost Reflection: The Alienation of the Image in Western and Polish Cinema* (London: Verso, 1985), 37.
22. Andrzej Wajda prepared a slightly different version of the film in 1995. He also produced a television series of *The Land of Promise*, eight one-hour-long episodes that premiered on Polish television in 1975 and 1976.
23. Wajda's adaptations are discussed extensively in Ewelina Nurczyńska-Fidelska's book, *Polska klasyka literacka według Andrzeja Wajdy* (Katowice: Śląsk, 1998). She focuses on *Ashes*, *The Land of Promise*, *Birchwood*, *The Wedding*, and *Danton*.
24. Discussed extensively in Dariusz Chyb, "Malarstwo w filmach Andrzeja Wajdy: Brzezina," *Kino* 11 (1988): 20–25.
25. Michałek, *The Cinema of Andrzej Wajda*, 138.
26. Nurczyńska-Fidelska, *Polska klasyka literacka według Andrzeja Wajdy*, 162.
27. Tadeusz Miczka's term in his "Polskie czary," *Kwartalnik Filmowy* 18 (1997): 72. One has to stress the role of the cinematographer, Witold Sobociński, and the set designer, Tadeusz Wybult.
28. The painterly aspect of Wajda's film is discussed by, among others, Tadeusz Miczka, "Inspiracje malarskie w *Weselu* Andrzeja Wajdy. Krążenie komunikatów plastycznych w artystycznych medytacjach o historii," in *Analizy i interpretacje. Film polski*, ed. Alicja Helman and Tadeusz Miczka (Katowice: Wydawnictwo Uniwersytetu Śląskiego, 1984), 131–158; and Dariusz Chyb, "Malarstwo w filmach Andrzeja Wajdy: *Wesele*," *Kino* 12 (1988): 24–28.
29. *The Land of Promise* received an Oscar nomination in the Best Foreign Film category; it also won the Festival of Polish Films in Gdańsk and film festivals in Moscow, Valladolid, and Chicago. In 1996, *The Land of Promise* was chosen the best film in the history of Polish cinema in a popular plebiscite in the Polish monthly *Film*. See *Film* 7 (1996): 10.
30. Aleksander Jackiewicz, *Moja filmoteka: kino polskie* (Warsaw: Wydawnictwa Artystyczne i Filmowe), 357.

31. The term was coined by Jerzy Płażewski and propagated by Janusz Gazda and Konrad Eberhardt. Werner, "Film fabularny," 12.
32. Jackiewicz, *Moja filmoteka: kino polskie*, 389.
33. Marszałek, "Film fabularny," 120–121. It has to be noted, however, that innovative films were also produced by some older filmmakers, such as Władysław Ślesicki (b. 1927), better known for his classic documentary films. In 1971 he directed *Ruchome piaski* (*Shifting Sands*, 1971) with Małgorzata Braunek and Marek Walczewski in the leading roles.
34. See David A. Cook, *A History of Narrative Film* (New York: Norton, 1996), 692.
35. For example by Michael Walker, "Jerzy Skolimowski," *Second Wave* (London: Studio Vista, 1970), 34–62.
36. See Mariola Jankun-Dopartowa, "*Rysopis* jako duchowa biografia pokolenia," *Kwartalnik Filmowy* 17 (1997): 101.
37. Skolimowski discusses his method of making films in a detailed conversation with Jerzy Uszyński, "Jerzy Skolimowski o sobie. Całe życie jak na dłoni," *Film na Świecie* 373 (1990): 3–47.
38. Walker, "Jerzy Skolimowski," 40.
39. Uszyński, "Jerzy Skolimowski o sobie," 8.
40. This aspect is indicated in the very title of Mariola Jankun-Dopartowa's essay, "*Rysopis* jako duchowa biografia pokolenia" [*Identification Marks: None* as a spiritual generational biography], 98.
41. Walker, "Jerzy Skolimowski," 48.
42. Paul Coates, *The Story of the Lost Reflection*, 140.
43. Bolesław Michałek and Frank Turaj stress this aspect of Zanussi by titling the chapter on him: "Krzysztof Zanussi: The Cinema of Intellectual Inquiry," *The Modern Cinema of Poland*, 173–195.
44. Tadeusz Sobolewski's term ("Zanussoid") used in his review of *The Touch*: "Zanussi: Posłaniec," *Kino* 10 (1992): 10–11.
45. Jackiewicz, *Moja filmoteka: kino polskie*, 421.
46. Marszałek, "Film fabularny," 118.
47. According to St. Augustine, our cognition does not depend on our intellectual activities or senses but on illumination granted by God. The philosophical aspect of the film is discussed by Łukasz Plesnar, "W poszukiwaniu absolutu (*Iluminacja* Krzysztofa Zanussiego)," in Helman and Miczka, *Analizy i interpretacje*, 179–191.
48. Krzysztof Zanussi, "Iluminacja: nowela filmowa," *Kino* 5 (1973): 25.
49. Jackiewicz, *Moja filmoteka: kino polskie*, 427.
50. Kluba's presentation of the conflict between the villagers and the communist authorities was the main reason behind the shelving of this film. The director had to change the ending three times before the film was released after five years. Marszałek, "Film fabularny," 91–92.
51. Grzegorz Królikiewicz is the author of a theoretical study on the off-screen space, "Przestrzeń filmowa poza kadrem," published in *Kino* 11 (1972): 25–28 [the text was written in 1968]. Królikiewicz is also known for a series of books—detailed examinations of film masterpieces.
52. For example, Jackiewicz, *Moja filmoteka: kino polskie*, 401.
53. Antoni Krauze previously made television films such as *Monidło* (1970), and *Meta* (*Shelter*, 1971, released in 1981), both adaptations of Jan Himilsbach's and Marek Nowakowski's fiction, respectively.
54. Kazimierz Kutz was born in 1929 in Szopienice (today part of Katowice). He was the founder and the head of the film studio Silesia between 1972–1978, and later the cofounder and head of the Silesian Film Society (1981–1988), as well as a lecturer at the Katowice Film School (1979–1982).
55. Elżbieta Baniewicz, *Kazimierz Kutz: z dołu widać inaczej* (Warsaw: Wydawnictwa Artystyczne i Filmowe, 1994), 177.
56. The First Polish Upising in Upper Silesia took place in August 1919; the third, which followed the March Plebiscite in Upper Silesia, broke out in May 1921.

57. The set design for the first two parts of the trilogy was created by Bolesław Kamykowski.
58. Marszałek, "Film fabularny," 66.
59. Baniewicz, *Kazimierz Kutz*, 166.
60. Ibid., 193.
61. Elżbieta Ostrowska, "Silesian Landscapes of Kazimierz Kutz," in *Polish Cinema in Ten Takes*, ed. Ewelina Nurczyńska-Fidelska and Zbigniew Batko (Łódź: Łódzkie Towarzystwo Naukowe, 1995), 90.
62. The Silesian themes return in Kutz's later films: *Na straży swej stać będę* (*I Will Stand on my Guard*, 1983), *Śmierć jak kromka chleba* (*Death as a Slice of Bread*, 1994), and *Zawrócony* (*The Turned Back*, 1994). To be discussed later in the book.
63. Alicja Helman, "Start i po starcie," *Kino* 4 (1971). Quoted from Iwona Rammel, "Dobranoc ojczyzno kochana, już pora na sen…. Komedia filmowa lat sześćdziesiątych," in Miczka and Madej, *Syndrom konformizmu?*, 63.
64. Rammel, "Dobranoc ojczyzno kochana …," 59. Citing figures from the 1976 *Kino* article by Edward Zajiček, Rammel remarks that several films labeled as "comedies" did not meet generic expectations—they were not funny.
65. Sylwester Chęciński's *Big Deal* and *Love It or Leave It* belong to the most popular films ever screened in Poland. According to 1987 figures, the former is listed twentieth and the latter seventeenth in popularity. Quoted from Hendrykowska, *Kronika kinematografii polskiej 1895–1997*, 427.
66. Rammel, "Dobranoc ojczyzno kochana …," 66–67.
67. Małgorzata Hendrykowska, "100 lat kina w Polsce: 1969–1970," *Kino* 3 (1999): 49.
68. Alicja Helman, "*Jak daleko stąd, jak blisko*: analiza kilku wybranych motywów," *Kino* 4 (1972): 18.

7

Camouflage and Rough Treatment
The "Cinema of Distrust," the Solidarity Period,
and Afterwards

> If we were to judge only by their films, the Poles would seem the most
> depressed people on earth.
>
> *Gerald Pratley*[1]

The era of relative prosperity under Edward Gierek was gradually coming to an end in the late 1970s. The strikes in June 1976, caused by the introduction of price increases, signaled the decline of the Gierek regime. The archbishop of Cracow, Karol Wojtyła, was elected pope as John Paul II in October 1978, and he made his first pilgrimage to Poland the following year. The workers' protest that erupted in August 1980 culminated in the emergence of a mass-supported movement, *Solidarność* (Solidarity), headed by the future Polish president Lech Wałęsa. In September 1980, Edward Gierek was replaced by Stanisław Kania as the new party first secretary. The period of Solidarity ended on 13 December 1981 with the imposition of martial law by General Wojciech Jaruzelski. Eighteen months of curfew and militarized administration were followed by the so-called "period of normalization" (1983–1986). Despite the name, this was an era of political struggle to change the system, an era of hopelessness, economic stagnation, and harsh living conditions.

The late 1970s in Poland signaled another generational change of guard in Polish cinema: the advent of filmmakers born after the war, whose first major political initiation were the March Events of 1968. The collection of essays written by two Polish poets, Julian Kornhauser and Adam Zagajewski, *Świat nie przedstawiony* (*The Unrepresented World*, 1974),[2] became the manifesto and the theoretical formula for the generation sometimes known as the "Young Culture" (*Młoda Kultura*) formation.[3] In an essay on postwar Polish literature, Zagajewski writes that the most basic disparity in Polish culture is between "what is and what should be; the disparity between the dreamed picture of the society, between the idealized picture of human personality and the actual state of things, full of conflicts and animosity in relations between people.... Due to the fact that what exists remains unrecognized, the very existence of reality is incomplete and lame, because to exist means to be described in culture."[4] Polish artistic life in the late 1970s was characterized by the presence of the official and the unofficial culture. The former was approved and censored by the state, and the latter existed in opposition to the communist regime. The lines between the two spheres of culture were often blurred.

The absence of life "as it is" on Polish screens prompted audiences to practice allegorical Aesopian reading.[5] The audiences often looked for references, frequently nonexisting ones, to Polish reality. The need to describe the unrepresented world, the world not present in official arts, had been advocated by a number of filmmakers. In publications and interviews they strongly manifested their generational bonds. Agnieszka Holland explains: "I know that this was the formation created thanks to a certain generational experience—the meeting of people sharing a similar sensibility and a strong need to receive feedback from the audience. This was not the film criticism that invented 'moral concern.'... This phenomenon was not artificial; it truly existed on the basis of 'social request.' It was created by the viewers."[6]

The corrupted side of communism was explored in the late 1970s by a group of films called the "Cinema of Moral Concern" (*Kino moralnego niepokoju*).[7] The term was coined by the filmmaker Janusz Kijowski (b. 1948), and Andrzej Wajda first used it in a public speech delivered at the 1979 Festival of Polish Films.[8] The term refers to realistic films that examine contemporary issues and were made primarily between 1976 and 1981 by, among others, established masters like Krzysztof Zanussi and Andrzej Wajda, and young filmmakers such as Krzysztof Kieślowski (1941–1996), Feliks Falk (b. 1941), Piotr Andrejew (b. 1947), Agnieszka Holland (b. 1948), Janusz Kijowski, and Janusz Zaorski.

Several Polish critics and filmmakers have objected to the term "Cinema of Moral Concern." Polish scholar Mariola Jankun-Dopartowa proposes a new label, "Cinema of Distrust" (*Kino nieufności*), to describe films characterized by contemporary themes, realism, and the social initiation of a young protagonist.[9] Jankun-Dopartowa explains that the term refers only to a group of selected films made during this period: Krzysztof Zanussi's *Camouflage* (1977); Feliks Falk's *Wodzirej* (*Top Dog*, 1978) and *Szansa* (*Chance*, 1980); Janusz Kijowski's *Indeks* (*Index*, 1977, released in 1981) and *Kung-fu* (1980); Agnieszka Holland's *Aktorzy prowincjonalni* (*Provincial Actors*, 1979); and Krzysztof Kieślowski's *Amator* (*Camera Buff*, 1979). Jankun-Dopartowa also includes Andrzej Wajda's *Bez znieczulenia* (*Rough Treatment*, 1978) and *Dyrygent* (*Conductor*, 1980); Marcel Łoziński's *Jak żyć?* (*How Are We to Live?* 1977, premiere in 1981); Piotr Andrejew's *Klinch* (*Clinch*, 1979); and the later continuations of the Cinema of Distrust:

Barbara Sass's *Bez miłości* (*Without Love*, 1980), and Janusz Zaorski's *Dziecinne pytania* (*Child's Questions*, 1981).[10]

This series of contemporary realistic films centers around the conflict between the state and the individual, and examines the massive gap between the "progressive" postulates and their implementation. Due to state censorship, the system is not attacked directly; the films target its institutions and functionaries, and focus on corruption and social maladies. The mechanisms of manipulation and indoctrination are examined on a metaphorical level. The summer camp in *Camouflage* and *How Are We to Live*, school in *Chance*, the world of show business in *Top Dog*, sport in *Clinch*, and the media in *Rough Treatment* and *Without Love* serve as a microcosm of Polish society. These films also portray the emergence of the arrogant communist elites, hypocrisy, conformity, and other social and political effects of the communist system. Often set in provincial Poland (perhaps to indicate that these problems are far from the center), they provide thinly veiled allusions to the political and social present.

In the second part of the 1970s, several documentary and narrative films attempted to uncover the unrepresented reality and to examine social issues. Interestingly, some of them were produced by Polish television, the institution usually associated with manipulation and indoctrination. Kieślowski's autobiographical *Personnel*,[11] for example, deals with the issue of being loyal to one's convictions in the manner of documentary cinema. Also, a group of television series were built around everyday problems, ranging from the problems of factory managers, *Dyrektorzy* (*Directors*, six episodes, 1975, Zbigniew Chmielewski), to the humorous depiction of life during the Gierek period, *Czterdziestolatek* (*The Forty-Year-Old*, twenty-one episodes, 1974–1976, Jerzy Gruza). Reality was far better represented in documentary cinema. A number of films dealing with everyday hardships, social pathologies, and the world of cynicism and incompetence were shelved by the authorities, and were not released until the Solidarity period. Some of the finest examples include: Marcel Łoziński's *Próba mikrofonu* (*Microphone Test*, 1980); Irena Kamieńska's *Robotnice* (*Female Workers*, 1980); Piotr Szulkin's *Kobiety pracujące* (*Working Women*, 1978); Krzysztof Kieślowski's *Z punktu widzenia nocnego portiera* (*From the Point of View of the Night Porter*, 1977); and Tomasz Zygadło's *Mikrofon dla wszystkich* (*Microphone for Everybody*, 1976). Later, Zygadło (b. 1947) made realistic narrative films, including *Rebus* (1977) and the more complex *Ćma* (*The Moth*, 1980). In the latter, Roman Wilhelmi stars as the broadcaster of an all-night radio talk show, whose own personal problems reflect those of his listeners. The concern for real life and authentic characters is also present in Krzysztof Wojciechowski's narrative films. In *Kochajmy się* (*Let Us Love*, 1974), and later in *Róg Brzeskiej i Capri* (*The Corner of Brzeska and Capri*, 1980), he employs a cast of nonprofessional actors and offers an almost "ethnographic experience" concerned with, respectively, the developing village and the impoverished working-class Warsaw suburb.[12]

In 1976 Kieślowski made two feature films that reflect the 1970s reality in Poland: *Blizna* (*The Scar*, 1976) and *Spokój* (*Calm*, 1976, released in 1980). Although critical about the former film (he calls it a socialist realist film *à rebours*),[13] Kieślowski succeeds in portraying a multifaceted, well-meaning manager of a huge chemical industrial complex, Bednarz (Franciszek Pieczka). The manager returns from Silesia to his small hometown to build a huge chemical industrial complex despite the opposition of the local residents. The realistic, sometimes even paradocumentary, portrayal of the Polish managerial class and the atmosphere surrounding typical "communist sites" are well balanced and devoid of clichés.

Jerzy Stuhr (b. 1947), who plays a supporting role in *The Scar* as an opportunistic assistant to director Bednarz, appears in the leading role in *The Calm*. He stars as Antoni Gralak, a simple man, recently released from prison, who wants to lead a calm life and stay out of trouble. He explains his dreams to his new colleagues: "[A] woman, children, a place of one's own." The reality, however, offers him no such chance. He is caught in the middle of the growing conflict between the director of the small plant, where he was employed in spite of his prison record, and his fellow workers. The protagonist is rejected by both sides—manipulated by the management, and beaten by his colleagues in the final scene of the film. The painful realism of Kieślowski's film and the inclusion of some forbidden images (a strike and prisoners working outside of a prison) resulted in the belated premiere of this modest yet superb film.

Zanussi's *Camouflage* and Andrzej Wajda's *Człowiek z marmuru* (*Man of Marble*)—two internationally known films that were made in 1976 and released at the beginning of 1977—had the biggest impact on the Cinema of Distrust filmmakers.[14] Wajda's search for a sincere picture of the Stalinist era, based on the script written by Aleksander Ścibor-Rylski, suffered from the restrictions imposed by the communist state. Although it was not banned, the film was shown in only a limited number of copies, and was not considered for awards by the jury at the Festival of Polish Films in Gdańsk.[15] Basically a film about Stalinism and disillusionment with the communist ideology, *Man of Marble* also serves as a portrait of the totalitarian mentality and manipulation in the 1970s. Two of the most forceful characters in Polish cinema are the model bricklayer Mateusz Birkut (Jerzy Radziwiłłowicz) and the young film director Agnieszka (Krystyna Janda), who uncovers the Stalinist era in Poland. Wajda's film later influenced a number of films dealing with the Stalinist past, made by a group of young filmmakers during the Solidarity period.[16]

Zanussi continued his cerebral, documentary-like style in *Camouflage*, a film set at a linguistics summer camp that portrays the conformity of the Polish intelligentsia. Unlike Zanussi's previous philosophical examinations of moral issues, *Camouflage* is more of a political and social satire. For the majority of Polish viewers in 1977, the film served as a clear metaphor for Polish society and an allegory of the corruptive nature of the system. Zanussi stresses, however, that this film has a universal meaning: "My film deals with a broader phenomenon, which I attempted to show in an individual case. This phenomenon refers not only to a university, and not only to our country."[17]

The film is built around a psychological struggle between two academics: the pragmatic and cynical middle-aged professor Jakub Szelestowski (Zbigniew Zapasiewicz), and the younger and idealistic teaching assistant Jarosław Kruszyński (Piotr Garlicki). Like other films by Zanussi, *Camouflage* examines the confrontation of two moral stands, perhaps just the two stages of the development of the same character. The cynical, almost devilish professor tests the young assistant, and tries to deprive him of illusions about life. Their conversations, often taking place in the tranquil milieu of the summer camp, form the main part of the film. In *Camouflage* both the students and their teachers are portrayed as pitiful characters who deserve their fate—conformists subjected to manipulation who change their colors rather than fight, and hide rather than attack. The title of the film introduces the theme of social and political mimicry—by referencing creatures who resort to camouflage to hide and stalk—and it is later reinforced by the professor's frequent comments on the natural

Figure 7.1 Zbigniew Zapasiewicz (Professor, on the left) and Piotr Garlicki (Teaching Assistant) in Krzysztof Zanussi's *Camouflage* (1977)

world. Marcel Łoziński depicts a similar milieu and theme of manipulation (set in a summer camp for young couples) in a paradocumentary film *How Are We to Live?*

The themes of manipulation and corruption appear in a number of films, for example, in Piotr Andrejew's *Clinch*, a film about the corrupt world of boxing, starring Tomasz Lengren.[18] The world of show business also serves as a metaphor for the Polish reality in Feliks Falk's *Top Dog*. This film narrates the story of Lutek Danielak (Jerzy Stuhr), the ruthless dance leader in a provincial town, and his climb to power in the world of Polish small town entertainment. Danielak's ambition is to lead an anniversary ball in his town, which will be broadcast by television. In order to get this job, he eliminates his rivals by employing blackmail, payoff, anonymous letters, and the betrayal of his friend, and by offering his sexual services. The emblematic Polish actor of the late 1970s, Jerzy Stuhr, known for his feel for everyday language, must be largely credited as the coauthor of this film. His monstrous yet sympathetic character never rests, running from place to place to entertain people, to give them "what they want."

The world of theater also serves as a coded image of the country and as a microcosm of Polish society. *Zdjęcia próbne* (*Screen Tests*, 1977), directed by Agnieszka Holland, Paweł Kędzierski, and Jerzy Domaradzki,[19] depicts young and aspiring film actors. Holland in *Provincial Actors* depicts a group of dissatisfied young actors unable to fulfill their artistic dreams. The relationship between Anna (Halina Łabonarska), a puppet theater actress, and Krzysztof (Tadeusz Huk), the most talented actor in a provincial theater, is permeated with an aura of hopelessness; their lives are full of professional and personal frustrations. The staging of Stanisław Wyspiański's classic, *Wyzwolenie* (*Liberation*), in spite of the initial outburst of creative freedom, brings Krzysztof only disappointment; his and other actors' hopes for personal liberation turn sour. The spectacle becomes yet another safe "avant-garde" event devoid of references to contemporary life.

The world of journalism (a traditional Polish villain during the late 1970s and afterwards) is portrayed in *Without Love*, the first feature film directed by Barbara Sass. The aggressive female journalist Ewa Bracka (Dorota Stalińska) yearns for a career at all costs. Like Danielak in *Top Dog*, she hurts other people and herself to achieve her goals. She loses her faith in love and other values to be "tougher then men." Stalińska (b. 1953), the star of Barbara Sass's early works, creates the portrait of a "liberated woman" who is "extremely dynamic, rarely reflects, instead works too much," and "tries not to show her weaknesses, even to herself."[20] Her next performances—as a sturdy young woman who is without family and real friends in *Debiutantka* (*Debutante*, 1982) and in *Krzyk* (*The Shout*, 1983)—were equally successful. The former film describes the professional initiation of a young female architect who is manipulated by her boss. The latter narrates the story of a young female ex-convict who is trying to get rid of her circle of friends and family and lead a normal life. Both films are set in 1981 and depict an unattractive reality. Although devoid of direct references to politics, they reflect the atmosphere of the Solidarity period.

Andrzej Wajda's *Rough Treatment* (aka *Without Anesthesia*) introduces another representative of the media, Jerzy Michałowski (Zbigniew Zapasiewicz), a middle-aged journalist who specializes in foreign affairs. A politically incorrect comment broadcast on television causes his fall from grace. The film centers on Michałowski 's professional and personal downfall: he no longer can lecture at the university, he loses some small personal privileges (for example, his supply of foreign newspapers), and his wife Ewa (Ewa Dałkowska) leaves him for her younger lover (Andrzej Seweryn), who is a career-oriented, hard-line party activist. Political and personal pressures prove too much for Michałowski, who falls into alcoholism and is consoled by a young female student. Ambiguity surrounds his loss of a career as well as his later death, supposedly accidental (an explosion of a gas stove). Co-scripted by Wajda and Holland, *Rough Treatment* deals with a Polish-style "conspiracy theory." When the protagonist's privileges are stripped away and he is deserted by his wife, he discovers the oppressive side of the system, which formerly favored him. "How are you going to prove what isn't true?" Ewa asks her manipulative divorce lawyer (Jerzy Stuhr). His response, "Proof is never a problem," aptly describes the presented reality.

The films of the Cinema of Distrust portray stories of the generation who experienced the 1968 March Events as students. For example, Janusz Zaorski's *Child's Questions* tells the story of six university friends, their political initiation in 1968, and their adult battleground—the Gierek era. Another film, Janusz Kijowski's *Index*, introduces a student, Józef Moneta (Krzysztof Zaleski), who is expelled from the university for defending a fellow student who participated in the March Events and was ousted from the university. Unwilling to compromise, Moneta works as a laborer and writes a novel. Later, as a high school teacher, the disillusioned protagonist punishes an equally rebellious student. The protagonists in both *Index* and *Child's Questions* are portrayed as struggling to maintain their moral views during the period of communist conformity.

Camera Buff, Kieślowski's first internationally acclaimed film, remains the most intricate work of that period. This deceptively simple story introduces an ordinary man working in a factory. Filip Mosz (Jerzy Stuhr) buys an 8mm camera and becomes preoccupied with the world around him. He begins with a home movie that documents the birth and the first months of his baby daughter. Then he becomes involved in making films about his factory and his small town. The camera enables him to see more, to go beyond the façade of things. He begins to read more, to learn, and to make films not necessarily expected by the small town bosses. Gradually, Filip learns the responsibilities of being a filmmaker. One of his films destroys the career of some other people, including his friend and supervisor Osuch (Jerzy Nowak). As a result, the shaken Filip destroys his new film produced for the television. His problems as a filmmaker are paralleled by his personal problems; the more he focuses on filmmaking, the more estranged he becomes from his wife, who finally leaves him, taking their daughter with her. In the frequently cited final scene, the disappointed protagonist takes his new 16mm camera and turns it on himself.

Kieślowski's film is self-reflective—a meditation on filmmaking, its pleasures and dangers, as well as the responsibilities of being an artist. When, in the last scene, the protagonist puts the camera in front of himself, Kieślowski explains that he "simply realizes that, as an amateur filmmaker, he's found himself in a trap and that, making films with good intentions, he might prove useful to people who'll use the films with bad

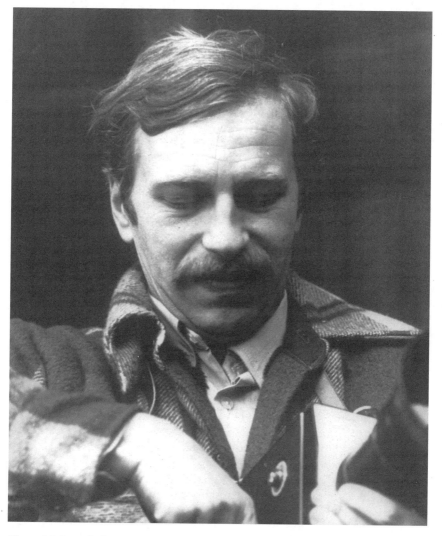

Figure 7.2 Jerzy Stuhr in Krzysztof Kieślowski's *Camera Buff* (1979)

intentions."[21] *Camera Buff* examines the impact of film on one's life, the process of self-discovery through the arts, and the pressures of censorship. The problems that the protagonist encounters parallel the problems of the Polish professional filmmaking community. As if to stress Zanussi's importance for the Polish film community, and for Kieślowski himself (he made *Camera Buff* for the Tor Studio headed by Zanussi since 1979), Zanussi participates in a meeting after a screening of his *Camouflage*, and comments on the filmmakers' moral obligations. Later Zanussi visits Filip's amateurish film club and offers some practical advice. The film also features Andrzej Jurga (a filmmaker and a professor at the Katowice Film School) as himself.

Several films made during the period in question share a number of thematic similarities with the Cinema of Distrust. For example, in his two films released in 1980, Zanussi deals with the issues of corruption, moral compromise, and moral choices. His *Kontrakt* (*Contract*) caricatures both the communist nouveaux riches and the corrupt Polish intelligentsia. Zanussi's satire tells the story of a wedding that does not happen (the bride escapes from the altar), but this development does not prevent the guests from celebrating. Described as "*The Wedding* of the Solidarity period,"[22] *Contract* mocks the morally bankrupt elites of the Polish People's Republic. Another "unattractively" titled film, *Constans* (*The Constant Factor*),[23] is more in line with the tone of Zanussi's earlier films. The young idealist of the film, Witold (Tadeusz Bradecki), wants to live honestly which proves difficult in a depraved reality: the people around him are involved in petty corruption. Unwilling to compromise his standards, Witold rejects the temptation of being involved in the world of communist conformity. Zanussi, however, reveals a sense of bitter irony in the film's finale, when the protagonist by accident causes the death of a young boy.

The representatives of the Cinema of Distrust frequently emphasized the utilitarian role of their films. "We took part in something important. I had the impression then that I was making something more than a film, something more than art. This was a kind of work for the society," recalls Feliks Falk.[24] In many cases, however, this functional attitude resulted in films that lack psychological or sociological depth. For instance, the world vision presented in Kijowski's *Kung-fu* or Falk's *The Chance* is uncomplicated and sketchy. Both films deal with the 1968 generation, and show how the students' riots impact on their lives. Psychological motivation in characterization is particularly bland in *Kung-fu*. Furthermore, social phenomena in the film are inadequately described: the group of young protagonists defend their nonconformist friend against the small town coterie by using the methods of their opponents. The pro-communist schematas are often reversed, proving that when fighting an established political system, one frequently falls into its way of thinking. *The Chance* narrates the conflict between two high school teachers who represent different moral values. The struggle for the "students' souls"—between a good history teacher and a simplistic and authoritarian physical education teacher—is heavy-handed, almost socialist realist in spirit. A similar scenario is played out in Andrzej Wajda's *Conductor*, a film about an old and famous orchestra conductor who is visiting his country of origin, Poland. The conflict between the old master and an opportunistic provincial orchestra conductor is presented as the struggle between the old and the new, between the sensitive music lover and the unscrupulous careerist.

In an interview conducted in 1993, Agnieszka Holland comments: "We were delighted that we could code the message in a film that 'evil is linked with communism.' It seems that this is the basic weakness of these films."[25] Several films suffered from this schematism. The clear divisions between the positive and the negative characters, inherited from socialist realism, frequently produce types rather than real-life characters. Maria Kornatowska distinguishes the following types present in Polish cinema in the late 1970s: "the old, 'sincere' party activist, cynical youth movement activist, career-oriented opportunist, pragmatic technocrat, vile representative of the mass media (primarily television), nouveau riche cosmopolitan, and neurotic member of the intelligentsia suffering from a complex of defeat and inability."[26] As in the world of socialist realist films, there is no love and no time for love in the reality presented in the Cinema of Distrust. In this world of predominantly male characters, who are slowly entering middle age and are usually portrayed without sympathy, the female supporting characters do not "stand behind their men." They are unwilling to understand the psychological torment of the protagonist; they betray and leave him.

The films of the Cinema of Distrust tell stories that were familiar to the majority of viewers. Maria Kornatowska comments about these films: "Employing the positivist, socialist realist viewpoint, they simplified the image of the world by cleverly avoiding issues and situations that were complicated. By and large, these films did not attempt to examine ambivalent, unclear complications of reality.... They were repeating some obvious truths, the pertinence of which nobody could question: neither the authorities tirelessly trying to 'restore the country,' nor the society that was, in its majority, passively waiting for that restoration."[27]

As if to stress generational and other links, the Cinema of Distrust filmmakers appear in each other's films. For example, Agnieszka Holland has a cameo appearance as a secretary in *The Scar* and a role in Ryszard Bugajski's *Przesłuchanie* (*Interrogation*, 1982, released in 1989); Tomasz Lengren and Tomasz Zygadło act in *Personnel*; Lengren also stars in Piotr Andrejew's *Clinch*, and Zygadło in *Provincial Actors*; Krzysztof Zanussi and Andrzej Jurga appear as themselves (filmmakers-mentors) in *Camera Buff*.

Two fine actors imprinted their mark on the Cinema of Distrust: Jerzy Stuhr and Zbigniew Zapasiewicz. The versatile Stuhr, with an ear for real-life dialogue (he is often credited as a writer)[28] created a panorama of characters ranging from uprooted careerists (*The Scar, Top Dog, Rough Treatment*) and people struggling with the pressure of politics and everyday hardship

(*Calm*) to passionate and sincere ordinary characters (*Camera Buff*). Zapasiewicz continued his characterization of a pragmatic intellectual that he introduced in Zanussi's *Next Door*. Zapasiewicz's portrayal of a journalist disenchanted with his professional and private life (*Rough Treatment*) and, in particular, that of a skeptical professor (*Camouflage*) became the classic characterizations of the period.

Solidarity Period

Although the spirit of Solidarity between 1980 and 1981 stimulated both the quality and quantity of locally made films, the film infrastructure in Poland was deteriorating. Comments such as "never before had Polish films attracted so much popular attention,"[29] although true regarding Western critics' interest, seem wishful thinking in the local context. For example, 144 million viewers visited Polish cinemas in 1976, including 45 million who saw Polish films. The gradual elimination of films from the West (fifty-five in 1975, and only fourteen in 1981) and the disintegration of the existing infrastructure contributed to the rapid decline in attendance. In 1981, only 88 million viewers went to cinemas, and only 31 million to Polish films. Between 1976 and 1982, 554 permanent cinema theaters and 150 mobile theaters ceased to exist.[30]

With their revolutionary atmosphere and uncertainty, the years 1980 and 1981 better suited documentary cinema. The documentary directed by Andrzej Chodakowski and Andrzej Zajączkowski, *Robotnicy '80* (*Workers 1980*, 1981),[31] was one of the most popular works produced and released in Poland during the Solidarity period. Probably the most sincere Polish narrative film about the working class is Kazimierz Kutz's *The Beads of One Rosary*, which was produced in 1979 and premiered in March 1980—months before the birth of the Solidarity movement. This modest film about the struggle for human dignity, depicting the clash between individualism and the power of the state, received the first prize at the 1980 Festival of Polish Films in Gdańsk.

Człowiek z żelaza (*Man of Iron*, 1981), Andrzej Wajda's sequel to *Man of Marble*, won the Palme d'Or (the grand prize) at the Cannes Film Festival and was the biggest critical success of the Solidarity period. *Man of Iron* preserves the narrative structure of its famous predecessor and relies on flashbacks to tell the story of Birkut's son Maciek Tomczyk (again, Jerzy Radziwiłłowicz), a Gdańsk shipyard worker and a Solidarity activist married to Agnieszka (Krystyna Janda). Another media man, the alcoholic journalist Winkiel (Marian Opania), who is being blackmailed by the state authorities, searches for Birkut's son in order to discredit him. The viewer learns about Tomczyk through the converted sinner Winkiel, who changes his views after meeting the Solidarity activists and learning about their goals. Wajda incorporates documents, newsreels, fragments of *Man of Marble*, television programs, and real-life political figures (such as

Lech Wałęsa) to produce an explicitly political work. The flashbacks in the film refer to the recent political events in Poland—the students' strikes of 1968 and the workers' protests in 1970; the father-son conflict, which is both political and generational in nature; and the death of Birkut in 1970.

The flashbacks provide a sense of the Solidarity movement's roots. As a work of art, however, the hastily made and edited *Man of Iron* does not belong to Wajda's foremost films. Time constraints and the demand for "the right film" resulted in the shallow, melodramatic aspect and one-dimensional characterization typical of socialist realist cinema. Only in flashbacks is Agnieszka dynamic and herself; when she marries the spotless hero Tomczyk, her dramatic role is finished—there is no place for her in this men-only world of Polish politics. Paul Coates aptly comments: "The tigress Krystyna Janda is miscast as a plaster saint of the overnight revolution, whilst the hero, played by Jerzy Radziwiłłowicz, has all the callowness of a socialist realist icon and none of the vibrancy he possessed in *Man of Marble*."[32] With some exceptions, Wajda portrays the clear divisions between "us" and "them." The party functionaries and security force members are depicted as caricatures—ruthless apparatchiks who are losing their ground. The ending of *Man of Iron* anticipates martial law.

Figure 7.3 Krystyna Janda and Jerzy Radziwiłłowicz in Andrzej Wajda's *Man of Iron* (1981)

The party apparatchik, played by Franciszek Trzeciak, tells Tomczyk that the recent agreement between the shipyard workers and the authorities is invalid because it was signed under pressure. Wajda's film may fail as a work of art, yet it fittingly captures the spirit of the times, which was both majestic and kitschy—full of passion, tragedy, and anxiety.

Gorączka (*Fever*, 1981), directed by Agnieszka Holland, and *W biały dzień* (*In Broad Daylight*, 1981), directed by Edward Żebrowski, return to the 1905 revolutionary movement in the Russian-controlled part of Poland. In these films Holland and Żebrowski are interested in psychological issues and the moral dilemmas of the revolutionaries, rather than historical reconstructions of past events. Holland adapts Andrzej Strug's now forgotten novel concerning the young Polish revolutionaries fighting the tsarist regime. Żebrowski examines the issues of political terrorism and fanaticism, telling the story of an assassin in an underground organization who is torn between obedience and conscientiousness, and who searches for truth concerning the guilt of his victim. Both films offer a number of references to the political situation in Poland during the Solidarity period.

Also in 1981 Agnieszka Holland produced for Polish television one of the darkest and most brutally honest films ever made in Poland: *Kobieta samotna* (*A Woman Alone*, released in 1988). Unfolding in a series of episodes, the film concerns a single mother, the postal worker Irena (Maria Chwalibóg), who struggles in a joyless Polish reality. Her new relationship with the equally unhappy, young but handicapped ex-miner Jacek (Bogusław Linda) offers her a chance to change her life. Desperate, Irena steals money from her workplace, buys an old car, and decides to move abroad with Jacek. After giving her son to an orphanage, they travel toward the border, but the voyage ends in an accident. When Irena confesses to Jacek that she has stolen the money, he strangles her. Jacek Petrycki's cinematography portrays the hopeless existence of the protagonists—victims of social and political circumstances. It stresses unfriendly landscapes, gloomy reality, and everyday hardship.

While the early narratives by Kieślowski demonstrate his fascination with capturing life as it is, they go beyond the ramifications of narrowly understood realism. *Przypadek* (*Blind Chance*, 1981, released in 1987), which attained dissident cult status after the introduction of martial law in Poland, portrays an undergraduate medical student, Witek (Bogusław Linda), whose future is determined when he jumps by chance onto a moving train. This is the beginning of Witek's three completely different life paths: he is a young party apparatchik manipulated by old party functionaries, a dissident activist involved in underground publishing, and a person isolated from others by his desire for privacy. In each case, an accidental element determines Witek's life. Kieślowski questions the "us" and "them" division that organized Polish political as well as cultural life under communist rule. He expresses disillusionment with life in Poland and favors uninvolvement—the model of life revolving around the personal rather than the public.

Figure 7.4 Bogusław Linda and Maria Chwalibóg in Agnieszka Holland's
A Woman Alone (1981)

Blind Chance might be considered a pessimistic philosophical parable on human destiny shaped by occurrences beyond individual control. On the one hand, Kieślowski's treatment of the matter stems in large part from his documentary beginnings; in this light, the film could be considered a political essay. On the other hand, by introducing the element of chance (perhaps destiny) into his protagonists' actions, the director is able to deal with questions present in his later, internationally acclaimed films, starting with *Dekalog* (*Decalogue*, 1988).

Another film by Kieślowski, *Krótki dzień pracy* (*Short Working Day*), made in 1981 for Polish television but with a possible theatrical release in mind, was immediately shelved by the authorities and never released. *Short Working Day* retells the workers' strike in the city of Radom in 1976 in an unusual manner—through the eyes of a local Communist Party secretary. Kieślowski often stressed the weaknesses of this film and, in the course of time, was against its release. The film premiered on Polish television after Kieślowski's death.[33]

Neglected Cinema?

Critical works on Polish cinema after 1976 tend to examine political films or films of social concern at the expense of other genres. For example, Gustaw Moszcz (Gary Mead) speaks of the makers of "the mass of dull literary adaptations and trivial costume dramas" as opposed to those who "are working towards a revitalization of the industry under the impetus of Solidarity."[34] Literary adaptations, however, constitute the most popular Polish films. For example, in 1979 two such successful films were released: Wojciech Marczewski's *Zmory* (*Nightmares*), based on Emil Zegadłowicz's anticlerical novel, and Andrzej Wajda's *Panny z Wilka* (*The Maids of Wilko*), another (after *Birchwood*) adaptation of Jarosław Iwaszkiewicz's prose. *Nightmares* tells the coming-of-age story of a sensitive boy in a small Galician town (then part of the Austro-Hungarian monarchy). Set at the beginning of the twentieth century in a brutal junior high school environment, the film is about the boy's confrontation with some sadistic teachers, his brief fascination with socialist ideology, and his first erotic fascinations. This first film by Marczewski (b. 1944), although set in the past, offers a number of relevant discourses on topics including educational methods, maintaining one's individuality at all costs, and the dangers of totalitarianism. Wajda's *The Maids of Wilko* introduces the forty-year-old protagonist Wiktor Ruben (Daniel Olbrychski), who is depressed after the death of a friend and moves to the village of Wilko to revive happy memories from his first visit there before World War I. The erotic and moody photography (by Edward Kłosiński) evokes a Chekhovian atmosphere. The feeling of nostalgia and the theme of the impossibility of reversing time permeate this story of the "five unhappy women from Venus and a tired man from Mars."[35]

Another prominent group of films consists of works that refer to Polish history, such as *Śmierć Prezydenta* (*Death of a President*, 1977), directed by Jerzy Kawalerowicz, and *Gdziekolwiek jesteś, Panie Prezydencie* (*Wherever You Are, Mr. President*, 1978), directed by Andrzej Trzos-Rastawiecki. Kawalerowicz's film depicts the 1922 assassination of the first Polish president Gabriel Narutowicz (Zdzisław Mrożewski) by a nationalist fanatic (Marek Walczewski). The film portrays the turbulent political climate in Poland, the dirty campaign directed against Narutowicz by the political right, and the outburst of hatred that resulted in the assassination. Another successful historical reconstruction, *Wherever You Are, Mr. President* describes the life of the legendary prewar Warsaw president Stefan Starzyński (Tadeusz Łomnicki). In September 1939, Starzyński was arrested in his office by the Germans, and later perished during the war. Trzos-Rastawiecki employs black-and-white photography and archival footage to produce a documentary-like experience. Unlike the historical reconstructions by Kawalerowicz and Trzos-Rastawiecki, Ryszard Filipski's *Zamach stanu* (*Coup d'état*, 1980) and Bohdan Poręba's *Polonia Restituta* (1981), both massive (by Polish standards) historical epics, offer

Figure 7.5 A scene from Wojciech Marczewski's *Nightmares* (1979)

unsophisticated chronicles of the events that led to Marshal Józef Piłsudski's coup d'état in 1926 and Poland's independence (*Polonia Restituta*). Often absent in critical works on Polish cinema of that period are popular comedies directed by Stanisław Bareja (1929–1987). In Bareja's films, generally undervalued both then and now, the absurdity of Polish life under communist rule was appropriately reflected. His bitter satires, such as *Co mi zrobisz jak mnie złapiesz* (*What Will You Do with Me When You Catch Me*, 1978) and *Miś* (*Teddy Bear*, 1981), reveal more about that period than the whole roster of politically oriented Polish cinema. Both films portray situations that are surrealist in spirit, people whose stupidity is of epic proportions, and an everyday existence that is kitschy, ridiculous, and painful.

In the late 1970s, Polish critics coined the term "creative cinema" (*kino kreacyjne*) to distinguish between those filmmakers who focused on everyday problems and politics, and those who were more interested in cultural issues and formal concerns. Polish critic Czesław Dondziłło coined a more appropriate term in 1979—"the cinema reflecting on culture" (*kino kulturowej refleksji*)—to contrast the "journalistic cinema" of the politically minded filmmakers and a group of films that were "oneiric, sophisticated, and aesthetically refined."[36] As the best examples, he briefly discusses Marczewski's *Nightmares*, Filip Bajon's *Aria dla atlety* (*Aria for an Athlete*, 1979), Piotr Szulkin's *Golem* (1980), and Tadeusz Junak's *Pałac* (*The Palace*, 1980).

Aria for an Athlete by Bajon (b. 1947) and Bajon's later films—*Wizja lokalna 1901* (*Inspection at the Scene of the Crime, 1901*, 1981) and *Magnat* (*The Magnate*, 1987)—deserve attention. Polish critic Waldemar Chołodowski writes: "Bajon does not employ a social background; he manages without it. His cinematographically well-defined protagonists are located in a culture of street songs and kitchen romances (*Aria*), and in the law-abiding culture (*Inspection*). These films are closer to a circus tradition or theatrical conventions; closer to decorativeness than an authentic story about life."[37] *Aria for an Athlete* introduces a nostalgic look at the turn of the twentieth century. The story, scripted by Bajon,[38] revolves around a freestyle wrestling champion, Władysław Góralewicz (Krzysztof Majchrzak), his rise to fame from a humble beginning in a provincial circus, and his love for the opera. The painterly quality and the mood of the film owe a lot to the stylish cinematography by Jerzy Zieliński, who also worked on the next two films by Bajon.

Inspection at the Scene of the Crime, 1901 reconstructs a school strike that happened in 1901 in the small town of Września, then part of Germany. Bajon portrays the fight to use the Polish language at school without resorting to national stereotyping and without imitating Polish sentimental patriotic films. The very title of the film indicates an attempt at an objective representation of past events. The symbolic nature of several scenes, their painterly quality, and the meticulous composition of the frame distinguish Bajon's film from the dominant "journalistic" tone and style of several Polish films made at that time. Stylish ventures into the past became Bajon's trademark. His *The Magnate*, which deals with Polish-German relations, provides references to actual events and places. The demise of the German aristocratic family von Teuss in Upper Silesia is the central story of *The Magnate*, an epic film covering the first half of the century. Jan Nowicki, who plays the family patriarch, leads a cast of several known Polish actors in this film in which the family saga merges with a careful re-creation of actual historical events.

Known for a series of painfully contemporary science fiction films, Piotr Szulkin (b. 1950) began his career with *Golem* (1980), based on Gustav Meyrink's writings and the Golem legend. This dystopian fiction describes the problem of dehumanization and portrays an animal-like existence in a futuristic, postnuclear world. *Golem's* cold beauty of painterly images (cinematography by Zygmunt Samosiuk) is repeated in Szulkin's next film, *Wojna światów: następne stulecie* (*War of the Worlds: Next Century*, 1981, released in 1983). Dedicated to H. G. Wells and Orson Welles, the film depicts another futuristic society as revealed during the landing of the Martians. It is not surprising that Szulkin made a film about a totalitarian system that uses television as its main tool of control. The emerging Polish filmmakers, including Szulkin, often cast the media in the role of the traditional Polish villain. "Reality—we create it," reads the slogan in the film. Roman Wilhelmi stars as a television anchor manipulated by "the system," thus allowing for numerous allusions to the 1981 political situation in Poland. Due to obvious parallels between the film's images and its political context, it was banned after the introduction of martial law.[39]

Polish cinema in the late 1970s and during the Solidarity period also paid attention to sociological observations and moral issues, often without linking them to current politics. For example, Grzegorz Królikiewicz's *Tańczący jastrząb* (*Dancing Hawk*, 1978), based on Julian Kawalec's novel, is about social advancement and its consequences—social uprooting. The film tells the story about the rise of an ambitious villager (Franciszek Trzeciak), who graduates from a university, breaks links with his roots (divorcing his first wife and marrying a socialite), and sacrifices everything for his career, with tragic repercussions. *Dancing Hawk's* cinematographer was Zbigniew Rybczyński, later known for a series of experimental films, including *Tango*, for which he received an Oscar award in 1983 in the Best Short Film category.[40] Sociological observations also dominate films made by Ryszard Czekała: *Zofia* (1976), and *Płomienie* (*Flames*, 1979). Both deal with generational conflicts, the disintegration of traditional values, and the confrontation between different (city/village) values.[41]

In the highly political atmosphere in Poland, films devoid of politics were often overlooked by critics. Among them were two distinct films set before the war: a down-to-earth comedy that utilizes the folklore of Silesia, *Grzeszny żywot Franciszka Buły* (*The Sinful Life of Franciszek Buła*, 1980, Janusz Kidawa), and a moody thriller, *Wśród nocnej ciszy* (*Silent Night*, aka *In the Still of the Night*, 1978), produced by Tadeusz Chmielewski, a filmmaker better known for his classic film comedies. Krzysztof Zanussi's *Spirala* (*Spiral*, 1978), a continuation of his earlier meditations on death, is also unique in the context of the Cinema of Distrust. Instead of social or political issues, in this film Zanussi tackles moral and philosophical dilemmas. The film's protagonist Tomasz (Jan Nowicki), a middle-aged professional man, faces a terminal disease. The grief-stricken Tomasz rebels against death and society. He escapes from the hospital to die on his own terms—climbing in the Tatra Mountains. The film poses a number of questions concerning the process of dying and the intimacy of death.

The Cinema of Martial Law and Afterwards

Leaving its political implications aside, the implementation of martial law in December 1981 seriously affected the cinema in Poland. The film land-scape in Poland was changed by the communist ban on "unwanted" Polish films, by the emigration of young filmmakers such as Ryszard Bugajski (b. 1943) and Agnieszka Holland,[42] and by the silence ("internal exile") of oth-ers, such as Wojciech Marczewski. Accused of oppositional activities, Andrzej Wajda was removed as the head of the film studio X in April 1983, together with his close collaborators—the producer Barbara Pec-Ślesicka and the literary director Bolesław Michałek. Wajda also resigned as the head of the Polish Filmmakers Association, which was suspended, like the majority of other Polish associations, after December 1981.

   The political situation after 1981 deepened the divisions between the filmmakers who supported the introduction of martial law and those who opposed it. Comments such as "Poland's quality cinema is now either silent or working in exile"[43] certainly simplify the problem, yet aptly reflect the heated atmosphere, with its intensified divisions between "us" and "them." Once again the political aspects became more important than the films themselves. The unofficial boycott of certain pro-communist filmmakers and the attempt to boycott filmmaking in general—and film-making for state television in particular—were unsuccessful. The boycott did not affect established filmmakers (some of whom were working abroad) and negatively influenced the careers of young, emerging film-makers and actors. The latter either were unable to produce films or had to comply with the dominant aesthetics in order to be considered true artists. Film director Waldemar Krzystek (b. 1953) comments sarcastically: "Immediately after martial law, it was not the best time to break with the artistic preferences of 'moral concern.' The country was again in need, the nation suffered, and the mothers shed tears."[44]

   A number of films that had been made and released during the brief Solidarity period were immediately banned by the authorities, among them *Man of Iron* and Wojciech Marczewski's *Dreszcze* (*Shivers*), which pre-miered on 12 December 1981—one day before the declaration of martial law. The same thing happened to a group of films finished at the beginning of 1982, including Janusz Zaorski's *Matka Królów* (*The Mother of Kings*, released in 1987) and Ryszard Bugajski's *Interrogation* (released in 1989). *The Mother of Kings*, based on Kazimierz Brandys's novel, is a saga about a working-class family led by a hard-working, widowed mother, Łucja Król (Magda Teresa Wójcik). Unlike Brandys's story, about a communist activist who is disenchanted after the end of the Stalinist period, Zaorski's powerful film covers more than twenty years of Polish history by focusing on the mother. Bugajski's *Interrogation* (discussed in chapter 9), perhaps the most famous Polish film of the 1980s, was seen by viewers in Poland on illegal video copies. After the introduction of martial law, Bugajski, unable to produce films in his own country, was forced to emigrate.[45] Due to the absence of locally made films that expressed dissenting views, distorted pro-communist interpretations of recent events were propagated in films such as *Godność* (*Dignity*, 1984, Roman Wionczek). This film tells the story of an old worker, a party member, who is humiliated by Solidarity activists.

A penetrating observer of the new Polish cinema, critic Tadeusz Sobolewski comments: "The experiences of martial law developed ritual reactions within the Polish culture: poetry was composed to commemorate particular occasions, along with paintings depicting the martyrdom of victims of the regime, Romantic Messianism came back to life, or rather the parody of it."[46] The banning of several Polish films, the reduction of Western films in Poland (only nine such films in distribution in 1982),[47] and the impact of the (mostly pirated) video market, which heavily promoted commercial cinema, alienated a number of sophisticated Polish viewers. The elimination of politically minded cinema in distribution and the growing importance of locally made popular genre films prompted several Polish critics, who supported the thematic preoccupations of the Cinema of Distrust, to speak of the danger of imminent commercialization. Comments such as Tadeusz Lubelski's "the picture of a viewer-partner was replaced by the hypothesis viewer-client"[48] overstate the danger of the specter of commercialism at the beginning of the 1980s.

The first films by Juliusz Machulski (b. 1955), very popular among audiences, have to be mentioned in this context: *Vabank* (*Va Banque*, 1982), its sequel *Va Banque II* (1985), and *Seksmisja* (*Sex Mission*, 1984). A former leading actor in Kieślowski's *Personnel*, a film heralding the Cinema of Distrust, Machulski is nevertheless openly critical about his colleagues' films. He accuses Polish filmmakers, with the exception of Holland and Kieślowski, of superficiality and the lack of professionalism.[49] Machulski's films refer to Western cinema rather than a national context, to cinema conventions rather than life "as it is." His *Va Banque*, a retro-gangster comedy set in the 1930s in Warsaw, was clearly influenced by American films such as *The Sting* (1973, George Roy Hill). It tells the story of a professional safecracker Kwinto (Jan Machulski, the director's father), who, with the help of his new friend "Duńczyk" (Witold Pyrkosz), avenges the betrayal by his former partner, a respected banker, who convinced Kwinto to rob his bank to cover misappropriations, but then called the police. *Sex Mission* is a science fiction farce about a futuristic society formed after a nuclear disaster by (as it appears later) an impotent older man disguised as a woman. In this females-only world, men are excluded because they are blamed for the disaster. When two hibernated male protagonists (Jerzy Stuhr and Olgierd Łukaszewicz) awaken, a series of comic situations develop that provide some clear references to gender politics in Poland and the Polish political reality.

Despite the popularity of Machulski's films and films like *Znachor* (*Quack*, 1982, Jerzy Hoffman), *Wielki Szu* (*The Big Rook*, 1983, Sylwester Chęciński), and *Yesterday* (1985, Radosław Piwowarski), Polish cinema theaters recorded a steady decline in attendance. In 1985 only 9 million viewers visited cinemas to watch Polish films,[50] compared with 31 million in 1981, and 45 million in 1976. The exceptional situation occurred in 1984, when a record number of viewers visited Polish cinemas—127.6 million; Polish films were seen by as many as 56.6 million. The popularity of *Sex Mission* (13 million viewers) and a children's film, *Akademia pana Kleksa* (*Mr. Blot's Academy*, 1984, Krzysztof Gradowski), with 10 million viewers, helped to achieve such results.[51]

Polish critics, by and large favoring politically committed cinema, wanted to protect this type of cinema against the growing importance of commercially minded films. Some critics saw the appearance of popular cinema as a cynical move on the part of state authorities to divert the attention of Polish viewers to matters of secondary importance. They did not object to Machulski's films or the unpretentious *Yesterday*, a sentimental and comic coming-of-age story about Beatlemania in Poland. Their prime target remained films such as the erotic *Thais* (1984, Ryszard Ber) and *Widziadło* (*Phantom*, 1984, Marek Nowicki); a barrack comedy set in 1918, *C.K. Dezerterzy* (*Deserters*, 1986, Janusz Majewski); and an erotic comedy, *Och, Karol* (*Oh, Charles*, 1985, Roman Załuski). The problem, however, was not a group of genuinely popular films, but rather the mass of mediocre products—neither popular, nor artistically or politically minded—that were swiftly rejected by new audiences that, by means of pirated videos, had been educated by American popular cinema.

* * * *

In the early 1980s a number of established filmmakers released their major films. The films include: *Konopielka* (1982), directed by Witold Leszczyński; *Danton* (1983), Andrzej Wajda's Polish-French coproduction; *Na straży swej stać będę* (*I Will Stand on My Guard*, 1983), Kazimierz Kutz's continuation of his Silesian themes; *Austeria* (aka *The Inn*, 1983), directed by Jerzy Kawalerowicz; and *Prognoza pogody* (*Weather Forecast*, 1983), by Antoni Krauze. The black-and-white *Konopielka*, based on a popular novel by Edward Redliński, portrays a grotesquely backward rural community. The appearance of a beautiful, young female teacher (Joanna Sienkiewicz) brings energy and a breath of fresh air into the village. Under her influence, the film's central character, Kaziuk (Krzysztof Majchrzak), begins to question old customs, taboos, and superstitious practices. The multilayered structure of the film and its bizarre humor, mocking observations, and sensuality result in a film that equals Leszczyński's classic debut—*The Life of Matthew*.

Stanisława Przybyszewska's play *Sprawa Dantona* (*The Danton Affair*), which premiered in 1931, provided a literary source for Wajda's *Danton*, one of the best films of his career. It is a complex historical drama about the French Revolution of 1789, set during its crisis in the spring of 1794. Unlike Przybyszewska, who portrayed Maximilien Robespierre as a hero, Wajda shifts his sympathy toward Georges-Jacques Danton. He juxtaposes the likeable and mass-supported Danton (Gérard Depardieu) and the ascetic doctrinaire Robespierre (Wojciech Pszoniak), who is obsessed with his ideas about the revolution and is unwilling to compromise. Like many other Polish films in the past, *Danton* was read by viewers in Poland as an allegorical reference to the country's political situation.[52] The political and physical similarities between the two leaders (Jaruzelski as Robespierre and Wałęsa as Danton), their confrontation, and the situation of revolutionary chaos and food shortages in 1981 prompted such a double reading. *Danton* depicts people who set the revolution in motion, but are crushed when it spins out of control. For a number of critics in Poland, this is a film, born out of the experience of the Solidarity movement, about the "birth of modern totalitarianism."[53]

Weather Forecast, another film that premiered in 1983, also provides commentary on the turbulent year 1981. Set in the fall of that year, this "seniors' road movie" tells the story of the boarders of a seniors' home who escape and regain some freedom and dignity while wandering through Poland. They escape because they fear for their lives. After watching a television news program that forecasts extremely harsh winter conditions, they secretly observe their director (Witold Pyrkosz) helping to transport some coffins to their home during the night. The seniors' panic is stronger than their fear of leaving the safety of their house. After a few days of enjoying their freedom and encountering different people, including young drug addicts, the seniors are found by militia using helicopters and sent back to their home. Clear references to the atmosphere preceding martial law, the theme of distrust toward authorities, and the idea of regaining one's freedom at all costs make this film a political metaphor of the year 1981.

The year 1981 saw the foundation of the new experimental production collective, the Karol Irzykowski Film Studio, where several significant films were made by younger filmmakers, such as *Kartka z podróży* (*A Postcard from the Journey*, 1984), by Waldemar Dziki (b. 1956), and *Nadzór* (*Custody*, 1985), by Wiesław Saniewski (b. 1948). *Custody* is one of the most important Polish films made in the mid-1980s. This prison film, set in a women's penitentiary, traces the life of Klara (Ewa Błaszczyk), who is arrested at her wedding in 1967, accused of misappropriating money, and sentenced to life in prison, which is then changed to twenty-five years. Klara's struggle for dignity and internal freedom and her attempts to see her born-in-prison child are at the center of the film. *Custody* also deals with the issue of manipulation and the psychology of female prisoners. The film's dark portrayal of the prison reality (a topic untouched by Polish films, with the exception of *Interrogation*) contributed to the limited release of this powerful film. Wiesław Saniewski, a former film critic (the author of three books of film criticism) and a reporter, also directed *Wolny strzelec* (*The Freelancer*, 1981, released in 1988) and *Sezon na bażanty* (*The Season of Dead Birds*, aka *The Stalking Season*, 1986).

Krzysztof Kieślowski's *Bez końca* (*No End*, 1985), which reflects the martial law reality, avoids easy, generic classification. It contains elements of psychological drama, political film, ghost story, romance, and metaphysical film. Kieślowski tells the story of mourning after the death of a lawyer Antoni Zyro (played by the symbol of Solidarity cinema, Jerzy Radziwiłłowicz), who defended political prisoners. He dies in 1982

Figure 7.6 Ewa Błaszczyk in Wiesław Saniewski's *Custody* (1985)

leaving his confused and grieving wife Urszula (Grażyna Szapołowska) and a young son. The metaphysical element, present earlier in Kieślowski's *Blind Chance*, dominates the story in *No End*. The ghost of the lawyer, who introduces himself in the opening scene, intervenes with daily matters; his widow feels his presence. The reality of 1982 is indicated in the film only because the psychological reality is more important here; it is not politics but a personal loss that matters to Urszula. The more she learns about the world of her deceased husband, the more she loves him. Her suicide can be read as her will to be reunited with him. Kieślowski's film was attacked by Polish critics, regardless of their political stand. This can be attributed to the film's complex poetics, its mood of despair and defeat, the importance of the metaphysical component, and the retreat from the paradocumentary realism—much praised by critics—that was characteristic of Kieślowski's earlier productions.[54]

Rok spokojnego słońca (*Year of the Quiet Sun*, 1985), Krzysztof Zanussi's tale of unfulfilled love, remains the classic Polish film of the mid-1980s. It portrays an impossible love between two lonely middle-aged people: an American soldier Norman (Scott Wilson) and a Polish war widow Emilia (Maja Komorowska). Both are battered by the war. Norman, who is a former prisoner of a German POW camp, works for the Allied War Crimes Commission investigating the death of captured American pilots. Emilia takes care of her ailing mother (Hanna Skarżanka). Their chance meeting in a small town deserted by the Germans, now part of the Polish "Regained Lands," offers them an opportunity to overcome the burden of the past. The language barrier (they have to communicate through interpreters) is not an obstacle to their love. Emilia, however, does not follow her heart and decides to stay in Poland, even though her mother died earlier and everything was ready for her escape abroad. Suffering unnecessarily, Emilia gives up her love and her chance to be free. The lovers are united only after death in a powerful symbolic last scene showing them dancing at Monument Valley.

Zanussi's reconstruction of the postwar period is devoid of the optimism present in a number of Polish films. He is not interested in political but in personal dilemmas; he does not focus on divisions between Poles and Germans, but rather between honest and devious people. Poland's small town in the "Regained Lands" is portrayed as a drab, sinister place populated by crooks, gangsters, prostitutes, and people lost in this reality like Emilia and her mother. Sławomir Idziak's camera captures inhospitable, chilly landscapes, brownish images of an unfriendly town, as if providing a bitter comment on the "year of the sun." Despite its careful balance between melodrama, psychological drama, and formal beauty, Zanussi's film was not very well received in Poland due to its mood of despair, its uncommitted portrayal of the postwar reality, and the presentation of the postwar situation as the end of the world instead of the beginning of a new one. Its success at the 1984 Venice Film Festival (Golden Lion) only raised suspicions that the award was politically motivated (as in the case of *Man of Iron*).

Figure 7.7 Norman Scott and Maja Komorowska in Krzysztof Zanussi's
Year of the Quiet Sun (1985)

Intimate psychological dramas and safe literary adaptations formed
the canon of Polish cinema in the mid-1980s. The oppressive, highly
politicized atmosphere of these years better suited films like the winner
of the 1985 Festival of Polish Films, *Kobieta w kapeluszu* (*A Woman with a
Hat*, 1985), scripted and directed by Stanisław Różewicz. It is a subtle
morality play, devoid of direct references to Polish political reality, that
tells the story about a young actress, Ewa (Hanna Mikuć), who lives an
unfulfilled dream of becoming a successful actress. Another film
released in 1985, Andrzej Barański's *Kobieta z prowincji* (*A Provincial
Woman*, aka *Life's Little Comforts*, 1985), introduces a sixty-year-old
woman Andzia (Ewa Dałkowska) living in a small town. Her difficult
yet not unhappy life is portrayed in a series of lengthy flashbacks. The
film registers her modest everyday life devoid of politics and stresses
the simplicity of her existence—its hardships and life's little comforts—
and the old-fashioned charm of ordinary, banal situations. An interest in
"simple people," sympathy (without sentimentality) for the underprivi-
leged, and a warmth emanating from characters like Andzia became
Barański's trademark.

Among thirty-five Polish films released in 1986, the most significant were adaptations of national literature: *Cudzoziemka* (*Foreigner*), by Ryszard Ber, based on Maria Kuncewiczowa's novel; *Kronika wypadków miłosnych* (*Chronicle of Amorous Accidents*), by Andrzej Wajda, based on Tadeusz Konwicki's novel; *Jezioro Bodeńskie* (*Bodensee*), by Janusz Zaorski, based on Stanisław Dygat's novel; *Siekierezada* (*Axiliad*), Witold Leszczyński's film based on Edward Stachura's novel; and *Dziewczęta z Nowolipek* (*The Girls from Nowolipki*) and its continuation *Rajska jabłoń* (*Crab Apple Tree*), both adaptations of Pola Gojawiczyńska's novel by director Barbara Sass. The popular novel by Gojawiczyńska was already successfully adapted before the war by Józef Lejtes in 1937. Faithful to the literary source, Sass tells the story about four Warsaw girls before World War I (the 1920s in the *Crab Apple Tree*). Reflecting Sass's interest in feminist issues and gender relations, these films, though basically melodramas, provide a sociological examination of the girls' background. Their youthful aspirations are tempered by sombre reality as they search for love with the disappointments that it brings. The most popular film screened in 1987 in Poland, with six million viewers, was another adaptation, *Nad Niemnem* (*On the Niemen River*), directed by Zbigniew Kuźmiński and based on Eliza Orzeszkowa's novel.[55]

* * * *

In 1978 a second film school was established in Poland, originally for the television industry exclusively—the Katowice Film School.[56] It emerged as a competitor for the well-known Łódź Film School, and was essential in invigorating the Polish film industry. By the end of the 1980s, it was dominating its famous rival by "producing" such talented graduates as Maciej Dejczer, Waldemar Krzystek, and Piotr and Magdalena Łazarkiewicz, to name just a few. The strength of the Katowice school also lay in its teachers, some of whom were "unwanted" at the Łódź Film School for political reasons. They included Krzysztof Kieślowski, Kazimierz Kutz, Andrzej Wajda, and Krzysztof Zanussi. Critics in Poland often juxtaposed the documentary-oriented style of Katowice with the formal concerns of Łódź. The competition between the two film centers has produced some engaging artistic results. The young filmmakers, sometimes labeled in Poland "the Martial Law Generation,"[57] had a difficult start in the mid-1980s. Caught in political divisions among the filmmakers, they produced their crucial films in the late 1980s and after the 1989 return of democracy.

Figure 7.8 A scene from *The Girls from Nowolipki* (1986, Barbara Sass)

Notes

1. Gerald Pratley, "Gdańsk: Metaphors for Poland," *Sight and Sound* 59, no. 1 (1989): 4.
2. Julian Kornhauser and Adam Zagajewski, *Świat nie przedstawiony* (Cracow: Wydawnictwo Literackie, 1974).
3. The term "Young Culture" (*Młoda kultura*) refers to the title of a Cracow periodical.
4. Adam Zagajewski, "Rzeczywistość nie przedstawiona w powojennej literaturze polskiej," in Kornhauser and Zagajewski, *Świat nie przedstawiony*, 32.
5. Michał Głowiński describes the weak foundations of the communist system in his seminal works, and analyzes the use of language—the Orwellian "newspeak." See, for example, Głowiński 's *Nowomowa po polsku* (Warsaw: PEN, 1990); *Rytuał i demagogia: trzynaście szkiców o sztuce zdegradowanej* (Warsaw: OPEN, 1992), and *Peereliada: komentarze do słów 1976–1981* (Warsaw: Państwowy Instytut Wydawniczy, 1993).
6. Tadeusz Sobolewski, "Wyzwoliłam się: mówi Agnieszka Holland," *Kino* 12 (1992): 8.
7. The term *kino moralnego niepokoju* is translated differently by various authors as the Cinema of Moral Anxiety or the Cinema of Moral Unrest. Daniel Bickley prefers another term: the Cinema of Moral Dissent. See his "The Cinema of Moral Dissent: A Report from the Gdańsk Film Festival," *Cineaste* 11, no. 1 (1980–1981): 10–15.
8. Janusz Kijowski is cited in a number of sources as the one who coined the term "Cinema of Moral Concern." It is also acknowledged by his fellow filmmakers, for instance by Feliks Falk. See, for example, Tadeusz Sobolewski, "Braliśmy udział w czymś poważnym: mówi Feliks Falk," *Kino* 12 (1992): 11.
9. Mariola Jankun-Dopartowa, "Fałszywa inicjacja bohatera. Młode kino lat siedemdziesiątych wobec założeń programowych Młodej Kultury," in *Człowiek z ekranu: Z antropologii postaci filmowej*, ed. Mariola Jankun-Dopartowa and Mirosław Przylipiak (Cracow: Arcana, 1996), 108.
10. Ibid., 109.
11. Like the film's protagonist, played by the future film director Juliusz Machulski, Kieślowski completed the Warsaw College for Theater Technicians (Państwowe Liceum Techniki Teatralnej) in 1962, and spent one year working as a tailor at the Warsaw Contemporary Theater (Teatr Współczesny).
12. Krzysztof Wojciechowski (b. 1939) is the author of educational films, television films and programs, and documentary films. He became known for his documentary classic *Wyszedł w jasny, pogodny dzień* (*He Left on a Bright, Sunny Day*, 1971). In 1997 he made *Historia o proroku Eliaszu z Wierszalina* (*The Story of Prophet Elijah of Wierszalin*)—another "ethnographic film" set before the war in the Polish eastern provinces.
13. Danusia Stok, ed., *Kieślowski on Kieślowski* (London: Faber and Faber, 1993), 99.
14. *Man of Marble* is discussed in length in chapter 9 of this volume.
15. This aspect is discussed, among others, by Bolesław Michałek and Frank Turaj, *The Modern Cinema of Poland* (Bloomington: Indiana University Press, 1988), 158.
16. See chapter 9.
17. Quoted from Marek Radziwon, "Barwy ochronne nie wyblakły," *Kwartalnik Filmowy* 18 (1997): 134.
18. Tomasz Lengren (b. 1945) is also a film director, the author of the medium-length *Choinka strachu* (*The Christmas Tree of Fear*, 1982, released in 1989), and the full-length *Tanie pieniądze* (*Cheap Money*, 1986).
19. After making several films in Poland, including *Bestia* (*The Beast*, 1979) and *Planeta krawiec* (*The Planet Tailor*, 1984), Jerzy Domaradzki (b. 1943) continues his career in Australia. In that country he directed *Struck by Lightning* (1990), and *Lilian's Story* (1996).
20. Joanna Korska, "Barbara Sass-Zdort: kobiety pod presją w Polsce lat osiemdziesiątych," in *Kobieta z kamerą*, ed. Grażyna Stachówna (Cracow: Wydawnictwo Uniwersytetu Jagiellońskiego, 1998), 82–83.
21. Stok, *Kieślowski on Kieślowski*, 112.
22. Aleksander Jackiewicz, *Moja filmoteka: kino polskie* (Warsaw: Wydawnictwa Artystyczne i Filmowe, 1983), 517.

23. I am referring here to films such as *Illumination* or Zanussi's films made abroad: *Imperative* (1982) and *Paradigm* (1985).

24. Sobolewski, "Braliśmy udział," 10.

25. Sobolewski, "Wyzwoliłam się," 8.

26. Maria Kornatowska, *Wodzireje i amatorzy* (Warsaw: Wydawnictwa Artystyczne i Filmowe, 1990), 184.

27. Ibid., 173.

28. See Piotr Litka, "Najważniejszy jest dialog" [interview with Jerzy Stuhr], *Kino* 12 (1999): 22–24.

29. Tomasz Warchol, "The End of the Beginning," *Sight and Sound* 55, no. 3 (1986): 190.

30. Ewa Gębicka, "Sieć i rozpowszechnianie filmów," in *Encyklopedia kultury polskiej XX wieku: Film i kinematografia*, ed. Edward Zajiček (Warsaw: Instytut Kultury and Komitet Kinematografii, 1994), 442–444. The number of films from the Western countries was even lower in 1982—nine out of the eighty-seven imported films. Figures from Jerzy Płażewski, "Film zagraniczny w Polsce," in Zajiček, *Encyklopedia kultury polskiej*, 348.

31. The title of *Workers 1980* refers to an earlier documentary, *Robotnicy '71: nic o nas bez nas* (*Workers 1971: Nothing about Us without Us*, 1972), directed by Krzysztof Kieślowski, Tomasz Zygadło, Wojciech Wiszniewski, Paweł Kędzierski, and Tadeusz Walendowski.

32. Paul Coates, *The Story of the Lost Reflection: The Alienation of the Image in Western and Polish Cinema* (London: Verso, 1985), 152.

33. See Stok, *Kieślowski on Kieślowski*, 115–116.

34. Gustaw Moszcz (Gary Mead), "Frozen Assets: Interviews on Polish Cinema," *Sight and Sound* 50, no. 2 (1981): 87

35. "*The Maids of Wilko*: Five Unhappy Women from Venus and a Tired Man from Mars" is a translation of the title of Teresa Rutkowska's Polish text, "*Panny z Wilka*: Pięć nieszczęśliwych kobiet z Wenus i zmęczony mężczyzna z Marsa," *Kwartalnik Filmowy* 18 (1997): 141–152.

36. Czesław Dondziłło, *Młode kino polskie lat siedemdziesiątych* (Warsaw: Młodzieżowa Agencja Wydawnicza, 1985), 92.

37. Waldemar Chołodowski, *Kraina niedojrzałości* (Warsaw: Czytelnik, 1983), 121.

38. Filip Bajon is also a novelist and is the scriptwriter of all of his films.

39. The representation of a television reporter, Winkiel, in *Man of Iron* serves here as a good example. The issues of manipulation by "the system" also appear in *Czułe miejsca* (*Sensitive Spots*, 1981), by Piotr Andrejew, and in Szulkin's next films: *O-bi, o-ba. Koniec cywilizacji* (*O-bi, o-ba: End of Civilization*, 1985), and *Ga, Ga. Chwała bohaterom* (*Ga, Ga: Glory to the Heroes*, 1986).

40. Zbigniew Rybczyński (b. 1950) graduated from the Fine Arts Academy in Warsaw in 1968 and the Łódź Film School in 1973. In Poland he made, among others, *Nowa książka* (*New Book*, 1975) and *Oj! Nie mogę się zatrzymać* (*I Cannot Stop*, 1975). After his emigration to the United States in 1983, he made a number of films, including *Steps* (1987), *The Fourth Dimension* (1988), and *The Orchestra* (1990).

41. Ryszard Czekała (b. 1941) started his career in the late 1960s with a series of animated films that were well received by Polish critics. In the 1970s animated films flourished in Poland. Apart from Czekała and Rybczyński, one has to mention, among others, the ascetic and philosophical films by Jerzy Kucia and the noncamera films by Julian Józef Antonisz. The early 1980s mark the appearance of the first animated films by Piotr Dumała and Aleksander Sroczyński, among others.

42. After the declaration of martial law, Agnieszka Holland decided to remain in France. She directed a number of internationally acclaimed films in Germany, France, and the United States. In Germany she made *Angry Harvest* (1985) and *Europa, Europa* (1991), and in France *To Kill a Priest* (1988), *Olivier, Olivier* (1992), and *Total Eclipse* (1995, French-English coproduction). Her Hollywood films include *Secret Garden* (1993), *Washington Square* (1997), *The Third Miracle* (1999), and *Shot in the Heart* (2001).

43. Gary Mead, "Volksfilm for the 1980s: Prospects for Polish Cinema after Martial Law," *Sight and Sound* 52, no. 4 (1983): 231. Mead's article reflects the spirit of the time. He singles out certain filmmakers, the party members, whose works are not screened in the West "largely because we have superior tripe factories." He also claims that the work of Ryszard Filipski, Bohdan Poręba, and Ewa and Czesław Petelski "is disliked in Poland, too, since there it stands out as even more artificial and contrived." He accuses them of mediocrity and wrongly attributes to them "humourless comedies and imitative thrillers," among other things. Ibid., 231.

44. Waldemar Krzystek, "Było sobie kino," *Kino* 12 (1995): 8.

45. Ryszard Bugajski settled in Canada where he directed *Clearcut* (1991). Back in Poland in the mid-1990s, he produced *Gracze* (*Players*, 1996), a political drama set during the first presidential elections after the fall of communism.

46. Tadeusz Sobolewski, "Peace and Rebellion," in *Polish Cinema in Ten Takes*, ed. Ewelina Nurczyńska-Fidelska and Zbigniew Batko (Łódź: Łódzkie Towarzystwo Naukowe, 1995), 133.

47. Płażewski in Zajiček, *Encyklopedia kultury polskiej XX wieku*, 348. As an example of the situation, Płażewski points out that between 1982 and 1989 Poland imported only six films from Italy (p. 349).

48. Tadeusz Lubelski, "Film fabularny," in Zajiček, *Encyklopedia kultury polskiej XX wieku*, 165.

49. For example, Zdzisław Pietrasik, "Klasa i kasa. Rozmowa z Juliuszem Machulskim, reżyserem filmu *Girl Guide*," *Polityka* 8 (1996): 46.

50. Gębicka, "Sieć i rozpowszechnianie filmów," 445,

51. Figures from Edward Zajiček, "Kinematografia," in Zajiček, *Encyklopedia kultury polskiej XX wieku*, 91.

52. I refer extensively to my own recollections concerning this period. I have experienced the Solidarity period and martial law firsthand, having lived at that time in Poland.

53. Jan F. Lewandowski, *100 filmów polskich* (Katowice: Videograf II, 1997), 158.

54. Kieślowski says that his film "was terribly received in Poland. Terribly. I've never had such unpleasantness over any other film as I had over this one. It was received terribly by the authorities; it was received terribly by the opposition, and it was received terribly by the Church. Meaning, by the three powers that be in Poland." Stok, *Kieślowski on Kieślowski*, 136.

55. The figure is quoted from Małgorzata Hendrykowska, *Kronika kinematografii polskiej 1895 – 1997* (Poznań: Ars Nova, 1999), 427.

56. Precisely, the Radio and Television Faculty at the University of Silesia in Katowice (Wydział Radia i Telewizji Uniwersytetu Śląskiego w Katowicach).

57. Piotr Wasilewski, *Świadectwa metryk* (Cracow: Powiększenie, 1990), 8.

8

Landscape after Battle
The Return of Democracy

Toward the end of the 1980s, the communist system in Poland started to show signs of decline. Round table discussions were arranged between the communists and the representatives of the opposition at the beginning of 1989 to find solutions to Poland's political problems and poor economy. The negotiations led to a compromise that, consequently, enabled the change of the political formation. The summer of 1989 is usually cited as a turning point in Polish history, marking the peaceful transition from the totalitarian system to democracy. Tadeusz Mazowiecki formed the first noncommunist government in Polish postwar history after the stunning election victory of Solidarity's Civic Committee in June 1989. Although Wojciech Jaruzelski still remained the president, the communists' monopoly had been brought to a decisive end. Lech Wałęsa's presidential victory in December 1991 definitively ended one-party rule and started a new era in Polish history.

Cinema Industry: From the State Monopoly to Free Market

The year 1989 was also a turning point for the Polish film industry. Once again, it was not a cinematic movement but rather a political transformation—this time a bloodless one—that defined the new period. The nationalized and centralized film industry, entirely dependent on government funding, was transformed into a free market economy subsidized by the state. In post-totalitarian Poland, filmmakers and other artists are relieved from their traditional duties to the nation, liberated from political pressures and commitments. The political role commonly reserved for artists has returned to politicians, political commentators, and historians. Film-making has once again become a strictly professional endeavor and exists somewhere on the margin of mainstream Polish life.

The year 1987 brought new legislation that abolished the state monopoly in the sphere of film production, distribution, and the purchase of foreign films. This act, more fully introduced after 1989, transformed the state-owned and controlled film industry, based on film units—the core of the local film business since 1955—into independent studios. The new legislation and the abolition of censorship in 1990 made film producers and directors responsible for both the content and the financial success, or failure, of their products. On the one hand, this decision gave considerable freedom to the companies mainly in the sphere of coproductions and distribution in the West. On the other hand, in spite of limited government subsidies via the Cinema Committee of the Ministry of Culture and Arts (also established in 1987), this independence forced the companies to concentrate on the commercial aspect of their productions. At the beginning of 1992, the following film studios functioned: Filip Bajon's Dom, Jerzy Kawalerowicz's Kadr, Tadeusz Chmielewski's Oko, Janusz Morgenstern's Perspektywa, Bohdan Poręba's Profil, Krzysztof Zanussi's Tor, Juliusz Machulski's Zebra, Jerzy Hoffman's Zodiak, and the Karol Irzykowski Film Studio managed by Jacek Skalski and Jerzy Bugajski.[1]

The process of democratization began with the releasing of a number of films shelved by the previous regime, among others Ryszard Bugajski's *Interrogation*, Jerzy Domaradzki's *Wielki bieg* (*The Big Run*, 1981), Agnieszka Holland's *A Woman Alone*, Krzysztof Kieślowski's *Blind Chance*, and Janusz Zaorski's *The Mother of Kings*. These films deal with the psychosocial pressures of Stalinism—the period euphemistically called by Communist Party authorities in Poland "the age of mistakes and blunders." Films concerned with Polish-Russian history, like Tadeusz Chmielewski's adaptation of *Wierna rzeka* (*Faithful River*, 1983), the classic novel by Stefan Żeromski about an anti-Russian uprising in 1863, had also been suppressed.

The move toward a market economy in Poland coincided with the universalization of coproductions in Europe and the incorporation of American popular cinema into that market. The end of a fully subsidized and centralized Polish film industry controlled through state censorship and the emergence of a new audience, for whom not only communism but Solidarity are history, have brought some inevitable changes to film production and distribution, as well as to film thematics and stylistics. Coproductions, multinational enterprises, competition with Hollywood, a plurality of styles and genres are all changing the film landscape in Poland.

The transition to a market economy in Poland has not been an easy process. At the beginning of the 1990s there were symptoms of a deep economic crisis in the film industry. Figures show that the number of cinema theaters decreased rapidly, from 1,830 toward the end of the 1980s to 1,195 in 1991 and 755 in 1993 (compared with 1,200 in the Czech Republic, 3,709 in Germany, and 4,397 in France in 1993). Another alarming figure was the extremely low average for the number of cinema visits per inhabitant: 0.35 in 1993 compared with 1.26 in Hungary, 2.06 in the Czech Republic, and 2.15 in Germany.[2]

Some Polish critics and filmmakers believed that free market reforms had created a situation in which Polish films could not compete with American products. With the gradual Americanization of the local market, it was also difficult to see Western European films, and almost impossible to see Central European and Russian works. For instance, between 1991 and 1995 only six Italian, nineteen German, forty-one English, and forty-five French films were released in Poland. Interestingly, there was not a single Russian film among 122 new titles exhibited in Poland in 1992.[3]

In accordance with expectations, American films clearly dominated the market: more than 60 percent of the Polish repertoire consisted of American films (as much as 73 percent in 1992). They were heavily promoted and well distributed. The average number of prints used for the release of an American film ranged from twenty to fifty. Only five to fifteen copies of films from Poland and other parts of Europe were distributed at release. Polish films accounted for only 18 percent in 1991, 14 percent in 1992, 20 percent in 1993, 12 percent in 1994, and 10 percent in 1995 of the total number of films released in Poland. The number of local films distributed in Poland does not, however, match their market share. Due to lower inflation rates and increasing cinema ticket prices (between US $2 and $3 in 1995), the total box office has been steadily growing and reached US $40 million in 1995. The percentage earned by Polish films has been low, ranging from 9.4 in 1991 to 5.2 in 1995.[4]

At the beginning of the 1980s, the film industry in Poland was a workplace for almost ten thousand people, half of whom were employed by state institutions. Throughout the 1990s, this number decreased rapidly. For example, the Film Production Company in Łódź, whose personnel numbered 1,100 in the 1980s, employed only 350 in 1992.[5] While the transfer of Poland's economy from the public to the private sector has been conducted in quite an efficient manner, the privatization of the film industry has proved difficult.

To stimulate and protect the indigenous film industry, the following three government funding bodies were created in 1991: the Script, Production, and Distribution Agencies.[6] The goal of the Script Agency (Agencja Scenariuszowa) is to create a market for film scripts in Poland by supporting script development and pre-production work. Currently, more than 50 percent of Polish scripts originate with the agency's financial support.

The Film Production Agency (Agencja Produkcji Filmowej) is involved financially in the production of feature, documentary, animated, and educational films. Its main goal is to cofinance projects that are "of cultural value." The selection process is carried out by a panel of experts appointed by the chairman of the Cinema Committee. Each feature project is evaluated by a commission of nine experts picked randomly from a group of fifty-seven. The commission is always composed of two critics or scriptwriters, two production managers, two distributors, and three cinema managers. The agency coproduced seventeen features in 1992, eighteen in 1993, and fifteen in 1994.

The main task of the Film Distribution Agency (Agencja Dystrybucji Filmowej) is to stimulate the distribution of films that are considered to be important from the point of view of the state's cultural policy. This is done through the financial participation of the agency in the distribution mostly of Polish films, but also of artistically significant foreign films. With the help of this agency, Polish cinemas have screened films by directors such as Jim Jarmusch, Derek Jarman, and Peter Greenaway, as well as the majority of Polish features.

Given the difficulties of the transitional period, it is worth noting that the Polish film industry has consistently been able to produce more than twenty feature films yearly. Every year during the 1990s, at least two or three films were made independently, without the state's involvement. Since the crisis at the beginning of the 1990s, the number of cinema theaters has been increasing slowly but steadily. In 1992 Poland joined the Eurimages Foundation (established in 1989), which sponsors European films. Krzysztof Kieślowski's last films were made with its help.

The future of Polish cinema, however, is more and more dependent on television. In 1995, state-run television participated in the production of almost all feature films in Poland, and acted as a sole producer of four. Three films were coproduced by the private television network Canal+. Certain acclaimed filmmakers, for example Andrzej Barański and Jan Jakub Kolski, made all of their films with the help of state television.

These changes have been introduced to create a new system in which state patronage coexists with private initiatives. The main task is to defend the national film industry; in a country with a population of almost thirty-nine million, it is understandable that virtually no local film can recoup its cost without foreign sales. Statistics show that one hundred thousand viewers in cinema theaters are considered high by Polish standards of the 1990s. For example, if we look at Polish films released in 1996, only five of them have achieved these results: Władysław Pasikowski's *Słodko-gorzki* (*Bitter-Sweet*) leads with 340,000 viewers, then Juliusz Machulski's *Girl Guide*, Andrzej Żuławski's *She-Shaman*, Krystyna Janda's *Pestka* (*Pip*), and Marek Koterski's *Nic śmiesznego* (*Nothing Funny*). Many films, often made by internationally renowned directors, have only a limited audience; for instance, Andrzej Wajda's *Wielki Tydzień* (*Holy Week*) had eight thousand viewers, Krzysztof Zanussi's *Cwał* (*In Full Gallop*) five thousand, and Jerzy Kawalerowicz's *Za co?* (*For What?*) only one thousand.[7] During the mid-1990s in Poland it was still easier to produce a film than to exhibit it in movie theaters.

Filmmakers after the Wall Came Down

In Robert Gliński's 1989 film, *Łabędzi śpiew* (*The Swan's Song*) a successful Polish scriptwriter returns from abroad only to learn that his ideas for future films have nothing to do with the changed reality around him. He tries to survive this difficult time by producing some desperate "postmodern" versions of Polish history and by cannibalizing American models. The effect is unintentionally comic, absurd, and out of place.

For many filmmakers in Poland, as was the case for Gliński's protagonist, the new reality has come as somewhat of a shock; the relationships between the state and the artist as well as between the artist and its audience have changed dramatically. The traditional antagonist (the totalitarian state) has disappeared and with it a polarized world in which the only meaningful distinction was between the pro-communist side ("them") and the "right side" ("us"). The artistic criteria in Poland were repeatedly subordinated to political criteria. To be a dissident meant to be a true artist; some artists were canonized simply because their work was incompatible with the communist system. For some, being on the right (dissident) side was enough reason to be hailed as a great artist. In a sense, it was an anachronistic, romantic Polish extension of the artist-as-torch-bearer myth. In this context, the quality of artistic output was often of minor importance. In Wajda's classic *Ashes and Diamonds*, the two Home Army survivors engage in a conversation that could easily be a commentary on the situation of a filmmaker in post-1989 Poland. "Those were the days!" says Maciek recalling his dead friends. "We knew what we wanted, and what was expected of us," responds Andrzej.[8]

Given the complexity of Polish history, cinema—and, for that matter, all Polish art—has generally been regarded as more than just entertainment. The artist's "mission" was that of a prophet and teacher bringing a message to society. Film and other art forms acted as safety valves in the controlled, corrupt political system. Filmmaking was a platform on which political debates were sometimes argued openly, and sometimes in an Aesopian language. Politically active filmmakers were always at the foreground of Polish life. The artists felt an immense responsibility. Conversely, they were also accustomed to a situation in which their voices were heard and analyzed by the people and by the authorities.

At present, film ideology is of minor significance and will remain so until a new antagonist is found. Economics supersedes politics. New audiences demand new films. The marginalization of traditional filmic themes like Polish martyrology and history (only two of the films at the 1996 Festival of Polish Films in Gdynia dealt with such themes) proves that the time has come for the Polish cinema to be free from political and social obligations. But what does this freedom mean—queries Andrzej Wajda in his 1991 diagnosis of the state of Polish cinema—in these changed political, economic, and social situations? He ironically suggests that such freedom is a freedom from the audience, criticism, authority, ideology, and artistic criteria.[9]

Filmmakers now have to defend themselves exclusively with their films. They have to fight for audiences that they depend on to exist. State-run political censorship has been replaced by the economic censorship of the producer, which, in many aspects, is even harsher. Polish film critic Tadeusz Sobolewski states that many filmmakers and critics started out believing in the victory of freedom but immediately felt disappointed with it.[10] One of the leading Polish Catholic intellectuals, Józef Tischner, states this concern bluntly in the title of his book: *Nieszczęsny dar wolności* (*The Unhappy Gift of Freedom*).[11]

A new market came into being. Nevertheless, Kazimierz Kutz maintained at the beginning of the 1990s that the quality of Polish cinema had reached rock bottom. For him, Poland was allowing itself to be flooded with anonymous international coproductions, rather than supporting national films.[12] In his view, the production of films was becoming exclusively an opportunity for grabbing money; the producers were behaving in the manner of the capitalists from early Soviet cinema.[13] Others, like the influential *Kino* critic Jerzy Płażewski, claimed that coproductions would guarantee survival for the local film industry.[14] The figures, which show the increasing number of coproductions, support the critic's claim: between 30 and 40 percent of Polish films are international coproductions.

After the 1989 freedom shock, there were claims—supported by leading Polish filmmakers such as Wajda and Zanussi—that Polish cinema was in danger of becoming commercialized, especially after Western distributors entered the Polish market. Some believed that free market reforms would create a situation in which Polish films could not compete with Western "B" products, such as "the collected works" of Chuck Norris. Another concern was the feigned reorientation of Polish filmmakers toward commercialism. For many critics and filmmakers, the specter of commercialism haunted Polish cinema. Disappointed with the first flood of commercially minded products, some filmmakers went so far as to emphasize the positive role of state censorship in the totalitarian period.[15] For instance, Kutz asserted that political censorship was one of the main factors behind the origins of artistic cinema in Poland. He maintained that there were some positive aspects to political censorship, which motivated the best artists to work harder and to speak in purely visual terms. For him, this laid the foundation of the Polish School in the late 1950s and early 1960s. According to Wajda, the figurativeness of Polish cinema was one of the crucial elements in its fight against political censorship. In contrast to dialogue, symbolic pictures are very difficult to censor, claims Wajda, giving examples from his *Ashes and Diamonds*.[16] Commenting on censorship, Kieślowski once remarked that filmmakers in Poland "were in a luxurious and unique situation. We were truly important ... precisely because of censorship. We're allowed to say everything now but people have stopped caring what we're allowed to say."[17]

The whole discussion about the current state and the future of the Polish film industry vacillates between voices emphasizing the importance of the national character of Polish films and those advocating the universal, cosmopolitan nature of art. Taking the first perspective, Polish film critic and writer Anita Skwara states that, "Polish cinema stands a chance of survival and development only when it is national in character, when it arises directly from the traditions, culture and myths forming Polish awareness."[18] Some directors, however, go beyond the limits of narrowly understood "national themes" or the "Polish perspective" and focus on what can be called "a European consciousness."[19] The popular slogan in Poland, "catching up with Europe," expresses a desire to create new post-totalitarian art that, while addressing some universal issues, will reflect national uniqueness. The problem facing new cinema, not only in Poland but in all of Central Europe, is to find a new voice to adequately express the "national" while incorporating other cinematic discourses.

Some established filmmakers are unable to find a new voice in this changed situation. For instance, Feliks Falk's *Koniec gry* (*End of the Game*, 1991) and *Daleko od siebie* (*Far from Each Other*, 1996), are full of clichés from the poetics of the Cinema of Distrust. *End of the Game* portrays a young, sensitive mathematician (who resembles the early protagonists of Zanussi) and tells the story of his uneasy love affair with the female leader of a political party. The world vision presented in the film is journalistic and sketchy, in line with the bland psychological characterization of the protagonists. An old master, Jerzy Kawalerowicz, experienced similar problems with two films released after the Wall came down. *Jeniec Europy* (*The Prisoner of Europe*, 1989) and *For What?* (1996) were poorly received by critics and ignored by audiences. This is also a factor that contributed to the indifference met by some of Wajda's more recent films: *The Ring with a Crowned Eagle*,[20] *Holy Week*, and *Panna Nikt* (*Miss Nobody*, 1996).

For self-declared cosmopolitan filmmaker Krzysztof Zanussi, recent years have been very productive. He has made a series of television films, several documentaries, and a number of feature films: *Stan posiadania* (*Inventory*, 1989), *Życie za życie* (*Life for Life*, 1990), *Dotknięcie ręki* (*The Silent Touch*, 1992), and *In Full Gallop*. In 2000, Zanussi's *Życie jako śmiertelna choroba przenoszona drogą płciową* (*Life as a Fatal Disease Sexually Transmitted*), a continuation of his earlier meditations on death (for example, *The Death of a Provincial* and *Spiral*), was announced the winner of the Moscow Film Festival and the Festival of Polish Films in Gdynia.

Films made by Zanussi in the late 1980s and the 1990s do not provoke the same disputes and controversies as his earlier works. In *Inventory*, for example, Zanussi centers on three characters: two women, representing two different world-views as well as two different groups of the Polish society ("us" versus "them"), and a sensitive young man acting as a mediator. Improvised elements play a major role in this ascetic film characterized by the minimal use of cinematic techniques and an emphasis on moralizing dialogues. In *Inventory*, Zanussi pushes his style to the extreme. The film seems too verbal at the expense of imagery and too artificial in its construction of the conflict.

After *Life for Life*, almost a hagiography of the saint Maksymilian Kolbe, Zanussi directed a multinational (Polish, British, Danish) production, *The Silent Touch*, arguably his best film in recent years. The film tells a familiar story: a young musicologist from Cracow (Lothaire Bluteau) has a dream about an unknown musical masterpiece. He writes down its basic tones and travels abroad to an old eccentric composer (Max von Sydow), once famous and worldly, now living in seclusion, to convince him to write the piece. The composer has been silent for almost forty years, withdrawn from the musical life. The young messenger from Poland has to awaken him from artistic inertia, to awaken his sexuality to enable him to compose the work of his life. (The film includes Wojciech Kilar's magnificent score.)

Reclaiming the Recent Past

The post-totalitarian period is characterized by an effort to overcome the previous modes of thinking. Filip Bajon's *Bal na dworcu w Koluszkach* (*Ball at the Koluszki Station*, 1990), Feliks Falk's *End of the Game*, Janusz Kijowski's *Stan strachu* (*State of Terror*, 1990), Waldemar Krzystek's *Ostatni prom* (*The Last Ferry*, 1989) and *Zwolnieni z życia* (*Dismissed from Life*, 1991), and particularly Andrzej Trzos-Rastawiecki's *Po upadku* (*After the Fall*, 1990) were made too late. Viewed after 1989, they had lost their relevance and, as a result, their audience.

The success of Wojciech Marczewski's *Ucieczka z kina "Wolność"* (*Escape from "Freedom" Cinema*, 1990) is merely an exception to the rule that political films are now difficult to market in Poland.[21] On the surface, Marczewski's film looks like a tribute paid to Woody Allen's *The Purple Rose of Cairo* (1985). The story is set in a movie theater called "Freedom" in which a fictitious Polish film titled *Jutrzenka* (*Morning Star*) is shown. The characters in the film rebel against the roles they have to perform; they do not follow the script and, in an act of defiance, utter their own words. They cannot be subjected to any external pressures. The mutiny on the screen spreads rapidly; real people from the street, regardless of their political standing, sing Mozart's *Requiem* as a way of showing their resistance. A government censor (Janusz Gajos, in an impressive performance) is unable to do anything and eventually falls under the spell of the film. Finally, afraid that the copy of the film will be burnt, the screen characters escape to the roof of the cinema theater building.

On the simplest level, *Escape from "Freedom" Cinema* can be taken as a story about a disillusioned censor, rejected by his family, who comes to fathom the misery of his present life. On another level, however, this multilayered film clearly serves as an allegory of the situation in the 1980s, a reminder of the supremacy of politics over people's lives, or, perhaps, as an allegorical story about rebellion. Marczewski's film is not as visually refined as his earlier *Nightmares* or *Shivers*. The emphasis is on direct political references, and on an examination of the near past from the perspective of a newly regained freedom. With its clear divisions between what is right and wrong, between the rulers and the ruled, *Escape from "Freedom" Cinema* accurately reflects the spirit of the former period. But intellectually, for these same reasons, it also belongs to that era.

One might well have expected a flood of artistic works reclaiming the past after the political events of 1989. Indeed, at the beginning of the 1990s, the distribution of major awards at festivals of Polish films demonstrated a consistent preference for honoring films that dealt with various aspects of Polish history. Awards were presented to Robert Gliński's *Wszystko, co najważniejsze* (*All That Really Matters*, 1992), an examination of the fate of Polish citizens deported by Stalin to Kazakhstan after the outbreak of World War II, and to Grzegorz Królikiewicz for his study of Polish history as seen through the eyes of a handicapped person in an unsuccessful search for his unknown mother in *Przypadek Pekosińskiego* (*The Case of Pekosiński*, 1993). Other well-received films dealing with recent history include, among others: *300 mil do nieba* (*300 Miles to Heaven*, 1989), by Maciej Dejczer; *Kornblumenblau* (1989), by Leszek Wosiewicz; *Pokuszenie* (*Temptation*, 1995), by Barbara Sass; *Pułkownik Kwiatkowski* (*Colonel Kwiatkowski*, 1996), by Kazimierz Kutz; and *Gry uliczne* (*Street Games*, 1996), by Krzysztof Krauze.

The film *300 Miles to Heaven* won the European Film Award (the "Felix") in 1989 as the Young European Film of the Year. This well-made and moving film, scripted by Dejczer and Cezary Harasimowicz and based on real events, tells the story of two young brothers who, during martial law, escape to Sweden hidden on the underside of a huge truck. In spite of the tendencies inherent in such topics, Dejczer (b. 1953) avoids sentimentality and never resorts to stereotypes or filmic clichés. The first part of the film portrays a hopeless picture of Polish "socialist" reality—the ugliness of the environment, the corruption, the futile struggles with authorities—and serves as justification for the boys' desperate departure from the country. The second part shows the two alienated teenage protagonists in prosperous, though cold, "capitalist" landscapes. The final scene, a telephone conversation between the two boys and their parents in Poland, is among the most powerful sequences in Polish cinema. "Don't ever return here," their father states. This cruel sentence might serve as one of the strongest criticism of the communist regime.

In *Kornblumenblau*, Leszek Wosiewicz (b. 1947) offers a completely different treatment of Polish martyrology—a different look at World War II and wartime suffering. *Kornblumenblau* also works against the romantic tradition that permeates Polish literature and film. Moreover, since the film is set in a concentration camp and its protagonist's name is Tadeusz, it is inviting to treat it as another reading of the laconic postwar prose of Tadeusz Borowski. In Borowski's world, all characters are infected by the devastating degeneration of human values. Everyday existence is marked by compromises and resignation, and is viewed through a personal philosophy adopted in order to survive. Likewise, in Wosiewicz's film, the focus is not on the psychology but on the physiology of the dehumanized hero. Tadeusz (Adam Kamień) survives by instinct: he tries to be loyal to the guards and to stay on good terms with the other inmates. For them, he remains an enigma. "Is he a sly dog or an imbecile?" wonders one of his fellow prisoners.

The film starts with a skillfully edited pre-credit, slapstick-like sequence that summarizes the early stages of Tadeusz's life. Wosiewicz employs old documentary footage and fragments of a Polish prewar film, intercut with original footage (also in sepia tones) showing the protagonist's parents, his birth, and the beginnings of his career as a musician. This silent part of the film (only a few captions are employed) ends with the outbreak of the war and the protagonist's being sent to a concentration camp for his supposed political activities.

It is tempting to read *Kornblumenblau* in broader terms, as a parable on the situation of an artist in a totalitarian state, but the film's protagonist is quite pragmatic, a chameleon-like person able to fit into different situations, an amiable conformist. Tadeusz fulfills his parents' dream by becoming an artist, but to secure his future, he also becomes an engineer. As if to emphasize this aspect of his personality, in the last symbolic scene, after the liberation of the camp, he voluntarily joins a group of Soviet soldiers and starts entertaining them.

Street Games, by Krzysztof Krauze (b. 1953), centers on an event in recent Polish history—the death of Stanisław Pyjas, a student and also a member of the opposition, who was murdered in 1977. According to the film, the mystery surrounding Pyjas's death does not belong to a faded past. In *Street Games*, the past affects the present. The ghosts from the past emerge as important players in contemporary political life. These include not only members of the disgraced Security Force (SB) but also a former dissident with an obscure past as a collaborator and informer, who is possibly involved in the murder. The young television reporter Janek (Redbad Klijnstra) investigates the past, although the subject initially seems to be too removed for him. Gradually, he develops a spiritual bond with the murdered student, becomes almost obsessed with the case, and, finally, has to die.

The look of Krauze's film is American, but its content is unmistakably Polish; it is a classic political thriller set in contemporary Poland. Łukasz Kośmicki's stylish cinematography creates a cinematic trip into the complexities of the past. *Street Games* is clearly a modern political film, successful in its attempts to capture the change of political systems and the spirit of the communist past. Similar to Agnieszka in Wajda's *Man of Marble*, Janek from *Street Games* also goes back almost twenty years and investigates the 1970s. In both cases, the past emerges in its dangerous intricacy and overshadows the present. The mosaic stylistics of Krauze's film (e.g., the insertion of animated clips into the realistic story), references to American cinema, and the use of modern Polish rock music clearly target young viewers.

Krauze's recent film, *Dług* (*Debt*, 1999), awarded the Grand Prix at the 1999 Festival of Polish Films, also refers to a well-publicized event. A group of young businessmen, who are being blackmailed by a gangster trying to collect a nonexistent debt, kill the blackmailer and his bodyguard out of desperation. The protagonists, who took the law into their own hands, receive long-term sentences. Although the psychological relations between the victims and the victimizer are at the center of Krauze's film, it takes part in a national discussion in Poland concerning the weakness of the law, the helplessness of ordinary citizens facing a corrupt underworld, and the links between organized crime and the political elite. A number of other films portray the Polish reality in a similar manner, among them *Poniedziałek* (*Monday*, 1998), which was directed by the accomplished cinematographer Witold Adamek.

A prominent member of the Polish School generation, Kazimierz Kutz continues to be one of the key figures in Polish cinema. Despite his harsh criticism of the new reality, he seems to have had no problems adjusting to it. Active in theater and television, and in the mid-1990s a regular contributor to a much-discussed column in the journal *Kino*, Kutz has directed, among others, *Zawrócony* (*The Turned Back*), the winner of the 1994 Festival of Polish Films; *Death as a Slice of Bread*, Special Award of the Jury at the same festival; and *Colonel Kwiatkowski*, one of the best Polish films released in 1996.

The Turned Back and *Death as a Slice of Bread*, films scripted by Kutz, are set in Silesia shortly before and after the introduction of martial law. The director, independent as usual and unconcerned with current political and aesthetic fashions, deals with the myth of Solidarity and the political atmosphere of 1981. Both films differ distinctly in their treatment of the subject. The tragedy and pathos of *Death as a Slice of Bread* is replaced by the almost farcical events of *The Turned Back*. For Kutz, these two films also mark a return to his favorite Silesian themes, which are present in his earlier best-known works.

The sit-in strike at the coal mine Wujek is the subject of *Death as a Slice of Bread*. The film is a faithful reconstruction of those events: it starts with the introduction of martial law and the arrest of the mine's Solidarity leader, and ends with the brutal pacification of the mine, during which nine people were killed. Working on the project for almost ten years, Kutz was faced with the challenge of making a film that would neither trivialize the events nor fall into the now obsolete category of "patriotic picture." The result is an almost documentary record of those events, a tragedy without individual heroes. The film lacks a typical narrative yet is laden with pathos in its celebration of everyday situations. Its characters are simple yet dignified, as if taken from a Solidarity poster. Kutz's film alienates the viewer with its refusal to introduce distinguishable characters. In the current period, characterized by the depreciation of the myth of Solidarity, Kutz's film goes against the trend by attempting to animate a myth that is already dead. *Death as a Slice of Bread* is, arguably, a powerful farewell to the epoch of Solidarity.

The Turned Back tells a tragicomic story about an ordinary man, the simple worker and party member Tomasz Siwek (Zbigniew Zamachowski), who, sent as a communist informer to a Solidarity demonstration, returns as a changed man (the title of the film is a play on words: in Polish *zawró-cony*=turned back is close to *nawrócony*=converted). At the gathering, Tomasz is overwhelmed by the exhilarating atmosphere and starts to sing religious and patriotic songs. Barely escaping the pursuit of militia special forces, he is later mistakenly identified as an active agitator and brutally interrogated by the secret police. Finally, the disillusioned Tomasz finds his own direction and protection in the Catholic Church.

The above account may be understood in symbolic terms as a story about political initiation. The protagonist is not an opportunist but a simple man lost in the complex reality of 1981. He is an ordinary man who comes from a village and feels alienated in a new industrial environment. Manipulated by representatives of the communist system and, accidentally, involved in Solidarity's actions, he starts the rapid process of self-education. Tomasz is not a converted sinner, but a person who is "turned back" from being an object of manipulation. Kutz stresses the grotesque, tragicomic aspect of his protagonist's adventures, particularly in the famous slapstick-like sequence in which Tomasz is chased by a group of riot militia.

Comedies

At the beginning of the 1990s, a few attempts to make deliberately commercial films resulted in some miserable releases. Intended as commercial endeavors, some films by formerly respected, artistically inclined directors proved to be both artistic and commercial failures, for example, Janusz Zaorski's *Panny i wdowy* (*Maidens and Widows*, 1991) and Barbara Sass's *Pajęczarki* (*Spider Women*, 1992). Fortunately, there were some exceptions. Apart from Radosław Piwowarski and Juliusz Machulski, who succeeded in making intelligent and apt popular films, other directors made single films that enjoyed commercial and critical success. These include Jerzy Domaradzki's *Łuk Erosa* (*Cupid's Bow*, 1988), Jan Łomnicki's *Wielka wsypa* (*The Big Giveaway*, 1993), and Filip Bajon's *Lepiej być piękną i bogatą* (*It's Better to Be Beautiful and Rich*, 1993).

Since his first feature film, *Aria for an Athlete*, Bajon has made a number of highly original, artistically sound films. Bajon's *It's Better to Be Beautiful and Rich*, a modern version of the Cinderella story with a distinct Polish flavor, is his successful first venture into mainstream commercial cinema. His young female protagonist, a weaver played by Adrianna Biedrzyńska, works in a declining factory that is permanently on strike. One day, she learns that she has inherited the factory. The implausible becomes possible in the film, which meanders toward an unavoidable happy ending that implicitly mocks popular films on success stories. The film has two layers: a melodramatic success story and an ironic commentary on the new Polish dream of becoming rich overnight. Bajon also plays with stereotypical Polish images of the West and of the "Wild East" (Ukraine; Bajon's film is a Polish, French, and Ukrainian coproduction). The film features a number of excellent Polish actors—among others, Daniel Olbrychski, Anna Prucnal, Bronisław Pawlik, and Marek Kondrat—who act (perhaps overact) in the manner of American prime-time television productions. The music and flamboyant photography emphasize the fairy-tale-like aspect of the film.

The award-winning *Kolejność uczuć* (*The Sequence of Feelings*, 1993), by Radosław Piwowarski (b. 1948), tells the story of a famous aging actor (Daniel Olbrychski) who comes to a provincial theater in Silesia to direct *Romeo and Juliet* and subsequently has a romance with a teenager, Julia (Juliet). The love story is set, atypically, against the background of industrial Silesia. This lyrical but unsentimental film, at times reminiscent of American romantic screwball comedies of the 1940s and 1950s, plays with Olbrychski's own star persona, which he earned in the late 1960s and the 1970s. His performance (a near mockery of "Olbrychski," a figure he created during his long career) also comes as a refreshing turn in his career.

Polish cinema is not internationally known for its comedies. The atmosphere of Polish films is usually serious, in keeping with the topics presented in these films: politics, social issues, and Polish history. Sylwester Chęciński's film about the introduction of martial law, *Rozmowy kontrolowane* (*Controlled Conversations*, 1992) brings some hope that in Poland it may finally be possible to laugh at matters normally reserved for serious treatment. Chęciński's fine comedy, scripted by a former contributor to Stanisław Bareja's comedies, Stanisław Tym (who also acts the main role), is set shortly before and after the implementation of martial law in Poland. Significantly, its innovation lies in its mockery of both sides. The protagonist (Tym), entangled in events that overwhelm him, unwillingly becomes a hero of the underground Solidarity. His undeserved fame spreads. Chęciński's mockery of Polish-style heroism and worn-out romantic gestures belongs to the tradition started by Andrzej Munk's antiheroic *Eroica*. The likeable hero of *Controlled Conversations* is involved in farcical adventures in the gloomy reality of the early 1980s in Poland. There is no ambiguity about him; he is a simple-minded, career-seeking individual, a product and a victim of the system.

Two later films, though lacking the strength of Chęciński's work, deal with similar issues told in a similar fashion. Marek Piwowski, the maker of the Polish cult film *The Cruise*, directed in 1993 the irreverent and uneven *Uprowadzenie Agaty* (*The Kidnapping of Agata*), based on a true story, about a politician who abuses his power to get rid of his daughter's lover. The new political situation, with its hastily created political elites, and the Catholic Church are the object of laughter and mockery. Piwowski's film, in spite of its satirical and comic potential, loses its initial impetus and turns out to be a collection of humorous yet disconnected and visually dry cabaret sketches. Konrad Szołajski's *Człowiek z ...* (*Man of ...*, 1993) goes so far as to mock Wajda's *Man of Marble* and *Man of Iron* and ridicule the "men of styrofoam," the descendants of brave dissidents turned new-style apparatchiks. Apart from direct references to Wajda's films, this sadly ineffective film tries to laugh at the current state of affairs, which is portrayed as corrupt, manipulated, and hopeless. In this world there are no ideas, and there is no protagonist to identify with.

Although the majority of contemporary comedies deal with the current political situation, there are also films focused more on characters than on politics. The exhibitionist film *Nothing Funny*, by Marek Koterski (b. 1942), is such an example. The film starts with an image of the deceased filmmaker, who tells the sad story of his life. One misfortune follows another from the time he is in diapers. Cezary Pazura plays the unfortunate loser, who goes through a midlife crisis and suffers from permanent artist's block. *Nothing Funny* can also be taken as a parody of the filmmaking community in Poland: several (sometimes crude) gags ridicule its alleged lack of professionalism and stupidity. Koterski blends fine humor and well-observed situations with lavatory jokes and unsophisticated imagery. Laughing at the state of the film industry, yet exhibiting a lack of filmic refinement himself, the director falls victim to his own mockery.

Dzieci i ryby (*Seen but Not Heard*, 1996) and *U pana Boga za piecem* (*Snug as a Bug in a Rug*, 1998), by Jacek Bromski (b. 1946), belong to the most interesting comedies made in recent years. *Seen but Not Heard* is the story of a forty-something generation trying to find itself in the new Polish reality. It narrates the story of a romance between a well-to-do woman (Anna Romantowska), running her own advertising business and raising a daughter, and her old romantic interest (Krzysztof Stroiński), once an aspiring scientist, now a provincial teacher.

Personal Films

Contemporary Polish cinema also originates with auteurs making low-budget, personal, easily recognizable films. Andrzej Barański and Jan Jakub Kolski deal with "provincial" Poland and the small, "insignificant" characters populating this landscape. Between 1989 and 1995, Kolski and Barański were the most prolific of Polish filmmakers, with six feature films, produced mostly by state television. Exceptional in the context of Polish cinema is the case of Andrzej Kondratiuk's *Wrzeciono czasu* (*The Spinning Wheel of Time*, 1995) and *Słoneczny zegar* (*The Sundial*, 1997), both low-budget, personal films produced by the director's family and friends.

Kondratiuk (b. 1936) started his career in 1965 with the television film *Monolog trębacza* (*The Trumpeter's Monologue*), and made several films in the 1970s, including *Dziura w ziemi* (*The Hole in the Ground*, 1970), *The Ascended*, and *Pełnia* (*Full Moon*, 1979). Kondratiuk and his wife actress Iga Cembrzyńska (b. 1939) made, in the 1990s, *The Spinning Wheel of Time* and *The Sundial*, both semiautobiographical stories about an aging filmmaker obsessed with the passage of time, cinema, and a young woman. These films are a continuation of Kondratiuk's earlier *Cztery pory roku* (*Four Seasons*, 1984), a work resembling a family album that portrays the Kondratiuks vacationing in their secluded family cabin. These films, however, are not "family movies," nor are they narcissistic pictures of the Polish intelligentsia. The discourse on aging, temporality, family bonds, and art is enhanced by the films' exhibitionist style, the creation of characters who border on being pretentious, and the inclusion of clever dialogues about existential problems. *The Spinning Wheel of Time*, in particular, succeeds in capturing the grotesque aspect of life as well as its poetry.[22] Critics in Poland labeled this type of cinema "private/separate cinema." The film's slow-paced scenes, unmistakable self-mockery, sarcastic humor, and visual beauty and Kondratiuk's perseverance in pursuing his vision were honored with the Special Award of the Jury at the 1995 Festival of Polish Films.

Since his impressive *A Provincial Woman*, Andrzej Barański (b. 1941) has made several notable films, including at the beginning of the 1990s *Kramarz* (*The Peddler*, 1990), *Kawalerskie życie na obczyźnie* (*A Bachelor's Life Abroad*, 1992), and *Dwa księżyce* (*Two Moons*, 1993). He is not a storyteller but rather a philosopher interested in the banality of everyday life. His films, although frequently set in the 1950s and the 1960s, ignore politics and are devoid of Polish romantic clichés. They resemble intimate miniatures, naive pictures that put everyday banality on the pedestal of art. Barański shows his protagonists' lives as heroic, tough but charming. His pragmatic protagonists are preoccupied with work and life; they do not shape history, ask "important questions," or fight/build the communist system. Instead, they approach life as a task to accomplish. They retain their composure when confronting everyday reality and survive day by day.

Barański's subtle version of realism has no predecessors in Polish cinema; it also differs from a version of realism developed in the early films of Jiří Menzel and Miloš Forman. The uniqueness of Barański's poetics is seen at its best in *The Peddler*. The protagonist Chruścik (Roman Kłosowski) is another de-romanticized, hard working individual who is not preoccupied with politics or history but with the everyday struggle for survival. Barański tells the story of his life in an extended flashback. Before the court, Chruścik narrates the futility of his past exertions, his failed attempts to fulfill the dream of his life (to own a small house), as well as his struggles with provincial authorities and unfair competition. The protagonist endures all of the hardships of life, yet, surprisingly, his account of Polish postwar history is devoid of politics. Politics plays a role in his life not unlike that of the elements, and is treated accordingly. A perpetual optimist with no luck on his side, Chruścik never complains.

Figure 8.1 Roman Kłosowski in Andrzej Barański's *The Peddler* (1990)

The Peddler is permeated with images of provincial Poland and the slow-paced lives of the province-dwellers. Due to the nature of his work (as an itinerant salesman), Chruścik moves from one small place to another. The camera follows him in these colorful places avoided by mainstream Polish cinema: country fairs and sleepy provincial towns. The importance of Barański's work lies in his painstaking re-creation of the material aspect of the Polish communist past. In this film, the paraphernalia of the Catholic Church and the communist system blend together into an idiosyncratic mélange characteristic of postwar Polish reality. Answering a question about the alleged banality of his films, Barański remarks: "It is not that I love banal aspects of life. I am, however, charmed by a certain order. Such an order with which one can live and die."[23]

Trained as a cinematographer, Jan Jakub Kolski (b. 1956) is probably the most important newly emerging figure in contemporary Polish cinema. He has made a number of highly original films since his well-received 1991 debut, *Pogrzeb kartofla* (*The Burial of Potato*). This success was followed by *Pograbek* (1992); *Jańcio Wodnik* (*Johnnie the Aquarius*, 1993); *Cudowne miejsce* (*Miraculous Place*, 1994); *Szabla od komendanta* (*The Sabre from the Commander*) and *Grający z talerza* (*The Plate Player*), both films released in 1995; the winner of the 1998 Festival of Polish Films, *Historia kina w Popielawach* (*The History of Cinema Theater in Popielawy*); and a recent film, a story about the Holocaust, *Daleko od okna* (*Away from a Window*, 2000). His slow-paced films are characterized by their fine cinematography (by Piotr Lenar) and stylized acting, particularly from Franciszek Pieczka (b. 1928), Mariusz Saniternik, and Grażyna Błęcka-Kolska (the director's wife). Kolski's films resemble in atmosphere Witold Leszczyński's classic *The Life of Matthew*, also starring Pieczka, and his later film *Konopielka*. Kolski's films share with *The Life of Matthew* the same obsession with mythologized rural communities and down-to-earth yet multidimensional protagonists who feel a sense of mystery when close to nature. In some of his films, however, the protagonists have more in common with characters depicted in *Konopielka*—characters who are backward, ignorant, and xenophobic. Kolski creates a private world, a mythical village, and protagonists who are outside of history. However, he does not make "rural films," as he frequently declares, but rather films that are set in a rural milieu; the problems they touch upon have universal appeal.

Kolski's prolific nature and his obsession with the private world lead inevitably to a certain mannerism, apparent in his *The Sabre from the Commander* and *The Plate Player*. To be sure, from a "personal director" we expect an "authorial style," and this frequently involves the repetition of themes, structures, and cinematic devices. Writer-director Kolski (all scripts are his own) is haunted by the same picturesque landscapes and characters, and by the presence of the religious/supernatural element in the lives of his down-to-earth yet unique characters.

The direct political references present in Kolski's first film, *The Burial of Potato*, gradually disappear from his later works, replaced by metaphysical meditation and folk wisdom combined with a unique version of lyricism and humor. Kolski is interested in oversensitive, weird, and marginalized characters whose worlds end with the horizon. His protagonists live as if outside of history; they are not political animals but simple people whose often banal and uneventful lives are limited to their village or small town and a marginal profession. Their aspirations follow suit. In Kolski's world, supernatural events are everyday phenomena, and Christianity coexists with remnants of Slavic pagan beliefs.

Johnnie the Aquarius is the essence of Kolski's stylized poetic, perhaps magic, realism. The film portrays a village thinker, Jańcio (Johnnie), who discovers his unusual ability to "control" water, which, under his power, is no longer constrained by the laws of gravity. Blessed with miraculous abilities and driven by a sense of mission, Jańcio leaves his secluded village and his pregnant, faithful wife Weronka for the outside world. Prosperity and fame change his life forever, endangering his marriage and, finally, bringing unhappiness to him and to those whom he loves. His son, born in a barn, has a devilish tail, the result of a spell thrown by a beggar for somebody else's wrongdoing. Desperate, Jańcio tries to reverse time and to repair the damage he has done to Weronka. He loses the battle with time, but, by accepting things as they are, he finds peace of mind while surrounded by his family.

With its multilayered construction and many references to religion, politics, and literature, *Johnnie the Aquarius* could be taken as a philosophical, political, or poetical parable, depending on a critic's predilection. Kolski's unusual story has no equivalent in Polish cinema; it has the appeal of a chromolithograph, of "primitive poetry," and of a philosophical folktale. Stylized dialogues and songs commenting on the action are combined with tableaux-like compositions of a world ruled by mysticism. The frequent use of slow motion stresses the importance of the moment and of the characters inscribed in a rural landscape.

Kolski's poetics and his portrayal of the farmers' class, as well as Barański's vision of provincial life, are not challenged in Poland. An important stream of so-called "Polish rural literature" has no filmic counterparts. For instance, Ryszard Ber's adaptation of Wiesław Myśliwski's prose, *Kamień na kamieniu* (*Not One Stone upon Another*, 1995), resulted in a disconnected picture devoid of the epic scope of the novel (interestingly, Myśliwski is credited as a scriptwriter of the film). Practically, the only

Figure 8.2 Franciszek Pieczka in Jan Jakub Kolski's *Johnnie the Aquarius* (1993)

picture that has to be mentioned here is *Śmierć dziecioroba* (*Death of the Kidsmaker*, 1991), by Wojciech Nowak (b. 1957). This film belongs to a different kind of realism. Like Kolski's *The Burial of Potato*, it is a cruel, merciless picture of the province. The reality Nowak presents is loathsome, peopled by grotesque, vulgar characters. The film's protagonist, a provincial Don Juan, refuses to marry a pregnant security officer's daughter. His refusal is not a nonconformist act, not a Don Juan's revolt, nor a political gesture. Instead, he is at pains to emphasize his separation from a world he despises, but of which he is paradoxically a part. The film's mise en scène stresses the ugliness and trashy characteristics of a degraded world.

Female Filmmakers

In recent years, several films made by female Polish filmmakers have enjoyed critical and/or commercial success, including works by Dorota Kędzierzawska, Teresa Kotlarczyk, Magdalena Łazarkiewicz (Agnieszka Holland's younger sister), and, in particular, Barbara Sass.

Dorota Kędzierzawska (b. 1957) started her career with *Koniec świata* (*The End of the World*, 1988, television film) and *Diabły, diabły* (*Devils, Devils*, 1991). Her subsequent films, *Wrony* (*Crows*, 1994) and *Nic* (*Nothing*, 1998), have been very popular on the international film festival circuit. *Crows* tells the story of a lonely twelve-year-old girl, who kidnaps a two-year-old toddler, plays at being her mother, and then returns her many hours later. The slow narration centers entirely on the two girls and their journey; other characters appear and then quickly fade away in this film about the need for love. The film's simple, poetic narrative is beautifully visualized by Artur Reinhart; his splendid cinematography captures sophisticated images of an old town, of beaches, and of the sea—the scenery of the journey. In these beautiful yet cold landscapes, the older girl's desperate search for love becomes almost a cry in the dark.

Another promising female director who started her career in the 1990s is Teresa Kotlarczyk (b. 1955). She is the author of *Zakład* (*The Reformatory*, 1990), an intriguing film dealing with the problem of manipulation and, on a different level, with moral questions involved in filmmaking. Kotlarczyk's *Odwiedź mnie we śnie* (*Visit Me in My Dream*, 1996) is the Polish equivalent of *Ghost* (1990). Ala, a beautiful and successful writer, dies in a car accident, leaving her three children and husband unable to come to terms with their loss. The parallel action portrays Ala in a kind of heavenly waiting room reconsidering her past life and watching her family on earth learning to live anew. In an emotional finale, she returns to earth disguised as a different woman and is recognized by her family. Kotlarczyk's most recent film, *Prymas. Trzy lata z tysiąclecia* (*The Primate: Three Years Out of the Millennium*, 2000), tells the story of the internment of the Polish Catholic primate Stefan Wyszyński by the communist authorities during the Stalinist period.

Magdalena Łazarkiewicz (b. 1954) is chiefly known for the youth-oriented *Ostatni dzwonek* (*The Last Bell*, 1989), the politically oriented *Odjazd* (*Departure*, 1992, directed with her husband, Piotr Łazarkiewicz), and *Białe małżeństwo* (*White Marriage*, 1993). The last film deals openly with young female sexuality as well as female psychology. Set against the backdrop of the idyllic scenery of prewar Poland—a picturesque country landscape with a pleasant manor, marching cavalry men, and burgeoning girls in virginal white dresses—the film mixes subjective and objective reality, dreams and waking reality, and also various genres. The young female protagonist rebels against her own gender and the traditional role prescribed for her. She despises and is afraid of matrimonial sex without love, with all of its biological connotations, and does not want to follow the example of other women in her family. *White Marriage* can be taken as an intelligent discussion of female sexuality with strong Freudian overtones, something of a rarity in Polish cinema.

In the shadow of Poland's internationally known filmmakers, Barbara Sass (b. 1936) has developed her own personal style. After working as an assistant director on films by Wajda, Has, and Skolimowski, she started her independent career in 1980 with the film *Without Love*. Following the success of this film, she developed a body of work characterized by thematic unity (she is also a scriptwriter) and by a simple documentary-like visual style (her husband, Wiesław Zdort, always participates as a cinematographer). Like Márta Mészáros of Hungary, Sass presents a feminist perspective and confronts issues largely ignored in overtly political Central Europe: the plight of women and gender relations. Like Mészáros and the majority of Central European female filmmakers, Sass also objects to narrow feminist interpretations of her films. Nevertheless, given Sass's manifest interest in feminist issues, her works almost force critics to take a feminist perspective. For instance, her early works—starting with *Without Love* through *The Debutante*, *The Shout*, and *The Girls from Nowolipki* and its sequel *Crab Apple Tree*—portray young women struggling to achieve their goals in spite of political and psychosociological pressures. These films center more on characters than on action or psychosociological backgrounds. Sass appropriately calls her early films "psychological portraits narrated in a rhythm corresponding to that of the contemporary world: dynamic, sharp, and fast."[24]

In the 1990s Sass completed four films: *Historia niemoralna* (*An Immoral Story*, 1990), *Tylko strach* (*Only Fear*, 1993), *Temptation*, and *Jak narkotyk* (*Like a Drug*, 1999). *An Immoral Story* comments on the creative process of filmmaking. Featuring the star of Sass's early films, Dorota Stalińska, the film tells a fictional story about an actress and reflects on being an artist (actress/filmmaker) at the same time. Throughout the film, a female director (perhaps Sass herself) comments off-screen to her editor on several scenes from her film in the making. *An Immoral Story* is full of intertextual references to Sass's early films, to Polish cinema, and to Stalińska's career as an actress. In spite of its significance, this intricate work did not receive the critical acclaim it deserves in Poland. After *Only Fear*, the story of a successful television journalist, Katarzyna (Anna Dymna's winning performance), struggling to overcome alcoholism, Barbara Sass directed one of the finest Polish films produced in 1995, *Temptation* (discussed in chapter 9).

Krzysztof Kieślowski

Krzysztof Kieślowski, born in 1941 and arguably the best-known contemporary Polish filmmaker, died in March 1996. His *Dekalog* (*Decalogue*, 1988), a ten-part series of contemporary television films loosely based on the Bible's Ten Commandments, was hailed as a great achievement and incontestably placed its director in the realm of renowned filmic authors. *Krótki film o zabijaniu* (*A Short Film about Killing*) and *Krótki film o miłości* (*A Short Film about Love*), the extended feature versions of two parts of *Decalogue*, were exceptionally well received in Europe. Kieślowski's last films, *Podwójne życie Weroniki* (*The Double Life of Véronique*, 1991) and his trilogy *Three Colors: Blue, Red, White* (1993–1994), consolidated his position as a distinguished European auteur.

A closer look at Kieślowski's oeuvre and his artistic persona reveals that he does not fit the traditional image of a "great Central European auteur" obsessed with politics and history. His films are also unique in the context of Polish cinema, which is usually preoccupied with the local romantic tradition. For a number of critics who are used to Polish film functioning, for the most part, as an expression of Polish history and political tensions, Kieślowski's films (especially his 1990s international coproductions) can be puzzling. I argue that Kieślowski's last films embrace many stylistic and thematic obsessions characteristic of European art cinema and, therefore, should be examined in a larger than national context.

As opposed to other internationally known Polish filmmakers, such as Andrzej Wajda or Krzysztof Zanussi, Kieślowski was never directly involved in politics nor was he ever explicitly political in his films or in public appearances. Although persistently subjected to an Aesopian reading by Polish critics and filmgoers alike, his early, still underappreciated films, such as *Camera Buff* or *Blind Chance*, do not demonize the communist system. Rather, they show the system as an obstacle to achieving happiness and, to use the title of his 1976 film, *Calm*. Discussing Kieślowski's career, Tadeusz Sobolewski points out the problem that Kieślowski's "apolitical" stand generated in Poland: "None of the critics in Poland had the foresight to perceive the uniqueness and specificity of Kieślowski's films, except in terms of their being a function of social, political or religious aspirations. The Polish critic persistently forces the artist to answer the questions concerning social issues."[25]

Perpetually independent, Kieślowski operated outside of mainstream Central European aesthetics. Within this highly politicized culture, in which political choices were of greater importance than aesthetic priorities,

Kieślowski was clearly an outsider, not afraid of expressing unpopular views concerning, for example, religion and political commitment. Kieślowski frequently stressed his disillusionment with politics. In 1994, explaining his surprising decision to retire from filmmaking at the age of 53, he claimed that "one of the reasons of my departure from the cinema is my dislike for fulfilling public roles, and a longing for privacy."[26]

Kieślowski's move to international coproductions and his subsequent critical recognition were considered by some Polish critics as suspicious.[27] Unlike other Polish artists, Kieślowski achieved his international auteur status without relying on the Polish romantic tradition, which, as Bolesław Michałek says, is characterized by its "battle for social justice, and its preoccupation with gaining independence, the tradition in which dilemmas are solved by a single gesture. Kieślowski indicates that a dilemma is something you live with."[28] Michałek's statement closely resembles Paul Schrader's distinction between American movies, which are "based on the assumption that life presents you with problems," and European films "based on the conviction that life confronts you with dilemmas—and while problems are something you solve, dilemmas cannot be solved, they're merely probed or investigated."[29] Kieślowski's films certainly deal with dilemmas.

In spite of its religious connotations, *Decalogue* is not an exploration of supernatural phenomena but an acute analysis of pre-1989 Poland. The ten-part film, written by Kieślowski with Krzysztof Piesiewicz (his regular co-scriptwriter since 1984), portrays a pessimistic picture of a harsh world in which moral choices have to be made against the pressure of politics and economics. Kieślowski's "entomological observations" of Polish society give *Decalogue* the sense of a semidocumentary film. The ugliness and grayness of the dehumanized urban landscape dominate the filmic landscape, together with close-ups of people surviving these harsh conditions. The Bergmanesque dilemmas depicted here are appropriate for Kieślowski, who is known for his admiration of some of Bergman's films, *The Silence* (1963) in particular. (Interestingly, in his 1995 interview, trumpeted as "the last one," Bergman listed *Decalogue* as one of the five contemporary films that he "most benefited from.")[30]

The semidocumentary aspect of *Decalogue* is particularly evident in *A Short Film about Killing*, which alludes to the Fifth Commandment. The film tells the story of a young drifter, Jacek (Mirosław Baka), who commits the brutal murder of a taxi driver, is sentenced to death for his crime, and is hanged. Kieślowski plays with three distinct viewpoints: that of the murderer, that of his victim, and that of the young lawyer who prepares for the lawyer's bar examination and later gets his first case—defending the killer. Kieślowski, as usual, brings into focus small details and stresses the dreadful aspect of both the murder of the taxi driver and the execution authorized by the state.

Kieślowski's Polish-French coproductions, starting with *The Double Life of Véronique*, are often read allegorically by Western critics as commentaries

Figure 8.3 Mirosław Baka (left) and Jan Tesarz in Krzysztof Kieślowski's *A Short Film about Killing* (1988)

on the relationship between Poland and Western Europe. *The Double Life of Véronique*, Kieślowski's breakthrough film, is a rare "art film" dealing with the subject of doubleness. This is presented in the story of two young women, Weronika in Poland and Véronique in France, both memorably played by Irène Jacob (winner of the Best Actress award at Cannes), who do not know each other but whose lives have many mysterious parallels. The element of chance is a driving force in the film. The protagonists' "double life" is intensified by Sławomir Idziak's remarkable cinematography and Zbigniew Preisner's poignant score.

This slow-paced enigma, beautifully crafted and governed by a sense of mystery, appears to be almost the essence of "European art cinema," due to its personal character, sensuality, and self-referentiality and to the fact that it is saturated with art film clichés. Kieślowski's episodic film, full of unexplained occurrences, relies heavily on magnification, enigmatic doubling, and symbolism. Its elliptical narrative construction, which is mysterious to the point of teasing the spectator, resists any explicit interpretation. The story about duality is told with the extensive use of mirrors that not only multiply space but also make the whole film a spectacle of ambiguity. The film's energy and breadth does not allow it,

Figure 8.4 Irène Jacob in *The Double Life of Veronique* (1991, Krzysztof Kieślowski)

however, to be another "fairly conventional box of ontological tricks, recycling traditional metafictional paradoxes."[31]

Kieślowski's formalist exercise probably did to art films in the 1990s what Sergio Leone's "spaghetti Westerns" did to the Western in the 1960s—the accumulation and intensification of features characteristic of the "genre." The accumulation of symbolic associations and other art cinema qualities in *The Double Life of Véronique* prompted Gaylyn Studlar to remark that it looks almost like "a virtual parody of all the established stereotypes of Continental filmmaking associated with an earlier generation of filmmakers, such as Ingmar Bergman and Alain Resnais."[32]

For Kieślowski, this film also marks a radical departure from his early filmic essays to polished international and "nonpolitical" coproductions. This is a turn toward privacy and "calmness," a retreat from the pressure of politics that is openly manifested in the Polish part of the film. For instance, Weronika does not notice a huge statue of Lenin being towed away on a truck, signaling, perhaps, the fall of communism. In another scene, when Weronika stares at her double among the tourists, she seems totally unaware of the political demonstration and the riot police surrounding her at Cracow's Main Square. Weronika is as free from politics as is the film, to the astonishment of many critics.

Kieślowski's *Three Colors*, a major cinematic achievement of the 1990s, is a trilogy inspired by the French tricolor, in which blue stands for liberty, white for equality, and red for fraternity. In spite of these connotations, Kieślowski does not seem to be particularly interested in politics or social issues; instead, once again, he deals with protagonists facing moral dilemmas, with their individual quests for the three values embodied in the French flag.

The first part of the trilogy, *Blue*, tells the story of Julie (Juliette Binoche) who endures the death of her husband and child in a car accident. The camera captures Julie's grief, her attempts to detach herself from her friends, to free herself from the past. When Julie accidentally learns about her husband's infidelity, she gradually embraces the life she has attempted to suppress. As in *The Double Life of Véronique*, the striking musical score by Zbigniew Preisner, Kieślowski's composer since *No End*, dominates the trilogy, especially the *Blue* part. It replaces dialogue and strengthens the narrative. *Blue*, in fact, is also about music. Julie's late husband was a famous composer who left an unfinished piece devoted to the idea of Europe's unification. At the end of the film, Preisner's music explodes with the "European Concerto," which employs St. Paul's Letter to the Corinthians.

White, the "Polish" part of *Three Colors*, portrays Karol (Zbigniew Zamachowski), a Polish hairdresser living in Paris and going through a bitter divorce with his French wife Dominique (Julie Delpy). After Karol is (improbably) smuggled into Poland in a suitcase, he quickly amasses a fortune by speculating on land. In order to get even with his French wife, he fakes his own death. When Julie appears in Poland to claim his legacy, she is arrested and accused of murdering Karol. The second part of the trilogy is frequently seen by Western critics as commenting on the ties between Poland and the West. For Paul Coates, for instance, *White* "dramatizes Polish fears of exclusion from Europe," and "Karol's impotence may be that of a Pole confronting locked European doors...."[33] Such political interpretations of the film seem to be valid—the film includes some penetrating, humorous references to Polish "capitalist reality"—yet this is not the tone of the majority of reviews published in Poland. *White* is discussed there as merely a "comic interlude" within the trilogy, a film devoid of serious examination of Polish reality and filled with suspicious art house clichés.[34]

Kieślowski's *Red*, probably the most sophisticated part of the triptych, tells the story of a young fashion model, Valentine (Irène Jacob), and her chance encounter with a retired judge (Jean-Louis Trintignant) who is obsessed with illegal electronic surveillance. The complex relationship that develops between them is at the center of the film. Another character is also introduced, Valentine's neighbor, Auguste, a young law student whose life mirrors that of the old judge. At the end of the film, Valentine and Auguste are among the seven survivors rescued from a ferry accident. In an attempt to sum up the trilogy, the film also lists additional survivors whose names include other protagonists of the trilogy.

Kieślowski's *Three Colors*, which premiered at major European festivals (an important aspect, because it shows Kieślowski's aspirations) is ostensibly self-reflective and self-referential. As in *Decalogue*, characters appear and reappear in the trilogy; "Van den Budenmayer's" music (actually composed by Preisner) is quoted extensively. Kieślowski remarks that these interconnections are "for the pleasure of some cinephiles who like to find points of reference from one film to another."[35] The director employs chance scenes with no apparent link to the story, rejects causal narrative, and peoples his films with familiar supporting characters (for example, elderly ladies slowly crossing the street, perhaps reminding the protagonist of the fragility of life). The same tendency toward mannerism is evident in the cinematography and mise en scène, including the extensive use of the films' key colors to stress the films' themes, and the reliance on mirror images, filters, and views through windows and doors. Kieślowski made films for cine buffs; there are more questions than answers in his cinema, and everything here is geared toward mystery.

Tadeusz Szczepański comments that "Kieślowski ingeniously multiplies subtle refrains, parallelism, counterpoints, correspondences, symmetries, echoes, and mirror effects not only on the level of narrative threads, situations, characters, or props in the roles of *res dramatica*, but also in the mise en scène and in the use of color, sound, and, of course, music."[36] Another Polish scholar, Grażyna Stachówna, lists recurrent motifs in the trilogy that also refer to Kieślowski's earlier films: "colors, slogans of the French Revolution, blind chance, Van den Budenmayer, voyeurism and eavesdropping, an old woman with a bottle, the final cry of the protagonists, windows, beads made of glass, two frank coin, loneliness, jealousy, humiliation, contempt, sex, suicide."[37]

The semantic richness of Kieślowski's trilogy is not, however, taken by all Polish film scholars and critics as a sign of art. For instance, Mariola Jankun-Dopartowa claims that *Three Colors* cannot be described within the existing boundaries of art cinema. According to her, the trilogy is somewhere between the domain of Bergman's cinema and videoclip or "pretentious" European production. She accuses Kieślowski of bordering on kitsch sensibility, telling stories familiar from numerous soap operas and "magazines for thinking women," and abandoning his earlier film poetics.[38]

For a number of Polish critics, Kieślowski seems to be the true hero in his films. Tadeusz Sobolewski writes that in spite of Kieślowski's often declared agnosticism, his films are imbued with strong religious overtones. For instance, the judge in *Red* "becomes simultaneously the figure of Kieślowski and the Lord God, as imagined by common folk." The same critic notes that Kieślowski abandoned "tales of fictitious characters, much in the same way he had once abandoned the documentary for fiction, for something in a way of an 'inner documentary' attempting to render inexpressible, agnostic states."[39]

* * * *

Although Kieślowski's films are unique in the Polish context, one may see a continuation of his cinema in the recent films made by Jerzy Stuhr: *Spis cudzołożnic* (*The List of Adulteresses*, 1994), *Historie miłosne* (*Love Stories*, 1997), *Tydzień z życia mężczyzny* (*A Week in the Life of a Man*, 1999), and *Duże zwierzę* (*The Big Animal*, 2000).[40] *The List of Adulteresses*, with Stuhr in the leading role, tells the story of a middle-aged academic who thinks back on his old girlfriends and women from his past during the official visit of a Swedish academic. Stuhr's film offers not only a nostalgic journey into one man's past but also a loving introduction to the unique character of Cracow.

One of Kieślowski's favorite actors, Stuhr also wrote and directed the 1997 winner of the Festival of Polish Films, *Love Stories*. In this film, dedicated to Kieślowski, Stuhr presents four parallel stories with four different protagonists: a university teacher, a priest, an army officer, and a convicted thief (all played by Stuhr). They have to choose between love and career, between the complications that love might introduce into their lives and the boredom of illusory stability. Stuhr employs an "art film atmosphere," down-to-earth characters facing moral choices, and mysterious, otherworldly figures like the "Master-Pollster," who questions the four protagonists about the true nature of their choices. *Love Stories* resembles a morality play permeated with the very metaphysical ingredients that are so characteristic of Kieślowski's last films.

In *A Week in the Life of a Man*, Jerzy Stuhr casts himself as public prosecutor Adam Borowski, who is eager to prosecute others, yet in his private

Figure 8.5 Jerzy Stuhr and Irina Alfiorova in *Love Stories* (1997, Jerzy Stuhr)

life is equally guilty. He has an extramarital affair, attempts to avoid paying taxes, and does not understand his wife's (Gosia Dobrowolska) urge to
adopt a child. The contrast between the public and private sphere of life
and the subtle criticism of the emerging post-communist middle class in
Poland are stressed by the ironic use of a line from *Hamlet*, sung in a song
by Wojciech Kilar. The choir, to which the prosecutor belongs, rehearses
several times "What a piece of work is a man," an ironic comment on the
duality of the main protagonist. Stuhr's most recent film, *The Big Animal* is
based on a script written by Kieślowski in 1973. It tells the story about a
simple office worker who, despite problems with his neighbors and the
authorities, takes care of a camel that had been abandoned by a wandering
circus. The camel clearly serves as a poetic metaphor of tolerance and personal freedom in Stuhr's realistic observations of small-town mentality.

* * * *

Political and economic transformations profoundly affected the Polish
film industry in the 1990s. The transition to a market economy changed
the relationship between the filmmakers and the state, and also between

the filmmakers and their audiences. After a period of noticeable crises at the beginning of the 1990s, recent years have brought some moderate optimism: Polish films have started to compete successfully with Hollywood's products on Polish screens. Some of the established filmmakers have regained their popularity. And emerging innovative auteurs like Kolski, Krauze, and Stuhr have found loyal audiences and critical recognition. A new cinema and new names have surfaced in Poland since 1989. If debuts testify to the rank and health of any national cinema, then the current state of Polish cinema is not as dark as sometimes portrayed.

The current situation in the Polish film industry indicates that the future belongs to those filmmakers who are too young to be "tainted" by the past and to those whose experiences liberated them from the clichés and preoccupations of the pre-1989 cinema. The future also belongs to films that are always popular among Polish audiences—adaptations of the national literary canon. Jerzy Hoffman's *Ogniem i mieczem* (*With Fire and Sword*), based on Henryk Sienkiewicz's historical epic novel, and Andrzej Wajda's *Pan Tadeusz*, an adaptation of Adam Mickiewicz's book-length poem, both released in 1999, proved to be the most successful films to have premiered in Poland after 1992.[41]

Notes

1. See Edward Zajiček, "Kinematografia," in *Encyklopedia kultury polskiej XX wieku: Film, kinematografia*, ed. Edward Zajiček (Warsaw: Instytut Kultury and Komitet Kinematografii, 1994), 93.
2. Monique van Dusseldorp and Raphaël Loucheux, eds., *Towards the Digital Revolution: European Television and Film between Market and Revolution* (Liege: The European Institute for the Media, 1994), 50 and 53.
3. Figures from the *Polish Film Guide 1996/97* (Warsaw: Film Polski, 1997), 9; and Barbara Hollender, "Kronika. Bilans roku 1992 w kinach," *Kino* 1 (1993): 2.
4. Ibid.
5. Zajiček, "Kinematografia," 92 and 97.
6. *The Catalogue of the XX Festival of Polish Feature Films in Gdynia* (Gdynia, 1995), 111–115. Also, "Jak powstaje film" *Kino* 11 (1994): 14–16.
7. "Popularność filmów polskich 29.12.95 – 29.08.96," *Film Pro* 10, no. 18 (1996): 11.
8. This fragment of *Ashes and Diamonds* was also mentioned by Wajda in his address at the Congress of Polish Film. Andrzej Wajda, "Co się stało z polskim kinem?" *Kino* 2 (1997): 5.
9. Andrzej Wajda, "Wolni od czego?" *Kino* 1 (1992): 3–5.
10. Tadeusz Sobolewski, "Filmy polskie mówią: w tym kraju nic się nie zmieni" [a statement of the Polish critic at the Forum of the Polish Filmmakers Association in Gdynia, 1991], *Kino* 1 (1992): 2.
11. Józef Tischner, *Nieszczęsny dar wolności* (Cracow: Znak, 1996).
12. Kazimierz Kutz, "Przestaliśmy istnieć" [fragment of a discussion: "Co z polskim kinem?"], *Kino* 11 (1992): 21.
13. Kazimierz Kutz's column "Z mojego młyna," *Kino* 7–8 (1995): 70.

14. Wanda Wertenstein and Jerzy Płażewski, "Współprodukcje: hydra czy szansa," *Kino* 6 (1993): 6–9.
15. For instance, opinions expressed in the special edition of *Reżyser* [Film Director], "Tren na śmierć cenzora," 11 (1992): 1–8. Published with *Kino* 11 (1992). Also, an interview with writer and filmmaker Tadeusz Konwicki: "Wróżby z dnia dzisiejszego," *Kino* 1 (1991): 5–6.
16. "Tren na śmierć cenzora," 2.
17. Danusia Stok, ed., *Kieślowski on Kieślowski* (London, Boston: Faber and Faber, 1993), 151–152.
18. Anita Skwara, "Film Stars Do Not Shine in the Sky Over Poland: The Absence of Popular Cinema in Poland," in *Popular European Cinema*, ed. Richard Dyer and Ginnette Vincendeau (London, New York: Routledge, 1992), 230.
19. See Krzysztof Zanussi's comment, "Obrona kosmopolityzmu," *Kino* 2 (1992): 16–18.
20. *The Ring with a Crowned Eagle* is, in a sense, an appendix to Wajda's famous *Ashes and Diamonds*.
21. Marczewski's film was the winner of the 1990 Festival of Polish Films in Gdynia. After the introduction of martial law in Poland, as a sign of protest, the director had remained silent for almost ten years ("internal exile" was the Polish term to describe such acts).
22. *The Spinning Wheel of Time* is virtually a family enterprise. Andrzej Kondratiuk is the writer-director-star and co-cinematographer of this film. His wife Iga Cembrzyńska, a well-known actress-singer, acts as producer-star. Among the few actors in this intimate film is Janusz Kondratiuk (b. 1943), Andrzej's brother, a director known mostly for his distinguished television films made in the spirit of an early Miloš Forman, for example, his cult film in Poland, *Dziewczyny do wzięcia* (*Marriageable Girls*, 1972). He also made full-length films in the 1990s, including *Głos* (*The Voice*, 1992) and *Złote runo* (*The Golden Fleece*, 1997).
23. Tadeusz Sobolewski, "Realizm Andrzeja Barańskiego" [an interview with Barański], *Kino* 11 (1992): 12.
24. Maciej Maniewski, "Między miłością a dojrzałością" [an interview with Barbara Sass], *Kino* 6 (1996): 6.
25. Tadeusz Sobolewski, "Peace and Rebellion: Some Remarks on the Creative Output of Krzysztof Kieślowski," *Polish Cinema in Ten Takes*, ed. Ewelina Nurczyńska-Fidelska and Zbigniew Batko (Łódź: Łódzkie Towarzystwo Naukowe, 1995), 124.
26. Ibid., 125.
27. Mirosław Przylipiak writes about the reception of Kieślowski's films in Poland, "Filmy fabularne Krzysztofa Kieślowskiego w zwierciadle polskiej krytyki filmowej," *Kino Krzysztofa Kieślowskiego*, ed. Tadeusz Lubelski (Cracow: Universitas, 1997), 213–247; idem, "Monter i studentka," *Kino* 3 (1997): 6–9 and 50.
28. Sobolewski, "Peace and Rebellion," 126.
29. Paul Schrader, quoted in Thomas Elsaesser, "Putting on a Show: The European Art Movie," *Sight and Sound* 4, no. 4 (1994): 24.
30. Kieślowski's fascination with Bergman is discussed extensively in Tadeusz Szczepański's essay, "Kieślowski wobec Bergmana, czyli Tam, gdzie spotykają się równoległe," in Lubelski, *Kino Krzysztofa Kieślowskiego*, 163–171. [Szczepański quotes Jannike Åhlund's interview with Bergman, "Sista intervjun med Bergman," *Expressen* (23 November 1995).]
31. Jonathan Romney, "The Double Life of Véronique," *Sight and Sound* 1, no. 11 (1992): 43.
32. Gaylyn Studlar, "The Double Life of Véronique," *Magill's Cinema Annual 1992: A Survey of the Films of 1991*, ed. Frank N. Magill (Pasadena and Englewood Cliffs: Salem Press, 1992), 120.
33. Paul Coates, "The Sense of Ending: Reflections on Kieślowski's Trilogy," *Film Quarterly* 50, no. 2 (1996–1997): 23–24.
34. See, for instance, Tadeusz Sobolewski, "Równanie w dół: Trzy kolory: Biały," *Kino* 2 (1994): 10–11; and Mariola Jankun-Dopartowa, "Trójkolorowy transparent: Vive le chaos!" *Kino* 6 (1995): 4–7.

35. Serge Mensonge, "Three Colours: *Blue, White* and *Red.* Krzysztof Kieślowski and Friends" [interview], *Cinema Papers* 99 (1994): 30.
36. Szczepański, "Kieślowski wobec Bergmana," 165.
37. Grażyna Stachówna, *"Trzy kolory:* wariacje na jeden temat," in Lubelski, *Kino Krzysztofa Kieślowskiego,* 102.
38. Jankun-Dopartowa, "Trójkolorowy transparent," 4–7.
39. Sobolewski, "Peace and Rebellion," 136 and 123.
40. Jerzy Stuhr is a well-known theatrical and film actor associated with the famous Teatr Stary in Cracow. He has appeared in several celebrated films made by, among others, Andrzej Wajda, Feliks Falk, Krzysztof Kieślowski, and Juliusz Machulski. Apart from Stuhr, directorial careers started such established actors as Bogusław Linda with *Seszele* (*Seychelles*, 1989), Krystyna Janda with *Pestka* (*Pip*, 1996), Olaf Lubaszenko with *Sztos* (*Making the Sting*, 1997), and Marek Kondrat with *Prawo ojca* (*Father's Law*, 1999).
41. According to the Polish weekly *Polityka, With Fire and Sword* (released in February 1999) remains the most popular film premiered in Poland between 1992 and June 1999 with 6,747,000 viewers. *Titanic* (1998) remains second with 3,516,000 viewers; *Jurassic Park* (1993), third with 2,742,096; *The Lion King* (1994), fourth with 2,722,000; and another Polish film, *Kiler* (1997), is ranked fifth with 2,201,502 viewers. *Polityka's* report does not include *Pan Tadeusz*, which premiered in October 1999 and was quickly seen by six million viewers. [The editorial board of *Polityka*], "Raport *Polityki*: 10 lat na wolności," *Polityka*, 5 June 1999, 24. In 1999, Polish films shared an unprecedented 60 percent of the local market. The successes of Polish films prompted the *Rzeczpospolita* film critic, Barbara Hollender, to title her review article "Hoffman and Wajda Won over Hollywood." Barbara Hollender, "Hoffman i Wajda wygrali z Hollywood," *Rzeczpospolita*, 26 January 2000, 8.

9

The Representation of Stalinism in Polish Cinema

Focusing on the past seems almost natural in Polish cinema. Like Central European cinema in general, it has familiarized viewers with its political contexts and messages through the presentation of Central Europeans as victims of a dark history. In the novel political situation in Central Europe after 1989, one could expect "the return of the repressed" in cinema and other art forms, the return of history, and a certain boldness in a critical reappraisal of the not-so-distant past. The thorough transition from communism to democracy appears impossible without an exhaustive understanding of the past. In a time of considerable political openness, in which (almost) everything can be said candidly, the double talk and subversive messages provided by the old Polish cinema are no longer needed.

Several openly political films, made at the beginning of the 1990s, referred to recent Polish history, but reflected immorality and corruption in 1980s terms—they were both commercial and artistic failures. Some attempts to reconstruct events experienced under martial law never received the critical or public acclaim they deserve. Kazimierz Kutz's passionate film about the tragedy at the Wujek coal mine, *Death as a Slice of Bread*, is just one example of a political work that has gone largely unnoticed. Polish audiences and critics alike seem to have grown tired of history, politics, and national martyrology. In spite of that, films featuring recent Polish history that attempt to recover long-suppressed levels of "national memory" do exist in post-1989 Polish cinema. Among them are films dealing with complex Polish-Jewish relations and works portraying the Stalinist past.

Due to strict political censorship, the question of the legacy of Polish Stalinism remained virtually untouched until the mid-1970s.[1] The process of unveiling the Stalinist years started in Polish as well as in Hungarian cinema in the late 1970s and was followed by the "perestroika films" in the 1980s in the former Soviet Union. Earlier, a group of distinguished films made in the former Czechoslovakia—Jaromil Jireš's Žert (The Joke, 1968), Jiří Menzel's Skřivánci na niti (Larks on a String, 1969), and Vojtěch Jasný's Všichni dobří rodáci (All My Good Countrymen, 1969)—had dealt with this problem.

Hungarian filmmakers, in particular, contributed extensively to this "genre." In the late 1970s they were quite politically blunt and moved out of the safe territory of Aesopian language. The denunciation of Stalinism was reflected in such critically acclaimed films as Péter Bacsó's The Witness (released in 1978 after being "shelved" for almost nine years), András Kovács's Ménezgazda (The Stud Farm, 1978), Pál Gábor's Angi Vera (1978), and Márta Mészáros' Napló gyermekeimnek (Diary for My Children, 1982) and Napló szerelmeimnek (Diary for My Loves, 1987). Károly Makk's Egymásra nézve (Another Way, 1982) and Péter Gothár's Megáll az idö (Time Stands Still, 1981) put the issues of sexual nonconformity and political nonconformity into the foreground.[2] David Paul aptly observed that the relative openness of the Hungarian regime allowed filmmakers to explore the Stalinist period in Hungarian history. The number of these films and their reception in Hungary prompted Paul to say: "Ironically, just when the Soviet cinema began at last to peel back the layers of restriction that had so long buried the past, Hungarian moviegoers considered Stalinism old hat."[3]

Stalinism also appears as a filmic genre on its own in the former Soviet Union, starting with Tengiz Abuladze's Pokayanie (Repentance, 1987), the film that, as Anna Lawton puts it, "brought the vampire out of its bunker for all to see."[4] In recent Russian cinema, Stalinism and Stalin himself have become almost "fashionable." For Svetlana Boym, Stalin is "a mythical fetish of the new Soviet cinema." She claims that "Stalin's cinematic repertoire includes the tragic and the farcical, the sublime and the ridiculous, the terrifying and the banal, fiction and documentary."[5]

Return of the Repressed: *Man of Marble* and Its Followers

At the beginning of the 1970s a number of Polish documentary films tried to uncover the Stalinist past. Wojciech Wiszniewski's stylized documentary film about the Stalinist period, Opowieść o człowieku, który wykonał 552% normy (The Story of a Man Who Produced 552 Percent of the Norm, 1973), portrays the life of a coal miner-Stakhanovite, Bernard Bugdoł, "the Polish People's Republic Citizen Kane."[6] This and other films by Wiszniewski that examine the Stalinist work competition—Wanda Gościmińska—włókniarka (Wanda Gościmińska, the Textile Worker, 1975) and Stolarz (Carpenter, 1976)—were banned from distribution and not released until 1981. Krzysztof Kieślowski's Murarz (Bricklayer, 1973) and Ryszard Bugajski's Słowo o Wincentym Pstrowskim (A Word on Wincenty Pstrowski,

1973), both released in 1981, also deal with the exemplary workers of the Stalinist era.

One of Andrzej Wajda's best-known works, *Man of Marble* (1977), is a pioneer narrative film that denounces Stalinism and retells the 1950s. The film deals with cynical manipulation and repression, and successfully captures the atmosphere of the 1950s. Its protagonist, Mateusz Birkut (Jerzy Radziwiłłowicz), is an honest bricklayer at the Nowa Huta steelworks near Cracow; he is an exemplary worker, courted and exploited by the communist authorities as a national hero. The structure of *Man of Marble*, as pointed out by many scholars, resembles that of Orson Welles's *Citizen Kane* (1941) The film student Agnieszka, played by Krystyna Janda, performs the role of Thompson, the reporter in search of Rosebud. While making her student documentary about a model worker, Birkut, she discovers secrets of the real Birkut and learns the true history of the Stalinist period. A marble statue of Birkut that she finds in the basement of the museum initiates her search for the "man behind the mask." Like Thompson, Agnieszka starts with the "official truth" (a newsreel featuring her protagonist), but as she gradually learns the story behind the façade, a more complete picture of the period emerges. Agnieszka approaches people who used to know Birkut—those who loved him, surrounded him, and spied on him. Extensive flashbacks portray the rise of the simple-minded worker to communist stardom and expose the hypocrisy and dirty politics of Stalinism. Unlike Thompson, Agnieszka encounters political obstacles while attempting to unveil the truth about her protagonist. She is told by her opportunistic producer that she should instead choose another topic because "nobody has touched the 1950s."

As the first powerful political, as well as artistic, work dealing with Stalinism, *Man of Marble* established a certain method of approaching that period in Polish history. To venture into the forbidden past, Wajda employs authentic black-and-white newsreels, a number of flashbacks in color, and skillfully made black-and-white pseudo-documentaries and newsreels that are virtually undistinguishable from the real ones. The fabricated footage is presented as recently unearthed documents, and Wajda's imitations of the official communist propaganda style are as effective as the actual propagandist work.[7] Wajda reproduces past modes of representation not to make his film look more "real," but rather to examine the past—to search for the roots of Polish Stalinism and to capture the mood of that period. As Janina Falkowska explains: "[T]he Stalinist totalitarian spirit is referred to in every discursive layer of the film, and it monologically conditions and manipulates the spectator's reaction toward the film. The Polish spectator, living most of his or her life under the influence of the Stalinist aura, felt especially overwhelmed by the hopelessness and oppressiveness of some scenes."[8]

A number of scenes in *Man of Marble* stress the paranoia, cynicism, and oppressive nature of Stalinism. This is a Kafkaesque world ruled by manipulation and fear, the world of accusations fabricated by the Urząd

Figure 9.1 Jerzy Radziwiłłowicz in Andrzej Wajda's *Man of Marble* (1977)

Bezpieczeństwa (Office of Security), show trials, and sinister cabinets of security officers—the places where people disappear without a trace. Wajda not only re-creates the 1950s by referring to that period's propaganda newsreels, but also by alluding to classic socialist realist paintings and the most popular Polish socialist realist film, *An Adventure at Marienstadt*.[9] Manipulative diegetic and nondiegetic music[10] and a stern voice-over in a pseudo-documentary expose "traitors" and refer to the socialist realist discourse. In many cases, the ironic use of music, especially the sarcastic use of well-known musical pieces from the 1950s,[11] and visual references to 1950s arts border on mockery of the socialist realist concerns. According to Stephen Schiff, Wajda's style in *Man of Marble* is "a perfect distillation of the tricky game that is survival in Poland. Wajda's camera feints, winks, jabs, and then drops back, as if to avoid reprisal, and beneath every shot one can feel the turbulent energy of an artist rein-ing in his rage."[12]

Man of Marble also serves as a statement on the filmmakers' responsi-bility for the distorted images of the Stalinist era. In a propagandist "film within a film" (*Architects of Our Happiness*), credited to the young and determined director Burski (perhaps Wajda's alter ego), Wajda lists him-self as an assistant director. The film portrays a sharp contrast between Agnieszka's youthful, committed, and, as a result, perhaps naive ap-proach and Burski's conformist, communist, celebrity-like lifestyle.

Wajda's film inspired a number of Polish films made during the brief Solidarity period. In 1981, for example, these included: *Shivers*, by Woj-ciech Marczewski; *Niech cię odleci mara* (*The Haunted*, released in 1983), by Andrzej Barański; *Był jazz* (*There Was Jazz*, released in 1984), by Feliks Falk; *The Big Run* (released in 1987), by Jerzy Domaradzki; and a televi-sion film, *Wahadełko* (*Shilly Shally*, released in 1984), by Filip Bajon. In 1982, after the introduction of martial law, two prominent films were fin-ished and promptly shelved by the authorities: *The Mother of Kings* (released in 1987), by Janusz Zaorski, and *Interrogation* (released in 1989), by Ryszard Bugajski. The same happened to a medium-length film, *Niedzielne igraszki* (*Sunday Pranks*, finished in 1983, released in 1988), by Robert Gliński. Had these temporally dislodged films been released ear-lier, all may well have played an important role in Polish cultural and political life.

Commenting on the "Cinema of Moral Concern," Frank Turaj sees the emergence of films examining the Stalinist epoch in the following way: "There continued to be a fascination with the Stalinist years, partly because that period is intrinsically interesting but also because Stalinism is a good target. It is a way of criticizing the system without being blamed for criticizing the system. It is permissible to denigrate Stalinism, as long as it is Polish Stalinism (any criticism involving the Soviets is the ultimate taboo), since it was officially acknowledged as an erroneous phenome-non."[13] The majority of films made during the brief Solidarity period denounce the Stalinist system and follow the poetics of *Man of Marble*. As Turaj accurately observes, they focus exclusively on the Polish aspect of Stalinism. Due to 1980s censorship practices in Poland, nobody openly criticized the Soviet involvement in Polish politics.

Wojciech Marczewski's *Shivers*, a coming-of-age story set in the 1950s, deals with institutionalized indoctrination and manipulation. Tomasz Hudziec, also the protagonist of Marczewski's earlier film *Nightmares*, stars as a young teenage boy, Tomasz, who is sent to a scouts' camp after Stalin's death. In the camp, designed to train future party activists, Tomasz falls under the spell of the communist ideology despite the fact that his father is a political prisoner. His enchantment with the new ide-ology parallels Tomasz's erotic fascination with a young woman, an ide-alistic counselor from the communist youth organization (ZMP), played by Teresa Marczewska.

Figure 9.2 Tomasz Hudziec as Tomasz, the protagonist of Wojciech Marczewski's *Shivers* (1981)

In the beginning of the film, Marczewski paints a picture of Tomasz's family and friends, creating a world devoid of emotions and populated by young adolescents framed by a cold landscape. Heavy, sometimes too obvious, symbolism permeates *Shivers*: a photograph of Karl Marx is shown with tears in his eyes, and in the final scenes of the film the same picture is seen in the mud. The oppressive atmosphere of *Shivers* distinctly resembles that of *Nightmares*; both films are set in an oppressive environment (Austro-Hungarian Galicia at the turn of the century in *Nightmares*), both deal with a combination of erotic and political fascinations, and both introduce demonic teachers/manipulators (a Catholic priest in *Nightmares*).

Marczewski's tale about indoctrination was followed by Bugajski's *Interrogation*, a shocking portrayal of ruthlessness and dehumanization set in early 1950s Poland. *Interrogation* is arguably the strongest work on the Stalinist past ever made in Central Europe. This film was a battering ram, revealing hidden taboos; like a bulldozer, it demolished existing images about the Stalinist period.

Interrogation is the preeminent Polish film of the early 1980s. It describes the imprisonment and torture of an innocent young woman, Tonia (Krystyna Janda), wrongly charged by the Stalinist secret police. In an interview, Janda said:

[T]he story was really based on the lives of two real women who lived through the Stalinist hell: Tonia Lechmann and Wanda Podgórska, the secretary to Władysław Gomułka [former Communist Party Secretary—M.S.]. Mrs. Podgórska, who spent six years in prison, including two in an isolation cell, served as my consultant on the film.... We had to make sure that we documented the film very well because we had to defend everything we did in front of a review board. That is why the French reaction at the Cannes festival showing, that the film was unreal, made me angry. It was remarkably factual.[14]

Interrogation, set predominantly in a prison, graphically shows the horror and brutality of the times. Bugajski's film is built around the sharp opposition between the oppressive Stalinist system (represented by the interrogators) and its innocent victims (exemplified by Tonia and her prisonmates). The protagonist of *Interrogation* suffers enormously, even attempts suicide, but refuses to help fabricate evidence against her friend (who is killed in spite of her silence). Tonia's confrontation with the Stalinist system brings her a Pyrrhic victory—after years behind bars she is released and can be reunited with her young daughter who had been born in the prison hospital and taken away from her. The girl's father is one of the interrogators, who, influenced by Tonia, begins to doubt the communist dogma and eventually shoots himself. Bugajski avoids the black-and-white characterization found in many postwar Polish productions. He abstains from merely reversing the stereotypical images of brave functionaries of the communist system who clash with the "reactionary elements," and creates an intricate nightmarish film about the rituals of Stalinist questioning.

Another film, Barański's *The Haunted*, portrays a provincial town some-where in central Poland in 1951. The film's personal, almost nostalgic tone stands in sharp contrast to the explicitly political works of that period. As in his other works, Barański is preoccupied with small people in small places and their personal versions of history. The film depicts the strug-gles of a store owner to keep his family business alive under communist rule. After several years of futile struggle, he loses the store and ends up working for the state.

The film introduces a different perspective on Stalinism. The story is narrated by the shopkeeper's son Witek (Marek Probosz), who tells about his father, an opportunist defeated by the system. Black-and-white flash-backs and dream sequences peer into periods before, during, and immedi-ately after the war. These recollections from the past provide information about the town itself (for example, that half of the prewar population was Jewish), and about the intrusion of postwar politics into the town's sleepy atmosphere. The last scenes of *The Haunted* clearly indicate that the com-munist takeover in this Polish provincial town at the beginning of the 1950s changed life forever. When the shopkeeper gives up his struggles to maintain his business, his store is transformed into a warehouse for the local branch of the Communist Party. The final camera pan over commu-nist paraphernalia (red flags, portraits of communist leaders, socialist realist portraits) reveals the "landscape after the battle."

Given the similarities between the Stalinist period and the situation after the introduction of equally oppressive martial law and before the transitional year of 1989, it was inevitable that films about Stalinism would be almost impossible to make. In *W zawieszeniu* (*Suspended*, 1987), Waldemar Krzystek, returning to the Solidarity poetics, tells the story of a former Home Army member who is sentenced to death, but escapes from prison, moves to a provincial town, and hides several years in the cellar of the house belonging to his wife, whom he had secretly married during the war. Like his predecessors, Krzystek directly condemns Stalinism while indirectly criticizing the communist system. To stress the link between his film and works by Andrzej Wajda, he casts in the main roles two of Wajda's actor-symbols, Krystyna Janda and Jerzy Radziwiłłowicz. Krzystek, however, is not interested in the epic scope and the "poetics of red banners" of *Man of Marble* or *The Mother of Kings*. Like Barański, he focuses on the everyday ugliness of Stalinism and its impact on ordinary yet heroic people. He is not interested in disillusioned or mesmerized communists but in people whose lives were destroyed by history.

Interestingly, in comments made about *Suspended* in 1990, Krzystek indicates that he does not view this work as a "historical film" but rather as a film relevant to the present. He claims that the Stalinist system still permeates many spheres of Polish life: "[W]e now barely fight its founda-tions. By reaching the roots of degeneration I wished to show that the reconstruction will not be helped by repainting the buildings, but that thorough changes are needed."[15]

Contemporary Films about Stalinism

After 1989, history became the domain of documentary rather than narrative cinema. A great number of documentary films made in Poland examine the Stalinist mentality, hypocrisy, and indoctrination. Many of the films dealing with earlier "forbidden topics" in Polish history have been seen by some critics and filmmakers as "cheap shots at the past." A film director and a sharp polemicist, Konrad Szołajski says in a 1995 article: "Historical films continuously dominate the screens. Their makers demonstrate the courage that they did not show ten or fifteen years ago. The new filmmakers, cherished by television bosses, mainly denounce the Stalinists' crimes and other sins of the Polish People's Republic or fill the screens with terribly boring pictures of pilgrimages and sanctuaries."[16]

This is not the case with Andrzej Fidyk's *Defilada* (*The Parade*, 1989), a film depicting the nature of totalitarianism in North Korea. Fidyk portrays preparations for the celebration of the fortieth anniversary of Kim Il Sung's Korea. Every person appearing before the camera seems to be under the spell of the communist dictator; everybody seems to be happy in this totalitarian system. The tone of *The Parade* resembles an entomological documentary. Fidyk's camera dispassionately portrays the complete subordination of any individuality within the personality cult of Kim Il Sung—"the Great Leader," as Fidyk's interlocutors call him. Equally interesting was this film's reception, which deserves a separate chapter. *The Parade* has been applauded in North Korea as a great propagandist film. For Polish audiences, or any Western audiences, for that matter, Fidyk's film clearly uncovers the true nature of the Stalinist regime.

Reviewing Krzysztof Zanussi's 1996 film *In Full Gallop*, Jerzy Płażewski asserts: "[A]fter *Shivers* or (in another dimension) *Interrogation*, it is more and more difficult to reveal something about the Stalinist system that captivated minds. That system has always been the same. More interesting, however, are the reactions of people who survived the system."[17] The shift from political to personal, suggested by Płażewski, may be observed in several contemporary Polish films that describe the reactions of ordinary people surviving or even outsmarting the system. The martyrological tone of former films is replaced by cathartic humor, epic scope by personal qualities. These films include intimate psychological dramas set in the 1950s, such as Barbara Sass's *Temptation*, and films giving a panorama of Polish history, including Stalinism, such as Grzegorz Królikiewicz's *The Case of Pekosiński*. Some are comedies taming the past or films with grotesque or comic touches, such as *In Full Gallop*, by Zanussi; *Colonel Kwiatkowski*, by Kazimierz Kutz; and *Cynga* (*Scurvy*, 1993) and *Kroniki domowe* (*Family Events*, 1997), both by Leszek Wosiewicz. *Poznań 56* (*Street Boys*, 1996), by Filip Bajon, and *The Ring with a Crowned Eagle*, by Andrzej Wajda, are examples of historical reconstructions devoid of irony and humor.

As if to illustrate the burden of history, the protagonist of *The Case of Pekosiński* is a hunchback—an older, ill, and alcoholic man, who appears in the film playing himself. He is a man without a family and without any knowledge of who he is. Everything about him is symbolic: his date of birth is the outbreak of World War II; his place of birth is the Nazi concentration camp where he miraculously survived being pushed through a barbed wire fence by his mother; and his surname is an acronym of a charitable institution (PKOS). Taking all this into account, the protagonist serves as another Central European victim of history.

Known for his bold experiments, Królikiewicz is not afraid to employ the authentic person to reconstruct episodes and scenes from his life and, consequently, to block the viewer's identification with the protagonist. Pekosiński does not act in the film (apart from some basic tasks); he is only the object of actions and manipulations by several people who surround him. From that perspective, however, as Mirosław Przylipiak writes, the director's name could be added to a long list of persons who simply exploited Pekosiński.[18] Interestingly, Jan Kidawa-Błoński's uneven *Pamiętnik znaleziony w garbie* (*Memento Found in a Hunched Back*, 1993) shows another handicapped, hunchbacked protagonist reflecting on his past. The film is set in Polish Silesia and looks at the complex history of this region via the personalized story of two brothers and their uneasy relationship.

The Stalinist past also returns in intimate and intense psychological dramas set in the harsh political climate of the 1950s. Barbara Sass directed what was arguably the finest Polish film produced in 1995, *Temptation*. The film, set in 1953, tells the story of a young nun, Anna (Magdalena Cielecka's award-winning debut performance), who is transferred from a prison to a remote location where a high-ranked Catholic priest is being held. They had known each other; he had convinced her to become a nun, and her decision to enter a convent was partly motivated by her love for him. The secret police try to take advantage of their relationship and pressure the nun to inform on the man she loves. To a certain extent, Sass's film is inspired by the factual experience of the Polish Roman Catholic primate Stefan Wyszyński. The director, however, is more preoccupied with the personal than with the political, more interested in the situation between a man and a woman than in the political circumstances.

Temptation differs distinctly from other Polish films about the Stalinist period, especially those made before 1989. Its story is told without ridiculing the system. Wiesław Zdort's camera portrays a gloomy picture deprived of the sun and dominated by the darkness of the priests' and nuns' frocks, the dirty green colors of the soldiers' uniforms, and the faded color of the old brick buildings. In the last scene, the female protagonist—oppressed by two systems—is left at the train station and given an opportunity to make a choice concerning her life.

As mentioned earlier, the accusatory tone of many earlier films dealing with the Stalinist past is no longer employed by the newest Polish cinema. Sporadic returns to earlier Solidarity poetics have been met by indifferent audiences and mixed critical reviews. This happened, for instance, to

Bajon's semiautobiographical *Street Boys*,[19] which, through the perspective of two boys, narrates the story of the violent workers' protest in Poznań in June 1956. During the strike, which concerned the reduction of work norms and salary increase, riots started, and the army and the security force opened fire.

Another film, Wajda's *The Ring with a Crowned Eagle*, which discusses issues the director first addressed in *Ashes and Diamonds*, was both a critical and box-office failure.[20] The opening sequence of Wajda's film introduces the Warsaw Uprising of 1944; the action then cuts abruptly to the last days of the uprising and moves quickly to the postwar period. After the war, a young officer from the uprising, Marcin, attempts to take care of his surviving soldiers and secure their future in Soviet-occupied Poland. "To collaborate with the communists or not" is the issue posed by the film. To stress the link between *The Ring with a Crowned Eagle* and *Ashes and Diamonds*, Wajda even reconstructs the famous symbolic scene in a bar with the flaming glasses of alcohol, each symbolizing a fallen member of the protagonist's Home Army unit. In the last scene, the politically naive protagonist, now bitter and disillusioned, leaves the Office of Security (UB) building and hides on the street, realizing that he is no longer in his own country.

More popular among the critics and moderately popular among audiences are comedies that tame the past. In the center of Zanussi's semiautobiographical film *In Full Gallop* is an aging female protagonist played by Maja Komorowska. She is proud, yet willing to compromise—a Catholic at heart and a communist on the surface.[21] The doubleness of the protagonist has a symbolic dimension: it represents the double talk and double behavior of the majority of her compatriots. If we take this into account, we realize that this could be a film about surviving in the Stalinist period, about political mimicry. Jerzy Płażewski writes that, in spite of its apparent autobiographical nature, this film is about a "philosophy of survival" in an era unfriendly to humans.[22]

Kutz's recent *Colonel Kwiatkowski* shares similar features. Its protagonist, a picaresque hero, is Kwiatkowski (Marek Kondrat), an army physician who assumes the false identity of a high-ranked officer in the secret police. Accompanied by a small group of friends, he travels throughout Poland and releases political prisoners, causing consternation among provincial functionaries. His actions, however, are not motivated by patriotic or political impulses. He takes this new identity to save himself after an argument with a Soviet officer, and maintains it to impress his girlfriend.

The film works against Polish national stereotypes and romantic myths, which demand that the protagonist sacrifice his life for a noble nationalist cause. As in the majority of his films, starting with *Cross of Valor*, Kutz prefers to focus on ordinary people absorbed by history, rather than on history epitomized by individual cases. Kutz's film laughs at issues usually reserved in Poland for martyrological works. His supposedly real story (as indicated by the credits) introduces a character unusual by Polish standards. This character is not another victim of history but almost a folk hero who beats the system with wisdom and wit.

Leszek Wosiewicz emphasizes the grotesqueness of history in his *Scurvy*, a film about the fate of Poles who, after the September 1939 German and Soviet aggression, found themselves in Soviet-occupied territories and were deported by Stalin to Siberia. Wosiewicz utilizes a montage of documentary footage to reveal the historical context and, in broader terms, to show his protagonist surfing on the wave of history. In the final sequence, the protagonist returns from a Soviet concentration camp to Poland and is promptly arrested by the Polish military as a spy (a fact indicated in documents fabricated by the Soviet security service). He is kept in a former German concentration camp, now a place for POWs and alleged collaborators, including Polish freedom fighters. Trying to escape, he finds himself in a crematorium and hides in a furnace, where he is spotted by two soldiers, a Russian and a Pole. With its stress on the grotesque, absurdist aspect of history, *Scurvy*, like Wosiewicz's earlier *Kornblumenblau*, shares many characteristics with *Europa, Europa* (1991), the acclaimed film by Agnieszka Holland. Wosiewicz's recent film, *Family Events*, differs distinctly from his previous works. It is a semiautobiographical story set in a small town during the Stalinist years. Wosiewicz divides the film into five chronological chapters and offers an almost idealistic evocation of childhood, despite the troubled political time.

Iconography

The Stalinist period continues to attract filmmakers not only for political but also for purely artistic reasons. Robert Gliński, the maker of *Sunday Pranks*, a film exposing the brutal, grotesque banality of Stalinism, comments that "this was the period extremely abundant with human dramas; there were clashes of different attitudes, a different model of life prevailed. Conflicts between new and old were distinct. Furthermore, the iconography of that period was extremely filmic."[23]

The cinematic images of Stalinism have been created in Poland predominantly by younger filmmakers such as Gliński who, unlike Wajda and Kutz, do not know Stalinism firsthand, having been being born in the late 1940s and the 1950s. They rely heavily on socialist realist aesthetics. The kitsch iconography of that period, as represented in Polish cinema, is very filmic indeed: communist slogans; red banners; portraits of Lenin, Stalin, and Bierut; May Day parades; sports parades; monumental construction sites; red stars; the masses of people enthusiastically greeting the leaders; black limousines of the infamous security service; and members of the communist youth organization in uniforms. Socialist realist songs, associated with May Day parades, and the phraseology of the period fill the soundtrack.

Flashbacks into the Stalinist past are usually constructed of stylized images employing a similar color palette: usually gray or blue, with elements of red (for banners, posters, etc.). Several Polish films utilize sequences resembling images associated with that period; frequently, to heighten their verisimilitude, they incorporate actual newsreels and other documentary materials into their narrative (in *The Mother of Kings*, a black-and-white film, Zaorski extensively employs prewar and postwar newsreels). To stress the oppressive nature of Stalinism further, these films frequently are set in places of confinement such as prisons (*Interrogation*; many sequences of *The Mother of Kings*), labor camps (*Scurvy*), internment sites (*Temptation*), hiding places (*Suspended*), and schools and scouts' camps (*Shivers*).

There is nothing fascinating about the Polish version of Stalinism, nothing seductive; the only discernible nostalgia is for lost innocence. Stalinist kitsch is an object of ridicule. Polish cinema shows Stalin's image in white uniform as he appears in documentary clips, billboards, and portraits. A scene from Jerzy Skolimowski's 1967 film *Hands Up*, banned until 1985, is symptomatic in this respect. In this film, once ambitious students in the

Figure 9.3 From the left: Magda Teresa Wójcik, Andrzej Zaorski, and Zbigniew Zapasiewicz in Janusz Zaorski's *The Mother of Kings* (1982)

1950s (now conformists addressing each other by the names of their cars) recall an incident from their youth involving Stalin's image. While preparing parts of an enormous portrait of Stalin for a state event, they paint an extra pair of eyes by mistake. When the portrait is assembled and raised publicly, Stalin appears with four eyes. He is sinister (no one can escape his scrutiny) and grotesque.

A mixture of fear and an almost surrealist quality is also inseparably linked with contemporary images of Stalin and other communist leaders. Deprived of their threatening aura, they appear almost like Grand Guignol characters: farcical, devilish, grotesque. For example, in the ironic *Femina* (1991), a film abundant with symbols, Piotr Szulkin mocks the emptiness of Polish political and religious rituals. He debunks the ritual aspect of Polish culture and its martyrological character. The female protagonist, played by Hanna Dunowska, is torn between the Catholic religion and the communist ideology: oneiric flashbacks full of bizarre images reveal the oppressiveness of her childhood. The reappearing image in the film is that of Stalin hanging from a chandelier.[24] This treatment of totalitarianism is new to Szulkin's works. His earlier antitotalitarian science fiction films employed barely hidden political messages that were easily deciphered by his audiences.

Conclusion

After years of the mythologization of history, Polish postwar history belongs to Polish screens. Although primarily the domain of documentary cinema, the Stalinist past also appears in mainstream narrative films. Coming to terms with the past has produced some interesting films. The Stalinist period is safely distant enough to enable some "filmic fascination" with these years, yet close enough to provide a number of strong parallels with the present.

For years Polish postwar history has attracted a number of leading filmmakers whose struggles with state censorship and other political obstacles were frequently as absorbing as their completed works. Now they can freely deal with various formerly taboo themes. The irony is that the new audiences seem to be tired of politics and do not care what the filmmakers have to say.

Notes

1. One of the first attempts to examine the Stalinist period was Janusz Morgenstern's *Życie raz jeszcze* (*Life Once Again*, 1965), based on Roman Bratny's novel.
2. Discussed in Marek Haltof and Donald Smith, "An Aborted Revolution, A Stillborn Generation: Generational Politics and Gender Relations in Péter Gothár's *Time Stands Still*," *Canadian Journal of Film Studies* 6, no. 2 (1997): 51–64.

3. David Paul, "Hungary: The Magyar on the Bridge," in *Post New Wave Cinema in the Soviet Union and Eastern Europe*, ed. Daniel J. Goulding (Bloomington and Indianapolis: Indiana University Press), 207.

4. Anna Lawton, "The Ghost That Does Return: Exorcising Stalin," in *Stalinism and Soviet Cinema*, ed. Richard Taylor and Derek Spring (London and New York: Routledge, 1993), 188.

5. Svetlana Boym, "Stalin Is with Us: Soviet Documentary Mythologies of the 1980s," in Taylor and Spring, *Stalinism and Soviet Cinema*, 201.

6. Tadeusz Sobolewski, "100 lat kina w Polsce: 1974–1976," *Kino* 5 (1999): 52.

7. This aspect of *Man of Marble* is discussed by Wiesław Godzic, "Metafora polityczna: *Człowiek z marmuru* Andrzeja Wajdy," in *Analizy i interpretacje. Film polski*, ed. Alicja Helman and Tadeusz Miczka (Katowice: Wydawnictwo Uniwersytetu Śląskiego, 1984), 106–121.

8. Janina Falkowska, *The Political Films of Andrzej Wajda: Dialogism in* Man of Marble, Man of Iron, *and* Danton (New York: Berghahn Books, 1996), 74.

9. The influence of socialist realist paintings and *An Adventure at Marienstadt* is apparent mostly in scenes with the young Birkut at the construction site (low-angle shots against the sky).

10. The use of music in *Man of Marble* is extensively discussed by Iwona Sowińska-Rammel, "Emocjonalna i ideologiczna funkcja muzyki w *Człowieku z marmuru* Andrzeja Wajdy," in Helman and Miczka, *Analizy i interpretacje*, 122–129.

11. For instance, "Murarski walczyk" (The Little Waltz of Bricklayers), played by the Gypsy band when drunken Birkut throws a brick at the state (perhaps security service) building.

12. Stephen Schiff's review of *Man of Marble* in *Foreign Affairs: The National Society of Film Critics' Video Guide to Foreign Films*, ed. Kathy Schulz Huffhines (San Francisco: Mercury House, 1991), 254.

13. Frank Turaj, "Poland: The Cinema of Moral Concern," in Goulding, *Post New Wave Cinema*, 160.

14. Michael Szporer, "Woman of Marble: An Interview with Krystyna Janda," *Cineaste* 18, no. 3 (1991): 14.

15. Piotr Wasilewski, *Świadectwa metryk. Polskie kino młodych w latach osiemdziesiątych* (Cracow: Oficyna Obecnych, 1990), 224.

16. Konrad Szołajski, "Świat nie przedstawiony," *Kino* 7–8 (1995): 13.

17. Jerzy Płażewski, "Przetrwać cwałem," *Kino* 4 (1996): 18.

18. Mirosław Przylipiak, "Pekosiński jako znak," *Kino* 1 (1994): 44–45.

19. Filip Bajon discusses the autobiographical aspect of *Street Boys* in a book-length interview: Włodzimierz Braniecki, *Szczun* (Poznań: W drodze, 1998), 132–148.

20. I am referring here to the critics' indifference and, as a consequence, to the fact that Wajda's film did not have a successful theatrical distribution in Poland. This is not the whole picture, however. Polish films may fail on a big screen, yet they are present and also very popular on Polish television. Sometimes, as statistics show, they have ten million or more viewers. When *The Ring with a Crowned Eagle* was shown on Channel 1 (Polish State Television), it had 17.6 million viewers. In spite of that record number, Wajda's film did not stir any major debates. Jolanta Rodziewicz-Rayzacher, "Raport z Agencji," *Reżyser* [published with *Kino*] 1 (1997): 2–3 and 4.

21. At the 1996 Festival of Polish Films in Gdynia, *In Full Gallop* received several awards, including the Best Actress award for Maja Komorowska and the Special Award ex aequo with *Street Boys* by Filip Bajon and *Street Games* by Krzysztof Krauze (there was no Grand Prize in 1996).

22. Płażewski, "Przetrwać cwałem," 18.

23. Wasilewski, *Świadectwa metryk*, 101.

24. Mirosław Przylipiak writes that, in some of the scenes, the image of Stalin resembles that of Lech Wałęsa. Mirosław Przylipiak, "Egzorcyzmy nad niedojrzałością," *Kino* 4 (1992): 7.

10

National Memory, the Holocaust, and Images of the Jew in Postwar Polish Films

What will I tell him, I, a Jew of the New Testament,
Waiting two thousand years for the second coming of Jesus?
My broken body will deliver me to his sight
And he will count me among the helpers of death:
The uncircumcised.

Czesław Miłosz[1]

Since the return of democracy in Central Europe, a great number of narrative and documentary films, as well as literary and academic works dealing with Jewish themes have surfaced. The quantity of works focusing on Polish-Jewish relations seems to be unprecedented and is usually interpreted as an indication of a will and commitment to come to terms with the complex and frequently suppressed past. In her article on the recent emergence of Hungarian films that bear witness to history, Catherine Portuges explains that "the need to mourn and to remember what was on the verge of being forgotten ... has perhaps only now begun to be integrated, in the psychoanalytic sense of remembering, repeating, and working through, and in the Barthesian sense of 'discours de l'absence.'"[2]

Portuges aptly views the treatment of Jewish history as a significant element of 1990s cinema in Central Europe. She also points out that under communist rule "the story of the Jews was largely the story of their absence."[3] The Jews practically disappeared from the Central European landscape and almost completely from the screen. For instance, in Polish cinema, Portuges states, Jewish figures were limited to "supporting roles in movies of wartime suffering."[4] While agreeing with Portuges's perceptive comments, I tend to consider her remark about Polish cinema as an overstatement. Jewish history has never been forgotten in Poland. Although at times silenced by communist authorities, the topic surfaced periodically, reflecting political maneuvers, and was always treated (when treated) as one of the most politically sensitive subjects. In democratic Poland—with the disappearance of the traditional antagonist, the totalitarian state—history is being reevaluated, looked at from a different perspective. This reevaluation has resulted in, among other things, the emergence of a significant number of films that deal with Polish-Jewish relations at a level of intensity unparalleled by earlier works.

The aim of this chapter is neither to look for political explanations of a complex Polish-Jewish history, nor to address the notion of the "truthfulness" of images emerging in post-1989 Poland. My objective is to discuss recent attempts to recover long-suppressed levels of "national memory," to deal with a culture and its members who, after the war, disappeared from the Polish landscape but not from its memory. "The Holocaust has been both repressed and 'canonized' in the recent past …," states Dominick LaCapra.[5] For many filmmakers and theorists, to represent the Holocaust is an attempt to represent the unrepresentable; visual images seem incapable of portraying its horror. Polish filmmakers who confront the theme of the Holocaust face the same difficulty as filmmakers elsewhere: Is it better to speak or to remain silent? Is it possible to create a cinematic language adequate to convey the enormity of human suffering, a language that will in no way trivialize the Holocaust?[6]

Jewish Characters in Early Postwar Cinema

The vibrant, multicultural mosaic of prewar Polish culture was destroyed during World War II. Poland lost more than six million of its inhabitants, about 22 percent of the entire population. That number includes about three million Polish Jews who perished during the war. Like other European countries, Poland was subsequently able to rebuild its economy and to redevelop its culture. The disappearance of the Jewish culture in Poland, however, was almost complete. Lucy S. Davidowicz reminds us in her book, *The Holocaust and the Historians*, that "the annihilation of six million of European Jews brought an end with irrevocable finality to the thousand-year-old culture and civilization of Ashkenazic Jewry, destroying the continuity of Jewish history."[7] As she states, "The Germans used Poland as their gigantic laboratory for mass murder, not (as has sometimes been wrongly charged) because the Nazis counted on Polish anti-Semitism, but because that was where most of Europe's Jews were concentrated and where the Germans expected to settle for a long time."[8] Today, there are probably no more than ten thousand Jews living in Poland, compared with 3.3 million before the war. With the war, as Eric Goldman writes, "Poland ceased to be one of the great centers of Yiddish life and culture; instead it became its burial ground."[9]

In postwar, Soviet-dominated Central Europe, Jewish figures often appeared in Polish films, though not necessarily in works dealing with wartime suffering. These films were mostly adaptations from the Polish literary canon, works dealing with Polish history and martyrology. Jewish figures functioned mostly as supporting characters, completing a panorama of human types. There were, however, some notable exceptions to this rule, which will be discussed later in more detail.

The first two prestigious successes of postwar Polish cinema—*The Last Stage*, by Wanda Jakubowska, and, in particular, *Border Street*, by Aleksander Ford—deal openly with Jewish subject matter.[10] After the creation of the state of Israel in 1948, the Communist Party in Poland began to treat Jewish issues extremely delicately. Nevertheless, in the 1950s, Jewish characters peopled war films, as in *The Hours of Hope*, by Jan Rybkowski, a film heralding the phenomenon of the Polish School. Another film, Stanisław Różewicz's *The Birth Certificate* (1961), shows the occupation through the eyes of a child. In the third episode of this three-part film, *Kropla krwi* (*Drop of Blood*), a young Jewish girl hides out in an orphanage where she is told by some Nazi "experts" that she has some typical features of the Aryan race.

A lesser known film by Jerzy Zarzycki, *White Bear* (1959), portrays a young Jewish scientist, Henryk Fogiel (Gustaw Holoubek), who escapes while being transported to a concentration camp. He hides in the mountain resort of Zakopane where he makes his living by acting as a prop for a local photographer, posing with tourists in a bearskin. The motif of hiding, common to many Holocaust narratives, appears also in a film underestimated by critics, *The Beater* (1964), by Ewa and Czesław Petelski, and in *Wniebowstąpienie* (*Ascension Day*, 1969), by Jan Rybkowski. Another film dealing with a similar theme, Janusz Nasfeter's *Długa noc* (*The Long Night*), was produced in 1967, but not released until 1992. The Six-Day War between Israel and the Arab states in June 1967 and the tense situation within the Soviet bloc (which supported the Arab states) were the main reasons for this film's shelving. A number of memorable Jewish characters on Polish screen have been created by actor Włodzimierz Boruński—the master of supporting roles. His finest film characters include Goldapfel in *All Souls Day*, Blumenfeld in *Somersault*, and Gold in *Jealousy and Medicine*.

The Holocaust motif is powerful in Andrzej Munk's incomplete *The Passenger*,[11] based on Zofia Posmysz's novel. At the center of the film is the relationship between the oppressor at Auschwitz (an SS woman, Liza, played by Aleksandra Śląska) and the oppressed (a Polish inmate, Marta, played by Anna Ciepielewska). Years after, a chance meeting between the two on a luxury liner brings back memories of the suppressed past. Liza's attempt at self-justification, which is verified by Marta's own version of what happened, prompts Annette Insdorf to assert that "a major question raised by *The Passenger* is whether postwar justifications by Germans are trustworthy or merely self-serving."[12] Certain aspects of Munk's film, such as the role of repressed memories and the portrayal of what almost is a sexual attraction between the victimizer and the victim, to a certain extent carry associations with later works, such as Liliana Cavani's exploitative *Il portiere di notte* (*The Night Porter*, 1974).

Since the beginning of his career, Andrzej Wajda has frequently cast his films with Jewish characters. In some of his works they are the leading characters: Jakub Gold (Serge Merlin) in *Samson* (1961); Nina (Stanisława Celińska), a young Jewish woman branded by the war in *Landscape after Battle*; Moryc Welt (Wojciech Pszoniak) in *The Land of Promise*. Jewish supporting characters also appear in some of Wajda's other films—for example, in *A Generation* and *The Wedding*—and are always portrayed as members of Polish society. Wajda states that Jewish characters and the Jewish topic are present in his films because they are present in Polish lives. "One cannot be a Polish filmmaker and completely disregard this matter."[13]

In 1973 three notable films were made, all based on well-known literary works, that featured either "a Jewish world" or prominent Jewish characters: *Hospital under the Hourglass*, *The Wedding*, and *Jealousy and Medicine*.[14] *Hospital under the Hourglass*, directed by Wojciech J. Has, deserves closer attention. It was inspired by the well-known writer Bruno Schulz's (1892–1941) short stories, which portray a Jewish community in southeast small-town Poland before World War II. Schulz's prose seems to be almost unadaptable for the screen; it would be like making a film based on paintings by Marc Chagall. Has, however, succeeds in representing Schulz's moody evocation of the lost Jewish world. Like Schulz, he creates a poetic, almost surreal landscape peopled by characters who move as if in a dream. Time is Has's obsession; he blends the past and the present, the living and the dead. The richness of the images, the panorama of characters, and the lyricism of this vision permeated by nostalgia contribute to the artistic success of *Hospital under the Hourglass*.

In the early 1980s, two significant films examined the Jewish history: *Austeria* (1983), by Jerzy Kawalerowicz, and *A Postcard from the Journey* (1984), by Waldemar Dziki.[15] *Austeria*, based on Julian Stryjkowski's novel of the same title, is a nostalgic account of a lost world. In an interview, the director confesses that he "fantasized a film about an extinct world, a community now dead, its culture, customs, habits, religion...."[16] *Austeria* portrays the idealized Jewish world of a small eastern Galician town at the outbreak of World War I. Its protagonist, Tag (Franciszek Pieczka), the innkeeper at Austeria, witnesses diverse communities who gather in his inn on the eve of the war. The last scene of this stylized film shows the destruction of Jews, in a sense heralding events that would happen thirty years later.

One of the most impressive debuts was Waldemar Dziki's *A Postcard from the Journey*, based on a novel by the Czech writer Ladislav Fuks. The film, set in 1941 in the Warsaw ghetto, portrays a middle-aged Jew, Jakub Rosenberg (Władysław Kowalski, in a superb performance), preparing for death. While awaiting deportation to the concentration camp, he

Figure 10.1 Wojciech Pszoniak and Franciszek Pieczka (right) in Jerzy Kawalerowicz's *Austeria* (1983)

methodically, almost obsessively, pays attention to small practical details to battle his fear and prepare for the inevitable day.

Looking at the aforementioned films, one could argue that, without denying their artistic merits, they are not at a level comparable with the Slovak feature *Obchod na korze* (*The Shop on Main Street*, 1965). Ján Kadár's and Elmar Klos's Oscar-winning film, set in the fascist Slovak state during World War II, shows "ordinary people" whose insensibility and opportunism contribute to the tragedy of the Jews. In Kadár's and Klos's film, this is not Central European cinema's mysterious "history" or "fate," but small people in small places bearing the guilt. Moreover, Polish films about the Holocaust have never constituted an impressive group, as have the Czech and Slovak films of the 1960s, such as *The Shop on Main Street*; *Démanty noci* (*Diamonds of the Night*, 1964), by Jan Němec; *Transport z raje* (*Transport from Paradise*, 1963) and *A pátý jezdec je strach* (*The Fifth Horseman Is Fear*, 1965), both films by Zbynek Brynych; and several others.

With the possible exception of *Border Street*, the majority of Polish films dealing with this issue avoid the accusing tone of the Czech and Slovak films. Instead, they seem preoccupied with either presenting nostalgic images of the lost past, of an almost harmonious world of multiplicity and peacefully coexisting cultures, or showing the martyrological aspect of Jewish history. Open discussions on Polish-Jewish relations are generally avoided because they are considered politically "delicate."

"The Poor Poles Look at the Ghetto"

The Polish approach to the common Jewish-Polish history changed toward the end of the 1980s.[17] The television screening of Claude Lanzmann's *Shoah* (1985; "Shoah" is Hebrew for "the annihilation") stimulated a heated debate in the Polish media. Although generally praised for his forceful account of the Holocaust, Lanzmann has been accused by many Polish commentators of being biased in his selection of material and, thus, of presenting an incomplete picture of the occupation in Poland. As some authors observed, Lanzmann's partial emphasis on anti-Semitic traits in Polish society prevented him from telling a more balanced version of what really happened.[18]

Another important event was the publication of an essay by Jan Błoński, "The Poor Poles Look at the Ghetto," which appeared in 1987 in the Catholic weekly *Tygodnik Powszechny*.[19] In it, Błoński explores the repression of the Jewish tragedy by the Poles and the degree to which the Polish people are morally responsible, as "silent witnesses," for what happened on their soil. In this now classic text—the title of which refers directly to Czesław Miłosz's poem, "A Poor Christian Looks at the Ghetto"—Błoński focuses on the question of repressed "national memories" and the necessity of mourning the dead. He also poses a crucial question: Can the Poles be blamed for their indifference? Błoński pronounces that the Polish soil was tainted, desecrated, and needs to be exculpated from guilt. What remains now, he says, is to see the Polish past truthfully.

In his intense essay, Błoński also refers to another well-known poem by Miłosz, "Campo dei Fiori," which the poet wrote in Warsaw in 1943. It shows the indifference of Poles to what happened in the Warsaw ghetto at the time of the Jewish uprising. In this poem, Miłosz compares the fate of Giordano Bruno, burned to death as a heretic in the presence of an unconcerned mob at Rome's Campo dei Fiori, and the fate of Polish Jewry. He writes in stanzas three and four:

> I thought of Campo dei Fiori
> In Warsaw by the sky-carousel
> one clear spring evening
> to the strains of a carnival tune.
> The bright melody drowned
> the salvos from the ghetto wall,
> and couples were flying
> high in the cloudless sky.[20]

Later in the poem Miłosz writes about "the loneliness of the dying," about the indifference of the outside world, and ends with the image of the only witness and the uncompromising truth-teller: the poet. Miłosz's image of a carousel close to the ghetto wall is very emblematic, almost the essence of the problem. The carousel, as Błoński explains, is a historical fact. It was installed at the Krasińskis' Square in Warsaw just before the uprising in the ghetto and was in operation for its duration.[21] It is no wonder that this very image is employed in two films discussed later in this chapter. Janusz Kijowski uses the image of the carousel extensively in *Tragarz puchu* (*Warszawa 5703*, 1992, a Polish-French-German production), and it is also present in Andrzej Wajda's *Wielki Tydzień* (*Holy Week*, 1996).

The Holocaust and Jewish-Polish relations are also explored in major literary works recently published in Poland. The past returns in several critically acclaimed books translated into English: for example, *The Final Station: Umschlagplatz*, by Jarosław Marek Rymkiewicz; *The Beautiful Mrs. Seidenman*, by Andrzej Szczypiorski; *Who Was Weiser David?* by Paweł Huelle; and *Annihilation*, by Piotr Szewc.[22] Szczypiorski's novel, in particular, as one of the reviewers appropriately noticed, comprises, "in a symbolic sense, an act of national catharsis. It is a powerful work that reflects upon the Polish national character: its strengths, its many flawed perceptions, and its prejudices fully exposed."[23] In *The Beautiful Mrs. Seidenman*, Szczypiorski attempts to portray the solidarity and harmony of the traditionally good Jewish-Polish relations, yet he depicts both cultures' disparity and prejudices as well. The book is peopled with a collection of Polish, Jewish, and German characters. This broad spectrum of viewpoints enables Szczypiorski to produce, in a sense, a treatise on the complexities of Central European history.

The return of democracy has enabled Polish filmmakers to freely explore areas that were taboo under the previous political order. Like its Central European neighbors, Poland is a history-conscious nation; films dealing with the past were and are the core of serious mainstream cinema.

Since the 1989 "freedom shock," a prominent group of feature films about Jewish-Polish history has been released: *Korczak* (1990) and *Holy Week*, by Andrzej Wajda; *Warszawa 5703*, by Janusz Kijowski; *Pożegnanie z Marią* (*Farewell to Maria*, 1993), by Filip Zylber; *Jeszcze tylko ten las* (*And Only This Forest*, 1991), by Jan Łomnicki; and *Deborah* (1995), by Ryszard Brylski. The Holocaust theme is not limited to the aforementioned films. It also appears in *Kornblumenblau*, by Leszek Wosiewicz; *All That Really Matters*, by Robert Gliński; and *The Burial of Potato*, by Jan Jakub Kolski.

In several films, for instance, Kolski's debut, *The Burial of Potato*, the Holocaust does not appear explicitly. In Kolski's film, which combines poetic metaphors with grotesque images of Polish postwar reality, a former concentration camp prisoner, played by Franciszek Pieczka, faces a hostile village after his unexpected and unwanted return. The village has already taken possession of his belongings and is after his land. He is rejected as an alien and as a Jew, although he is neither. The essence of the film is his struggle for acceptance, not the political reality of postwar Poland. Kolski demythologizes Polish farmers. While in the majority of literary and filmic works farmers function as the defenders of traditional nationalistic values, in *The Burial of Potato* they are portrayed as brutal, superficially religious, anti-Semitic caricatures, almost in the manner of Jerzy Kosinski's literary achievement *The Painted Bird*.[24]

To make the list of films dealing with Polish-Jewish relations complete, one must also take into account films dealing with the 1968 anti-Semitic campaign in Poland: *Marcowe migdały* (*March Almonds*, 1990), by Radosław Piwowarski, and *1968: Szczęśliwego Nowego Roku* (*1968: Happy New Year*, 1993), by Jacek Bromski. It is also essential to mention foreign films shot in Poland and with a strong Polish involvement (most notably Steven Spielberg's *Schindler's List*, 1993) and films made abroad by Polish filmmakers, for instance, Agnieszka Holland's German-made film *Bittere Ernte* (*Angry Harvest*, 1985) and *Europa, Europa* (1991, a French and German coproduction).[25]

Wajda's *Korczak* and *Holy Week*

"Everything I made after *Danton*, I consider films of wasted opportunities," claims Andrzej Wajda, in a statement that attempts to explain the mixed public and critical reactions to some of his recent films.[26] Wajda's *Korczak*, scripted by Agnieszka Holland, is a perfect example. It portrays a figure of great importance for both Polish and Jewish cultures—Dr. Janusz Korczak (in reality, Józef Goldszmit), a famous writer, a well-known physician, and a devoted pedagogue who in his writings and in practice always stressed the dignity of childhood. He died in the gas chamber of Treblinka with two hundred of "his orphans" from a Jewish orphanage. In the film, Korczak is described by one of his senior pupils as "the world's greatest Pole ... and the greatest Jew, too." His devotion to children, regardless of their race and nationality, and his fight for children's rights is shown in a scene in which he is asked, "What will you do after the war?" His response is quick: "I'll look after German orphans."

Wajda is chiefly interested in Korczak's martyrdom and legend; therefore, he swiftly moves to the final stages of his life. The film starts immediately before the war and briefly signals the intricacy of Polish-Jewish relations. The war is announced by a few street scenes intercut with Polish documentary footage showing the burning King's Castle in Warsaw. A cut to an image of marching Polish prisoners of war announces the stage of resignation and despair. "Everyone has betrayed us," remarks Korczak (played memorably by Wojciech Pszoniak). "This is the uniform of the betrayed soldier," and he refuses to take off his own Polish uniform. The film cuts from the marching POWs to scenes introducing the terror of the occupation: the creation of the Warsaw ghetto on 13 September 1940.

From the beginning, Wajda insists on an almost "documentary" quality for his film, chiefly by choosing black-and-white photography and by inserting newsreels and documentary footage, both Polish and German. The film is filled with "realistic" images of the ghetto. The director intercuts documentary material that is frequently indistinguishable from Robby Müller's grayish photography. As if taking part in a discussion concerning the ambiguity and appropriateness of images to describe the

Holocaust, Wajda questions whether such material should ever be filmed. In a short scene he shows images of the German newsreel cameramen at work, attempting to frame the disarray around them, searching for "photogenic" images, and not visibly bothered by the misery and death.

The film introduces familiar images of ghetto life: hunger, brutality, overcrowding, death in the streets. Wajda, however, is not afraid to show the less familiar side of the ghetto: Jewish police and Jewish martyrs, rich and poor Jews, Polish anti-Semites, and those who risked their lives to help the Jews. He also portrays the tragedy of Adam Czerniakow, the chairman of the Jewish Council (*Judenrat*) in the Warsaw ghetto. Polish characters appear only as supporting figures in *Korczak*, particularly in the first, prewar sequences. Their attitudes toward the Jews and the separation between the Poles and the Jews range from passive sympathy and active help (punished by death) to silent approval.

The last sequence shows the deportation of the orphans from the ghetto to the camp at Treblinka. The Jewish orphans, led by Korczak, who refuses to abandon his children, carry a flag with a star of David as they march to meet their doom. In the symbolic and emotional final scene, shown in slow motion, they jump from the mysteriously disconnected wagon and fade into a peaceful rural landscape. When the image whitens a sentence appears leaving no doubt about their actual fate: "Korczak died with his children in the gas chambers of Treblinka in August 1942." With his death the legend was born.

Figure 10.2 A scene from *Korczak* (1990, Andrzej Wajda). Wojciech Pszoniak as Dr. Korczak leading the orphans from the ghetto to the camp of Treblinka

Korczak, although well received in Germany and in Israel (among other countries), stirred many controversies in France.[27] Wajda and his scriptwriter, Agnieszka Holland (herself half-Jewish), were accused by some French critics and filmmakers (like Lanzmann) of being anti-Semites and of misrepresenting the Holocaust, and were castigated for their choice of a polonized Jew as a hero. Ewelina Nurczyńska-Fidelska, a Polish scholar, has noted that "the accusations of his [Wajda's] anti-Semitism which appeared in the world press in connection with *The Land of Promise* and *Korczak* are the evidence of a curious ill-will. The plight of Polish Jews in Wajda's films is a part of Polish history without which the picture of Polish history would be incomplete."[28]

Undeterred by some negative responses to *Korczak* (or perhaps because of them), in *Holy Week* Wajda returns once again to an examination of Polish-Jewish relations. *Holy Week* is based on Jerzy Andrzejewski's short story written soon after the Warsaw Ghetto Uprising.[29] It was probably the first literary attempt to examine the behavior of Poles faced with the Holocaust that occurred on their own soil.

Like the short story, the film is set during the Easter Week of 1943, during the first seven days of the uprising in the ghetto. Its Jewish protagonist, Irena Lilien (Beata Fudalej), seeks sanctuary on the safer (but not completely safe) side of the ghetto with her Polish friend, Jan Małecki (Wojciech Malajkat), and his wife. During the film, Irena spends several days in her hiding place, feeling constantly threatened by the outside world, and in the final scene she returns to the ghetto, now in flames and almost destroyed. Earlier the same day, Małecki had died while attempting to recover Irena's belongings from her former hiding place. This happens on Good Friday, the day Christ died. The parallel between the Jewish tragedy and the meaning of Easter Week provides an artistic framework carefully devised and developed by Wajda.

The director portrays the film's protagonist in an unconventional way: she is not a sympathetic character, not a typical Holocaust victim. Unlike most of the figures in Holocaust narratives, Irena refuses to remain silent and obedient, out of German sight, and she questions the attitude of her Polish hosts. "The more death you see, the more you want to live," says Irena. "Suffering makes you a worse person, a much worse person."

The film provides an examination of Polish morality, of the Polish experience of the Holocaust. The core of the film consists of conversations between Irena and her hosts, and between Poles themselves. These discussions exhibit Polish attitudes toward Jews, acknowledging their moral obligation toward them. As in his first films from the Polish School period, Wajda emphasizes the tragic aspects of life: powerlessness and the inescapableness of fate. However, unlike in his early films, he tones down all emotions and reinforces, rather than questions, the myth of the Polish intelligentsia and Polish Catholicism. In *Holy Week* Wajda does not go beyond the stereotypes of the bad lumpenproletariat, good intelligentsia, and heroic young fighters marked by death. The symbolic image of the carousel in front of the ghetto wall appears in the film, but not only to stress the indifference of the Poles. Young Polish fighters, probably members of the Szare Szeregi (The Gray Ranks) movement, employ the carousel to look behind the wall before entering the ghetto to help the Jewish insurgents.

Warszawa 5703

Warszawa 5703 (a Polish-French-German coproduction), by Janusz Kijowski, deals with events taking place at the same time as those in Wajda's *Holy Week*. It tells the story of a young couple escaping through sewers from the Warsaw ghetto and finding refuge on the Polish side of the wall in an apartment owned by Stefania (Hanna Schygulla), a half-German, middle-aged woman whose Polish husband is in a POW camp. Stefania is allowed "freedom" because she gives blood to make a vaccine against typhus. Alek (Lambert Wilson), who first gets to the hiding place, becomes Stefania's lover. To prolong his and his wife Fryda's (Julie Delpy) stay at Stefania's place, and because he is afraid to tell the truth, he pretends to be Fryda's brother, in spite of her violent objections ("I can't live over there and here I don't want to"). In the film's finale, Alek follows a desperate, unstable Fryda back into the sewers to return to the burning ghetto, while Stefania's apartment is searched by the Gestapo, the result of her denouncement by the then departed Fryda.

Warszawa 5703 opens with several negative images showing mysterious faces and characters. It then cuts to an image of a photographer surreptitiously taking pictures of the horrors transpiring in the ghetto. He gives the negatives to Alek, hoping that he will deliver them to a Polish photographer on the Aryan side. The photographer, however, had been arrested (and probably killed) for hiding a Jew, and this situation forces Alek to accept Stefania's help. After these brief, promising initial scenes, the action moves to Stefania's apartment. From this point on, the film relies heavily on the three leading stars, and more and more resembles a theatrical play: most scenes are set in brownish interiors. The camera rarely ventures outside of Stefania's apartment, and when it does, the results are sketchy and unconvincing, such as two scenes, set in the sewers, that invite comparisons with Wajda's *Kanal*. The nightmarish external circumstances only serve to bring the three characters more intimately, claustrophobically together. "To ostatnia niedziela" (This is our last Sunday), a famous nostalgic prewar hit by Jerzy Petersburski, enhances the film's melodramatic atmosphere.

The image of the carousel on the Polish side of the ghetto wall appears several times throughout the film. The carousel, which separates Stefania's apartment building from the ghetto wall, is in operation almost all of the time—even during the outbreak of the uprising, when it is covered with smoke but still running. Unlike Wajda, Kijowski employs it exclusively as a symbol of the outside world's indifference and of the indifference of Poles living on the Aryan side of the wall.

The subtle Polish title of Kijowski's film *Tragarz puchu* means, in direct translation, "a person who carries downy feathers." This title would be more appropriate for this intimate psychological drama than the adopted English title *Warszawa 5703*, which suggests a film of almost epic proportions. A television film with the same Polish title, directed by Stefan Szlachtycz, had been made in 1983 and presented the next year at the Festival of Polish Films in Gdańsk. Kijowski's multinational production, though far superior in almost every aspect, shares the same weaknesses as its predecessor. To put it bluntly, Kijowski exploits the Holocaust theme to produce a schematic psychological melodrama, a love triangle set in the atypical circumstances of the Holocaust.

Deborah

Ryszard Brylski (b. 1950) similarly fails with *Deborah*, a film based on Marek Sołtysik's short story titled "Debora" that was barely noticed by critics in Poland. The action of the film is set before the outbreak of World War II in a small Polish provincial town with a significant Jewish population. The vision of the end of a certain world preoccupies Brylski. By employing stylish photography and Michał Lorenc's music (with its sad Jewish overtones), he aims at the creation of an atmosphere of despair.

The film's protagonist, a Polish painter, Marek Wawrowski (Olgierd Łukaszewicz), is preoccupied with restoring the newly uncovered frescoes in a local Catholic church. Rumors about war enhance the feeling of fear in the sleepy town. The Jewish population is afraid of what looms ahead. At the outbreak of the war, the married painter begins an affair with a young, beautiful Jewish woman, Deborah Grossman (Renata Dancewicz). After the war begins, he hides Deborah in an empty apartment, then in a cellar, while the Jewish population of the town, including Deborah's father and friends, are being exterminated by the Germans.

The imminent war and then its reality overshadow the characters' actions. Poles are generally shown to be sympathetic to the plight of the Jews; the majority are depicted helping the Jews, with many being killed by the Germans as a result. The theme of deeply rooted anti-Semitism is introduced by an anti-Jewish tale portrayed in the church's frescoes ("We work on the same theme," the Nazi officer says to the Polish painter). In Brylski's film, however, the Holocaust functions as the background for a tale about a passionate love, doomed from its very inception. Like Kijowski's *Warszawa 5703*, *Deborah* attempts to exploit the Holocaust, to incorporate it into mainstream cinema formulae.

Farewell to Maria

The first feature film by Filip Zylber (b. 1960), *Farewell to Maria*, based on a classic, powerful short story by Tadeusz Borowski,[30] differs from other films dealing with the occupation, the war, and Polish-Jewish relations. Modern jazz compositions by Tomasz Stańko and sophisticated stylized photography by Dariusz Kuc stress the morbid melancholy initially introduced by edifying dialogues about love, war, and poetry. Slow-motion photography, used consistently throughout the film, functions here not as a clichéd cinematic device but as a means of building atmosphere.

This is not to say that Zylber builds an atmosphere at the cost of aestheticizing the Holocaust. The film offers a new reading of a classic text and of history. Zylber does not follow the partly autobiographical, laconic, and verging-on-cynical vision of Borowski. In Borowski's world, there is no distinction between good and evil; all characters are infected by the devastating degeneration of human values. Everyday existence is marked by compromises, resignation, and the adoption of pragmatic personal philosophies useful in the struggle for survival. In its thematics, the film is the story of two Jewish women who manage to escape from the ghetto. The older of the two (Danuta Szaflarska), thanks to her prewar connections on the "Aryan side," escapes from the ghetto, but later, choosing inevitable death, she returns to be with friends and relatives. The young and beautiful Sara (Katarzyna Jamróz) performs a different role. According to Zylber, she "propels the action, circles like a moth, perturbs people. In a sense, she provokes her own death."[31] Like Irena in *Holy Week*, Sara serves as a reminder of what is going on behind the wall in the ghetto. She "upsets" people by her very presence.

In Borowski's short story, the emphasis is on the old Jewish woman; the nameless young one performs only a marginal role. This characterization was repeated by Jerzy Antczak in his memorable 1965 television adaptation of the story with Ida Kamińska (the star of *The Shop on Main Street*) in the leading role. Tadeusz Lubelski calls Zylber's film "a drama of helplessness" and Borowski's short story "a drama of mutual responsibility."[32] According to Lubelski, the filmic *Farewell to Maria* creates two distinct realms: the realm of private rituals and the realm of death. Young Polish intellectuals attending the wedding of their friends know that the nightmarish world behind the ghetto wall exists, but they feel unable to do anything about it. Insulated from the realm of death by their artificial rituals, they can only powerlessly watch the death of Sara, killed by a Polish *granatowy* (navy blue) policeman.

And Only This Forest

Jan Łomnicki's *And Only This Forest* is a Polish anti-*Schindler's List*: low budget, antispectacular, with an ordinary hero performing ordinary

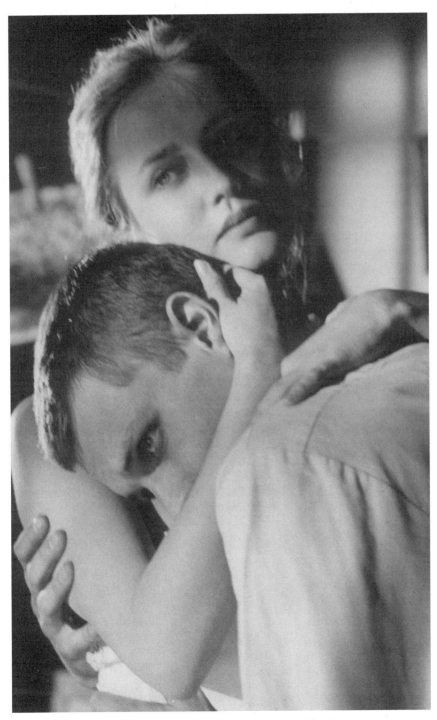

Figure 10.3 Marek Bukowski and Agnieszka Wagner in Filip Zylber's *Farewell to Maria* (1993)

deeds in exceptional circumstances. The opening scenes, set in the Warsaw ghetto in June 1942, show an elderly woman wandering fearfully
through impoverished streets. The impassioned camera portrays an over-
crowded ghetto in an almost semidocumentary manner. A washer-
woman, Kulgawcowa (the outstanding Ryszarda Hanin), is introduced
clearly as an outsider, an observer of a world that is far removed from her
own. This simple woman, previously employed by a rich Jewish doctor
and his family, is now about to help them. She is asked to take their only
child, the young girl, Rutka, out of the ghetto. The film shows their dangerous journey beyond the ghetto wall and, later, to a village where Kulgawcowa hopes to hide Rutka.

And Only this Forest does not portray a favorable picture of Polish reality. The Poles in the film are presented as poorly educated people, as a collection of low Polish types, blackmailers, and anti-Semites. Łomnicki's
aim is not to present a well-known figure (like Korczak in Wajda's film)
nor an "important topic" in an artificial theatrical setting (as in Kijowski's
film). Rather, he is interested in small, insignificant people overwhelmed
by history. These people are the center of this modest film. Whereas Wajda
gives a lesson (presented in an almost didactic manner) on history and
Jewish-Polish relations, Łomnicki creates characters and situations
entrenched in realism with seemingly contemporary dilemmas. The
scriptwriter, Anna Strońska, comments on this aspect of the film: "[We]
did not want to make a film about the martyrology of a nation. This had
to be a matter between people, between particular people, yet typical, like
the situation between the Irish and the English, the Palestinians and the
Israelis. Contrary to our expectations, the world of the twentieth century
has become an arena of nationalisms and chauvinisms. And this human
aspect was the core of our film and not, as somebody unwisely has said,
that Poles have anti-Semitism coded in their genes."[33]

The Year 1968

The year 1968 in Poland, as elsewhere in Europe, was marked by student
demonstrations. The ban on Adam Mickiewicz's classic romantic drama
Dziady (*Forefathers*) and the brutality of the police provoked student
demonstrations.[34] These events were used by some Communist Party
members to get rid of old guard communists, many of whom were of Jewish origin. The so-called "Zionist elements" were blamed for the eruption
of political protests directed against the party. The "anti-Zionist" campaign resulted not only in purges within the party, but also in attacks on
people of Jewish origin in other spheres of life. Some filmmakers of Jewish origin left for the West or Israel, including the controversial "father of
Polish postwar cinema," Aleksander Ford.

The political atmosphere in 1968 is reflected in two films: *March Almonds*
and *1968: Happy New Year*. Both films re-create those events through the

eyes of young protagonists, high school and university students, respectively, who experience their political initiation and are forced to make their first adult choices.

In *March Almonds*, Piwowarski tells the story in his usual, lyrical style, a style that had already emerged in his earlier films, such as *Yesterday*—a film that considers the Beatles phenomenon in Poland. In both films Piwowarski deals with coming-of-age problems, and both stories are set in small provincial towns against the backdrop of the political atmosphere of the late 1960s. The action of *March Almonds*, as the title suggests, is set in March 1968—the infamous, turbulent period in Polish politics. There are also clear references to events that happened soon afterward in Czechoslovakia with the invasion of the Soviet-led Warsaw Pact troops that brutally ended the "Prague Spring."

The peaceful atmosphere of the small town ends abruptly with the intrusion of politics. Generational conflicts merge with political ones. Though marginalized and ridiculed by Piwowarski, politics start to overshadow the characters' lives. One of the protagonists, Marcyś (Piotr Siwkiewicz), learns that he is of Jewish origin and is eventually forced to leave the country with his father. At the beginning of the film, Marcyś, supposedly unaware of his Jewishness, carries an anti-Semitic slogan at the small-town gathering in support of the official party line. Gradually, politics completely takes over Marcyś's life: anonymous voices in the local paper point out "the others" who are disguised as "true Poles" but plot against them; an anonymous hand paints the word "Żyd" (Jew) on the doors of Marcyś's home.

March Almonds is also a nostalgia film for the 1960s, Piwowarski's generation. To enhance this mood, the film features 1960s music groups from the West as well as their Polish counterparts, such as Breakout and Czerwone Gitary (Red Guitars). In one of the scenes, at an old, deserted Jewish cemetery, the film's narrator Tomek (Olaf Lubaszenko) is asked by a girl he is in love with, "So, there are no longer Jews in our town?" "No," he answers. "A pity," she responds. Soon after Marcyś's expulsion, a likable but conformist teacher remarks that "now, only amongst us, everything will work." At the film's end, the song "Ta nasza młodość" (That our youth) is heard, and a brief postscript describing the fates of the nonfictional characters who inspired their screen counterparts passes before the viewer.

There are clear political allusions in the film's final scene at the railway station. While Marcyś's train is about to leave, the school is awaiting its patron, a partisan nicknamed Leśny Władek (Władek from the Forest)—a reference to the advent of the Polish nationalists headed by General Mieczysław Moczar, the leader of the so-called "partisans' faction" within the Polish Communist Party. In many respects, the atmosphere created in *March Almonds* resembles that of some Czech films of the 1960s: the characters are likable, warm, mildly grotesque but not villainous. Piwowarski's film, in spite of the director's hazardous tendency to sentimentalize, may

Figure 10.4 From the left: Robert Gonera, Piotr Siwkiewicz, and Olaf Lubaszenko in *March Almonds* (1990, Radosław Piwowarski)

serve as a good example of the new political films emerging in Poland. Contrary to pre-1989 works, *March Almonds* avoids martyrological gestures and clear divisions between good and bad. It also offers a satirical look at political opportunism, primitive indoctrination, and doublespeak.

Conclusion

The theme of the Holocaust is not limited to feature films. It is chiefly present in contemporary Polish documentary films, such as *Chasydzi polscy* (*Polish Hasidic Jews*, 1993), by Krzysztof Wojciechowski, or *Kronika powstania w getcie warszawskim według Marka Edelmana* (*Chronicle of the Warsaw Ghetto Uprising According to Marek Edelman*, 1993), by Jolanta Dylewska. Dylewska creatively employs footage shot by the Germans in the Warsaw ghetto in 1943. The materials were brought to Poland by Jerzy Bossak, who used them in his classic documentary *Requiem for 500,000*. Later, this footage appeared in many other films, but Dylewska treats it differently. She creates new images from old ones, editing "within" a frame; by magnifying and slowing frames, she accentuates details missed by previous filmmakers. Through this process she transforms anonymous victims, deprived of humanity, into suffering but dignified characters. The only surviving member of the Jewish underground leadership, Marek Edelman, narrates this powerful documentary.[35]

The growing interest in the Jewish part of Polish history is further illustrated by the number of other cultural events referring to the Jewish cultural heritage and the Jewish contribution to Polish culture. The 1993 Polish presentation of Jewish art, "Shalom," was also partly devoted to cinema. The presentation featured some well-known prewar Yiddish classics such as *The Dybbuk*; lesser known Yiddish films made in Poland before the war by, among others, Aleksander Ford; little-known postwar Jewish films made in Poland by the cooperative Kinor (films by Natan Gross); as well as Polish documentary films on Jewish history.

In Polish films dealing with Polish-Jewish relations, Jewish characters are portrayed almost exclusively as figures emerging from the past. History is presented either as a nightmare everybody would like to forget or as an almost nostalgic picture stressing the multinational character of prewar Poland. It is not surprising to note the lack of contemporary Jewish (and for that matter other national) characters in contemporary Polish film. In an almost homogenized contemporary Poland, other resident nationalities are marginalized and scarcely portrayed in mainstream film.[36]

The sense of loss of the colorful Jewish culture appears genuine. One leading Polish journalist, Ewa Berberyusz, expresses it well: "The absence of Jews, whom I still remember but who are now gone, leaves me, for one, with a sense of irreplaceable loss. I voice here not just a sentiment in which is enshrined an idealised memory of old Poland, but rather an awareness of the real, manifest impoverishment of Polish culture. Poland has lost a very important creative contribution."[37]

Poland, traditionally a haven for Jews, has no significant Jewish presence now.[38] The repossession of the common Polish-Jewish heritage and the incorporation of Jewish culture into Polish memory entails the disturbing operation of confronting the past. The recognition of Poland's Jewish history and the struggle with the legacy of the Holocaust involves an unavoidable process of redefining the national Polish character, of redefining Polishness. As Harold B. Segel explains: "[T]he Poles cannot morally tolerate empty pages in their history as a nation. Hence the ongoing postcommunist archaeology of the Jewish past in Poland."[39]

Notes

1. Czesław Miłosz, "A Poor Christian Looks at the Ghetto," *The Collected Poems 1931–1987* (London and New York: Viking, 1988), 64–65. [Originally published in 1945 in a volume *Ocalenie (Rescue)*.]
2. Catherine Portuges, "Exile and Return: Jewish Identity in Post-Communist Hungarian Cinema," *Discourse* 17, no. 3 (1995): 24–25.
3. Ibid., 29.
4. Ibid.
5. Dominick LaCapra, *Representing the Holocaust: History, Theory, Trauma* (Ithaca and London: Cornell University Press, 1994), xi.
6. These and several other problems of a filmic, historical, and ethical nature have been discussed in great depth by many scholars. For instance, Annette Insdorf, *Indelible Shadows: Film and the Holocaust* (Cambridge and New York: Cambridge University Press, 1989); Ilan Avisar, *Screening the Holocaust: Cinema's Images of the Unimaginable* (Bloomington: Indiana University Press, 1988); André Pierre Colombat, *The Holocaust in French Film* (Metuchen: Scarecrow Press, 1993).
7. Lucy S. Davidowicz, *The Holocaust and the Historians* (Cambridge, Mass.: Harvard University Press, 1981), 14.
8. Ibid., 93.
9. Eric A. Goldman, *Visions, Images, and Dreams: Yiddish Film Past and Present* (Ann Arbor: UMI Research Press, 1983), 109.
10. Both films are discussed in chapter 3 of this volume.
11. Munk was killed in 1961 in a car accident while returning from the set of *The Passenger*. The film, edited by Munk's friends, had its premiere on the second anniversary of Munk's death, 20 September 1963. It was presented as an unfinished statement by the tragically deceased director. The material left by Munk was added, as well as commentary on the making of the film.
12. Insdorf, *Indelible Shadows*, 56.
13. Maria Malatyńska, "Siedmioramiennie" [an interview with Andrzej Wajda], *Tygodnik Powszechny* 9 (1996): 7.
14. The year 1973 was a very good one for Polish cinema. Apart from the films mentioned, several notable films were made, for instance, *Hubal* (Bohdan Poręba), *Illumination* (Krzysztof Zanussi), *Through and Through* (Grzegorz Królikiewicz), and *God's Finger* (Antoni Krauze).
15. Tadeusz Sobolewski discusses four films dealing with the Holocaust presented at the 1984 Festival of Polish Films in Gdańsk. Apart from Kawalerowicz's and Dziki's films,

these were *Tragarz puchu* (*A Down Carrier*, television production), by Stefan Szlachtycz, and *Wedle wyroków twoich* (*According to the Decrees of Providence*), by Jerzy Hoffman. Sobolewski calls Szlachtycz's and Hoffman's productions "kitsch works on the Jewish theme." Tadeusz Sobolewski, "Czy film współczesny jest możliwy," *Kino* 1 (1985): 8.

16. Quoted from Bolesław Michałek and Frank Turaj, *The Modern Cinema of Poland* (Bloomington: Indiana University Press, 1988), 112.

17. In the mid-1980s, two films dealing with Polish-Jewish relations were released: *Nie było słońca tej wiosny* (*There Was No Sun That Spring*, 1984), directed by Juliusz Janicki, and *W cieniu nienawiści* (*In the Shadow of Hatred*, 1986), directed by Wojciech Żółtowski.

18. For example, see the discussion in Colombat, *The Holocaust in French Film*, 299–344, and in Stefan Korboński, *The Jews and the Poles on World War II* (New York: Hippocrene Books, 1989), 107–125.

19. Jan Błoński, "Biedni Polacy patrzą na getto," *Tygodnik Powszechny* (11 January 1987), 1 and 4. For the translation of Błoński's essay and the discussion it initiated in Poland, see Anthony Polonsky, ed., *My Brother's Keeper? Recent Polish Debates on the Holocaust* (London and New York: Routledge, 1990).

20. Czesław Miłosz, "Campo dei Fiori," in *The Collected Poems*, 33. [Originally published in 1943 in the underground anthology *Z otchłani* (*From the Abyss*), composed by poets living on the "Aryan side" and dedicated to the Warsaw Jews.]

21. Błoński, "Biedni Polacy," 1.

22. Jarosław Marek Rymkiewicz, *Final Solution: Umschlagplatz*, translated by Nina Taylor (New York: Farrar, Straus and Giroux, 1994) [originally published in Polish as *Umschlagplatz* (Paris: Instytut Literacki, 1988)]; Andrzej Szczypiorski, *The Beautiful Mrs. Seidenman*, translated by Klara Główczewska (New York: Grove Weidenfeld, 1989) [originally published as *Początek* (Paris: Instytut Literacki, 1986)]; Paweł Huelle, *Who Was David Weiser?* translated by Michael Kandel (Orlando: Harcourt, 1994) [originally published in Poland as *Weiser Davidek* (Gdańsk: Wydawnictwo Morskie, 1987)]; Piotr Szewc, *Annihilation*, translated by Ewa Hryniewicz-Yarbrough (n.p.: Dalkey Archive Press, 1993) [originally published as *Zagłada* (Warszawa: Czytelnik, 1987)].

23. Robert DiAntonio's review of *The Beautiful Mrs. Seidenman*, *World Literature Today* 65, no. 1 (1991): 145.

24. Jerzy Kosiński, *The Painted Bird* (New York: Harcourt Brace Jovanovich, 1970).

25. Holland's *Angry Harvest* received an Academy Award nomination for Best Foreign Film. Its examination of the psychological and social mechanisms behind the relationship between a Polish farmer, Wolny, and a Jewish fugitive, Rosa, prompts Karen Jaehne to write that "it explores the peasant/Jew relationship with more insight and less self-righteousness than all nine and a half hours of *Shoah*." Karen Jaehne, "Angry Harvest," *Cineaste* 15, no. 1 (1986): 39. *Europa, Europa* received a Golden Globe award for Best Foreign Film. The subject matter of this factual odyssey of the survival of Solomon Perel, with its blending of humor and horror and its almost absurdist yet true story, perhaps prompted the Germans to decline to nominate *Europa, Europa* for an Academy Foreign Film Award.

26. Tadeusz Lubelski, "Wajda: albo *Pana Tadeusza* albo *Pannę Nikt*" [an interview with Andrzej Wajda], *Kino* 2 (1995): 9.

27. Colombat, *The Holocaust in French Film*, 113–116. Also Tzvetan Todorov, "Umrzeć w Warszawie," *Kultura niezależna* 49 (1989), reprinted in *Kino* 7 (1991): 41–42 (translated by Jagoda Engelbrecht).

28. Ewelina Nurczyńska-Fidelska, "Romanticism and History: A Sketch of the Creative Output of Andrzej Wajda," in *Polish Cinema in Ten Takes*, ed. Ewelina Nurczyńska-Fidelska and Zbigniew Batko (Łódź: Łódzkie Towarzystwo Naukowe, 1995), 12.

29. Jerzy Andrzejewski, *Wielki Tydzień* (Warszawa: Czytelnik, 1993). Fragments of Andrzejewski's work in Harold B. Segel, ed., *Stranger in Our Midst: Images of the Jew in Polish Literature* (Ithaca and London: Cornell University Press, 1996), 338–362

30. Tadeusz Borowski, "Pożegnanie z Marią," the title piece of a collection of short stories, *Pożegnanie z Marią*, first published in Warsaw in 1947.

31. Bożena Janicka, "Coś zostało w powietrzu—mówi Filip Zylber," *Kino* 3 (1994): 13.
32. Tadeusz Lubelski, "Borowski na dziś," *Kino* 3 (1994): 15.
33. Tadeusz Sobolewski, "Rozmowy po kinie: Przełamywanie obcości," *Kino* 7 (1991): 20.
34. The play *Dziady* was adapted for the screen in 1989 by Tadeusz Konwicki as *Lawa: Opowieść o Dziadach* (*Lava: The Story of Forefathers*).
35. Marek Edelman is also the narrator of one of the most powerful accounts of the Warsaw Ghetto Uprising, a book by Hanna Krall, *Zdążyć przed Panem Bogiem* (Cracow: Wydawnictwo Literackie, 1977). This book is translated into English as *Shielding the Flame: An Intimate Conversation with Dr. Marek Edelman, the Last Surviving Leader of the Warsaw Ghetto Uprising*, translated by Joanna Stasińska and Lawrence Weschler (New York: Henry Holt, 1986).
36. For instance, the Gypsies are portrayed in a single film, Dorota Kędzierzawska's *Devils, Devils*. There are no contemporary films featuring Belarusian or Ukrainian national minorities. Certain topics, such as the postwar Polish-Ukrainian relations, are still unexplored, probably because they remain troubling to examine.
37. Ewa Berberyusz, "The Black Hole: Conversation with Stanisław Krajewski, 'a Pole and a Jew in One Person,'" in Polonsky, *My Brother's Keeper?* 108.
38. This aspect is stressed, for instance, in the very title of Małgorzata Niezabitowska's volume, *Remnants: The Last Jews of Poland* (New York: Friendly Press, 1986).
39. Segel, *Stranger in Our Midst*, 1.

11

Polish Films with an American Accent

∽

In the aftermath of World War II, cinema in Poland was generally regarded as more than just entertainment. There was no place for commercial cinema within the framework of socialist art. Film's task was to communicate, educate, and perform other social duties.

Although it had the support of an audience, genre cinema in Poland never constituted a distinct part of national film production. This type of cinema was also rarely supported or treated seriously by Polish film critics, who looked for great authors dealing with great themes. Similarly, this cinema was ignored in the West, which was chiefly interested in films that gave insight into Central European politics. For a number of critics, certain popular genres, such as the crime film, were impossible to make in the highly politicized climate of communist Poland. Adam Zagajewski comments on the absence of certain popular genres in totalitarian states: "Murder mystery novels are impossible here: everyone always knows who the guilty party is—the state."[1] Zagajewski observes that in totalitarianism the state monopolizes every aspect of life—including its evil dimensions—and, as a consequence, becomes "by necessity" the only wrongdoer.

In spite of the political obstacles, there were several attempts to make genre cinema—American in form but with "socialist" overtones and messages. For example, the adaptations of "militia novels"[2] resulted in a peculiar version of the detective genre, "militia films," frequently known as "democratic thrillers." Janusz Majewski's 1969 film *The Criminal Who Stole a Crime* serves as probably the best example of that genre. In it, Zygmunt Hübner portrays Captain Siwy, an MO (militia) officer who successfully continues his search for justice after his retirement. Unlike the protagonists in other Polish crime films, Siwy's character is more than a stereotyped militia officer; he is a multifaceted individual with strengths and weaknesses, a tired hero of socialist work.

Figure 11.1 Zygmunt Hübner (right) and Ryszard Filipski in Janusz Majewski's *The Criminal Who Stole a Crime* (1969)

Unlike their Western counterparts, Polish popular genres had to perform several political duties outlined in the state's propagandist cultural
policy. In her analyses of Polish crime films of the 1960s, Agnieszka
Ćwikiel lists the various social roles these films had to perform. First of all,
they had to be ambitious, artistic works that scrupulously reflected life in
Poland and contained the truth about its inhabitants. Another task of
these films was to show the achievements of the militia and thereby serve
as a form of crime prevention. Finally, they had to entertain.[3] Thus the
"popular genres" belonged to the domain of "ambitious cinema"; they
had to be didactic, touching upon political and social issues to justify their
existence. For filmmakers, it was an almost impossible task to meet the
demand of making an entertaining film that would also be apologetic
toward the state and its representatives in blue uniforms.

The political correctness of that time required the modification of
imported formulae by establishing the militia as the main protagonist.
The educational tasks of the "militia genre" were achieved by including
several stereotyped elements: the emphasis on the futility of crime
("crime does not pay"), the emphasis on the infallibility of the system, and
the presentation of militia officers as dignified yet sympathetic characters
with proper (usually working-class) backgrounds and beliefs. These
attributes were seldom questioned. An example of this type of film would
be Marek Piwowski's *Przepraszam, czy tu biją?* (*Foul Play*, 1976), a crime
picture starring two boxing champions (Jerzy Kulej and Jan Szczepański)
as two unconventional police inspectors who are not afraid to employ
brutal yet apparently successful methods in their investigative work.

Politics aside, the malfunctioning Polish economy proved to be another
obstacle for the production of local popular genres. The colorless reality
produced equally unglamorous, paltry crimes. The boring, politically correct militia officers represented an equally boring political system. High-
speed chases, car crashes, and luxurious clothes and interiors belonged to
a different world. Local audiences could only dream foreign dreams.

Polish Action Films after 1989

The lack of a popular cinema tradition in Poland is emphasized by the
title of Anita Skwara's essay, "Film Stars Do Not Shine in the Sky Over
Poland: The Absence of Popular Cinema in Poland."[4] In this work, written before the appearance of the wave of Polish action films, Skwara states
that "the poetics of American genre cinema transplanted to Poland turned
out to be dysfunctional, alien, astonishingly naive or vulgar, and simplistic."[5] Harsh in her criticism of the "Polish-made American films" (a term
used in Poland to describe the local versions of Hollywood), Skwara
stresses that these "clumsy imitations" were not made for the more
sophisticated viewer and, deprived of a Polish national context, had no
chance of survival.

The number and popularity of recent genre films in Poland suggest the opposite. The poetics of Hollywood transferred to Polish reality is seen at its best in such action films as Wojciech Wójcik's *Zabić na końcu* (*To Kill at the End*, 1990), Jacek Skalski's *Miasto prywatne* (*The Private Town*, 1993), Jarosław Żamojda's *Młode wilki* (*Fast Lane*, 1995), Maciej Dutkiewicz's *Nocne graffiti* (*Night Graffiti*, 1997), and, in particular, in Władysław Pasikowski's *Kroll* (1991), *Psy* (*The Pigs*, 1992), and its sequel, *Psy 2—Ostatnia krew* (*The Pigs 2: The Last Blood*, 1994). Also, the most recent action films incorporate the poetics of American action films. This is evident in films like *Demony wojny według Goyi* (*The War Demons According to Goya*, 1998) and *Operacja Samum* (*Operation Samum*, 1999), both directed by Pasikowski, as well as the most effective, *Prawo ojca* (*Father's Law*, 1999), directed by Marek Kondrat, and *Ostatnia misja* (*The Last Mission*, 2000), directed by Wojciech Wójcik.

The adoption of the genre cinema formulae is, of course, not restricted to genuine action films. For example, the return of melodrama can be observed in *Tato* (*Daddy*, 1995), a debut film by Maciej Ślesicki (b. 1964). His *Sara* (1997) goes even further with its incorporation of Hollywood formulae; it cannibalizes many genres and cleverly plays with cinematic clichés. The Polish-Czech production, *Zabić Sekala* (*To Kill Sekal*, 1998), directed by Vladimir Michálek, successfully transplants the poetics of the Western to the war reality of the Protectorate of Bohemia and Moravia.

In box-office terms, action films were the most successful Polish films of the early 1990s, and were the only works effectively competing with American products. For instance, if we look at the Polish films released between 1991 and April 1997, the top three seen by viewers are action films: *The Pigs 2: The Last Blood* (684,000 viewers), *Fast Lane* (541,000), and *Night Graffiti* (500,000). Their popularity on video matches that of American action films. The title of Zdzisław Pietrasik's article in the influential weekly *Polityka* emphasizes the preferences of Polish audiences clearly: "Defend Yourself: Most of All We Enjoy Watching Polish-Made American Films."[6] If we take into account films released in the 1990s, as many as seven among the most popular ten are action films. Machulski's *Kiler* is listed third with 2,179,865 viewers, right after two historical epics, *With Fire and Sword* and *Pan Tadeusz*.[7]

Awards at the Festival of Polish Films in Gdynia indicate a change of direction favoring genre cinema: the 1993 award went to a romantic comedy by Radosław Piwowarski, *The Sequence of Feelings*; the 1994 festival winner, *The Turned Back*, was a political comedy by Kazimierz Kutz; and the 1995 award went to Juliusz Machulski's *Girl Guide*. Also, a growing number of young Polish directors are interested in telling stories and in making commercial, well-narrated films. As they often insist, their goal is not to perform any national or social mission, discuss "important issues," or focus on traditional filmic themes like Polish history. They want cinema to be free from political and social obligations. Their films are no longer made for the young Polish intelligentsia. The word "art" seems to be forbidden in these young filmmaking circles. Sporadic voices stressing the importance of art cinema sound as if they were taken from a previous political reality.[8]

The transfer of Hollywood poetics to Polish reality is primarily visible in popular Polish television series, such as *Ekstradycja* (*The Extradition*, 1995–1998, twenty five episodes), directed by Wojciech Wójcik. In this production, Marek Kondrat stars as Olgierd Halski, a Warsaw police inspector fighting international drug gangs that smuggle heroin and amphetamines from Russia via Poland to the West. Kondrat plays an aging, almost stereotypically hard-bitten cop who uses brutal methods in his work. In the film, the Polish viewer encounters clear references to contemporary political and criminal affairs, like the well-publicised racketeering in Warsaw's Old Town. *The Extradition* demonizes the Russians, the Russian mafia, and former KGB officers, now involved in large-scale criminal activities. It also stresses the helplessness of the Polish police and the corruption of its high-ranking officers. Another successful television series, *Akwarium* (*The Aquarium*, 1995, four episodes, a Polish-German-Ukrainian coproduction), directed by Antoni Krauze, goes even further with its morbid fascination with the Soviet secret services. Based on Victor Suvorov's famous account, *The Aquarium* is a psychological, rather than an action, film about espionage.

There is no doubt that the popularity of certain action films is partly due to their exploration of realms that, until recently, could not be depicted in a negative fashion. For instance, Pasikowski's *Kroll* and Feliks Falk's *Samowolka* (*AWOL*, 1993) create a dark picture of a formerly taboo topic, the military. The vulgar language of the screen protagonists reflects an unrefined actual Polish life based on corruption, depravity, and primitive indoctrination. *AWOL* is less action oriented and more a journalistic film made in the Cinema of Distrust tradition. Falk's film is organized around the conflict between new soldiers and the old guard about to retire from active duty. The older soldiers, led by a criminal nicknamed Tiger, rule the garrison and drill the newcomers in order to avenge their own earlier humiliation. Everything happens with the silent approval of the officers. In spite of its popularity in the Polish video market, this type of cinema—a substitute for independent media before 1989—is rife with clichés and does not go beyond common knowledge of the subject.

The opening scenes of *Kroll* suggest a typical Polish "war film": in a dark rainy atmosphere soldiers load heavy tanks onto a train. Vulgar language and scenes showing the humiliation of a young soldier introduce a reality never before seen in Polish cinema. What follows is the suicide of the victimized soldier, which is falsely reported as an accident to avoid controversy. His distraught friend and protector, Kroll (Olaf Lubaszenko), leaves the barracks illegally and goes to see his own family. Lieutenant Arek (Bogusław Linda) and one of his soldiers, Wiaderny (Cezary Pazura), try to bring Kroll back so that he will not be prosecuted. The worlds in and out of the barracks contain the same ugly features: corruption, violence, alcoholism, betrayal.

Kroll sets the tone for subsequent films by Pasikowski. It introduces a harsh, violent world reserved for equally violent and tough men with clear misogynist attitudes. The film also stresses the message that is present in almost all Polish action films: the friendship between males matters more than anything else. Kroll's friend Kuba, who has a romance with Kroll's wife, finally saves Kroll and their friendship by taking on the identity of the AWOL soldier. In the final scene, Kuba asks the lieutenant, who knows of the switch and accepts the deception, "How is it here?" The lieutenant's spasmatic laughter is the only answer—and an excruciating comment on the situation in the Polish armed forces.

Pasikowski's *The Pigs*

The incorporation of American models is seen at its best in *The Pigs*, directed by Władysław Pasikowski (b. 1959). The film, set in 1989, incorporates many factual events into its narrative. Pasikowski draws heavily on the formula of American police/gangster films and quotes extensively from several makers of quality action films. The mise en scène is distinctly American; there are American references in nearly every scene. The viewer encounters "American" locations (luxurious interiors, rainy streets, underground parking lots, a deserted factory), excessive violence shown in extreme slow motion, vulgar language, and tough talk in the world of rough men. The film relies on action instead of dialogue, an unusual feature compared to the majority of Polish productions. The cinematographer, Paweł Edelman, captures images with a tracking camera. These images are frequently displayed in slow motion and are sometimes portrayed as tableaux-like compositions.

Despite the aforementioned features, this film is "very Polish." Pasikowski shows Poland in a process of transition from one political system to another, in which all principles are shaken and everything is possible. In Poland, 1989 was the year marked by verifications of the former members of the secret police (SB), by burnt secret police files, and by open corruption. The film also portrays a world in which colleagues from the former Soviet KGB, East German STASI, and Polish SB join forces to fight for control of the illegal, but lucrative, drug market. The film reveals the escalation of crime that before 1989 was a rarely publicized fact, but which now makes front-page news.

The protagonist of *The Pigs*, Franciszek (Franz) Maurer (played memorably by Bogusław Linda), a lieutenant in the secret police, tries to survive in an "age of verifications," lost privileges, and his own personal problems. Truth and lies coexist in this world; it is impossible to distinguish between the two. "Commissions change but you remain their member," the protagonist tells the cunning chairman of the verification commission.

The protagonist is introduced in the first pre-credit scene of *The Pigs* in which the color red dominates the frame. Franz Maurer, dressed formally but without a tie, sits nonchalantly before the verification commission, smoking a cigarette and listening to his work record. The camera portrays him frontally, from the point of view of the commission. The viewer learns that Franz is thirty-seven, married to a daughter of the former vice-minister of internal affairs, and has one child. In his professional career, he was honored but also disciplined several times and almost discharged from the police force. The most serious crime he has been accused of is the killing of Captain Nowakowski, who tried to establish free trade unions in the police force in 1980, the year of Solidarity. Franz defends himself by saying that Nowakowski was a mentally unstable person who killed his wife and dragged his daughter onto the roof of a building demanding the registration of the trade unions and an increase in his salary. Franz proudly admits that he shot him from 220 meters with a Mauser 7.8 mm. After bragging about his marksmanship ("I shot his head off"), he adds in a poignant voice: "He was my colleague."

With Michał Lorenc's music evoking spaghetti Westerns and gangster classics, the camera cuts to the building that houses the Ministry of Internal Affairs. Franz and his colleagues from the security force pack confidential documents and police files onto a truck, and later burn them at an abandoned dumping ground. In one of the scenes, Franz approaches some barking police dogs in their cages. The dogs bark viciously, but are contained, alluding to the situation of the secret police members—once above the law but now controlled by the former dissidents.[9] The film shows the end of a certain political formation; its now unwanted pretorians fight for survival. At the dumping ground, Franz's friend Olo (Marek Kondrat) tells a police newcomer (Cezary Pazura), who spies on them: "When you grow up, you'll understand that politics is not the evening news. We are the politics, here on this dumping ground. Either we manage to get out of this or we stay here forever."

In Pasikowski's world there is no longer a division between "us" and "them" but rather (almost a "discovery" in Polish cinema) between good and bad. Immediately after its release, *The Pigs* became a cult film for many young viewers in Poland, which confused some established film critics and filmmakers. Pasikowski's viewers side with a member of the disgraced former secret police, an individual whose world collapses, who was and is surrounded by corrupt politicians, and who exists in a world without moral values. The viewer sides with a classic loser: a lonely tough guy, betrayed by "his system," his wife, his best friend, and his girlfriend.

The protagonist, formerly in a position of power and money (indicated by his new BMW and luxurious house), finds himself deprived of his privileged status. He loses his loved ones and his material possessions, and his career comes under investigation. After destroying the police documents that relate to his professional past, Franz burns family documents and photographs in the backyard of his empty villa (his private past). "What are you doing here?" asks Angela, his girlfriend, after learning that Franz's wife and their child have left for America. "I'm cleaning up," is his answer.

Pasikowski's film was probably the first artistic work to capture the death of the Solidarity movement's ethos. In an opening scene, Franz relates that the free trade activist in the police force not only had mental problems but also had motives that were not political but rather purely economic. In a scene that aggravated some Polish film critics, the drunken members of the infamous security force carry one of their completely drunk colleagues on their shoulders toward the camera while singing "Janek Wiśniewski padł" (Janek Wiśniewski has fallen). The song was previously employed by Andrzej Wajda in his *Man of Iron* to refer to the Solidarity movement because of its associations with the 1970 strike in Gdańsk. The young audience of *The Pigs*, never exposed to political thinking prevalent in the communist era, appreciated the debunking of the oppositional myths. In a 1996 interview with Zdzisław Pietrasik, Wajda made the following observation on the scene from *The Pigs*: "I understood that something important had happened in Poland, something that may have unforeseeable consequences. That is why I was not surprised with the later election results [the defeat of the pro-Solidarity parties and the victory of the former communists, now labeled socialist democrats], not to mention the latest presidential elections [the defeat of Lech Wałęsa by Aleksander Kwaśniewski—the former Communist Party member]."[10]

According to some critics and filmmakers, *The Pigs* "preys on human disappointment, human helplessness."[11] For others, the film does not exploit the current situation but merely unveils the state of mind in post-communist Poland. For instance, Bogusław Linda says, "People have had enough of martyrology, veterans, selling out. They're angry about what is happening in the country. My role in *The Pigs* was born out of this anger and hatred towards the new reality."[12] Other voices defend *The Pigs*, stressing its moral dimensions. Piotr Lis, a film critic, titles his essay "Moralitet z klocków" (Morality play from building blocks).[13] Piotr Szulkin, a filmmaker, notes the similarities between Wajda's *Ashes and Diamonds* and *The Pigs*. Szulkin states: "*The Pigs* does not have the literary dimension of Andrzejewski's novel [the literary source of Wajda's film], but in a strange, discotheque-hamburger-like aesthetics, the film communicates similar astonishments that, for Andrzejewski, could have been a discovery but, for Pasikowski, are only a statement."[14]

The parallels between Maciek, the protagonist of Wajda's classic *Ashes and Diamonds*, and Franz, the protagonist of *The Pigs*, seem unlikely at first, but eventually appear legitimate. For different reasons, both bear the burden of the past and try to survive in a new political reality. Both suffer defeat. In one of the final scenes of the sequel to *The Pigs*, *The Pigs 2: The Last Blood*,[15] the wounded Franz runs into a field away from a train filled with ammunition. The way he moves and the way he is followed by the camera, as well as his groaning and exaggerated gestures, emulate Wajda's dying hero.

The Pigs 2, commercially one of the most successful Polish films of the 1990s,[16] reinforces images from the first part, images also present in other

Polish action films. The film opens with newsreel-like scenes of the Balkan War. A man whom the viewer later recognizes as Wolf (Artur Żmijewski), an arms dealer, poses in front of the camera with two severed heads. Another man briskly approaches, points a gun to the camera (and the viewer), and shoots. After a short period of blackness, the camera cuts to a prison cell that Franz Maurer shares with a convicted murderer who hastily reveals his crimes. In a scene likely referring to Krzysztof Kieślowski's *A Short Film about Killing*, the murderer is taken out of the cell by force to be executed.

Upon his release from prison, after serving several years, Franz is greeted by his former colleague from the police force, nicknamed Nowy (Cezary Pazura). Fired for not joining the strike in the factory and unable to find a permanent job, Franz pairs up with Wolf and together they become involved in an illegal international arms deal. For unclear reasons (perhaps conscience) Franz single-handedly prevents the sale of arms to the Balkans. In the film's finale, he blows up a train filled with firearms.

The Pigs and its sequel created a new charismatic Polish star, Bogusław Linda (b. 1952). He is another generational actor who follows two acting personalities known for their roles in Andrzej Wajda's films: Zbigniew Cybulski and Daniel Olbrychski. Like his predecessors, and unlike the majority of Polish actors, he is known exclusively for his filmic roles. Linda is also a film and theater director; in 1989 he made his first feature film, *Seszele* (*Seychelles*), which was well received by young audiences. He started his acting career at the beginning of the 1980s in a series of acclaimed political films, including Agnieszka Holland's *Fever* and *A Woman Alone*, Andrzej Wajda's *Man of Iron* and *Danton*, Krzysztof Kieślowski's *Blind Chance*, and Janusz Zaorski's *Mother of Kings*. He became one of the idols of the Solidarity generation, although most of the films he appeared in were shelved by the censor.

Linda changes with his audience. In the 1990s, he has become an icon for another generation, the post-Solidarity generation, and represents its nihilism and disillusionment with the new reality. His lupine smile reflects his inner passion. The tough guy aura and the cynical attitude of the protagonists he portrays reflect the reality of the first period of unfettered Polish capitalism. Linda's nickname, Bogie, which refers to his first name as well as to Humphrey Bogart, exemplifies his popularity in Poland. At the 1994 Festival of Polish Feature Films in Gdynia, he was honored with a special retrospective of his films.

Linda often stresses that the evolution of his image, from romantic, frequently antitotalitarian heroes to the fallen angel of the old system in the 1990s, is intentional, an integral part of his artistic development: "The time came when I felt that I had had enough of roles of an intellectual. I felt that such a person, without any major life experiences, torn by idealistic differences, was not a hero for the present."[17] Nevertheless, this shift has prompted some Polish critics to accuse the actor of betraying his initial image. Tadeusz Lubelski, for instance, declares that contemporary Linda "remains merely a caricature of himself."[18]

Figure 11.2 Bogusław Linda in *The Pigs 2: The Last Blood* (1994, Władysław Pasikowski)

The character portrayed by Linda in *The Pigs* is a tough policeman and a great sharpshooter. These facts are emphasized in the opening scene of part one and reaffirmed in a Western-like target shooting in part two. As played by Linda, this character becomes a completely new hero, different from any former Polish screen star. The protagonist representing the young intelligentsia has been replaced by a tough guy, passivity by action. Male solidarity and money are what really matter for the new hero; male bonding and a foreign car are more important than political ideals and lasting male-female relationships. Like some of his American predecessors (beginning with Clint Eastwood's Dirty Harry), the new Polish action hero does not want to wait for justice; he does not even believe that it exists. Rather, he takes the initiative and the law into his own hands. Franz Maurer is not a vigilante, however. In a manner resembling Dirty Harry, in *The Pigs 2* he claims: "I am nobody. I only remove weeds." Also in part two, parodying Dostoevsky (perhaps a Dostoevsky for the masses), Franz remarks, while standing next to the body of the Russian mafia boss whom he has just killed: "If there is no god, what kind of a satan are you?"

Both parts of *The Pigs* and the majority of Polish action films are male-oriented films, masculine spectacles celebrating Polish-style machismo. They show the breakdown of law and order that prompts the characters to resort to violent methods. They evoke sympathy for the criminals. These films can be classified as male melodramas, notable for their sense of melancholy. The protagonists are always males, usually bearing foreign names such as Kroll, Maurer, Wolf, or Kossot. With the exception of *Fast Lane*, which portrays inexperienced teenagers tempted by the big money that can be made almost overnight by smuggling, the protagonists are tough middle-aged men, usually former security agents, military men, or sometimes petty criminals (*The Private Town*). Customarily dressed in black suits and dark ties, they resemble FBI agents or stereotypical businessmen. According to Polish folk wisdom, gangsters and businessmen have a lot in common in the post-1989 period; their moralities fuse.

In *The Pigs*, Pasikowski shows a degraded world with clichéd female characters. His clichés, however, have more to do with stereotypes found in American action cinema than with stereotypes of women in Polish films. Piotr Szulkin, who contributes to this discussion with his film *Femina*, points out that women in Polish films never had time for love because they were busy making national banners.[19] Pasikowski is not interested in this aspect of Polishness; his films also do not explore notions such as love, friendship, loyalty. Like some of their American counterparts from the 1980s, both *Pigs* films represent female characters as voiceless figures who inhabit male-dominated landscapes. Their task is no longer to "stand by their men," as in classical Hollywood cinema, but to find a place for themselves in a ruthless world where only their sexuality matters.

In Pasikowski's films, men are active, powerful, and violent; women are passive, powerless, and blatantly sexual. In these films women are portrayed as sexual objects. According to the films' inner logic, the female characters deserve their fate due to their sexually provocative behavior, their unfaithfulness, and—a recurrent feature in Pasikowski's films—their inanity. "You are not that bad, you are simply immensely stupid," shouts Nowy to his wife in *The Pigs 2* when she does not want him to go out and help his friend Franz. Unfaithful women surround Pasikowski's protagonists: Kroll's battered wife has an affair with his best friend; Angela and

254 I *Polish National Cinema*

Nadia, though "belonging" to Franz, have affairs with his close friends. Women can also be bought and sold; for example, Nadia, in *The Pigs 2*, is Wolf's "war trophy." He bought her in Sarajevo for a case of Johnnie Walker and eventually sells her to Franz. In part one of *The Pigs*, Angela is taken by Franz from the reformatory and thus becomes his property. Male characters seem to need women only to enhance their prestige and as evidence of their manliness.

Similar treatment of female characters spreads across other genres. The melodramatic *Daddy* (directed by Maciej Ślesicki), for example, a film employing stars from *The Pigs* (Bogusław Linda and Cezary Pazura), tells the story of a bitter divorce case between a successful filmmaker and his wife, who shows signs of mental illness. This well-narrated film, full of references to contemporary American cinema, portrays a one-dimensional world with black-and-white divisions between genders. Ślesicki, who skillfully retains precise control of the mood and atmosphere of the film, portrays a clearly misogynist landscape where almost all of the female characters border on caricatures.

Machulski's *Déjà Vu*

Films by Juliusz Machulski, from his very well-received *Va Banque* (1981) to the recent box-office successes *Kiler* (1997) and its 1999 sequel *Kiler-ów 2-óch* (*Kiler 2*), are also inspired by American genre cinema. The commercial and critical success of these films in Poland relies on yet another important ingredient: formulaic structures that are saturated with numerous references to Polish politics and everyday life. When Machulski moves to the realm of "art cinema," as is the case with his historical drama *Szwadron* (*Squadron*, 1995), the result is less convincing.

One of Machulski's best films, *Déjà Vu* (1989, a Polish-Soviet coproduction), employs pastiche as a dominant form of expression. Set in 1925, *Déjà Vu* tells the story of Johnny Pollack (Jerzy Stuhr), an American gangster of Polish origin sent by mobsters from Chicago to Odessa. What follows are Pollack's adventures in a land governed by its own principles, principles incomprehensible to Westerners. Pollack's pragmatic professionalism is out of place in the land of the Bolsheviks.

The title *Déjà Vu* implies events "already seen ..., the illusion of having previously experienced something actually being encountered for the first time."[20] Indeed, Machulski builds his film from clichés, fills it with references to world cinema, and thus creates a film for cine-buffs. In this multilayered pastiche, he employs familiar images from numerous films and quotes both early Soviet and American cinemas extensively. He borrows from Lev Kuleshov and Sergei Eisenstein as well as from Boris Barnet's comedies about everyday life under the New Economic Policy (NEP) program. He also borrows heavily from burlesque and American gangster films set during the prohibition era. *Déjà Vu* is peopled with American

Figure 11.3 Cezary Pazura (left) and Jerzy Stuhr as Johnny Pollack in Juliusz Machulski's *Déjà Vu* (1989)

gangsters bearing familiar names (like Cimino, Pacino, Scorsese, Coppola, etc.) and icons of an early Soviet culture: Vladimir Mayakovsky, Lili and Osip Brik, and Sergei Eisenstein. In the most famous sequence, frequently cited by scholars, Johnny Pollack, who is pursuing another gangster, finds himself on the steps of Odessa during Eisenstein's shooting of *Battleship Potemkin* (1925). Because Pollack is wearing a stolen officer's jacket, he is mistaken by the film crew for an actor who is supposed to be playing a commanding officer on the steps. Eventually, Chicago gangsters watch Pollack as he leads the Cossacks in the released version of *Battleship Potemkin*. With the exception of Zbigniew Rybczyński's *Steps* (1987), this is probably the most intelligent utilization of Eisenstein's famous sequence.

Machulski's *Girl Guide* (the title refers to a stolen nuclear warhead guidance system named GIRL), winner of the 1995 Festival of Polish Films, is advertised as "an amusing story combining rock and roll, spies, and highland folk, with a thriller element."[21] As this brief description suggests, it is a film that employs elements of Hollywood genre cinema but fuses them with a distinctly Polish idiom. The film targets young Polish viewers with its postmodern references to world cinema, its depiction of the local rock scene (the Polish rock star Paweł Kukiz plays the leading role), and its mockery of Polish political life, as well as with its humor.

Recent Action Films

Polish action filmmakers today employ hybrid, transgeneric constructs to tell stories similar to those of numerous American films. These filmmakers, mostly first-time directors, create films predominantly for the younger generation who are untainted by the politically draining 1980s in Poland, people who grew up in the transitional period of the early 1990s. These young viewers seem to have grown tired of politics, and are no longer interested in the political complexity of the past and the problems experienced in the post-totalitarian period.

The ambition of action filmmakers in Poland (and anywhere else, for that matter) is to beat Hollywood on its own terms, yet, paradoxically, their films rely on the Polish social context for success. These films are saturated with many references to Polish politics and everyday life. They present a world ruled by corruption, disharmony, and violence. They refer to contemporary political, financial, and criminal affairs. They reflect the unstable political and economic life, as well as moral chaos. Even unsuccessful films, such as *The Private Town*, which shows a gang of small-town criminals who terrorize their own town, to a certain extent reflect the new Polish reality.

Some of the recent examples of Polish action cinema, for example *Night Graffiti* and *Father's Law*, continue a long tradition of films dealing with the necessity of taking the law into one's own hands. In *Night Graffiti*, an inconsistent yet popular film directed by Maciej Dutkiewicz, the captain of an elite army troop and his friends from the military fight a war against drug dealers. Captain Kossot (Marek Kondrat, in what is almost a continuation of his role from the television series *Extradition*) is an avenger in the inner-city asphalt jungle. *Night Graffiti* also shows the corruption of a high-ranking police officer who, in the film's finale, is killed in a cover-up to preserve the good name of the police force.

The first screen appearance of Kasia Kowalska, a young Polish rock star, as a troubled drug addict contributes to this film's commercial success. In spite of that, however, according to a *Kino* critic, *Night Graffiti* is "devoid of a scrap of probability, an ersatz youth action film."[22] One may certainly find a better example of an "ersatz youth action film" in Żamojda's directorial debut, *Fast Lane*, and its 1998 sequel, *Fast Lane 1/2* (Żamojda is a well-known cinematographer of the younger generation). The plot describes the dilemmas of the new generation, teenagers who face their first adult choices. "An intelligent person has money" is the advice given to Robert, the best student in a high school class, prompting the young wolf[23] to join a gang of smugglers operating between Poland and Germany. *Fast Lane* and *Night Graffiti* are works without secrets, clumsy imitations of American genres made purely for entertainment. When compared with them, the much criticized *The Pigs* appears not only professionally made but also multidimensional and very Polish, in spite of its borrowings from American cinema.

Marek Kondrat's directorial debut, *Father's Law* (in which he plays the role of a single father avenging his teenage daughter), develops the theme of police corruption and ineffectuality. In the final scenes of the film, the victorious yet wounded protagonist addresses the female prosecutor and the police officer: "Where are you when they kill people? Law is for ordinary people, not for bandits. Don't you understand that?!" The thematic similarities between *Father's Law* and *Dirty Harry* have been stressed by Polish critics; for example, Zdzisław Pietrasik titles his article in *Polityka* "Brudny Marek" (Dirty Marek).[24] The very title of Kondrat's film, with its biblical connotations, suggests that the father has the right to avenge his daughter's sufferings and to protect her. His methods, though not approved by law, help to restore "good, old values" endangered by the liberal policymakers. *Father's Law* received the audiences' award at the 1999 Festival of Polish Films in Gdynia, a sure testimony that this film, apart from its well-executed American accent, also articulates the pressing problems of the post-communist reality.

Action films made in Poland are frequently perceived by some filmmakers and critics as a threat to a national cinema that needs to speak with a discrete Polish idiom. Others, myself included, do not view the appearance of these films as an indication of a crisis within the Polish film industry. Rather, these films can be seen as a chance to rejuvenate Polish film—to make it well narrated and absorbing for the viewer.

Notes

1. Adam Zagajewski, *Solidarity, Solitude* [translated from the Polish by Lillian Vallee] (New York: Ecco Press, 1990), 140.
2. Stanisław Barańczak's term from his *Czytelnik ubezwłasnowolniony* (Paris: Libella, 1983), 96–132. Milicja Obywatelska (Civic Militia)—Polish police in the communist era.
3. Agnieszka Ćwikiel, "U nas na komendzie," in *Syndrom konformizmu? Kino polskie lat sześćdziesiątych*, ed. Tadeusz Miczka [assistant editor: Alina Madej] (Katowice: Wydawnictwo Uniwersytetu Śląskiego, 1994), 84.
4. Anita Skwara, "Film Stars Do Not Shine in the Sky Over Poland: The Absence of Popular Cinema in Poland," in *Popular European Cinema*, ed. Richard Dyer and Ginnette Vincendeau (London and New York: Routledge, 1992): 220–231.
5. Ibid., 230.
6. Zdzisław Pietrasik, "Broń się. Najbardziej lubimy oglądać amerykańskie filmy polskie," *Polityka* 15 (1997): 72–73.
7. Barbara Hollender, "Raport o kinie polskim," *Rzeczpospolita* 80 (4 April 2000). http://www.rzeczpospolita.pl/Pl-iso/gazeta/wydanie_000404/kultura/kultura_a_1.htm
8. For example, Mariusz Grzegorzek's defense of art cinema, "Żal tak młodo umierać," *Kino* 11 (1994): 12–13. Grzegorzek (b. 1962) is the director of *Rozmowa z człowiekiem z szafy* (*Conversation with a Person in a Wardrobe*, 1993), a film about an unusual case of motherly love, isolation, and rejection.
9. The Polish title of the film, *Psy*, literally means "the dogs." The connotation of the word "dog" in Polish is pejorative; the word, which implies servility and subhuman qualities, is frequently used to denigrate another person.

10. Zdzisław Pietrasik, "Andrzej Wajda: na moich warunkach" [interview with Wajda], *Polityka* 10 (1996): 70.
11. Tadeusz Sobolewski, "Andrzej Wajda: Pojedynek z dniem dzisiejszym" [interview with Wajda], *Kino* 4 (1993): 6.
12. *The Catalogue of the XIX Festival of Polish Feature Films in Gdynia* (Gdynia, 1994): 78. [Reprint from: Stanisław Zawiśliński, *Powiedzmy Linda* (Warsaw: Taurus, 1994).]
13. Piotr Lis, "Moralitet z klocków," *Kino* 5 (1993): 14–15.
14. Piotr Szulkin, "Psy wieszane non stop," *Kino* 5 (1993): 13
15. The title of the film, *The Pigs 2: The Last Blood*, clearly refers to the Rambo films of the 1980s: *First Blood* (1982, Ted Kotcheff) and *Rambo: First Blood Part II* (1985, George P. Cosmatos).
16. *The Pigs 2* is listed as the sixth most popular film in the 1990s with more than 684,000 viewers. Hollender, "Raport o kinie polskim."
17. *The Catalogue of the XIX Festival of Polish Feature Films in Gdynia*, 78–79.
18. Tadeusz Lubelski, "Bogie, na jakiego zasłużyliśmy," *Kino* 7–8 (1994): 41.
19. Manana Chyb, "Otoczony przez niemych Maurów. Rozmowa z Piotrem Szulkinem," *Kino* 4 (1992): 3.
20. *Webster's Encyclopedic Unabridged Dictionary of the English Language* (New York: Portland House, 1989), 381.
21. *The Catalogue of the XX Festival of Polish Feature Films in Gdynia* (Gdynia, 1995), 46.
22. Konrad J. Zarębski, "Zwyczajny cynizm" *Kino* 3 (1997): 34.
23. The original Polish title, *Młode wilki*, literally means "young wolves."
24. Zdzisław Pietrasik, "Brudny Marek. Samotny mściciel w polskich realiach," *Polityka* 6 (2000): 44–45.

Afterword

Since its humble beginnings in 1902, the Polish film industry has produced a diverse corpus of films. Often performing specific political and cultural duties for their nation, Polish filmmakers were perfectly aware of their role as educators, entertainers, social activists, and political leaders. Liberated from some of these roles after the fall of communism, they quickly managed to adjust to the new political reality and to produce some outstanding films. After overcoming the rough transitional period at the beginning of the 1990s, Polish filmmakers succeeded in winning back their audiences toward the end of the decade. Their commercial success came with films that have always been popular in Poland—adaptations of the Polish national literary canon. Thanks to Jerzy Hoffman's *With Fire and Sword* and Andrzej Wajda's *Pan Tadeusz*, which together had more than thirteen million viewers in 1999, Polish cinema shared an unprecedented 60 percent of the local market.

Due to this record number, several filmmakers and producers saw adaptations of classic Polish literature as the only way to fill the movie theaters. Poor financial results in the year 2000, in spite of a small group of remarkable films, were blamed on the lack of big-budget literary adaptations. This situation prompted some filmmakers to choose the much-traveled path and rely on well-known literary sources. Thus, the year 2001 has seen new adaptations of Henryk Sienkiewicz—*Quo Vadis*, by Jerzy Kawalerowicz, and *W pustyni i w puszczy* (*In Desert and Wilderness*), by Gavin Hood—as well as an adaptation of Stefan Żeromski's novel *Przedwiośnie* (*Early Spring*), directed by Filip Bajon. These (by Polish standards) blockbusters share the local market with, among others, *Weiser*, directed by Wojciech Marczewski, an adaptation of the critically acclaimed contemporary novel by Paweł Huelle, and local big-budget productions such as the fantasy film *Wiedźmin*, by Marek Brodzki. *Quo Vadis*, with its budget of $18 million, is clearly the most expensive Polish film ever made; the average cost of a mainstream Polish film remains at about $800,000.

Polish adapters of the national literary canon favor safe literary works set in an equally safe history. Their films do not deconstruct the past or stir up vitriol. Instead, they offer romantic-nostalgic images of bygone times and rely on the popularity of their literary sources for success. Aspiring to make big-budget "quality pictures," Polish filmmakers, however, produce films inferior to Hollywood products. The elaborate sets of these films and the appearance of well-known literary names in the credits provide the only signs of "art." Audiences are reassured rather than challenged. Despite the industry's large-scale publicity machine that stresses the contemporary relevance of a given literary work, audiences are taken to places that bear little significance to the present.

The commercial success of film adaptations in Poland is almost guaranteed. Regardless of their artistic merit, these films will serve many generations of Poles as handy, albeit sometimes naïve, illustrations of the national literature and the national past. Schools and public libraries will make an extensive use of them. Their artistic merit as films, however, is questionable. *Pan Tadeusz* and several other film adaptations fare poorly among those who lack familiarity with their literary sources and knowledge that pertains to their literary and political contexts. This, in turn, makes them specifically Polish products, incomprehensible to outsiders. The growing production costs, bigger budgets, and competition between Polish blockbusters may make it difficult for some of the Polish film producers to recoup the costs of their films through domestic sales alone.

Fortunately, although the most prominent in terms of popularity, film adaptations do not constitute the majority of films produced in Poland. Among the thirty-one films competing for awards at the 2001 Festival of Polish Films in Gdynia, some were inspired by Quentin Tarantino, such as *Sezon na leszcza* (*Sucker Season*), by Bogusław Linda; some bordered on self-parodies, such as *Reich*, by Władysław Pasikowski and starring Bogusław Linda; and others included the highly personal and poetic cinema of Lech Majewski (*Angelus*) and Witold Leszczyński (*Requiem*). The most visible, however, were twelve films directed by first-time directors, including six films made independently—outside of the existing funding system. The majority of independent films portray a gloomy picture of the new capitalist reality in Poland. The scenery from Kieślowski's *Decalogue*—ugly post-communist apartment buildings—returns powerfully in a group of films of uneven quality, often featuring nonprofessional actors, MTV-style editing, vulgar language, an abundance of social problems, and contempt for "quality cinema." *Blok.pl*, by Marek Bukowski, and ... *że życie ma sens* ... (... *That Life Makes Sense* ...), by Grzegorz Lipiec, and others deal with the plight of people who inhabit impersonal building complexes (*bloki*)—the pride of the former communist system.

The same degraded reality is present in a powerful film made by the established director Robert Gliński (b. 1952). His *Cześć Tereska* (*Hi, Tessa*), the 2001 winner of the Festival of Polish Films in Gdynia and also the award-winning film at the Karlove Vary Film Festival, is one of the best Polish films made in recent years. Featuring nonprofessional actresses in the leading roles, this black-and-white film deals with a tragic coming-of-age story. Although low cinema attendance in Poland makes it difficult for ambitious films to recoup their costs and reach more than one hundred thousand viewers, the future of artistic cinema will depend upon films such as *Debt, A Week in the Life of a Man, Life as a Fatal Disease Sexually Transmitted,* and *Hi, Tessa.*

The near future will likely bring some important structural changes to the existing film industry. The current system, which combines elements of the pre-1989 cinema and the free market economy, is less than perfect. The five state-owned and Warsaw-based film studios still remain active in Poland: Filip Bajon's Dom, Tadeusz Chmielewski's Oko, Janusz Morgenstern's Perspektywa, Krzysztof Zanussi's Tor, and Juliusz Machulski's Zebra. They produce films and also support themselves by having legal rights to films produced before 1989. Among numerous, but mostly small, private production companies, some play an important role in Polish cinema industry, for example, Dariusz Jabłoński's Apple Film Production, Lew Rywin's Heritage Films, and Waldemar Dziki's Pleograf. Television, both state-owned and private channels such as Canal Plus and HBO, play essential roles in invigorating the industry. For example, Polish State Television (Telewizja Polska SA) is, and probably will remain, the leading producer of films in Poland. Contrary to many dark prognoses, the current situation in the Polish film industry shows no signs of crisis.

November 2001

Selected Filmography

[Asterisks indicate films that are lost. Dates shown are the years of release. If a premiere was significantly delayed, the production year is given first, and the release date follows in brackets.]

1902   *Powrót birbanta* (*The Return of a Merry Fellow*), directed by
        Kazimierz Prószyński*

1908   *Antoś pierwszy raz w Warszawie* (*Antoś for the First Time in
        Warsaw*), Joseph Meyer*
        Pruska kultura (*Prussian Culture*), director unknown*

1911   *Dzieje grzechu* (*The Story of Sin*), Antoni Bednarczyk*
        Meir Ezofowicz, Józef Ostoja-Sulnicki (*fragments)

1912   *Krwawa dola* (*Bloody Fate*), Władysław Paliński*

1913   *Kościuszko pod Racławicami* (*Kościuszko at Racławice*), Orland*
        Wykolejeni (*Human Wrecks/The Led Astray*), Kazimierz Kamiński
        and Aleksander Hertz*

1914   *Niewolnica zmysłów* (*The Slave of Sin*, aka *Love and Passion*),
        Jan Pawłowski*

1915   *Żona* (*Wife*), Jan Pawłowski*

1916   *Ochrana warszawska i jej tajemnice* (*The Secrets of the Warsaw
        Police*), Wiktor Biegański*

1917   *Bestia* (*Beast*), Tadeusz Sobocki and Józef Galewski
        Carat i jego sługi (*The Tsarist Regime and Its Servants*), Tadeusz
        Sobocki and Józef Galewski*

1919   *Blanc et noir*, Eugeniusz Modzelewski*

1920   *Bohaterstwo polskiego skauta* (*Heroism of a Polish Boy Scout*),
        Ryszard Bolesławski*
        Dla ciebie, Polsko (*For You, Poland*), Antoni Bednarczyk*

1921   *Cud nad Wisłą* (*Miracle on the Vistula*), Ryszard Bolesławski

1922   *Rok 1863* (*Year 1863*), Edward Puchalski
        Tajemnica przystanku tramwajowego (*The Tram Stop Mystery*),
        Jan Kucharski*

1923   *Bartek zwycięzca* (*Bartek the Victor*), Edward Puchalski
        Niewolnica miłości (*The Slave of Love*), Jan Kucharski*

Otchłań pokuty (*The Abyss of Repentance*), Wiktor Biegański*
Syn szatana (*Satan's Son*), Bruno Bredschneider*
1924 *O czym się nie mówi* (*The Unspeakable*), Edward Puchalski*
Tkies Kaf (*The Vow*, 1924), Zygmunt Turkow (in Yiddish)*
1925 *Iwonka: tajemnica starego rodu* (*Iwonka: The Mystery of an Old Lineage*), Emil Chaberski*
Wampiry Warszawy (*The Vampires of Warsaw*), Wiktor Biegański*
1926 *Czerwony błazen* (*Red Jester*), Henryk Szaro*
Trędowata (*The Leper*), Edward Puchalski and Józef Węgrzyn*
1927 *Kochanka Szamoty* (*Szamota's Lover*), Leon Trystan*
Mogiła nieznanego żołnierza (*The Grave of an Unknown Soldier*), Ryszard Ordyński
Zew morza (*The Call of the Sea*), Henryk Szaro
Ziemia obiecana (*The Land of Promise*), Aleksander Hertz and Zbigniew Gniazdowski*
1928 *Huragan* (*Hurricane*), Józef Lejtes
Kropka nad i (*The Final Touch*), Juliusz Gardan*
Pan Tadeusz, Ryszard Ordyński
Szaleńcy (*Daredevils*), Leonard Buczkowski
1929 *Kobieta, która grzechu pragnie* (*The Woman Who Desires Sin*), Wiktor Biegański*
Mocny człowiek (*Strong Man*), Henryk Szaro
Policmajster Tagiejew (*The Police Chief Tagiejew*), Juliusz Gardan
1930 *Janko Muzykant* (*Johnny the Musician*), Ryszard Ordyński
Kult ciała (*Cult of the Body*), Michał Waszyński
Moralność pani Dulskiej (*The Morality of Mrs. Dulska*), Bolesław Newolin
Na Sybir (*To Siberia*), Henryk Szaro
1931 *Cham* (*The Boor*), Jan Nowina-Przybylski
Dziesięciu z Pawiaka (*The Ten from the Pawiak Prison*), Ryszard Ordyński
1932 *Biały ślad* (*White Trail*), Adam Krzeptowski
Dzikie pola (*Wild Fields*), Józef Lejtes*
Legion ulicy (*Legion of the Street*), Aleksander Ford*
Księżna Łowicka (*The Princess of Łowicz*), Janusz Warnecki and Mieczysław Krawicz
1933 *Dzieje grzechu* (*The Story of Sin*), Henryk Szaro
Każdemu wolno kochać (*Anybody Can Love*), Mieczysław Krawicz and Janusz Warnecki
Pod Twoją obronę (*Under Your Protection*), Edward Puchalski (in reality: Józef Lejtes)*
Przybłęda (*The Vagabond*), Jan Nowina-Przybylski
Wyrok życia (*Life Sentence*), Juliusz Gardan

1934   *Co mój mąż robi w nocy?* (*What Is My Husband Doing at Night?*),
       Michał Waszyński
       Córka generała Pankratowa (*General Pankratov's Daughter*),
       Mieczysław Znamierowski (in reality: Józef Lejtes)
       Czy Lucyna to dziewczyna (*Is Lucyna a Girl?*), Juliusz Gardan
       Młody las (*Young Forest*), Józef Lejtes

1935   *ABC miłości* (*ABC of Love*), Michał Waszyński
       Antek Policmajster (*Antek, the Police Chief*), Michał Waszyński
       Rapsodia Bałtyku (*The Baltic Rapsody*), Leonard Buczkowski

1936   *Barbara Radziwiłłówna*, Józef Lejtes
       Róża (*Rose*), Józef Lejtes
       Trędowata (*The Leper*), Juliusz Gardan
       Yidl mitn Fidl (*Yiddle with His Fiddle*), Jan Nowina-Przybylski and
       Joseph Green (in Yiddish)

1937   *Der Dibuk* (*The Dybbuk*), Michał Waszyński (in Yiddish)
       Dziewczęta z Nowolipek (*The Girls from Nowolipki*), Józef Lejtes
       Znachor (*Quack*), Michał Waszyński

1938   *A Brivele der Mamen* (*A Little Letter to Mother*), Leon Trystan with
       Joseph Green (in Yiddish)
       Granica (*Line*), Józef Lejtes
       Ludzie Wisły (*The People of the Vistula*), Aleksander Ford and
       Jerzy Zarzycki
       Profesor Wilczur (*Professor Wilczur*), Michał Waszyński
       Strachy (*The Ghosts*; aka *Anxiety*; aka *The Creeps*), Eugeniusz
       Cękalski and Karol Szołowski
       Wrzos (*Heather*), Juliusz Gardan
       Zapomniana melodia (*Forgotten Melody*), Konrad Tom and
       Jan Fethke

1939   *Czarne diamenty* (*Black Diamonds*, premiere in 1981),
       Jerzy Gabryelski
       Kłamstwo Krystyny (*Krystyna's Lie*), Henryk Szaro

1947   *Jasne Łany* (*Bright Fields*), Eugeniusz Cękalski
       Zakazane piosenki (*Forbidden Songs*), Leonard Buczkowski

1948   *Ostatni etap* (*The Last Stage*, aka *The Last Stop*),
       Wanda Jakubowska

1949   *Skarb* (*Treasure*), Leonard Buczkowski
       Ulica graniczna (*Border Street*), Aleksander Ford

1950   *Miasto nieujarzmione* (*Unvanquished City*), Jerzy Zarzycki

1951   *Warszawska premiera* (*Warsaw Premiere*), Jan Rybkowski

1952   *Gromada* (*The Village Mill*), Jerzy Kawalerowicz
       Młodość Szopena (*The Youth of Chopin*), Aleksander Ford

1954   *Celuloza* (*A Night of Remembrance*), Jerzy Kawalerowicz
       Piątka z ulicy Barskiej (*Five Boys from Barska Street*),
       Aleksander Ford

Pod gwiazdą frygijską (*Under the Phrygian Star*),
Jerzy Kawalerowicz
Przygoda na Mariensztacie (*An Adventure at Marienstadt*),
Leonard Buczkowski

1955 *Błękitny krzyż* (*Blue Cross*), Andrzej Munk
Godziny nadziei (*The Hours of Hope*), Jan Rybkowski
Pokolenie (*A Generation*), Andrzej Wajda

1956 *Cień* (*Shadow*), Jerzy Kawalerowicz

1957 *Człowiek na torze* (*Man on the Track*), Andrzej Munk
Kanał (*Kanal*), Andrzej Wajda
Koniec nocy (*The End of the Night*), Julian Dziedzina, Paweł
Komorowski, and Walentyna Uszycka
Prawdziwy koniec wielkiej wojny (*The True End of the Great War*),
Jerzy Kawalerowicz
Trzy kobiety (*Three Women*), Stanisław Różewicz
Zagubione uczucia (*Lost Feelings*), Jerzy Zarzycki
Zimowy zmierzch (*Winter Twilight*), Stanisław Lenartowicz

1958 *Dezerter* (*Deserter*), Witold Lesiewicz
Eroica, Andrzej Munk
Ewa chce spać (*Ewa Wants to Sleep*), Tadeusz Chmielewski
Ostatni dzień lata (*The Last Day of Summer*), Tadeusz Konwicki
with Jan Laskowski
Pętla (*Noose*), Wojciech J. Has
Pigułki dla Aurelii (*Pills for Aurelia*), Stanisław Lenartowicz
Popiół i diament (*Ashes and Diamonds*), Andrzej Wajda
Pożegnania (*Farewells*) Wojciech J. Has
Wolne miasto (*Free City*), Stanisław Różewicz

1959 *Baza ludzi umarłych* (*Damned Roads*), Czesław Petelski
Krzyż Walecznych (*Cross of Valor*), Kazimierz Kutz
Lotna, Andrzej Wajda
Orzeł (*The Submarine "Eagle"*), Leonard Buczkowski
Pociąg (*Night Train*; aka *Baltic Express*), Jerzy Kawalerowicz
Zamach (*Answer to Violence*), Jerzy Passendorfer

1960 *Krzyżacy* (*Teutonic Knights*), Aleksander Ford
Lunatycy (*Sleepwalkers*), Bohdan Poręba
Miasteczko (*Small Town*), Romuald Drobaczyński, Julian
Dziedzina, and Janusz Łęski
Niewinni czarodzieje (*Innocent Sorcerers*), Andrzej Wajda
Nikt nie woła (*Nobody Is Calling*), Kazimierz Kutz
Rok pierwszy (*First Year*), Witold Lesiewicz
Zezowate szczęście (*Bad Luck*; aka *Cockeyed Luck*), Andrzej Munk

1961 *Kwiecień* (*April*), Witold Lesiewicz
Ludzie z pociągu (*People from the Train*), Kazimierz Kutz
Matka Joanna od Aniołów (*Mother Joan of the Angels*), Jerzy
Kawalerowicz

1961   *Ogniomistrz Kaleń* (*Sergeant-Major Kaleń*), Ewa and
(cont.)   Czesław Petelski
        Samson, Andrzej Wajda
        Świadectwo urodzenia (*The Birth Certificate*), Stanisław Różewicz
        Zaduszki (*All Souls Day*), Tadeusz Konwicki
1962   *Głos z tamtego świata* (*Voice from the Other World*),
        Stanisław Różewicz
        Nóż w wodzie (*Knife in the Water*), Roman Polański
1963   *Gangsterzy i filantropi* (*Gangsters and Philanthropists*),
        Jerzy Hoffman and Edward Skórzewski
        Jak być kochaną (*How to Be Loved*), Wojciech J. Has
        Milczenie (*Silence*), Kazimierz Kutz
        Pasażerka (*The Passenger*), Andrzej Munk
1964   *Gdzie jest generał?* (*Where Is the General?*), Tadeusz Chmielewski
        Naganiacz (*The Beater*), Ewa and Czesław Petelski
        Prawo i pięść (*Law and Fist*), Jerzy Hoffman and
        Edward Skórzewski
        Żona dla Australijczyka (*The Wife for an Australian*), Stanisław Bareja
1965   *Popioły* (*Ashes*), Andrzej Wajda
        Rękopis znaleziony w Saragossie (*The Saragossa Manuscript*),
        Wojciech J. Has
        Rysopis (*Identification Marks: None*), Jerzy Skolimowski
        Salto (*Somersault*), Tadeusz Konwicki
        Walkower (*Walkover*), Jerzy Skolimowski
        Życie raz jeszcze (*Life Once Again*), Janusz Morgenstern
1966   *Bariera* (*The Barrier*), Jerzy Skolimowski
        Faraon (*The Pharaoh*), Jerzy Kawalerowicz
        Ktokolwiek wie (*Whoever Knows*), Kazimierz Kutz
        Niekochana (*Unloved*), Janusz Nasfeter
        Potem nastąpi cisza (*Then There Will Be Silence*),
        Janusz Morgenstern
1967   *Chudy i inni* (*Skinny and Others*), Henryk Kluba
        Kontrybucja (*Contribution*), Jan Łomnicki
        Ręce do góry (*Hands Up*, released in 1985), Jerzy Skolimowski
        Sami swoi (*All among Ourselves*), Sylwester Chęciński
        Słońce wschodzi raz na dzień (*The Sun Rises Once a Day*,
        released in 1972), Henryk Kluba
        Stajnia na Salwatorze (*The Barn at Salvator*), Paweł Komorowski
        Westerplatte, Stanisław Różewicz
1968   *Czterej pancerni i pies* (*Four Tankmen and a Dog*; first a television
        series), Konrad Nałęcki
        Lalka (*The Doll*), Wojciech J. Has
        Wilcze echa (*Wolves' Echoes*), Aleksander Ścibor-Rylski
        Żywot Mateusza (*The Life of Matthew*), Witold Leszczyński

1969   *Kierunek Berlin* (*Direction Berlin*), Jerzy Passendorfer
Pan Wołodyjowski (*Pan Michael*, aka *Colonel Wolodyjowski*), Jerzy Hoffman
Polowanie na muchy (*Hunting Flies*), Andrzej Wajda
Stawka większa niż życie (*Stake Higher Than Life*; first a television series), Janusz Morgenstern
Struktura kryształu (*The Structure of Crystals*), Krzysztof Zanussi
Wszystko na sprzedaż (*Everything for Sale*), Andrzej Wajda
Zbrodniarz, który ukradł zbrodnię (*The Criminal Who Stole a Crime*), Janusz Majewski

1970   *Abel, twój brat* (*Abel, Your Brother*), Janusz Nasfeter
Brzezina (*Birchwood*), Andrzej Wajda
Jarzębina czerwona (*The Rowan Tree*), Ewa and Czesław Petelski
Krajobraz po bitwie (*Landscape after Battle*), Andrzej Wajda
Rejs (*The Cruise*), Marek Piwowski
Sól ziemi czarnej (*Salt of the Black Earth*), Kazimierz Kutz

1971   *Kardiogram* (*Cardiogram*), Roman Załuski
Nie lubię poniedziałku (*I Hate Mondays*), Tadeusz Chmielewski
Trąd (*Leprosy*), Andrzej Trzos-Rastawiecki
Życie rodzinne (*Family Life*), Krzysztof Zanussi

1972   *Jak daleko stąd, jak blisko* (*How Far from Here, Yet How Near*), Tadeusz Konwicki
Ocalenie (*Deliverance*), Edward Żebrowski
Perła w koronie (*The Pearl in the Crown*), Kazimierz Kutz
Trzeba zabić tę miłość (*Kill That Love*), Janusz Morgenstern
Trzecia część nocy (*The Third Part of the Night*), Andrzej Żuławski
Uciec jak najbliżej (*Escape as Near as Possible*), Janusz Zaorski

1973   *Chłopi* (*Peasants*), Jan Rybkowski
Hubal, Bohdan Poręba
Iluminacja (*Illumination*), Krzysztof Zanussi
Na wylot (*Through and Through*; aka *Clear Through*), Grzegorz Królikiewicz
Palec Boży (*God's Finger*), Antoni Krauze
Sanatorium pod Klepsydrą (*Hospital under the Hourglass*), Wojciech J. Has
Wesele (*The Wedding*), Andrzej Wajda
Zazdrość i medycyna (*Jealousy and Medicine*), Janusz Majewski

1974   *Ciemna rzeka* (*Dark River*), Sylwester Szyszko
Nie ma mocnych (*Big Deal*), Sylwester Chęciński
Potop (*The Deluge*), Jerzy Hoffman
Zapis zbrodni (*Record of Crime*), Andrzej Trzos-Rastawiecki

1975   *Bilans kwartalny* (*Balance Sheet*; aka *A Woman's Decision*), Krzysztof Zanussi
Dzieje grzechu (*The Story of Sin*), Walerian Borowczyk
Noce i dnie (*Nights and Days*), Jerzy Antczak

1975 Zaklęte rewiry (Hotel Pacific), Janusz Majewski
(cont.) Ziemia obiecana (The Land of Promise), Andrzej Wajda
1976 Blizna (The Scar), Krzysztof Kieślowski
      Przepraszam, czy tu biją? (Foul Play), Marek Piwowski
      Spokój (Calm, released in 1980), Krzysztof Kieślowski
      Zofia, Ryszard Czekała
1977 Barwy ochronne (Camouflage), Krzysztof Zanussi
      Człowiek z marmuru (Man of Marble), Andrzej Wajda
      Indeks (Index, released in 1981), Janusz Kijowski
      Kochaj albo rzuć (Love It or Leave It), Sylwester Chęciński
      Śmierć Prezydenta (Death of a President), Jerzy Kawalerowicz
      Sprawa Gorgonowej (The Gorgon Affair), Janusz Majewski
1978 Bez znieczulenia (Rough Treatment, aka Without Anesthesia),
        Andrzej Wajda
      Co mi zrobisz jak mnie złapiesz (What Will You Do with me When
        You Catch Me), Stanisław Bareja
      Gdziekowiek jesteś, Panie Prezydencie (Wherever You Are,
        Mr. President), Andrzej Trzos-Rastawiecki
      Spirala (Spiral), Krzysztof Zanussi
      Tańczący jastrząb (Dancing Hawk), Grzegorz Królikiewicz
      Wodzirej (Top Dog), Feliks Falk
      Wśród nocnej ciszy (Silent Night, aka In the Still of the Night),
        Tadeusz Chmielewski
1979 Aktorzy prowincjonalni (Provincial Actors), Agnieszka Holland
      Amator (Camera Buff), Krzysztof Kieślowski
      Aria dla atlety (Aria for an Athlete), Filip Bajon
      Bestia (The Beast), Jerzy Domaradzki
      Lekcja martwego języka (The Lesson of a Dead Language),
        Janusz Majewski
      Panny z Wilka (The Maids of Wilko), Andrzej Wajda
      Szpital Przemienienia (The Hospital of Transfiguration),
        Edward Żebrowski
      Zmory (Nightmares), Wojciech Marczewski
1980 Bez miłości (Without Love), Barbara Sass
      Constans (The Constant Factor), Krzysztof Zanussi
      Golem, Piotr Szulkin
      Grzeszny żywot Franciszka Buły (The Sinful Life of Franciszek
        Buła), Janusz Kidawa
      Kontrakt (Contract), Krzysztof Zanussi
      Paciorki jednego różańca (Beads of One Rosary), Kazimierz Kutz
1981 Człowiek z żelaza (Man of Iron), Andrzej Wajda
      Dreszcze (Shivers), Wojciech Marczewski
      Gorączka (Fever), Agnieszka Holland
      Kobieta samotna (A Woman Alone, released in 1988),
        Agnieszka Holland

Miś (*Teddy Bear*), Stanisław Bareja
Niech cię odleci mara (*The Haunted*, released in 1983),
    Andrzej Barański
Przypadek (*Blind Chance*, released in 1987), Krzysztof Kieślowski
Wizja lokalna 1901 (*Inspection at the Scene of the Crime, 1901*),
    Filip Bajon
Wielki Bieg (*The Big Run*, released in 1987), Jerzy Domaradzki

1982   *Konopielka*, Witold Leszczyński
    Matka Królów (*The Mother of Kings*, released in 1987),
        Janusz Zaorski
    Przesłuchanie (*Interrogation*, released in 1989), Ryszard Bugajski
    Vabank (*Va Banque*), Juliusz Machulski

1983   *Austeria* (aka *The Inn*), Jerzy Kawalerowicz
    Danton, Andrzej Wajda (Polish-French coproduction)
    Prognoza pogody (*Weather Forecast*), Antoni Krauze
    Wielki Szu (*The Big Rook*), Sylwester Chęciński

1984   *Kartka z podróży* (*A Postcard from the Journey*), Waldemar Dziki
    Nie było słońca tej wiosny (*There Was No Sun That Spring*),
        Juliusz Janicki
    Seksmisja (*Sex Mission*), Juliusz Machulski

1985   *Bez końca* (*No End*), Krzysztof Kieślowski
    Kobieta w kapeluszu (*A Woman with a Hat*), Stanisław Różewicz
    Kobieta z prowincji (*A Provincial Woman*, aka *Life's Little Comforts*),
        Andrzej Barański
    Nadzór (*Custody*), Wiesław Saniewski
    Rok spokojnego słońca (*Year of the Quiet Sun*), Krzysztof Zanussi
    Yesterday, Radosław Piwowarski

1986   *C.K. Dezerterzy* (*Deserters*), Janusz Majewski (Polish-Hungarian
        coproduction)
    Cudzoziemka (*Foreigner*), Ryszard Ber
    Dziewczęta z Nowolipek (*The Girls from Nowolipki*), Barbara Sass
    Kronika wypadków miłosnych (*Chronicle of Amorous Accidents*),
        Andrzej Wajda
    Rajska jabłoń (*Crab Apple Tree*), Barbara Sass

1987   *Bohater roku* (*Hero of the Year*), Feliks Falk
    Magnat (*The Magnate*), Filip Bajon
    Nad Niemnem (*On the Niemen River*), Zbigniew Kuźmiński
    W zawieszeniu (*Suspended*), Waldemar Krzystek

1988   *Krótki film o miłości* (*A Short Film about Love*),
        Krzysztof Kieślowski
    Krótki film o zabijaniu (*A Short Film about Killing*),
        Krzysztof Kieślowski
    Łuk Erosa (*Cupid's Bow*), Jerzy Domaradzki
    Tabu (*Taboo*), Andrzej Barański

1989   Deja vu (Déjà Vu), Juliusz Machulski (Polish-Soviet
        coproduction)
        Kornblumenblau, Leszek Wosiewicz
        300 mil do nieba (300 Miles to Heaven), Maciej Dejczer
1990   Historia niemoralna (An Immoral Story), Barbara Sass
        Korczak, Andrzej Wajda
        Kramarz (The Peddler), Andrzej Barański
        Marcowe migdały (March Almonds), Radosław Piwowarski
        Ucieczka z kina "Wolność" (Escape from "Freedom" Cinema),
        Wojciech Marczewski
1991   Femina, Piotr Szulkin
        Jeszcze tylko ten las (And Only This Forest), Jan Łomnicki
        Kroll, Władysław Pasikowski
        Podwójne życie Weroniki (The Double Life of Veronique), Krzysztof
        Kieślowski (Polish-French coproduction)
        Pogrzeb kartofla (The Burial of Potato), Jan Jakub Kolski
        Śmierć dziecioroba (Death of the Kidsmaker), Wojciech Nowak
1992   Dotknięcie ręki (The Silent Touch), Krzysztof Zanussi
        Psy (The Pigs), Władysław Pasikowski
        Rozmowy kontrolowane (Controlled Conversations),
        Sylwester Chęciński
        Wszystko, co najważniejsze (All That Really Matters),
        Robert Gliński
1993   Cynga (Scurvy), Leszek Wosiewicz
        Jańcio Wodnik (Johnnie the Aquarius), Jan Jakub Kolski
        Kolejność uczuć (The Sequence of Feelings), Radosław Piwowarski
        Pożegnanie z Marią (Farewell to Maria), Filip Zylber
        Przypadek Pekosińskiego (The Case of Pekosiński), Grzegorz
        Królikiewicz
        Trzy Kolory: Niebieski (Three Colors: Blue), Krzysztof Kieślowski
        (Polish-French-Swiss coproduction)
1994   Cudowne miejsce (Miraculous Place), Jan Jakub Kolski
        Psy 2: Ostatnia krew (The Pigs 2: The Last Blood),
        Władysław Pasikowski
        Śmierć jak kromka chleba (Death as a Slice of Bread), Kazimierz Kutz
        Trzy kolory: Biały (Three Colors: White), Krzysztof Kieślowski
        (Polish-French coproduction)
        Trzy kolory: Czerwony (Three Colors: Red), Krzysztof Kieślowski
        (Polish-French-Swiss coproduction)
        Wrony (Crows), Dorota Kędzierzawska
        Zawrócony (The Turned Back), Kazimierz Kutz
1995   Bye, bye, Ameryka (Bye, Bye, America), Jan Schütte (Polish-German
        coproduction)
        Girl Guide, Juliusz Machulski
        Tato (Daddy), Maciej Ślesicki

Pokuszenie (*Temptation*), Barbara Sass
Wielki Tydzień (*Holy Week*), Andrzej Wajda
Wrzeciono czasu (*The Spinning Wheel of Time*),
    Andrzej Kondratiuk

1996   *Cwał* (*In Full Gallop*), Krzysztof Zanussi
Dzieci i ryby (*Seen but Not Heard*), Jacek Bromski
Gry uliczne (*Street Games*), Krzysztof Krauze
Poznań 56 (*Street Boys*), Filip Bajon
Pułkownik Kwiatkowski (*Colonel Kwiatkowski*), Kazimierz Kutz

1997   *Bandyta* (*Brute*), Maciej Dejczer
Farba (*The Paint*) Michał Rosa
Historie miłosne (*Love Stories*), Jerzy Stuhr
Kiler, Juliusz Machulski
Kroniki domowe (*The Family Events*), Leszek Wosiewicz
Księga wielkich życzeń (*The Book of Great Wishes*),
    Sławomir Kryński

1998   *Historia kina w Popielawach* (*The History of Cinema Theater in
    Popielawy*), Jan Jakub Kolski
U pana Boga za piecem (*Snug as a Bug in a Rug*), Jacek Bromski
Nic (*Nothing*), Dorota Kędzierzawska
Poniedziałek (*Monday*), Witold Adamek
Zabić Sekala (*To Kill Sekal*), Vladimir Michálek (Czech-Polish
    coproduction)

1999   *Dług* (*Debt*), Krzysztof Krauze
Ogniem i mieczem (*With Fire and Sword*), Jerzy Hoffman
Pan Tadeusz, Andrzej Wajda
Prawo ojca (*Father's Law*), Marek Kondrat
Tydzień z życia mężczyzny (*A Week in the Life of a Man*),
    Jerzy Stuhr
Wojaczek, Lech Majewski

2000   *Daleko od okna* (*Away from a Window*), Jan Jakub Kolski
Duże zwierzę (*The Big Animal*), Jerzy Stuhr
Ostatnia misja (*The Last Mission*), Wojciech Wójcik
Prymas. Trzy lata z tysiąclecia (*The Primate: Three Years Out of the
    Millennium*), Teresa Kotlarczyk
Życie jako śmiertelna choroba przenoszona drogą płciową (*Life as a
    Fatal Disease Sexually Transmitted*), Krzysztof Zanussi

2001   *Angelus*, Lech Majewski
Cześć Tereska (*Hi, Tessa*), Robert Gliński
Quo Vadis, Jerzy Kawalerowicz
Sezon na leszcza (*Sucker Season*), Bogusław Linda
Weiser, Wojciech Marczewski

Selected Bibliography

Afanasjew, Jerzy. *Okno Zbyszka Cybulskiego. Brulion z życia aktora filmowego połowy XX wieku.* Łódź: Wydawnictwo Łódzkie, 1970.

Andrew, Geoff. *The "Three Colours" Trilogy.* London: BFI Modern Classics, 1998.

Armatys, Barbara, Leszek Armatys, and Wiesław Stradomski. *Historia filmu polskiego 1930–1939* [vol. 2]. Warsaw: Wydawnictwa Artystyczne i Filmowe, 1988.

Armatys, Leszek, and Wiesław Stradomski. *Od Niewolnicy zmysłów do Czarnych diamentów. Szkice o polskich filmach z lat 1914–1939.* Warsaw: COMUK, 1988.

Avisar, Ilan. *Screening the Holocaust: Cinema's Images of the Unimaginable.* Bloomington: Indiana University Press, 1988.

Balski, Grzegorz, ed. *Directory of Eastern European Film-Makers and Films.* Westport: Greenwood, 1992.

Banaszkiewicz, Władysław, and Witold Witczak. *Historia filmu polskiego 1895–1929* [vol. 1]. Warsaw: Wydawnictwa Artystyczne i Filmowe, 1989.

Baniewicz, Ewa. *Kazimierz Kutz: Z dołu widać inaczej.* Warsaw: Wydawnictwa Artystyczne i Filmowe, 1994.

Benedyktynowicz, Zbigniew, ed. *Podróż do krainy niemożliwości.* Warsaw: Instytut Sztuki, 1993.

Bickley, Daniel. "The Cinema of Moral Dissent: A Report from the Gdańsk Film Festival." *Cineaste* 11, no. 1 (1980–1981): 10–15.

Biró, Yvette. "Landscape after Battle: Films from 'the Other Europe.'" *Daedalus* 119, no. 1 (1990): 161–182.

Bobowski, Sławomir. *Dyskurs filmowy Zanussiego.* Wrocław: Towarzystwo Przyjaciół Polonistyki Wrocławskiej, 1996.

Bocheńska, Jadwiga. *Polska myśl filmowa: Antologia tekstów z lat 1898–1939.* Wrocław: Ossolineum, 1975.

———. *Polska myśl filmowa do roku 1939.* Wrocław: Ossolineum, 1974.

Braniecki, Włodzimierz. *Szczun* [book-length interview with Filip Bajon]. Poznań: W drodze, 1998.

Bren, Frank. *World Cinema 1: Poland.* London: Flicks Books, 1986.

Cavendish, Phil. "Kieślowski's *Decalogue.*" *Sight and Sound* 59, no. 3 (1990): 162–165.

Chociłowski, Jerzy, ed. *Contemporary Polish Cinema.* Warsaw: Polonia, 1962.

Chołodowski, Waldemar. *Kraina niedojrzałości*. Warsaw: Czytelnik, 1983.

Chyb, Dariusz. "Inspiracje malarskie w filmach Andrzeja Wajdy." *Kwartalnik Filmowy* 15–16 (1996): 144–186.

Ciechowicz, Jan, and Tadeusz Szczepański, eds. *Zbigniew Cybulski. Aktor XX wieku*. Gdańsk: Uniwersity of Gdańsk Press, 1997.

Coates, Paul. "Exile and Identity: Kieślowski and His Contemporaries." *Before the Wall Came Down: Soviet and East European Filmmakers Working in the West*, ed. Graham Petrie and Ruth Dwyer. New York: University Press of America, 1990: 103–114.

———. "Forms of the Polish Intellectual's Self-Criticism: Revisiting *Ashes and Diamonds* with Andrzejewski and Wajda." *Canadian Slavonic Papers* 38, no. 3–4 (1996): 287–303.

———. "Karol Irzykowski: Apologist of the Inauthentic Art." *New German Critique* 42 (1987): 113–115 [excerpts from Irzykowski's *The Tenth Muse* in Coates's translation: 116–127].

——— ed. *Lucid Dreams: The Films of Krzysztof Kieślowski*. London: Flicks Books, 1999.

———. "Metaphysical Love in Two Films by Krzysztof Kieślowski." *The Polish Review* 37, no. 3 (1992): 135–144.

———. "Observing the Observer: Andrzej Wajda's Holy Week (1995)." *Canadian Slavonic Papers* 42, no. 1–2 (2000): 25–33.

———. "The Sense of an Ending: Reflections on Kieślowski's Trilogy." *Film Quarterly* 50, no. 2 (1996–97): 19–27.

———. "Shifting Borders: Konwicki, Zanussi and the Ideology of "East-Central Europe." *Canadian Slavonic Papers* 42, no. 1–2 (2000): 87–98.

———. *The Story of the Lost Reflection: The Alienation of the Image in Western and Polish Cinema*. London: Verso, 1985.

———. "Walls and Frontiers: Polish Cinema's Portrayal of Polish-Jewish Relations." *Polin: Studies in Polish Jewry* 10 (1997): 221–246.

Cornell, Katharine. "The Cinema of Ambivalence: Recent Films from Central and Eastern Europe." *Cineaste* 21, no. 3 (1995): 28–30.

Cowie, Peter. "Wajda Redux." *Sight and Sound* 49, no. 1 (1979–1980): 32–34.

Crnković, Gordana P. "Interview with Agnieszka Holland." *Film Quarterly* 52, no. 2 (1998–1999): 2–9.

DeNitto, Dennis, and William Herman. *Film and the Critical Eye*. New York: Macmillan, 1975 [chapter 15 on *Ashes and Diamonds*, 362–395].

Dondziłło, Czesław. *Młode kino polskie lat siedemdziesiątych*. Warsaw: Młodzieżowa Agencja Wydawnicza, 1985.

Eagle, Herbert. "Andrzej Wajda: Film Language and the Artist's Truth." *Cross Currents: A Yearbook of Central European Culture* 1 (1982): 339–353.

———. "Polanski." *Five Filmmakers*, ed. Daniel J. Goulding. Bloomington: Indiana University Press, 1994. Pp. 92–155.

Eberhardt, Konrad. *Zbigniew Cybulski*. Warsaw: Wydawnictwa Artystyczne i Filmowe, 1976.

———. *Wojciech Has*. Warsaw: Wydawnictwa Artystyczne i Filmowe, 1967.

Eidsvik, Charles. "Kieślowski's `Short Films.'" *Film Quarterly* 44, no. 1 (1990): 50–55.

Estève, Michel, ed. *Etudes cinématographiques: Andrzej Munk.* Paris: Minard, 1965.

———. *Etudes cinématographiques: Andrzej Wajda.* Paris: Minard, 1968.

———. *Etudes cinématographiques: Jerzy Kawalerowicz.* Paris: Minard, 1967.

———. *Etudes cinématographiques: Krzysztof Zanussi.* Paris: Minard, 1987.

Falkowska, Janina. *The Political Films of Andrzej Wajda: Dialogism in Man of Marble, Man of Iron, and Danton.* New York: Berghahn Books, 1996.

———. "'The Political' in the Films of Andrzej Wajda and Krzysztof Kieślowski." *Cinema Journal* 34, no. 2 (1995): 37–50.

Falkowska Janina, and Marek Haltof, eds. *The New Polish Cinema.* London: Flicks Books, 2002.

Fox, Geoffrey. "Men of Wajda." *Film Criticism* 6, no. 1 (1981): 3–9.

Fuksiewicz, Jacek. *Film and Television in Poland.* Warsaw: Interpress, 1976.

———. *Tadeusz Konwicki.* Warsaw: Wydawnictwa Artystyczne i Filmowe, 1967.

Garbowski, Christopher. "Kieślowski's Seeing I/Eye." *The Polish Review* 15, no. 1 (1995): 53–60.

———. "Krzysztof Kieślowski's *Decalogue*: Presenting Religious Topics on Television." *The Polish Review* 37, no. 3 (1992): 327–334.

———. *Krzysztof Kieślowski's Decalogue Series: The Problem of the Protagonists and Their Self-Transcendance* [*sic*]. Boulder: East European Monographs, 1996 [distributed by Columbia University Press in New York].

Gierszewska, Barbara. *Czasopiśmiennictwo filmowe w Polsce do 1939 roku.* Kielce: Wyższa Szkoła Pedagogiczna, 1995.

Giżycki, Marcin. *Awangarda wobec kina. Film w kręgu polskiej awangardy artystycznej dwudziestolecia międzywojennego.* Warsaw: Wydawnictwo małe, 1996.

———. *Walka o film artystyczny w międzywojennej Polsce.* Warsaw: Państwowe Wydawnictwo Naukowe, 1989.

Goban-Klas, Tomasz. *The Orchestration of the Media: The Politics of Mass Communications in Communist Poland and the Aftermath.* Boulder: Westview Press, 1994.

Głowa, Jadwiga, ed. *Zooming in on History's Turning Points: Documentaries in the 1990s in Central and Eastern Europe* [Conference Papers in Polish and English translations]. Cracow: Uniwersytet Jagielloński, 1999.

Godzic, Wiesław. *Film i psychoanaliza: problem widza.* Cracow: Wydawnictwo Uniwersytetu Jagiellońskiego, 1991.

———. "How to Be Loved." *MovEast* 3 (1993/1994): 128–143.

Goldman, Eric A. *Visions, Images, and Dreams: Yiddish Film Past and Present.* Ann Arbor: UMI Research Press, 1983.

Goulding, Daniel J., ed. *Five Filmmakers.* Bloomington: Indiana University Press, 1994.

———, ed. *Post New Wave Cinema in the Soviet Union and Eastern Europe.* Bloomington and Indianapolis: Indiana University Press, 1989.

Gow, Gordon. "Cult Movies: *Ashes and Diamonds.*" *Films and Filming* 23, no. 6 (1977): 22–25.

Gwoźdź, Andrzej, ed. *Nie tylko filmy, nie same kina.... Z dziejów X muzy na Górnym Śląsku i w Zagłębiu Dąbrowskim.* Katowice: Śląsk, 1996.

Haltof, Marek. "A Fistful of Dollars: Polish Cinema After 1989 Freedom Shock." *Film Quarterly* 48, no. 3 (1995): 15–25.

———. "Everything For Sale: Polish National Cinema After 1989." *Canadian Slavonic Papers* 39, no. 1 (1997): 137–152.

———. "Film Theory in Poland Before World War II." *Canadian Slavonic Papers* 40, no. 1–2 (1998): 67–78.

———. "The Representation of Stalinism in Polish Cinema." *Canadian Slavonic Papers* 42, no. 1–2 (2000): 47–61.

Helman, Alicja. "Andrzej Munk: *Cockeyed Luck.*" *MovEast* 2 (1992): 96–107.

———. *Dwadzieścia lat filmu polskiego. Film fabularny 1947–1967.* Warszawa: Wydawnictwa Artystyczne i Filmowe, 1969.

———. "The Masters Are Tired." *Canadian Slavonic Papers* 42, no. 1–2 (2000): 99–111.

———. "Polish Film Theory." *The Jagiellonian University Film Studies*, ed. Wiesław Godzic. Cracow: Universitas, 1996. Pp. 9–40.

———. *Słownik Pojęć Filmowych* [10 Volumes; volumes 3–10 edited by A. Helman]. Wrocław: Wydawnictwo "Wiedza o Kulturze," 1991–1998.

Helman, Alicja, and Alina Madej, eds. *Film polski wobec innych sztuk.* Katowice: Wydawnictwo Uniwersytetu Śląskiego, 1979.

Helman, Alicja, and Tadeusz Miczka, eds. *Analizy i interpretacje. Film polski.* Katowice: Wydawnictwo Uniwersytetu Śląskiego, 1984.

Hendrykowska, Małgorzata. "From the Phonograph to the Kinetophone." *Film History* 11, no. 4 (1999): 444–448.

———. *Kronika kinematografii polskiej 1895–1997.* Poznań: Ars Nova, 1999.

———. *Śladami tamtych cieni: Film w kulturze polskiej przełomu stuleci 1895–1914.* Poznań: Oficyna Wydawnicza Book Service, 1993.

———. "Was the Cinema Fairground Entertainment? The Birth and Role of Popular Cinema in the Polish Territories up to 1908." *Popular European Cinema*, ed. Richard Dyer and Ginette Vincendeau. London and New York: Routledge, 1992. Pp. 112–126.

Hendrykowski, Marek, ed. *Andrzej Kondratiuk.* Poznań: Apeks, 1996.

———, ed. *Debiuty polskiego kina.* Konin: Wydawnictwo "Przegląd Koniński," 1998.

———. "Kazimierz Prószyński and the Origins of Polish Cinematography." *Celebrating 1895: The Centenary of Cinema*, ed. John Fullerton. London: John Libbey, 1998. Pp. 13–18.

———. "Styl i kompozycja *Popiołu i diamentu.*" *Analizy i interpretacje. Film polski*, ed. Alicja Helman and Tadeusz Miczka. Katowice: Wydawnictwo Uniwersytetu Śląskiego, 1984. Pp. 72–91.

Insdorf, Annette. *Double Lives, Second Chances: The Cinema of Krzysztof Kieslowski.* New York: Hyperion, 1999.

————. *Indelible Shadows: Film and the Holocaust*. Cambridge and New York: Cambridge University Press, 1989.

Irzykowski, Karol. *Dziesiąta Muza. Zagadnienia estetyczne kina*. Cracow: Krakowska Spółka Wydawnicza, 1924) [reprints: 1957, 1960, 1977, 1982].

Jackiewicz, Aleksander. *Film jako powieść XX wieku*. Warsaw: Wydawnictwa Artystyczne i Filmowe, 1968.

————. *Moja filmoteka: kino polskie*. Warsaw: Wydawnictwa Artystyczne i Filmowe, 1983.

————. "Powrót Kordiana. Tradycja romantyczna w kinie polskim." *Kwartalnik Filmowy* 4 (1961): 23–37.

Janicki, Stanisław. *Aleksander Ford*. Warsaw: Wydawnictwa Artystyczne i Filmowe, 1967.

————. *Film polski od A do Z*. Warsaw: Wydawnictwa Artystyczne i Filmowe, 1973.

————. *Polscy twórcy filmowi o sobie*. Warsaw: Wydawnictwa Artystyczne i Filmowe, 1962.

————. *Polskie filmy fabularne 1902–1988*. Warsaw: Wydawnictwa Artystyczne i Filmowe, 1990.

————. *The Polish Film: Yesterday and Today*. Warsaw: Interpress, 1985.

Jankun-Dopartowa, Mariola, *Labirynt Polańskiego*. Cracow: Rabid, 2000.

Jankun-Dopartowa, Mariola, and Mirosław Przylipiak, eds. *Człowiek z ekranu. Z antropologii postaci filmowej*. Cracow: Arcana, 1996.

Jewsiewicki, Władysław. *Filmowcy polscy na frontach drugiej wojny światowej*. Warsaw: Wydawnictwa Artystyczne i Filmowe, 1972.

————. *Materiały do dziejów filmu w Polsce*. Warsaw: Państwowe Wydawnictwo Naukowe, 1952.

————. *Polska kinematografia w okresie filmu dźwiękowego (1930–1939)*. Łódź: Ossolineum, 1967.

————. *Polska kinematografia w okresie filmu niemego (1895–1929/1930)*. Łódź: Ossolineum, 1966.

Karpiński, Maciej. *The Theatre of Andrzej Wajda*. Cambridge: Cambridge University Press, 1989.

Kehr, Dave. "To Save the World. Kieślowski's *Three Colours* Trilogy." *Film Comment* 30, no. 6 (1994): 10–20.

Kibourn, R. J. A. "Toward a Non-Euclidean Cinema: Kieślowski and Literature." *Canadian Journal of Film Studies* 6, no. 2 (1997): 34–50.

Kieślowski, Krzysztof, and Krzysztof Piesiewicz. *Decalogue: The Ten Commandments* [transl. Phil Cavendish and Suzannah Bluh]. London: Faber and Faber, 1991.

————. *Three Colours Trilogy: Blue, White, Red* [transl. Danusia Stok]. London: Faber and Faber, 1998.

Kino: Polish monthly on cinema [articles, interviews, reviews].

Kluszczyński, Ryszard W. "Absolute Against Casuality: Zbigniew Rybczyński's Cinema (1972–1980)." *Exist: New Art in Poland* 3, no. 15 (1993): 608–611.

—————. "Avant-Garde Film and Video in Poland: An Historical Outline." *The Middle of Europe: Avant-garde Film and Video Art from Austria, Czecho-Slovakia, Hungary and Poland,* ed. Ryszard W. Kluszczyński. Warsaw: Center for Contemporary Art, 1991. Pp. 52–73.

—————. *Obrazy na wolności. Studia z historii sztuk medialnych w Polsce.* Warsaw: Instytut Kultury, 1998.

Kornatowska, Maria. *Eros i film.* Łódź: Krajowa Agencja Wydawnicza, 1986.

—————. "Polish Cinema." *Cineaste* 19, no. 4 (1993): 47–50.

—————. *Wodzireje i amatorzy.* Warsaw: Wydawnictwa Artystyczne i Filmowe, 1990.

Krzysztof Kieślowski. [special issue of] *Film na Świecie* 3–4 (1992).

Kwartalnik Filmowy 15–16 (1996/1997) [issue on Andrzej Wajda].

Kwartalnik Filmowy 17 (1997) [issue on Polish cinema, part 1].

Kwartalnik Filmowy 18 (1997) [issue on Polish cinema, part 2].

Lemann, Jolanta. *Eugeniusz Cękalski.* Łódź: Muzeum Kinematografii, 1996.

Lewandowski, Jan F. *Kino na pograniczu.* Katowice: Śląsk, 1998.

—————. *100 filmów polskich.* Katowice: Videograf II, 1997.

Lewis, Clifford, and Carroll Britch. "Andrzej Wajda's War Trilogy: A Retrospective." *Film Criticism* 10, no. 3 (1986): 22–35.

Liebman Stuart and Leonard Quart. "Lost and Found: Wanda Jakubowska's *The Last Stop.*" *Cineaste* 22, no. 4 (1997): 43–45.

Liehm, Mira, and Antonin J. Liehm. *The Most Important Art: Soviet and Eastern European Film After 1945.* Berkeley: University of California Press, 1977.

Lubelski, Tadeusz, ed. *Kino Krzysztofa Kieślowskiego.* Cracow: Universitas, 1997.

Lubelski, Tadeusz. *Poetyka powieści i filmów Tadeusza Konwickiego.* Wrocław: Wydawnictwo Uniwersytetu Wrocławskiego, 1984.

—————. *Strategie autorskie w polskim filmie fabularnym lat 1945–1961.* Cracow: Wydawnictwo Uniwersytetu Jagiellońskiego, 1992.

—————. "Wzlot i upadek wspólnoty, czyli kino polskie 1975–1995." *Kino* 1 (1997): 17–20.

Madej, Alina. *Mitologie i konwencje. O polskim kinie fabularnym dwudziestolecia międzywojennego.* Cracow: Universitas, 1994.

Madej, Alina, and Jakub Zajdel, *Śmierć jak kromka chleba. Historia jednego filmu.* Warsaw: PAN-Instytut Sztuki, 1994.

Marszałek, Rafał, ed. *Historia filmu polskiego 1962–1967* [vol. 5]. Warsaw: Wydawnictwa Artystyczne i Filmowe, 1985.

—————. *Historia filmu polskiego 1968–1972* [vol. 6]. Warsaw: Wydawnictwa Artystyczne i Filmowe, 1994.

Marszałek, Rafał. *Filmowa pop-historia.* Cracow: Wydawnictwo Literackie, 1984.

—————. *Polska wojna w obcym filmie.* Wrocław: Ossolineum, 1976.

Maśnicki, Jerzy, and Kamil Stepan. *Pleograf. Słownik biograficzny filmu polskiego 1896–1939.* Cracow: Staromiejska Oficyna Wydawnicza, 1996.

Matuszak, Remigiusz Włast. "Film." *Polish Realities: The Arts in Poland 1980–1989*, ed. Donald Pirie, Jekaterina Young, and Christopher Carrell. Glasgow: Third Eye Centre, 1990. Pp. 62–73.

Mazierska, Ewa. "Any Town? Post-communist Warsaw in Juliusz Machulski's *Girl Guide* (1995) and *Kiler* (1997)." *Historical Journal of Film, Radio and Television* 19, no. 4 (1999): 515–530.

———. "Non-Jewish Jews, Good Poles and Historical Truth in the Films of Andrzej Wajda." *Historical Journal of Film, Radio and Television* 20, no. 2 (2000): 213–226

Michalewicz, Kazimierz S. *Polskie rodowody filmu. Narodziny masowego zjawiska*. Warsaw: Polska Agencja Ekologiczna, 1998.

Michałek, Bolesław. *The Cinema of Andrzej Wajda*. London: Tantivy Press, 1973.

———. *Szkice o filmie polskim*. Warsaw: Wydawnictwa Artystyczne i Filmowe, 1960.

Michałek, Bolesław, and Frank Turaj, eds. *Le Cinéma polonais*. Paris: Centre Georges Pompidou, 1992.

Michałek, Bolesław, and Frank Turaj. *The Modern Cinema of Poland*. Bloomington: Indiana University Press, 1988.

Miczka, Tadeusz, ed. [assistant ed. Alina Madej]. *Syndrom konformizmu? Kino polskie lat sześćdziesiątych*. Katowice: Wydawnictwo Uniwersytetu Śląskiego, 1994.

Miczka, Tadeusz. "Cinema Under Political Pressure: A Brief Outline of Authorial Roles in Polish Post-War Feature-Film 1945–1995." *Kinema* 4 (1995): 32–48.

———. *Inspiracje plastyczne w twórczości filmowej i telewizyjnej Andrzeja Wajdy*. Katowice: Wydawnictwo Uniwersytetu Śląskiego, 1987.

———. *Wielka improwizacja filmowa. Opowieść o Dziadach Adama Mickiewicza: Lawa Tadeusza Konwickiego*. Kielce: Szumacher, 1992.

———. "'We live in the world lacking idea on itself': Krzysztof Kieślowski's Art of Film." *Kinema* 7 (1997): 23–47.

Możejko, Edward. *Der socialistische Realismus: Theorie, Entwicklung und Versagen einer Literaturmethode*. Bonn: Bouvier Verlag Herbert Grundmann, 1977.

Mruklik, Barbara. *Andrzej Wajda*. Warsaw: Wydawnictwa Artystyczne i Filmowe, 1969.

Negri, Pola. *Memoirs of a Star*. New York: Doubleday, 1970.

Nemes, Károly. *Films of the Commitment: Socialist Cinema in Eastern Europe*. Budapest: Corvina, 1985.

Nurczyńska-Fidelska, Ewelina. *Andrzej Munk*. Cracow: Wydawnictwo Literackie, 1982.

———. *Polska klasyka literacka według Andrzeja Wajdy*. Katowice: Śląsk, 1998.

Nurczyńska-Fidelska, Ewelina, and Bronisława Stolarska, eds. *"Szkoła polska" – powroty*. Łódź: Wydawnictwo Uniwersytetu Łódzkiego, 1998.

Nurczyńska-Fidelska, Ewelina, and Zbigniew Batko, eds. *Polish Cinema in Ten Takes*. Łódź: Łódzkie Towarzystwo Naukowe, 1995.
———. *W stulecie kina. Sztuka filmowa w Polsce*. Łódź: Centralny Gabinet Edukacji Filmowej Dzieci i Młodzieży, 1996.
Ostrowska, Elżbieta. "Filmic Representations of the 'Polish Mother' in Post–Second World War Polish Cinema." *European Journal of Women Studies* 5, nos. 3–4 (1998): 419–435.
———. "Obraz Matki Polki w kinie polskim: mit czy stereotyp?" *Kwartalnik Filmowy* 17 (1997): 131–140.
Palczewska, Danuta, and Zbigniew Benedyktowicz, eds. *Film i kontekst*. Wrocław: Ossolineum, 1988.
Palczewska, Danuta. *Współczesna polska myśl filmowa*. Wrocław: Ossolineum, 1981.
Paul, David. "Andrzej Wajda's War Trilogy." *Cineaste* 20, no. 4 (1994): 52–54.
———. *Politics, Art and Commitment in East European Cinema*. New York: St. Martin's Press, 1983.
Paul, David, and Sylvia Glover. "The Difficulty of Moral Choice: Zanussi's *Contract* and *The Constant Factor*." *Film Quarterly* 37, no. 2 (1983–1984): 19–26.
Petrie, Graham, and Ruth Dwyer. *Before the Wall Came Down: Soviet and East European Filmmakers in the West*. New York: University Press of America, 1990.
Pirie, Donald, Jekaterina Young, and Christopher Carrell, eds. *Polish Realities: The Arts in Poland 1980–1989*. Glasgow: Third Eye Centre, 1990.
Polanski, Roman. *Roman by Polanski*. New York: William Morrow, 1984.
Pryzwan, Mariola, ed. *"Cześć, starenia!": Zbyszek Cybulski we wspomnieniach*. Warsaw: MK, 1994.
Przylipiak, Mirosław. "Dokument polski wczoraj i dziś." *Kino* 6 (1997): 22–24.
———. *Poetyka kina dokumentalnego*. Gdańsk: Wydawnictwo Uniwersytetu Gdańskiego, 2000.
———. *Kino stylu zerowego*. Gdańsk: Gdańskie Wydawnictwo Psychologiczne, 1992.
Rammel [Sowińska], Iwona. "Van den Budenmayer i jemu podobni. O muzyce w ostatnich filmach Kieślowskiego." *Kwartalnik Filmowy* 6 (1994): 130–140.
Rogerson, Edward. "Polish Cinema: An Internal Exile." *Sight and Sound* 55, no. 3 (1986): 195–197.
Schlott, Wolfgang. "Der polnishe Film zwischen Kommerzialisierung und neuen ästhetischen Mustern." *Osteuropa* 7 (1995): 616–626.
———. "Wer rettet den polnischen Film?" *Osteuropa* 7 (1995): 406–417.
Skwara, Anita. "Film Stars Do Not Shine in the Sky Over Poland: The Absence of Popular Cinema in Poland." *Popular European Cinema*, ed. Richard Dyer and Ginette Vincendeau. London and New York: Routledge, 1992. Pp. 220–231.

Slater, Thomas J. *Handbook of Soviet and East European Films and Filmmakers.* New York: Greenwood Press, 1992.

Słodowski, Jan, ed. *Leksykon polskich filmów fabularnych.* Warsaw: Wiedza i Życie, 1996.

Sobański, Oskar. *Polish Feature Films: A Reference Guide 1945–1985.* West Cornwall: Locust Hill, 1987.

Sobolewski, Tadeusz. *Dziecko Peerelu. Esej. Dziennik.* Warsaw: Wydawnictwo Sic!, 2000

———. "Solidarność grzesznych. O *Dekalogu* Krzysztofa Kieślowskiego." *Na Głos* 1 (1990): 91–101.

Sobotka, Kazimierz, ed. *Film polski. Twórcy i mity.* Łódź: Łódzki Dom Kultury, 1987.

Sobotka, Kazimierz. "Robotnik na ekranie, czyli o tak zwanym 'filmie produkcyjnym.'" *Szkice o filmie polskim,* ed. Bronisława Stolarska. Łódź: Łódzki Dom Kultury, 1985.

Sosnowski, Alexandra. "Cinema in Transition: The Polish Film Today." *Journal of Popular Film and Television* 24, no. 1 (1996): 10–16.

———. "Polish Cinema Today: A New Order in the Production, Distribution and Exhibition of Film." *The Polish Review* 15, no. 1 (1995): 315–329.

Stachówna, Grażyna, ed. *I film stworzył kobietę.* Cracow: Wydawnictwo Uniwersytetu Jagiellońskiego, 1999.

———, ed. *Kobieta z kamerą.* Cracow: Wydawnictwo Uniwersytetu Jagiellońskiego, 1998.

———. *Roman Polański i jego filmy.* Warsaw and Łódź: Państwowe Wydawnictwo Naukowe, 1994.

———. "Równanie szeregów. Bohaterowie filmów socrealistycznych (1949–1955)." *Człowiek z ekranu. Z antropologii postaci filmowej,* ed. Mariola Jankun-Dopartowa and Mirosław Przylipiak. Cracow: Arcana, 1996.

Stok, Danusia, ed. *Kieślowski on Kieślowski.* London and Boston: Faber and Faber, 1993.

Stolarska, Bronisława, ed. *Szkice o kinie polskim.* Łódź: Łódzki Dom Kultury, 1985.

Taylor, Richard, Nancy Wood, Julian Graffy, and Dina Iordanova, eds. *The BFI Companion to Eastern European and Russian Cinema.* London: British Film Institute, 2000.

Toeplitz, Jerzy, ed. *Historia filmu polskiego 1939–1956* [vol. 3]. Warsaw: Wydawnictwa Artystyczne i Filmowe, 1974.

———. *Historia filmu polskiego 1957–1961* [vol. 4]. Warsaw: Wydawnictwa Artystyczne i Filmowe, 1980.

Tomasik, Wojciech. *Polska powieść tendencyjna 1949–1955. Problemy perswazji literackiej.* Wrocław: Ossolineum, 1988.

Trzynadlowski, Jan, ed. *Polska Szkoła Filmowa. Poetyka i tradycja.* Wrocław: Ossolineum, 1976.

Turaj, Frank. "Poland: The Cinema of Moral Concern." *Post New Wave Cinema in the Soviet Union and Eastern Europe*, ed. Daniel J. Goulding. Bloomington and Indianopolis: Indiana University Press, 1989. Pp. 143–171.

Wajda, Andrzej. *Double Vision: My Life in Film*. New York: Holt, 1989.

————. *Three Films* [*Ashes and Diamonds, Kanal, A Generation*]. London: Lorrimer, 1984.

————. *Wajda – Filmy*. Warsaw: Wydawnictwa Artystyczne i Filmowe, 1996.

Walker, Michael. "Jerzy Skolimowski." *Second Wave*. London: Studio Vista, 1970. Pp. 34–62.

Warchoł, Tomasz. "Polish Cinema: The End of a Beginning." *Sight and Sound* 55, no. 3 (1986): 190–194.

Wasilewski, Piotr. *Świadectwa metryk: Polskie kino młodych w latach osiemdziesiątych*. Cracow: Oficyna Obecnych, 1990.

Weiner, Steve. "Jan Lenica and Landscape." *Film Quarterly* 45, no. 4 (1992): 2–16.

Werner, Andrzej. *Polskie, arcypolskie...*. London: Polonia, 1987.

Wertenstein, Wanda. *Wajda mówi o sobie: wywiady i teksty*. Cracow: Wydawnictwo Literackie, 1991.

————. *Zespół filmowy X*. Warsaw: Wydawnictwo "Officina," 1991.

Wilson, Emma. "Three Colours: *Blue*. Kieślowski, Colour and the Postmodern subject." *Screen* 39, no. 4 (1998): 349–363.

Winchell, James. "Metaphysics of Post-Nationalism: La Double Vie de Krzysztof Kieślowski." *Contemporary French Civilization* 22, no. 2 (1998): 240–263.

Whyte, Alistair. *New Cinema in Eastern Europe*. New York: Dutton, 1971.

Włodarczyk, Wojciech. *Socrealism. Sztuka polska w latach 1950–1954*. Cracow: Wydawnictwo Literackie, 1991.

Zajiček, Edward. *Poza ekranem. Kinematografia polska 1918–1991*. Warsaw: Filmoteka Narodowa and Wydawnictwa Artystyczne i Filmowe, 1992.

————, ed. *Encyklopedia kultury polskiej XX wieku: Film i kinematografia*. Warsaw: Instytut Kultury and Komitet Kinematografii, 1994.

Zwierzchowski, Piotr. *Zapomniani bohaterowie. O bohaterach filmowych polskiego socrealizmu*. Warsaw: Wydawnictwo Trio, 2000.

Index of Names

Index of Film Titles

DEFA
East German Cinema 1946–1992

Edited by **Seán Allan** and **John Sandford**, both, University of Reading

"A useful appendix provides research sources. Written in clear prose, these essays should interest undergraduates and generalists as well as scholars and faculty." —**Humanities**

"The lucid style of all contributions ... makes this volume an accessible read to students ... this volume has also the bonus of offering an excellent appendix on sources for future research ... this collection of essays illustrates precisely why the quality of DEFA film-making should not be confined to the archives of history."
—**Journal of European Areas Studies**

1999. 336 pages, ills., bibliog., index
ISBN 1-57181-943-6 hardback
ISBN 1-571817530 paperback

POSTMODERNISM IN THE CINEMA

Edited by **Cristina Degli-Esposti**, Kent State University

"These essays ... provide interesting reading strategies and different systems of interpretations that may help us with the difficult task of being post-modern."
—**Film and Theory**

Contents: The Ideological, the Mnemonic, the Parodic, and the Media – Issues of Cross-Cultural Identity and National Cinemas – Postmodernism and Tourism, (Post)History, and Colonization – Auteurial Presences

1998. 272 pages, 13 ills., bibliog.
ISBN 1-57181-105-2 hardback
ISBN 1-57181-106-0 paperback

THE POLITICAL FILMS OF ANDRZEJ WAJDA
Dialogism in *Man of Marble*, *Man of Iron*, and *Danton*

Janina Falkowska, University of Western Ontario

Contents: Introduction – The Political Films of Andrzej Wajda – Issues of Methodology – Andrzej Wajda: The Carrier of the Political Message – The Historical Dialogue in Wajda's Films – Wajda and His *Dramatis Personae* – The Films' Dialogical Aesthetics – Conclusion – Appendix: Film Synopses of *Man of Marble*, *Man of Iron*, and *Danton*

1995. 256 pages, 12 photos, bibliog., index
ISBN 1-57181-005-6 hardback